Praise for *Defeating the Dictators*

'Remarkable. A thoughtful and perceptive book.'

Rt Hon Jeremy Hunt MP

'*Defeating the Dictators* is a rare book: a deeply researched and engaging work that both details the challenges democracies face, and offers us clear and persuasive solutions. Dunst's writing is as sharp as his argument is necessary. Anyone who believes in democracy – in the United States or anywhere else – should read his book.'

Senator Chris Coons (D-Delaware),
Chair of the US Senate Ethics Committee and
Member of the Senate Foreign Relations Committee

'This is an important and timely book which needs to be widely read. Charles Dunst makes a compelling case that democracy and individual freedom are no longer seen in many countries as the surest route to success. Crucially, he also gives us a plan of action to restore the tarnished reputation of the democratic model and to show that, when combined with effective governance, this still offers a far better future for humanity than any alternative.'

Peter Ricketts,
Former UK National Security Adviser, Chairman of the
Joint Intelligence Committee, Permanent Representative
to NATO and Ambassador to France

'This lively and thoughtful book provides a welcome and much-needed shot in the arm for supporters of democracy everywhere. No matter how much some may envy the power wielded by authoritarians, no matter the results they appear to achieve, Dunst reminds us that humanity will always flourish most when granted its deepest desire: freedom.'

Josh Glancy,
Special Correspondent for the *Sunday Times*

'A smart, sweeping and well-written book that makes the case for rebuilding democracy at home and defeating authoritarianism abroad. It is an important contribution and an urgent call to action for democracies everywhere.'

Ambassador Nancy Soderberg,
Former US Deputy National Security Advisor and
Alternative Representative to the United Nations

'America's founders understood that our republic would require constant nurturing. Charles Dunst's excellent book tells us how we can defeat the dictators, strengthen democracies and build a better future for generations to come. People everywhere who care about freedom should read this book and implement what the author recommends.'

Lt General H R McMaster (ret.),
Former US National Security Advisor and *New York Times* bestselling author of *Battlegrounds: The Fight to Defend the Free World*

'The central question of our global political age is the increasingly poor health of democracy worldwide. This is no less urgent than the struggle for freedom during the Cold War or the fight against fascism in the mid-twentieth century. Charles Dunst addresses this challenge head-on with lively on-the-ground reportage and an inspiring call to action. This is an essential book for our times.'

Arthur Snell,
Author of *How Britain Broke the World* and presenter
of the *Doomsday Watch* podcast,
former UK High Commissioner to Trinidad and Tobago

'At a time when democracy is under attack, Charles Dunst helps us understand the nature, scale and scope of the power grabs that are changing the world. Dunst also offers an insightful review of the options we have to restore, protect and strengthen democracy at home and abroad. A must-read.'

Moisés Naím,
Distinguished Fellow at the Carnegie Endowment for International Peace and author of *The Revenge of Power*

'Timely, thoughtful and thought-provoking, *Defeating the Dictators* reminds us that freedom and democracy cannot be taken for granted – they need to be nurtured and nourished every day of our lives.'

Azar Nafisi,
New York Times bestselling author of *Reading Lolita in Tehran*

'In *Defeating the Dictators*, Dunst convincingly shows that preserving and advancing liberalism abroad is possible only if democracies get their own houses in order. He marshals practical evidence from across the globe to offer a clear roadmap for fixing key challenges at home and abroad. In this turbulent era of rising strongmen, what could be more important?'

Admiral James Stavridis (ret.),
Retired four-star US naval officer and former Supreme Allied Commander of NATO, *New York Times* bestselling author

'No one knows the world like Dunst. He's lived the good and bad in other nations, and knows how to get our democracies back on track. His how-to manual on fighting autocracy and strengthening democracy is indispensable reading.'

Congressman Jim Cooper (D-Tennessee),
Former chair of the US House Subcommittee on Strategic Forces, dubbed the 'conscience of the House' by the *New York Times*

'A decade ago, democracies were confident that we could prevail against autocratic challengers simply by being democracies. But as Charles Dunst argues in his powerful new book, this confidence is a dangerous illusion. Democracies can stand up to autocracy only if we are ready to face our own vulnerabilities and the strength of our opponents. *Defeating the Dictators* is a great place to start – essential reading.'

Ivan Krastev,
Chairman of the Centre for Liberal Strategies in Sofia, Bulgaria, and Permanent Fellow at the Institute for Human Sciences in Vienna, contributing opinion writer for the *New York Times*, author of *After Europe* and co-author of *The Light That Failed*

'*Defeating the Dictators* is an extraordinary, compelling and pragmatic analysis of the authoritarianism versus democracy debate that builds its case by drawing on a wide range of illustrations from around the globe and throughout history. In this well-written, swiftly moving book, Charles Dunst clearly lays out the dangers of rising authoritarianism and the steps that must be taken by democracies to rebuild trust, restore accountability and deliver on their fundamental promise – all necessary if we are to prevail against the creation of a world order based on brute power, one that would supplant the rule of law, values-based order built in the wake of the Second World War. A necessary and thought-provoking read for policymakers, journalists and civil society leaders alike.'

Ambassador John Emerson,
Former US Ambassador to Germany,
Chairman of the American Council on Germany

'At a time in world history when too many countries veer towards autocracy, it is heartening to read that democracies still produce the happiest, most creative and longest-living citizens. Not only must Americans and democrats everywhere make this case abroad, but we must be confident that our messy democracies will yield the best possible future for our own citizens. In *Defeating the Dictators*, Dunst gives us a clear and incisive roadmap for securing ever-expanding self-governance for humankind. It gave me hope for the future of democracy, and will do the same for you, too.'

Congressman Don Beyer (D-Virginia),
Chairman of the US Congress Joint Economic Committee and former US Ambassador to Switzerland and Liechtenstein

'In *Defeating the Dictators*, Charles Dunst explains the threat posed by the rising popularity of authoritarians around the world. He makes the compelling case that our own national security – and the very concept of democracy – are at risk as they wield their successes at home to shape the international order in their favour.'

Barbara McQuade,
Professor from Practice at the University of Michigan Law School and former US Attorney for the Eastern District of Michigan

'Like Benjamin Franklin's cultivation of thirteen virtues in his quest for moral perfection, Charles Dunst breaks down political perfection into eight key democratic virtues, with best practices drawn from around the world for each. Dunst's analysis functions as a much-needed self-help guide for democracy in an age of rising authoritarianism. We would be wise to put his prescriptions into practice.'

Asha Rangappa,
Senior Lecturer at Yale University's Jackson Institute for Global Affairs and former FBI Special Agent

'A compelling and urgent case for why halting autocracy's spread first requires strengthening democracy where it already exists. A smart and timely read.'

Yasmeen Serhan,
Staff Writer at *TIME*

'In a moment when authoritarianism, led by the Chinese model, is gaining appeal, this carefully written book provides valuable perspective on a worrisome global trend. Dunst offers a much-needed survey on what ails democracies today and solutions on how to regain our place as the world's model. His sharp and engaging analysis is essential to understanding our crisis-riven age and how to navigate it.'

Ana Palacio,
Former Foreign Minister of Spain and Member
of the European Parliament

'Everybody knows that democracy is in trouble, both in the United States and in liberal societies abroad. With *Defeating the Dictators*, Dunst has provided a clear-eyed, deeply researched and accessible roadmap for fixing what ails us. His book could not be more timely, or more important. A must-read.'

Senator Tom Daschle (D-South Dakota),
Former US Senate Majority Leader and co-chair
of President Barack Obama's 2008 campaign

'Charles Dunst has presented a timely warning for democracies everywhere. Drawing on examples in Asia, the Middle East and elsewhere, he has highlighted advanced autocracies' ability to achieve stability by satisfying the desires of their populations – and democracies' troubling inability to do the same. I was the US Ambassador in one of the countries he examines, the United Arab Emirates, whose ruling family has navigated the challenges of succession without elections by generously providing for its citizenry. Dunst piercingly points out that democracies, on the other hand, are not adequately offering their own citizens a path to the good life. Our continued failure poses a grave threat for democracy.'

Ambassador Edward Walker,
Former US Ambassador to Israel,
Egypt and the United Arab Emirates,
former US Assistant Secretary of State

'In an era focused on the West's strategic competition with authoritarian states, much ink is spilled complaining about authoritarian misdeeds. But not enough attention is given to how to keep democracies vibrant, coherent and successful. Dunst leads us through some sharp and honest retrospection for today's democracies.'

Ambassador Kurt Tong,
Managing Partner at The Asia Group,
former US Ambassador for APEC and
Consul General in Hong Kong

'Charles Dunst's *Defeating the Dictators* offers a brutally honest and incisive account of the contemporary challenge posed by autocracy to democracy today, the dangers of complacency and how democracies can reverse the illiberal tide. The prescriptions in this book should serve as a wake-up call for all those who care about the shape of political affairs, individual rights and global security in the twenty-first century.'

Ambassador Derek Mitchell,
President of the National Democratic Institute and
former US Ambassador to Myanmar

'*Defeating the Dictators* provides the framing and motivation to move democracies back to the high ground, starting now. Renewing the conversation we all need to be having with ourselves and each other, this book is a call to action for all generations. Dunst is clear and compelling – this cannot wait.'

Bill Purcell,
Former Mayor of Nashville, Tennessee, and Director of the
Institute of Politics at the Harvard Kennedy School

'Doom has a certain aesthetic allure, claims the novelist Martin Amis. There is plenty to be pessimistic about if you are wedded to the democratic ideal. While not making light of the challenges to the democratic model, Dunst also offers reasons to be optimistic that the model will survive. He has written a book that makes clear how much is at stake for the world's leading democracies and the opportunities they still have to shape the future.'

Dr Christopher Coker,
Director of LSE IDEAS, author of *Why War?*

'At a time when liberal politics is under threat from without and within, Charles Dunst's *Defeating the Dictators* is a refreshing antidote to despair. He not only tells us why defeating authoritarianism is so important but, more importantly, how to do it. Could not be more timely.'

Dr Ashley J Tellis,
Tata Chair for Strategic Affairs at the Carnegie Endowment for
International Peace, former Senior Advisor to the US Ambassador
to India and Special Assistant to President George W Bush

'Charles Dunst has written a timely handbook for people who believe in the ideals of democracy. Not a moment too soon.'

Gerald Butts,
Former Principal Secretary to Prime Minister Justin Trudeau,
Vice Chairman at Eurasia Group

'Charles Dunst invites the reader for a long journey in space and in time: the book takes you to new places but also to cities and countries you think you know rather well – and it is fascinating to read the observations and comments of a younger traveller. A good read but the book makes you think hard about institutions, old and new, familiar and exotic, efficient and rigid, as well as about merits and meritocracy, democrats and democracy, about leaders in high jobs who may or may not be up to the standards of their office. There is no happy ending here, the journey never ends – but co-travellers may accept Charles's guarded optimism.'

Péter Ákos Bod,
Former Governor of the Hungarian National Bank and
Hungarian Minister of Industry and Trade

About the Author

Charles Dunst is deputy director of research and analytics at The Asia Group, a fellow at the Center for Strategic and International Studies, and a contributing editor of *American Purpose*, Francis Fukuyama's magazine. His reportage and analysis have appeared in the *New York Times*, the *Atlantic*, the *Washington Post* and *Foreign Policy*, among other outlets. A former foreign correspondent, he has reported from countries including Cambodia, Myanmar, Vietnam, Israel and the Palestinian territories, Hungary, Romania and Andorra. He holds degrees from the London School of Economics and Hamilton College. A native New Yorker, he lives in Virginia.

Defeating
the Dictators

How Democracy Can Prevail
in the Age of the Strongman

CHARLES DUNST

HODDER &
STOUGHTON

First published in Great Britain in 2023 by Hodder & Stoughton
An Hachette UK company

1

Copyright © Charles Dunst 2023

A CIP catalogue record for this title is available from the British Library

Hardback ISBN 978 1 399 70443 4
Trade Paperback ISBN 978 1 399 70444 1
eBook ISBN 978 1 399 70445 8

Typeset in Minion Pro by Hewer Text UK Ltd, Edinburgh
Printed and bound in Great Britain by Clays Ltd, Elcograf S.p.A.

Hodder & Stoughton policy is to use papers that are natural, renewable and recyclable
products and made from wood grown in sustainable forests. The logging and manufacturing
processes are expected to conform to the environmental regulations of the country of origin.

Hodder & Stoughton Ltd
Carmelite House
50 Victoria Embankment
London EC4Y 0DZ

www.hodder.co.uk

Contents

For Lee and Lisbeth, my first and forever champions

Introduction

Stepping off the plane at Singapore's Changi Airport, having flown in from Phnom Penh, is enough to make you think you've completely lost it. When I took that trip in 2019, I thought I was dreaming. There's nothing quite as disorienting as going from a developing country like Cambodia to one where every sixth household has a million US dollars in disposable wealth, in no more than the time it takes to ride the Eurostar from London to Paris.

But arriving at the USD 1.3 billion Changi Airport would be nothing less than astonishing wherever you were coming from. The Jewel complex, opened in 2019, lives up to its name. Here, a soaring waterfall descends 130 feet, seemingly raining down from the glass-panelled heavens. A forest of some 1,400 trees offers shade to weary jetsetters from Asia, Europe and beyond. A park offers nets for recreational bouncing, more than eighty feet above the ground. All the while, a plethora of retail and dining options wraps around the complex, offering luxury to those lucky enough to afford it.

Eye-catching as the extras were, it was the actual experience of *using* Singapore's airport that blew me away. Whenever I landed in the Cambodian capital of Phnom Penh, which I did frequently while living there in 2018 and 2019, I was immediately confronted by visa-on-arrival officials, to whom you must hand actual, physical dollar bills to enter the country (assuming you did not purchase an e-visa). Not cheques. Not a credit card. Just cold, hard US cash. In the Thai capital of Bangkok, meanwhile, the customs line snakes back and forth endlessly through the arrivals area, and it can take hours just to get your passport stamped. Even at New York's John F. Kennedy airport, the exit process can take hours. And the less we say about Britain – the spiritual home of the queue – the better.

Not in Singapore. After hopping off the plane and admiring the terminal with wide eyes, you reach the dreaded customs area. Only here you're confronted not with a long line or intimidating officials asking for your money, but with, at Terminal 4 at least, a bank of automated machines. You scan your fingerprints and passport, remove your hat and the first gate opens. Then you proceed to get a passport stamp from an actual human. This person probably doesn't speak to you; if they do, they say something nice. And that's it. Despite heavy traffic through the airport, the whole process takes less than twenty minutes and is even pleasant.

Welcome to Singapore.

Changi epitomises everything that Singapore has become: clean, safe, well-governed and, above all, a marvel. The city gleams with stainless steel. A glass greenhouse, one of the world's largest, attracts tourists and locals alike. Hundred-foot-tall 'supertrees' mimic photosynthesis, emitting a neon glow, much to the delight of both children and adults. Nowhere in the world looks quite like this place. To visit is to peer into an idealised future – one that is lush and immaculate, but never soulless or sterile. Singapore's multi-ethnic cultural heritage still shines at the Hawker centres with their delightfully tongue-searing chili crab, the Chinatown shops offering piping-hot *kway teow*, and the Little India curry houses whose aromas and tastes are pleasingly fresh and warm. Winding through these streets, you're just as likely to find a major financial office as you are a Chinese shrine, a Malay mosque or a Hindu temple. The future, it seems, will have room for the best of our respective traditions.

The nightlife thrives, too, despite most drugs being strictly illegal under penalty of death. From glitzy cocktail bars to clubs, partygoers in Singapore don't lack options. The booze, while highly

regulated, nonetheless flows, and getting home safely is no problem, either by cab or subway. The city-state's homicide rate is
incredibly low, at around 0.2 cases per 100,000 people[1] – roughly
650 times better than London's[2] and 2,500 times better than New
York's.[3]

Nor are the more humdrum bits of human infrastructure lacking. The city-state has an incredibly efficient and meritocratic
bureaucracy; its officials are seemingly incorruptible; the air is clean;
the schools are excellent; healthcare is affordable; the country's housing programme has worked so well that some of its subsidised apartments now resell for more than USD 700,000; and its per capita
income is among the highest in the world.

And yet, Singapore, so well governed, is an authoritarian state.
It was ruled by an out-and-out autocrat for twenty-five years after
independence, and by that same autocrat's party ever since. There's
that death penalty hanging over people's heads all the time. The
city's migrant workers are treated as second-class citizens.
Government policies prevent LGBTQ Singaporeans from purchasing affordable public housing until the age of thirty-five, while the
ban on gay marriage prevents LGBTQ Singaporeans from accessing the large housing subsidy available only for married couples.[4]
Inequality is on the rise.

Singapore is certainly a paradise for the privileged. It is a play-
ground, not for the migrant workers who keep Singapore running,
but for most, nonetheless. And for most, life in Singapore is pretty
good.

I wrote this book to understand how we can reconcile these two
sides of the city – a lack of freedom and an abundance of good living.
How can we in the West and other democracies grasp Singapore's
success, watching from such a different political value system? And,
ultimately, what do liberal democracies need to do to become so
successful that people in autocracies like Singapore will wish to

transform their own systems of governance – so they want to become like us, rather than the other way around? How can we become the world's model once again?

* * *

When Stamford Raffles, the British colonial administrator, founded Singapore in January 1819, it was nothing but a small fishing village comprising a few thousand Malay fishermen and some Chinese farmers. For years, it remained little more than a malaria-ridden harbour, its existence justified only by the transport needs of an empire. The city-state still is, as former Singaporean diplomat Kishore Mahbubani has written, 'absurdly small', occupying half the space of tiny Bahrain and containing no natural resources.[5] A further challenge in other parts of the world was its multi-ethnic and multi-religious population – Muslims, Hindus, Christians and Buddhists have not always coexisted peacefully.[6]

How, then, did Singapore get here? How did Singapore come to have a gross domestic product per capita nearly 35 per cent higher than that of its erstwhile coloniser – not to mention a higher standard of living and a longer life expectancy?[7] How did Singapore, ranked economically in 1965 on a par with Chile, Argentina and Mexico, come to have a gross national product four or five times theirs today?[8]

The answer, in short, is strong, adaptive and effective governance – namely by Lee Kuan Yew, the country's first prime minister and founding father.

Born in 1923, Lee lived through the British and Japanese colonial periods, and then a brief stretch during which Singapore was part of Malaysia, before his country achieved independence. Lee always had his eyes on the prize; he spent his youth and early career readying himself for the day colonialism in Singapore came to an end. He attended Britain's Cambridge University on a scholarship, graduating at the top of his class. After returning to Singapore in 1950, he worked as a lawyer before founding the People's Action Party (PAP) in 1954. After a few years as an opposition leader, Lee was elected prime minister in 1959, when Singapore gained full self-government from the British, albeit as part of Malaysia. Finally, in 1965, Singapore became an independent country, and while most of the population was unskilled and illiterate, Lee had what it took to make this new nation a success.[9]

From the outset, he prioritised development over democratic ideals, believing that Singaporeans wanted food, cash in their pockets and strong hospitals more than they wanted liberty. Democracy, he thought, could come only after people's stomachs were full and their ailments treated. But even then, he made clear, democracy was not a stand-alone good nor a prerequisite for success – what Lee called the 'basics' of economic growth were.[10]

Lee and his aides accordingly directed the government to focus on manufacturing: to build factories and other infrastructure while seeking foreign investment. They believed that high-grade, First World quality infrastructure and standards would prompt American, Japanese, European and other companies to bring their operations to Singapore, in turn boosting the tiny city-state's fledgling economy.

Their gamble paid off. By the 1970s, major multinational companies like Hewlett-Packard and General Electric had invested hugely in Singapore. Companies like these were expanding in the region anyway, given East Asia's growing population and talented workforce, but Lee's policies made Singapore far more attractive than the other mostly conflict-free nations nearby, like Thailand and Malaysia. The foundations Lee laid in the 1960s allowed Singapore to become a major electronics exporter by the time the 1970s rolled around.

Foreign companies came to Singapore not only for the infrastructure but because they trusted Lee's government. Singapore accomplished something few post-colonial countries were able to do so quickly: the city-state had a predictable government and a relatively clean economy that was manoeuvrable for foreign operators. There was a transparent tax regime; the bureaucracy was incorruptible and efficient; the legal framework was strong; and the country's geopolitical orientation was effectively neutral, favouring neither the Soviet Union, the United States, nor China, meaning that investors were unlikely to find themselves caught up in geopolitical storms. All of which made Singapore stable and attractive, unlike, say, Cambodia or Indonesia.

Lee planned ahead, too. He knew that building more state-of-the-art public infrastructure, along with excellent air and sea linkages, would bring further business to Singapore.

One anecdote is particularly telling. When the British completely withdrew from Singapore in 1971, they planned to destroy their naval dock. Most post-colonial leaders around the world would have been thrilled with British self-destruction – the perfect symbolic moment for a nationalist firebrand, like Ghana's Kwame Nkrumah or India's Jawaharlal Nehru, hoping to legitimise their nascent rule. But Lee was less interested in ideas, values or political imagery than he was in absolute progress for his country and people. So, rejecting a short-lived populist victory in favour of an actual win, he personally convinced the British not to destroy their dock. He later converted the naval dockyard for civilian use. This step was just one of many that would transform Singapore into one of the world's greatest trade centres. These days, Singapore boasts the world's busiest container transhipment hub, and the largest publicly owned port.

Relying on these building blocks – economic development, top-tier infrastructure and a transparent, reliable system open to business from just about anywhere – Lee turned Singapore into a major financial centre. By building top-class infrastructure and establishing a strong education system, while committing to keeping the Singaporean dollar stable through sound macroeconomics, Lee assured investors that Singapore was the place to be in the unpredictable Asian market. The country quickly became, in the words of journalist Louis Kraar, the 'Zurich of the East, an international haven for money and bankers'.[11]

Lee liked business and foreign capital for a reason: he ran Singapore very much like a corporation. He prioritised efficiency and outcomes above all else. Singapore's key criterion, as one top official defined it in 1974, was not that different from that of a Wall Street bank or top multinational: 'What good can we get out of it?'[12] Or as Lee put it later in his life: 'We are ideology-free. Does it work? If it works, let's try it. If it's fine, let's continue it. If it doesn't work, toss it out, try another one.'[13]

This approach put Singapore on a stunning trajectory. In Singapore's first nine years of full independence, the gross national product nearly tripled – raising the average per capita income to the second highest in Asia, trailing only Japan.[14] By the mid-1980s, many Singaporeans were enjoying a lifestyle rivalling those of the West.[15]

The point is clear: Lee Kuan Yew was that rare autocrat who really could be called at least relatively benevolent; he made life better for his people. He did not steal from them. He did not set up concentration camps or gulags. He certainly did repress them – Singapore is no bastion of liberty – but one cannot deny that he left his country far better than he found it. He transformed a tumultuous backwater into the pride of Southeast Asia, what he called a First World oasis in a Third World region.

'In the end,' he wrote, 'my greatest satisfaction in life comes from the fact that I have spent years gathering support, mustering the will to make this place meritocratic, corruption-free and equal for all races – and that it will endure beyond me, as it has.'[16]

It's not hard to see why he died a happy man.

* * *

And yet there's something deeply uncomfortable about acknowledging Lee's success, especially for a writer born in a liberal Western nation – and grateful for the privileges of being born American.

Despite graduating as the top law student in his class at Cambridge, a citadel of liberalism and democratic values, Lee never became enamoured with democracy. Quite the opposite: he cared little about liberty or freedom. He considered these values something of a Western fantasy and had no interest in transforming Singapore into a democratic nation. Rather, he championed stability and growth over liberty; he travelled for years around Asia, telling the Chinese, Vietnamese, Filipinos and others that they, too, could achieve stunning economic growth like Singapore's without the standard trappings of democracy, just at a time when the Americans, Brits and others were saying the opposite.

Throughout his life, Lee politely lambasted democracy, while still building strong ties with the United States, United Kingdom and other leading Western powers. Although he admitted to admiring some aspects of the United States, he deemed 'parts of it totally unacceptable', including guns, drugs and violent crime, saying 'the exuberance of democracy leads to undisciplined and disorderly conditions which are inimical to development'.[17] For him, development mattered more than liberty. Discipline, he argued, must come before freedom. Because he was in charge, nobody could tell him otherwise.

And if his government was the one to secure economic gains while imposing discipline by outlawing everything from gum to spitting on the street to meaningful political opposition, so be it. For years he arbitrarily detained hundreds of alleged communists and 'extremists' using the Internal Security Act, a remnant from Singapore's British colonial past.

Make no mistake about it, Singapore under Lee was an authoritarian country and remains one today. The government has long restricted a whole host of civil and political liberties, severely constraining any potential political competition. But he was an unusual autocrat. He focused on transforming his country into a genuinely better place – not on lining his own pockets like the autocrats of Cambodia and Zimbabwe. And there's no denying that he did make Singapore into the success it is today: 'An interconnected, fully wired, air-conditioned nanny state where everything is beautiful and nothing hurts,' as the chef, writer and presenter Anthony Bourdain once said.

Lee died in 2015, leaving behind a legacy of what is best described as authoritarianism-lite: Singapore may have occasional elections and limited civil freedoms, but the country effectively operates as a one-party state that brooks little criticism. If liberal countries are bothered by Singapore's illiberal streak, they have largely remained silent. The United States and United Kingdom remain close geopolitical partners. Western money flows into Singapore. The miracle chugs along.

For most, Singapore is today an idyllic little escape from the rough-and-tumble reality, not only of Southeast Asia, but of a democratic world struck by the discord of the US Capitol insurrection, Brexit and other destabilising events. It's not hard to see why American and British expats alike acclaim life in Singapore, even if they can't chew gum there.

It is not hard to see, too, why so many people abroad want their countries to look more like Singapore. Leaders in Silicon Valley, like Peter Thiel, have made it clear that they would prefer it if the United States operated in a top-down, authoritarian corporate way – that is, like Singapore.[18] This approach, they argue, is better for business, and therefore for the world. Brexiteers, in justifying the United Kingdom's exit from the European Union, argued similarly that their country could follow the 'Singapore model' to build a Britain that would become a low-tax, low-regulation and low-public-spending paradise.[19]

Even Bourdain, who gave airtime to freedom-seekers from Asia to Africa and beyond, could not help but admire the paradise that is Singapore. 'You look around the litterless streets, where everything seems to work just fine, and you think – or you could be forgiven for thinking – "Gee, maybe a one-party system is just what we need,"' he once said. 'It ain't my system, it's not the world I want, but damn, it has its appeal.'[20]

* * *

Democracy's Challenge

Singapore's rise – and its appeal – is emblematic of the autocratic challenge we face today, even if Singapore itself is a friendly country. Other autocracies, led by China, a not-so-friendly country, are increasingly trying to wield their successes at home to shape the international order in their favour.

Yet no matter how 'successful' China, Singapore or the Gulf States are, autocracies everywhere lack the benefits of true socio-political freedom – the context in which humanity produces its best innovations and where freedom flows. Some level of prosperity might not require democracy, as these and other countries have proved, but progress, contentment and freedom do. For all of autocracies' successes, the world's best still come from democracies.

Of the world's twenty-five richest countries, all but seven are democracies.[21] Only two autocracies rank among the top forty countries in life expectancy.[22] The average Japanese lives almost eight years longer than the average Chinese; the average Italian lives nine years longer than the average Saudi.[23] China and Singapore are the only autocracies that rank in the top twenty most innovative countries. Switzerland, Sweden, the United States, the United Kingdom, South Korea, the Netherlands and Finland all outrank Singapore. All of these countries – along with Denmark, Germany and France – outrank China.[24]

And while some may say otherwise, the world's best art comes from places where there is freedom of expression: democracies. There is a reason why people around the world clamour for American films, French friezes and Japanese novels. Haruki Murakami could not have written his masterful novel, *1Q84*, in an autocracy; Jackson Pollock could not have produced his wonderfully chaotic canvases under a one-party state. There is a reason why Chinese entertainment does not capture the world's imagination in the same way South Korean films like *Parasite* and pop bands like BTS have.

The social science paints a clear picture, too. If you live in a democracy, you will almost surely receive a better education, become wealthier, live longer and have a richer cultural life than your counterparts in autocracies around the world. We embrace the volatility, tumult and imperfections of democracy, and we're better for it.

Sometimes, in the angry, shaky era we're living through, that feels difficult to believe. This book, then, is about showing why democracy is a superior system – in spite of Singapore's clean streets and rapidly accumulated wealth. It's a book about beating back the autocratic challenge by getting our own houses in order: by outperforming autocracies to serve as an example for the rest of the world, because democracies can defeat dictators only with good governance at home. Only when people the world over think of the United States, Europe, Japan and other democracies as examples – as exemplary leaders that hold the path to the good life – can democracy triumph around the world.

Beating the drum for liberal values and economics abroad while these same principles appear to struggle at home will do us no good.

Trying to sell Singapore or Vietnam on democracy using only idealistic rhetoric in the wake of the January 6 insurrection in the United States is doomed to fail. Why would the stable regimes in Singapore or Hanoi want *that*?

What we need is a 'no-bullshit' approach to the future: we must commit not only to our values, but also to our practices and we must not buy into utopianism – into undue confidence in democracy's inevitable success and the self-assurance that reason will save us. We must convince the world in practical terms why our organising principles remain preferable to those of autocracies, both at home and abroad. We need to look our own failures in the eye, while learning from the success of others.

With this book, I will offer a roadmap to do just this: to reinstitute the basics of good governance to ensure that our democracies deliver on their promises and ultimately rise to meet this difficult moment. I'm going to look at examples of good governance from everywhere – past and present – to detail best practices for running a democratic country in the twenty-first century. This roadmap is not exhaustive, but it's a good start.

We'll look first at ancient China and modern Singapore, which democracies can emulate to make our own systems more meritocratic. Then we'll journey to France, Malaysia and South Korea on one end of the democratic spectrum, as well as Singapore and the United Arab Emirates on the other, to see how – and why – governments must hold themselves accountable. We'll look, too, at the unlikely suspect of Vietnam, a one-party state, to see why we must re-establish trust in government. We'll also study both the private sector and countries like China and Saudi Arabia to understand the importance of making long-term plans. Looking at Denmark, and its struggles in recent years, we'll grasp the importance of modernising our social safety nets. Moving west, we'll look to the United States and other success stories to learn why we must invest more in human capital – in the people and technology that will define our shared future. We'll learn from the Asian miracles, too, about the vital importance of building better infrastructure, from literal roads to digital ones. Finally, we'll explore why democracies must commit themselves to replenishing our well of talent and tax revenue by opening up our doors to immigrants – something that North America and much of Europe has done well but inconsistently, and that democracies everywhere can and must do better.

This roadmap is decidedly non-interventionist. I am not arguing that the West should overthrow governments in China or Vietnam to institute what we think is the right form of democratic governance. Attempts to do so have almost never succeeded elsewhere – just look at Western failures in Afghanistan, Iraq and Vietnam. Instead, this book offers a roadmap with which democracies can set an example to ensure that the world once again looks to us for a model of good governance and economic flourishing.

When we can offer a roadmap to prosperity, other countries will be more likely to follow our example in the long-term. Only by truly being the best option can we usher in a more democratic and peaceful world – one better organised around liberal principles of equality and fairness.

* * *

Why is this book necessary? Autocracies do not run the world. They still rely on the Western financial system – as Russia found out when it invaded Ukraine – and, to a lesser but still significant extent, Western technology. The bleak future of an autocratic global order has not yet come to pass, thanks to both democracy's astounding resilience and autocracy's own internal contradictions.

Yet democracies do continue to struggle, and autocracies seemingly continue to best us. From the COVID-19 response to social

13

safety nets to top-class infrastructure, democratic citizens increasingly wonder why efficiency and quality of life in their countries are seemingly lagging behind those of China, Singapore and the Gulf states. Some both in democracies and abroad would say that we have embraced too much tumult for our own good.

Modern autocracies may be fundamentally flawed but many have proven themselves quite durable; some have not just survived but thrived. They are nothing like the Soviet Union, whose system never performed effectively, let alone well. Part of the reason the West won the Cold War was because Soviet illiberalism was never successful; it was, as the German writer Hans Magnus Enzensberger said, 'the highest stage of underdevelopment'.[25] The system never achieved legitimacy at home or abroad because it never worked.

The same cannot be said of autocracies today. China is already the world's largest economy when adjusted for purchasing power parity; countries like Singapore and Vietnam have successfully married authoritarianism with market economics.[26] Autocracies account for some 35 per cent of global income – compared to only 12 per cent in 1992.[27] For the first time since 2004, there are today more autocracies than democracies.[28]

Public legitimacy is conditioned on government performance.[29] And because autocracies today increasingly seem to be performing better than democracies, even if these autocracies lack the benefits of true socio-political freedom – the context in which humanity produces its best innovations – a distressing number of people looking for new political visions are finding inspiration in autocracy.[30] As democracies struggle, hundreds of millions of people around the globe have already bought into the Chinese dream of 'authoritarian modernity', whose illiberal success testifies to the notion that prosperity no longer requires freedom – and that a key tenet of Western orthodoxy was, apparently, a mirage.[31]

Yet commentators in Berlin, London and Washington still argue that autocracy is inherently brittle and that the regimes running China and Singapore will eventually crumble and give way to democracy. They remain convinced themselves that the tides of history are flowing their way, that they are simply pushing on an open door.[32] They seem to forget that people everywhere increasingly consider autocracy ascendant and democracies impotent. They seem to forget that democracy is the anomaly and that we must fight to protect it. They seem to forget that most of human history has been made up of empires and despots – that autocracy is the norm and opposition to democracy is at the heart of Western civilisation: Plato's *Republic* is an eloquent pitch for authoritarianism – for the rule of benevolent philosopher-kings. And while there were early proto-democratic expressions of government in Athens, Carthage, Vaishali, San Marino, the Netherlands and Britain, it was not until the Age of Reason that these governments took forms similar to contemporary democracy.

Even the West does not have a natural predisposition to democracy. It is something that we created, but it is also something that we must maintain.

Most critically, champions of democracy who rely on some inherent flaw in autocratic government to bring it down seem to not understand that, unlike when democratic citizens visited the Soviet Union – our last great autocratic competitor – and saw how bleak Moscow or Nizhny Novgorod were, today they go to Dubai, Shanghai and Singapore and they think: 'I've seen the future, and I want *that*.'

* * *

Autocracy's Ills

Democratic government is a historical anomaly, but so too are the gleaming successes of Singapore. Most autocracies have not established the basics of good governance; most have been corrupt and

15

ineffective and truly vicious to their own people, also fomenting instability abroad.

In Russia, corruption pervades daily life, while outspoken journalists wind up dead. In Venezuela, hyperinflation skyrockets out of control and children suffer, prompting hundreds of thousands to flee to neighbouring countries. In these and most other illiberal countries, the building blocks of a good life are nowhere to be found. Autocracy in nearly all forms is a failure.

But a few countries have proved that autocracy is not always inimical to good governance. Recent years have demonstrated that some autocracies can govern well – all while democracies have seemed to struggle, with domestic discord preventing good decision-making or even a minimal standard of effectiveness.[33]

These strong autocracies are overwhelmingly in East Asia, a region blessed with historically high-quality (if undemocratic) institutions and social structures that leaders were able to rediscover after colonialism receded.[34] Chief among them is China, whose economic success is one of history's most remarkable stories.

Yet throughout the disastrous rule of communist founding father Mao Zedong, who combined quasi-Stalinism with a dangerous personality cult, China was poorer than most African countries, with an annual per capita income of about USD 90.[35] It was a nation of grinding poverty and deprivation that lacked even the most basic infrastructure; China was anything but a major player in global affairs. Now, China is the world's second-largest economy by most measures, and the first by several others. The average Chinese citizen lives a life of luxury that would have been inconceivable to their grandparents. China, in the last forty years, increased its per capita income twenty-five-fold, lifting more than 800 million people out of poverty.[36]

Vietnam, too, has had great success, emerging from decades of war with France, the United States and China to become one of the world's top forty economies. After introducing the 'Đổi Mới' reforms,

Vietnam since the 1990s has been one of the world's top five fastest-growing economies. It has steadily outperformed its quasi-democratic neighbours, like Thailand, Malaysia and the Philippines. By 2020, Vietnam's gross domestic product was more than twice that of those three countries. And in that year, when much of the world was in a recession thanks to COVID-19, Vietnam's economy grew by 2 per cent.[37]

Some autocracies of the Arabian Gulf have had similar success, harnessing their oil wealth and relying on the increasing demand for and price of energy to bolster their states and societies. It's easy for critics to say that of course these countries succeeded – they had oil! – but their success really should not be taken for granted. Many resource-rich countries find themselves mired in conflict and discord precisely *because* they have oil or rare earths. From Angola to Venezuela and beyond, vast natural resources lead to conflict, corruption and poverty, as weak institutions stifle growth and enable discord, often over who gets to control these resources.[38]

Yet the Gulf emirates emerged from the colonial era to become wealthy, glittering states. Within living memory, the cities and sheikhdoms of Qatar, Kuwait and Dubai were little more than fishing villages, smuggling havens or fuelling stations for their foreign colonisers. Their populations were nomadic; they lacked the traditions and national identities needed to form nations, let alone functioning, rich states with major roles in international politics.

These leaders' ability to transform their countries into what they are today in a matter of decades is nothing less than staggering. It was nearly impossible to imagine, for instance, that the impoverished, nomadic peoples of the *Rub'al-Khali* would eventually comprise Saudi Arabia, a country that is now one of the world's top twenty economies and a leading regional and global geopolitical player. Nobody writing in the early twentieth century could have expected this. Despite their vast oil wealth, the Gulf States' evolution is, as the scholar Rami Khouri has written, 'perhaps unprecedented in the entire history of human civilization'.[39]

So, if natural resources or well-controlled populations don't guarantee that autocracies will thrive, what sets some of them apart from the others?

* * *

The 'successful' autocracies described are of a similar type. They are authoritarian capitalist countries in East Asia and the Arab Gulf; they all combine relatively free markets and reasonably secure property rights; some but not at all count on natural resources for their wealth.[40]

But even these successes – impressive as they may be – are precarious.

Since Lee Kuan Yew died, several issues have plagued Singapore. Citizens, not just migrant workers, are struggling to make ends meet after losing their jobs during the pandemic; many have signed up for government skills training courses, but the provided income is barely enough to feed their families.[41] The city-state secured enough COVID-19 vaccines and promised to reopen after crossing an 80 per cent vaccination rate, but the government clamped down instead of opening up, and struggled to figure out how to live with the virus.[42]

There are structural problems, too. The country's fertility rate is steadily declining, leaving a smaller workforce, which could lead to weakened productivity. Inequality is on the rise, with the government failing to redistribute its stunning wealth even to the same extent as the more conservative United States.[43] Most worryingly, people lost a huge amount of faith in the government when Lee Kuan Yew died. The state was largely centred around him and his wisdom; without Lee Kuan Yew, people are less confident in their government and their future. The current prime minister, Lee Hsien Loong – Lee's son – is already in his seventies and has chosen a young, relatively unproven figure in Lawrence Wong as his likely successor. The Lee family has been a pillar of stability; without them, Singapore's future looks more rickety.

China's success could also be nearing its end. The Communist Party's goals – improving the economy, cleaning up the environment and meeting its people's ever-rising expectations – are proving harder and harder to reach. China's economy is slowing; juicing it is proving difficult, in no small part because the country is already deeply in debt. And because of China's massive 2008 economic stimulus, and the package it enacted during the COVID-19 crisis, the country's total debt has ballooned to over 250 per cent of GDP.[44]

Debt like this normally precedes a debilitating financial crisis. But because China controls its banks, a crisis is unlikely. This does not mean that China is out of the woods: if Chinese officials do not clean up their economic system, this debt could weigh down the economy for years with zombie firms and unpayable loans.[45] The economy will slow and house prices will fall; many of the loans owned by state-owned enterprises and property developers will be unpayable.

At the same time, Chinese income inequality is worse than in Europe – and only slightly better than in the United States.[46] China's population is also ageing rapidly due to Beijing's infamous 'one-child' policy. Today, pension contributions by workers no longer cover retiree benefits, forcing the government to fill that gap.[47] If current trends continue, China's population will peak at 1.44 billion in 2029 before entering an unstoppable decline, and then an era of negative population growth.[48]

Above all, it remains to be seen if Chinese President Xi Jinping's vision for governance is compatible with economic growth. It is hard to imagine that he can have it both ways: that he can be *more* communist and exert *more* control over society while maintaining the high level of economic growth that the Chinese people expect. It remains to be seen, too, if Xi – under whom Chinese foreign policy has become more and more aggressive – can keep China out of a disastrous war for Taiwan, which would almost surely see China lose access to the Western financial system and Western technology on which Beijing has long relied.[49]

Singapore and China are only two of many examples where autocracies are on the ropes, rather than in the clear. The gradual global phase-out of oil will eventually put huge economic pressure on the Gulf States; they will have to figure out how to provide their people with the high quality of life to which they have become accustomed without oil revenue. Climate change will wreak havoc on countries like Vietnam, also prompting mass waves of immigration that threaten to undermine even the most consolidated of autocracies. The list goes on. And of course, whereas democracies are willing to embrace the chaos – chaos that produces innovations like the internet and paintings like Pollack's – that drives us forward, autocracies snuff out that same chaos in the name of order, stifling potential progress in its infancy.

Democracies may have their problems. But autocracies do, too – and they don't have the solutions. We do.

* * *

Autocracy's Rise – and How to Beat It

In the Second World War's ashes, the United States and its allies created the liberal international order: an architecture of institutions, including the United Nations and World Trade Organization, designed to peacefully resolve conflicts, regulate global finance and, ultimately, ensure rules-based international exchange. Washington's hubris at times undermined the order – American policymakers seemingly extended the order's privileges of sovereignty and respect only to rich democracies, and not to states like Chile and Vietnam – but the order nonetheless brought unprecedented peace among the Great Powers and lifted billions out of poverty. Countries around the world, including China, understood that this way of life could provide them with the tools for advancement in a way that nothing else could. While the Soviet Union maintained its spheres of influence (and nuclear weapons) for the better part of the next half-century, the United States was the unquestioned leader of the free world. And when the Soviet Union collapsed, Washington become the unquestioned leader of just about the entire world.

This order cannot be taken for granted. Criticising it is easy, particularly given the West's militarised failures in places like Afghanistan and Vietnam, but the critic's task becomes harder once they are forced to compare it with what came before – the anarchy preceding the Second World War – or what China and Russia offer for the future.

In February 2022, Russia invaded a sovereign Ukraine, inflicting brutal violence against civilians and government officials alike. China has in recent years committed horrific crimes against the Muslim Uyghurs in the northwest region of Xinjiang, and an ethnic cleansing in Tibet, all while surveilling and brutally preventing any kind of dissent that might bubble up from the country's massive population – not to mention outright seizing of parts of the South China Sea and even Bhutan while also fomenting conflict with India. And, in a critical harbinger of what a China-led order might look like, Beijing has restricted trade with countries including Australia, Lithuania and South Korea for purely political reasons.

North Korea, meanwhile, continues its arbitrary killings and torture (among other atrocities). In Cameroon, the government tortures journalists to death and massacres children in English-speaking schools.

The list goes on: from Iran to Venezuela and everywhere in between, autocracy produces the truly macabre.

This might-makes-right illiberal alternative approach to both domestic governance and the world is quite clearly worth challenging.[50]

Yet autocracies seem to be on the rise. China and Russia have in recent years extended their influence around the world. This is in significant part because over the last decade, particularly in the Trump years, the United States withdrew from leadership and engagement in many areas of the world. Vietnam has consolidated its one-party state, while democracy has died in Myanmar (and possibly in Thailand, too). Even Hungary and Poland, countries at the heart of Europe, have backslid from democracy. Right-wing autocratic parties have gained ground in several other European countries in recent years, not to mention in Brazil as well. And India, the world's largest democracy, continues to experience spasms of ethnic- and religiously-motivated violence – often encouraged by government officials – that undermines the country's liberal foundations.

I've lived in Hungary, which is nowhere near as bad as China or Russia, but nonetheless has a prime minister, Viktor Orbán, who has rapidly done away with the rule of law to cement an autocracy at Europe's centre. I've marched through the streets of Budapest to protest against Orbán's evisceration of academic freedom. I've had the Hungarian government scuttle my plans to return to work in Budapest – because Orbánites in the government didn't like an article I wrote criticising Orbán's crackdowns on press freedom. I've travelled to and worked in other autocracies. I know what autocracy looks like; I know its brutal costs; and I certainly know that it is never justified.

Democracy and liberty are the goals; they are worthwhile pursuits on their own. 'Happiness', as pro-democracy protests in Myanmar have so bravely declared, 'is not born in the cage'.[51] There is no level of economic success that would change my mind on that point.

People in democracies might not realise how lucky they have been to live not only in liberal systems at home, but in a world governed by democracies – and by the rules-based order, flawed as it is. But we are at increasing risk of finding out how bad it will be to live in a world without such rules.

As China has grown more and more powerful, Beijing has steadily begun asserting its power around the world, seeking to refashion the international order around its own ideals. A Sino-centric order will be one organised around brute power, of which China will be the greatest holder, and in which the global trade and innovation networks that have long focused on the West will flow back and forth to China instead.[52] If the behaviour of China, Russia and others described above is anything to go by, an autocracy-led world is one in which democratic governments and their people will get the short end of the stick, over and over again.[53]

A world of autocracies will not be a world of friendly one-party states like Singapore; it will be one of antagonists like China and Russia, whose insecure leaders could plunge us into war – and cut us off from the global economy, if it does flow through them – at any moment. And even if autocracies do not entirely succeed in displacing democracies, the dictators' muddling of the international order will leave the world frayed, allowing for more disruptions and violence. Neither is an attractive option.

* * *

Less than a generation ago, scholars and policymakers believed that we had solved the problem of international order for good. The Soviet Union had collapsed; the United States stood, alone, at the tip of the global spear; it was, as former US secretary of state Madeleine

Albright called it, the 'indispensable nation'. And the United States would be, as another former secretary of state, Dean Acheson, once said, 'the locomotive at the head of mankind' driving history forward into a brighter age.

This, of course, did not come to pass. While the United States did lead the free world and more democracies did emerge following the Soviet Union's dissolution, the West did not take the steps necessary to cement our power. At home, we allowed our social safety nets to decline and money to seep into – and weaken trust in – our democracies. Abroad, we carried out ill-conceived wars in Afghanistan and Iraq that sucked up our resources and left the affected countries and regions in disarray. We promised countries like Hungary and Russia that by democratising and liberalising their economies they would become rich, but instead rapid deregulation left them in a state of shock and, in Russia's case, complete disaster. And by deregulating our financial systems at home, and allowing the extraordinary growth of financial trading without adequate oversight, we set the world up for the crises of 1997 and 2008, which only further weakened global confidence in liberal democracy.

At the same time, several autocracies – from China to Vietnam and beyond – grew and succeeded without democracy. Sure, they accepted certain liberal economic principles, but the leaders of these and other countries explicitly refused democracy. Western scholars and policymakers said that economic growth would create a middle class who would eventually demand and receive democracy. Instead, these same middle classes grew accustomed to their relative wealth and became comfortable with the autocratic regimes that brought them this material ease.[54] These countries' successes taught other leaders around the world that democracy was no longer a prerequisite for abundance. They proved that capitalism could succeed without liberal values – without freedom and democracy.

It should come as no surprise, then, that people throughout the democratic world, and particularly in the West, are increasingly clamouring for autocracy. It is no secret that a disturbing number of Americans would prefer an authoritarian strongman to a democratically elected president.[55] Many in democratic Europe feel the same. What is surprising, though, is just how many scholars, writers and others across the political spectrum are calling for autocracy.

Sohrab Ahmari, a right-wing American writer previously with major outlets like the *New York Post* and *Wall Street Journal*, has offered something of an anti-democracy or at least post-democracy position, arguing that religious conservatives should not adhere to liberal democracy while 'the overall balance of forces has tilted inexorably away from us', because conservative causes – opposing abortion and same-sex marriage – are so important that they must be pursued even beyond legitimate, democratic means.[56]

Of course, this position lacks logic: the current, governing values in much of the West, where people support abortion and same-sex marriage, were won only after decades of activism within a democratic system. If Ahmari wants to return religious conservatism to government, he need only run for office and win it back.

Arguably – despite Ahmari's anti-democratic position – American conservatives have been doing that for thirty years and it has paid dividends today. One might not like the Republicans' manoeuvring, but their ability to stack the Supreme Court, which eventually struck down *Roe v. Wade*, is in large part the result of their democratic victories. Ahmari clearly does not need to do away with democracy to make his wish a reality – at least in parts of the United States. Ironically, it is the Republicans' success *within* democracy that makes Ahmari's position look all the more ridiculous.

Another, somewhat more coherent school of anti-democratic thought comes from Georgetown University professor Jason Brennan. In his book *Against Democracy*, he argues that in terms of efficacy, democracies cannot provide competent governance, precisely because voters tend to be irrational and ignorant.[57] Brennan presents a few alternatives to democracy that all aim to 'the rule of the knowledgeable' (epistocracy), where only the most knowledgeable voters get to elect their countries' leaders.[58]

This is probably how the Chinese Communist Party's elites think of themselves. Every five years, the Chinese National People's Congress elects the country's president and vice president, the chairman of its Central Military Commission, and the president and chief justice of its Supreme People's Court. These officials would likely tell you that the most 'knowledgeable' Chinese were benevolently deciding their country's future – and that this governance system, coupled with its apparently successful authoritarian capitalism, is one to be emulated by nations the world over.

But Brennan's anti-democratic argument does not hold up. The overwhelmingly majority of autocracies, even those more traditionally epistocratic than China is, do not govern more effectively than democracies. Authoritarian governments frequently promise to be making headway on a whole host of fronts – from economic growth to green reforms – but they tend to undermine them in practice. And as inner circles tighten in personalist regimes, like that of North Korea or Russia or China today, information flows worsen, the leader becomes more and more aggressive, and underlings refuse to challenge them. The result is unwise, dangerous policy decisions, such as Putin's invasion of Ukraine.

Autocracy may seem to solve short-term problems, but it is just about always disastrous in the long-term.

A third view is put forward by what we might describe as eco-authoritarians. Confronted by the massive challenge of climate change, there's a view that governments must be granted special powers. We may have affection for democracy, but it is messy and slow – and decadent, as Xi Jinping or Lee Kuan Yew might put it. *Faced with an existential crisis*, these eco-authoritarians argue, *shouldn't we be willing to slay the sacred cows of freedom and democracy?*

'Climate change is bigger than democracy,' said Roger Hallam, a leader of Extinction Rebellion, back in 2019. Likewise, at a 2021 talk in Paris, Swedish academic Andreas Malm – the author of *How to Blow Up a Pipeline* – called for 'war communism' to deal with the climate crisis.[59] His debate partner, the prominent French economist Frédéric Lordon, called for 'neo-Leninism' for the same reason.[60] Malm and Lordon are careful to avoid saying that they are calling for armed revolution, but how else would Sweden or France move from peaceful capitalist democracy to war communism or neo-Leninism?

The pair are influential and thoughtful scholars, but they are also fundamentally wrong. What they are hoping for is an authoritarian magic wand, a wand that one strongman, or a cadre of a few selected strongmen, can wave and make the unbelievably complex issue of climate change go away. The chief problem with this theory is that if we authorised our state to coerce people into doing things that they do not want to do – even if we all recognise that it is in our collective interest – we would, by extension, authorise the state to punish those who do not obey those rules. It does not feel plausible that we would accept a government authority telling us whether we can go on holiday, or what food we could eat. That being the case, the said authority would have to fine or even imprison transgressors. To put it bluntly, then, neo-Leninism would need neo-Gulags.

Moreover, autocracy very clearly does not inexorably lead to the kind of good government necessary to combat climate change. Very often, it leads to the opposite. China is the world's biggest polluter not despite being an autocracy, but because of it. And, of course, if your green autocrat turns out to be corrupt – or not as interested in climate change as they seemed to be when trying to get into power – you have no mechanism by which to remove them.

So, while authoritarianism might seem seductive to elites lamenting the purportedly misguided voting behaviour of average citizens fed up with seemingly incompetent governments presiding over decline, autocracy decidedly does not offer a salve to our struggles. It is not the answer. It never will be.

Democracy is not our problem. But faith in its automatic functioning is.[61]

* * *

Yet people in Western democracies are particularly fed up, and in some cases fed up with democracy itself. While Japan, South Korea and Taiwan thrive or at least muddle through, it is Americans, Brits, Germans and others in the West who continue to express the most troubling, anti-democratic views, both in newspaper columns and at the ballot box. Studies show that global dissatisfaction with democracy is at an all-time high, with frustration notably high in the West.[62] People throughout the world, but specifically in the West, have high expectations, and they are furious that their governments are not delivering.[63]

Voters are inherently correct. They do, generally, have a rational view of their political institutions; they tell decision-makers what is working, what is not, and what desperately needs to be addressed.[64] For all the elite laments about their supposed ignorance, voters know what they want, whether that be lower taxes, greater personal agency, or improved healthcare. And what Brexit and Trump and Le Pen voters are telling politicians is that globalisation has failed them – that as their countries got richer, they did not.

From Ronald Reagan to David Cameron, our leaders did not ensure that globalisation's benefits would 'trickle down'. And when these benefits did not reach the average person, voters began to reject the elites on both the left and right who failed them.

This book, then, is a call to action: it is a call for democracies to beat autocracy both within and abroad by learning to perform and deliver for our people once again.

We need to combat the tendency towards autocracy – the sense among people around the world that when things go wrong, as they have for many since 2008, a strongman or Singapore-like authoritarian government can fix it. It's far too easy to say, when confronted with a big problem, that new powers are needed, that a so-called 'strongman' (and it invariably is a man) should come in and sort it out.

To combat the autocratic way of life, we will need to look far afield to emulate the countries that have successfully established meritocracies, developed accountable systems, won social trust, built top-class infrastructure and invested in human capital, all while embracing the volatility that is intrinsic to democracy and drives progress. We can learn as much from the Singaporean present as much as from the American past, from the United Arab Emirates as much as from Denmark, all while retaining the character of our own nations, our societies' openness, and strengthening democracy. We will need to find wisdom in what might seem like odd places. We must not assume that democracy is pushing to victory on a door ajar. Instead, we must act – because if we don't get this right, our failure will be democracy's failure, not only abroad, but at home, too.

If we fail, we will have left the door swung in the opposite direction, propped up and open for the autocratic-leaning politicians who would use domestic discontent to move us away from liberalism. We will hand would-be autocrats a golden opportunity – because when people are fed up with their governing elites for a failure to deliver the basics of the good life, they will not only vote these elites out but will also replace them with the most anti-elite, anti-status quo politicians on offer. And around the world, such politicians tend to be demagogues with authoritarian tendencies.

We shouldn't forget that this is essentially what happened in the United States when Trump got elected in 2016. Racial animus, and Trump's willingness to wield it, certainly helped vaunt him into power, but he made vital gains with people of all backgrounds who were more frustrated with economic inequality and globalisation than they were concerned about racism. We shouldn't forget, too, that Trump almost won in 2020 – in part because he improved his performance among minority voters, who were frustrated by the Democrats' purportedly high-tax, identity-focused agenda (and that when he lost, he tried to violently manoeuvre his way into power on January 6).

Complacency in the face of popular pain breeds demagoguery.

This is precisely what happened in Hungary, where left-wing ineptitude gave way to the authoritarian Viktor Orbán. It was the 2006 leaking of former left-wing prime minister Ferenc Gyurcsány's expletive-laden speech – in which he admitted that his government 'lied in the morning [and] lied in the evening' while campaigning and in office, particularly about the economy – that helped rejuvenate Orbán, who had been ousted from the premiership in 2002.[65] It was the leaking of this speech – one in which the prime minister declared, 'You cannot name any significant government measures that we can be proud of except pulling our administration out of the shit at the end. Nothing!' – that signalled the erstwhile end of the Hungarian left and Hungary's return to autocracy.[66]

Magyar Rádió broadcast the twenty-seven-minute speech, known as the 'Őszöd speech' after where it was delivered, on 17 September 2006. Protests erupted in Budapest soon after; Orbán helped lead the demonstrations, which saw 200 people injured in violent clashes.[67] Gyurcsány refused to quit, so Orbán and his allies took to the streets again in 2007, with the former and future prime minister declaring: 'We have assembled here today to show those in power that we cannot be held in fear.'[68]

Gyurcsány would finally step down in March 2009, but the

damage was done. Orbán's right-wing Fidesz party swept the 2010 parliamentary elections, winning – along with its allies – a super-majority needed to rewrite major laws, and even amend the country's constitutions. Orbán has been in power since, using this super-majority to undermine democracy by gerrymandering parliamentary districts and packing the courts, for starters.

In 2021, he made sure to mark the fifteenth anniversary of the Gyurcsány speech. He called the speech a 'terrifying moment', adding that Gyurcsány had 'created that situation, he delivered the speech, lied to the people and came to power through lies, took people's money and then drove the country to bankruptcy'.[69] Not new to this game, Orbán made sure to animate the threat once again. 'This is not past tense but the past still living with us and which keeps trying to return,' he said, insisting that the left had stripped the elderly of their 13th month pensions and stopped supporting families, while they 'doubled, tripled' the prices of household energy. But his government, Orbán said, had *of course* stepped in to reintroduce housing subsidies and wage hikes.

'Once pensioners get back their 13th month pensions,' he added, 'we can say that we have left behind the whole Őszöd speech.'[70]

* * *

The Hungarian example is extreme. A leak this damaging seems unlikely in many of our democracies. But it is not impossible. Nor is it the only way a feckless government makes way for the autocrats within. Orbán was such an attractive option precisely because the speech was coupled with actual economic pain and governmental incompetence.

Something similar could very well happen in democracies around the world today. It is not hard to see how failure to deliver in the United States, United Kingdom, Germany, South Korea or elsewhere could bring to power an anti-democratic populist. It could happen in your backyard – which is why we must shut the door on these would-be dictators as soon as possible.

To do so, we'll need to take urgent action. And above all, we will need to deliver good governance.

* * *

Some two hundred years ago, Alexis de Tocqueville, French diplomat and chronicler of the early United States, wrote, 'The greatness of America lies not in being more enlightened than any other nation, but rather in her ability to repair her faults.'[71] It was this willingness to contend with its flaws and failings that also made post–Second World War America so great.[72] It is this attitude that democracies desperately need today.

Only once we embrace this attitude, recognising and committing to fix our mistakes, can we truly stand up for democracy both at home and around the world. Only by reinvigorating what makes our democracies great – and by truly delivering for people – can we patch up the liberal international order and take the next step into a better world.

Only then can we defeat the dictators.

1

Merit

Ancient China's Wisdom

Liu Heng's name was one meant to be forgotten. A diligent and deferential man, the son of a lesser concubine, he became ruler of China's south-eastern Dai region in 196 BCE, at just seven years old. These were years of violence, with Dai at the forefront of foreign tribal raids against the ruling Han dynasty. Liu almost certainly did not expect much in life beyond this post – perhaps he dreamed of rising to a slightly more important job elsewhere on the dynasty's frontlines. He was not looking to write his name into the history books.

But in 180 BCE, after the Han empress died and officials deposed her clan, these same officials offered Liu the throne, believing his family to be humble and better suited for leadership than that of his rivals.[1] Ironically, it was the qualities that seemingly marked him for mediocrity that now launched Liu into history.

From the day he took power as emperor – with some hesitation, at just twenty-three years old – he lived up to the hopes of the king-makers: he cared for his people, not just for his clan and regime. Just a year into his rule, Liu, known now as Emperor Wen of Han, abolished a law that allowed the state to imprison criminals' families, created an economic assistance programme for those in need and made peace with a neighbouring kingdom.

And then, in 165 BCE, he introduced the reform that would not only strengthen his dynasty and the modern Chinese state that eventually emerged, but would also serve as a gift to the world at large.[2] It was in this year that Emperor Wen decided that civil servants should be recruited through exams – that is, chosen based on merit – rather than through the networks of acquaintance and influence that today we might call the 'old boys' club'.

Before Wen, government officials never sat for any kind of examination. Instead, local officials sent the names of prospective candidates, generally local elites, to the central government, which judged them based on little more than their reputation.

Wen's system was imperfect. Those who sat for the exams were the most educated, and likely those with connections and wealth. But these tests nonetheless institutionalised the concept of merit for the first time in recorded history – nearly two millennia before anyone in what would become the West did anything comparable.

* * *

For all its success, the Han dynasty eventually collapsed, as nearly all dynasties do. Hereditary regimes can rarely last longer than three generations. They are highly susceptible to individual incompetence: one poor successor can break the system that was handed to him (almost never her). Nearly every clan throughout history has been swept out of power or, at best, marginalised and commodified, as with England's current royal family.

But the Han dynasty nonetheless left behind a vital legacy: meritocracy.

Several hundred years after Wen's rule, in the sixth and seventh centuries CE, the Sui dynasty further improved the exam system, opening it to all people, regardless of social class and hometown. The Tang dynasty, ruling from the seventh to the tenth centuries, made the system even more merit-based, focusing less on family background and instead on 'physique and manners', along with 'talk and words' on contemporary policy issues.[3]

Through years of ingenuity and reform, Emperor Wen's testing system became China's civil-service exam, in which individuals were assessed and deemed capable before receiving what were generally coveted government jobs. The exam system resulted in good government and 'contributed to the development of a prosperous China' before colonialism, as the scholar Bernard Yeung has written.[4]

Chinese émigrés would soon spread this meritocratic system to Japan, Korea and Vietnam. Only two thousand years later did the system migrate to the West on horseback.[5] Now, virtually every modern bureaucracy replicates the ancient Chinese model, in which there is a centralised system of appointment and promotion based on clear ranks (as in the American General Service schedule).[6] Competitive national examinations became similarly vital to advancement in the United Kingdom, the United States and France through the eleven-plus, Scholastic Aptitude Test, and baccalaureate, respectively. These tests – in which students demonstrated their merit on paper – channelled people into the best schools and most prestigious careers.[7] Britain and France competed for years to produce the world's best civil service, which selected their servants by merit as well.

As history pressed on, the governments that ran the world increasingly fused democracy with meritocracy, moving from hereditary power and classes of favour-trading elites towards economic government and popular consent. When meritocracy works – when people understand that they can get ahead by working hard – citizens tend to bless the system.

But the fusion of meritocracy and democracy is neither necessary nor automatic. Both autocracies and democracies are at their best when they are most meritocratic, even if democracies are inherently *more* meritocratic, because in liberal societies everyone can aspire to lead their countries, unlike in autocracies, where that privilege is limited to a small, self-selecting cadre of party officials.

Yet democracies the world over today find their meritocracies in disrepair.

In fact, in most democracies today meritocracy is strongest not in politics, the public sector, or even the private sector – but in professional sports. No amount of money or connections will buy you a spot in a Premier League squad or etch your name in Major League Baseball's record books if you lack the requisite talent (which is why the steroid scandal, in which people *did* cheat their way into history, so angered Americans). But a nice family connection can get you a job in the White House or at a top bank in the City of London.

The best sporting teams, on the other hand, are those composed of the absolute best players and organised by the best manager, who was hired by the best executive – while the worst are those comprising players signed for personal reasons by a manager who, in turn, was hired by an executive because they went to Oxford or Harvard together. And when teams hire from the same pool of coaches and executives over and over again, rather than bringing in clearly talented new candidates, they tend to struggle, as the National Football League's racism row has demonstrated.[8]

Countries, too, are strongest when they build their civil and foreign services with the best people they can get: when they hire the proven data scientist or a truly skilful analyst, not the one who just happened to go to high school with the president's grandson. National success comes on the back of talented individuals who enter government (and the private sector) believing that they will be promoted if they work hard and succeed. National disaster comes when leaders stack their regimes with self-serving supporters and those with personal connections to the ruling clan, as in dictatorships across the globe – and in more than a few democracies.

Meritocracy, as this chapter will show, is the only proper way to run a state, particularly a democratic one whose legitimacy hinges on representing the public. It is ancient China that gave this legacy to the world. And today it is Singapore, another autocracy, that seems to have perfected the meritocratic system – all while the path to opportunity seems to have narrowed in democracies in both the West and beyond, with actual advancement seemingly a rite only of the already-privileged.

But democracies know how to get back on track.

Throughout ancient Chinese history, officials appealed for meritocracy not when things were going well, but 'when political hierarchies became frozen, and the governing body could not function well', as the political scientist Wang Pei has written.[9] Nepotism froze the system; meritocracy oiled its gears, pushing forward progress that corruption had stalled.

So too, today.

* * *

Our Ailing Meritocracies

Meritocracy is a system in which people are chosen to advance based on their ability. Regardless of privilege or connections, in a meritocracy, the cream rises to the top. Meritocracy is inherently unequal: a meritocratic system can provide equality of opportunity – as in the idealised American dream – but not equality of outcome, as in Karl Marx's vision. Some people are born with more talent than others. Not everyone is born with the physical build to be an Olympic diver or the intellectual capacities to a rocket scientist. (I'm 0-for-2 on those fronts.)

Yet meritocracy is the best system we have. As the *Economist*'s Adrian Wooldridge has written, such systems are those in which 'people are individuals before they are anything else: masters of their fates and captains of their souls'.[10] And, with masters and captains performing at their best in aggregate, meritocracy produces strong economic efficiency and material progress on a national level.

Meritocracy is never perfect in its execution. People are naturally inclined to help their families and clan, meaning that even the most well-intentioned, seemingly incorruptible officials may elevate or privilege their kin when given the chance. But at many times and in many places, meritocracy has thrived despite these challenges. A system imperfectly based on merit is still immeasurably preferable to one based on favouritism and connections or racial and ethnic quotas.

* * *

Meritocracy, like democracy, is far from permanent. Leaders must tend to its roots, lest the human inclination to help our own clans destroys it. China again offers a telling example.

For centuries, Chinese leaders understood the importance of meritocracy, so much so that when Sun Yat-sen established the Republic of China in 1912, he formed the 'Examination Yuan' (Ministry of Examination) as one of the five pillars of a modern Chinese government.[11]

But in the 1960s, Chinese communist leader Mao Zedong unleashed the anti-intelligentsia Cultural Revolution, instructing his supporters to attack the existing authorities, especially teachers, which they did with great zeal. Through this and other initiatives, Mao effectively reversed centuries of Chinese meritocratic progress to elevate his communist cadres, rather than the people most qualified to do the work, everywhere from the Ministry of Foreign Affairs to the education system.

It should come as no surprise, then, that Mao's leadership deprived China of expertise and ingenuity, and turned the once great country into a landscape of poverty. It should also come as no surprise that only once post-Mao China rediscovered meritocracy was the country able to get back on track and grow into the global power it is today.

* * *

Democracies, too, have struggled to maintain their meritocratic systems.

Over the years, poor governance has either weakened our meritocratic systems or allowed these systems to stagnate. Too often, and in too many countries, these systems entrench elites rather than refreshing their ranks with society's most talented people, whether they be the children of princes or paupers.[12] While something of a meritocracy operates *among* elites – those who perform best at the top-tier schools attend the best universities and are hired for the best jobs, and then compete for advancement within the top companies or in government – meritocracy does not operate for the overwhelming majority of democratic citizens.

While former British prime minister Theresa May declared her country a place where people have 'the chance to go as far as their talents will take them', study after study shows that most Brits go only as far as their family background will take them.[13] Teenagers from low-income households are significantly less likely to get into a university in the Russell Group, which comprises twenty-four of the United Kingdom's top institutions. The result is to further weaken their potential social mobility: graduates from the country's top universities earn 40 per cent more than other graduates and are far more likely to run the country.[14]

The UK's former prime minister, Boris Johnson, went to both Eton College (the fees for which are currently around USD 50,000 annually) and Oxford University, as did his last male predecessor, David Cameron. Theresa May, who served between them, did not attend Eton – which is a boys-only institution – but she too attended Oxford.

In fact, one-third of Britain's post–Second World War prime ministers have been Old Etonians, as were Johnson's previous business secretary Kwasi Kwarteng, the Leader of the House Jacob Rees-Mogg, and a host of other MPs, along with the Archbishop of Canterbury and many leaders across the arts and sciences.[15] Remarkably, every prime minister since Margaret Thatcher attended Oxford except John Major and Gordon Brown. Major, exceptionally among his fellow premiers, left school at fifteen; but Brown attended Edinburgh University, which is in the United Kingdom's and world's top tier for higher education. Given, too, that many of them are white (and nearly all at least upper middle class), it is safe to say that Britain's 'meritocracy' has produced a set of ruling elites who simply do not look like the people they're supposed to represent.

One could counter that Britain's rulers have always drawn from a specific, privileged segment of society; that is true enough, the country retains a unique aristocratic character. But it is hardly an excuse for accepting this flawed system as the norm, especially as other countries move in the right direction. The Netherlands and Sweden have proven themselves to be better than the United Kingdom at addressing inequality – because they've redistributed funds to break down class distinctions.[16]

Eton's spiking fees are one example of Britain's failure to seriously address this issue. Another is that, like in the United States, students with money – those who can afford tutors – remain more likely than their less privileged counterparts to post top scores on standardised tests.[17] These exams, conceived to *bust* privilege and level the playing field, are doing the opposite.

The ladder into the British elite was certainly never easy. Yet even as the country has become more diverse and dynamic over the last five decades, the path into this elite has remained far from the ordinary person's grasp, perhaps further now than in recent memory.

The British writer Musa Okwonga laments as much in his memoir, *One of Them*, published in 2021. Okwonga – the child of Ugandan immigrants – attended Eton, but he was hardly from Britain's elite. He was an Etonian of a certain, lost type: those from small towns with what he calls 'middle-class professionals' for parents.[18] But since Okwonga left Eton, fees have tripled, meaning that even doctors and civil servants cannot afford to send their kids there. Despite having secured what should be solid jobs that set their children up for success, these parents cannot spend the money to give their kids the leg-up that the super-rich can.

Eton today would 'be unaffordable for someone like my mother', he writes, meaning 'that most of the boys there will be drawn from an even narrower segment of society'.

'It is grim,' he adds, 'to think that the journey I took [. . .] is no longer possible for boys like me.' It would seem that today, 'mere academic excellence', as Okwonga writes, simply 'is not good enough'.[19]

* * *

Many high-minded Western assaults on meritocracy tend to come from well-meaning pundits and politicians concerned with inequality, particularly on racial and ethnic lines. But meritocracy's perversion by privilege is a more pernicious global problem rather than one limited to the West. Even in South Korea – a country once considered a paragon of meritocracy – the same issues crop up.

From the very start, South Korean children advance on what looks like merit. A top-tier elementary school performance gets you into an elite high school, where success funnels you into three of the country's best universities: Seoul National, Korea University and Yonsei. The graduates of these universities, particularly those at the top of their classes, feed into top jobs at South Korea's top firms and companies, as well as in the government.[20]

The key to Korean success may seem meritocratic, but as in much of the West, money greases the wheels to power. Parents with resources pay for foreign trips and language education, along with private tutoring – 'cram schools' – in which specialised teachers instruct lucky students on the content of upcoming exams. South Koreans spend some USD 15 million annually, or 20 per cent of their collective household income, on after-school private tutoring known as *hagwon*.[21] Some 75 per cent of children attend such classes.

As Dr Yoo Jung Kim writes, 'at the end of the day, there can only be so many winners'.[22] And in South Korea, those winners tend to be those with enough money to get ahead, not necessarily those with the most talent.

It should be no surprise, then, that the country has produced several films and television shows specifically about inequality, with strong references to how broken the country's purportedly meritocratic system is.

The 2021 Netflix hit show *Squid Game*, in which Koreans experiencing financial issues compete in deadly competitions to win millions of dollars, shines light on these issues through character 212, or Han Mi-nyeo. A conniving but clearly bright woman, she offers a striking, understated commentary on South Korea's declining meritocracy: 'I am very smart. [. . .] I just never got a chance to study.' This saying is common in Korean media and implies that while Han is 'street smart' and quick on her feet, she never had the opportunity to pursue formal education, let alone attend a *hagwon* or university.[23] Despite her merit, she simply never had a chance to succeed in South Korea.

* * *

When meritocracy works as intended, it allows people to overcome privilege. As a system, meritocracy has allowed the best – from all segments of society, regardless of race, class or gender – to rise to the top and replace stagnant and homogeneous elites.

At one point, the United States military was an example of this. The institution's meritocratic nature allowed people from all walks of life to succeed, regardless of their economic or ethnic background. It was this system that enabled Colin Powell, the child of working-class Jamaican immigrants growing up in the Bronx, to become a four-star general, and eventually US national security advisor, chairman of the Joint Chiefs of Staff, and US secretary of state.

Powell entered the military in 1958. He steadily worked his way up the ladder, earning promotions based on his decorated service. Being a Black man facing racism from his counterparts couldn't stop his rise – precisely because army promotions were based on merit, rather than skin colour or connections, unlike in the contemporary State Department, which for decades was stacked with Harvard and Yale graduates who all know one another from boyhood (and it was inevitably boyhood).[24] 'The only thing we care about in the military is performance and potential. If you perform and have potential, you'll move up,' Powell later said. 'If you don't, you won't.'[25] And because he performed and had evident potential, he moved up the ladder.

Something similar is true in at least parts of the US army today.

White, Black, Hispanic and all other active-duty male soldiers are almost equally as likely to earn promotion from O-1 (Second Lieutenant) to O-4 (captain), as well as from O-4 to O-6 (Colonel).[26] Black women are 15 per cent more likely to earn a promotion from O-1 to O-4 than white women, and around 10 per cent more than Hispanic or other women.[27] People of 'other' backgrounds and Hispanic women are more likely than white or Black women to earn promotion from O-4 to O-6.[28]

But white officers remain more likely than their counterparts to earn promotions as they move up the US army ladder, leading the Pentagon to suggest the removal of photos from promotion and selection boards to account for racial bias.[29] The army bureaucracy also remains outdated, stifling careers and prompting huge numbers of talented soldiers of all backgrounds to leave the military.[30] Veterans are on record as saying they would have stayed if the military was 'more of a meritocracy'.[31] The United States would be better off if they had stayed.

The army's troubles are reflective of our meritocracies' broader failures. Our systems are not busting as much privilege as they are supposed to, instead cementing a sclerotic elite, widening the income gap and, understandably, turning people against meritocracy. It is not hard to understand why progressives and conservatives alike, from Black Lives Matter protestors to Brexit voters, resent the broken versions of 'meritocracy' operating in their respective countries, or even why certain elites, from institutions like Harvard and Yale, have diminished meritocracy as 'tyranny' or a 'trap'.[32] Our broken meritocracies lay the groundwork for public frustration – frustration that tends to explode in waves of populist voting for the demagogue who promises to root out these elites, to 'drain the swamp' and replace it with a proper meritocracy in which *real* natives, not those only from the urban centres and fancy schools, have the chance to succeed.

But the problem is not meritocracy itself; and the solution is most definitely not to ban school admissions tests and use a lottery system for admission to top schools to make them more diverse, as tried by San Francisco's prestigious Lowell High School in 2021.[33] The result of that approach has been to disadvantage children who had demonstrated merit in the classroom, who in San Francisco are disproportionately Asian-Americans – meaning that an effort aimed at increasing diversity ended up hurting certain minorities.[34] The effort also failed to produce better outcomes for the more diverse class. Nearly 25 per cent of the school's 620 freshmen students received a D or an F in the 2021 fall semester, compared to only 7.9 per cent in the fall of 2020 and 7.7 per cent in the fall of 2019 – before the school adopted its lottery admissions system.[35]

By any measure, this system was a failure.

Yet this effort is only one of many to replace meritocracy with more lottery-like systems, which advocates say are better at promoting equity. These same advocates essentially argue that meritocracy stifles diversity, and that the two cannot coexist. But they can, and they must – because nobody has yet found a system that produces, nurtures and elevates more talent, whether Black, white, Asian or anything else. When done right, meritocracy remains the only way to progress, not just for the dominant group, but for all.

* * *

The problem, as this chapter aims to make clear, is that stagnant leadership and misgovernance have corrupted meritocracy, that a failing meritocracy will make for a failing democracy and that the problem is not meritocracy itself.

For all the attacks against meritocracy, there is no other way of organising society than through meritocratic means. And if you're inclined to disagree, think for a moment about your personal life. Ultimately, when your back is up against the wall, you will want to be operated on by a surgeon or flown by a pilot who graduated at the top of their class and achieved renown in their field through genuine merit – not through a lottery or connections. At some point, particularly when it is a matter of life and death, the buck always stops, and meritocracy always triumphs.

On an individual level, our governments are not a matter of life and death. The mid-level staffer who received their position because of nepotism is not necessarily going to cause any substantial harm, even if a better but less well-connected candidate was denied the opportunity. But staffing large swathes of one's government this way and failing to improve our meritocracies – as many democracies have – sets the stage for national misgovernance, and thus catastrophe. It also breeds public discontent, priming people to put in power those demagogues who promise to dismantle this patronage system, root and branch. (Of course, strongmen tend to simply install their own highly corrupt patronage systems.)

The result? To weaken democracy at home by boosting the would-be dictators within – and to weaken democracy's image abroad. Because if we can't maintain meritocracies strong enough to keep democracy alive, we will not seriously be able to claim ourselves as a model for anyone else.

The ancient Chinese, who invented and practised meritocracy long before it reached the West, have a solution. When their systems froze because of elite stagnation, some subset of officials raised their voice, making the case for meritocracy once again. So, too, should democracies worldwide. And unlike ancient China, we have a present model from which to learn: Singapore.

* * *

The Singaporean Model

It was early September 1992 in the humid Indonesian capital of Jakarta, and the world was ripe for change. The Berlin Wall had collapsed; the Soviet Union had dissolved; America – and its model of liberal democracy – had emerged from the Cold War's depths seemingly unchallenged.

Yet while the West and its partners cheered, the Non-Aligned Movement, founded in 1961, had existed for one specific reason: to gather developing countries that refused to choose a side in the Cold

War together in solidarity. With the Soviet Union's collapse, they found themselves without a purpose.

But the movement's leaders wisely decided to stay relevant.[36] Its members, whose governments then held two-thirds of the seats in the United Nations, dialled down the anti-West speeches that dominated previous meetings to instead take up serious development issues. In this new world, there were simply too many opportunities – and much money out there – to make the West mad. It was more important to get rich than to be right.

And so, the non-aligned countries searched for solutions, for ways to capitalise on all this new world had to offer. Unsurprisingly, they turned to Singapore, a member of the movement since 1970 and surely the most successful one.

Singapore was represented at this summit by Goh Chok Tong, who had taken over from Lee Kuan Yew only a few years earlier. Goh was a personable man, one who served as the 'velvet glove on the iron fist of an authoritarian government', as the journalist Philip Bowring later wrote.[37]

In Jakarta, non-aligned member movements sought him out. *How*, they wondered, *did Singapore, this tiny city-state, become such a power? How*, I imagine them thinking but politely not asking, *did this little country do so much better than we have?*

At least one official put the question to him. In Goh's telling, Nepali Prime Minister Girija Prasad Koirala asked simply for the secret of Singapore's success, as if Goh could offer a one-sentence answer with which Koirala could cure all that ailed his country. A soft smile spread across Goh's face, as the Singaporean basked in this admiration. Characteristically, he offered a one-sentence answer, but almost surely not the one his Nepali counterpart wanted: 'Lee Kuan Yew.'[38]

But Goh also offered more practical advice. He briefly explained the principles with which Lee governed and built Singapore, the ones that set the city-state up for its grand successes. Meritocracy was chief among them.

In a speech some months later to his party colleagues, Goh put it simply: the 'practice of meritocracy in the civil service, in politics, in business, and in schools' pushed Singaporeans 'to achieve excellence and to compete against others'. The result was to create institutions of a genuinely high calibre, ones run by what Lee called the 'good men' needed to have 'good government'.[39]

Much to his credit, Lee from the outset considered multiracialism and meritocracy as critical principles, even if his Singapore did favour those of Chinese heritage. His position was not popular at the time: when Singapore was still part of Malaysia, the Malaysian ruling elite wanted affirmative action for the Malay community, because they were the region's indigenous people, whereas many Singaporeans were of Chinese origin, their families having emigrated in the years, decades and even centuries prior.[40]

And while racial disparities persisted – with the Chinese getting the most plush jobs and owning the most prime real estate, the privileges of being Chinese operating like the privileges of whiteness in the United States – Lee's progressive attitude was real, if unusual for the time, and important. His approach to diversity served his country well and would inform Singaporean policy both throughout his life and after his death.

* * *

Perhaps you might be asking the same questions that the Nepali prime minister did. *How did multi-ethnic Singapore do it? How did this small country establish such a meritocratic system that government corruption is almost non-existent? And how did they do it without being a democracy?*

Education is the first answer.

Singapore has a national approach to education; countless other governments leave that responsibility to sub-national administrators. Singapore, gifted with a small population, looks at the system from above, invests heavily in education research, tests its reforms, and carefully applies new ideas and research to its schools. Education officials work carefully to create textbooks, worksheets and working examples before they ever see a classroom.

Singapore has also kept education fees affordable. An education at elite schools and national universities is never out of reach of the average Singaporean household; grants and scholarships are available for those unable to bear the full costs.[41] Affordability generally does not prevent the smartest Singaporeans from rising to the top, unlike in the United States, where one year of college costs, in some cases, close to USD 80,000 – nearly double what the average American makes annually, and far more than most can afford.

Singapore's education system also differs from those of the West by not prioritising a traditional college education for everyone. Instead, Singapore focuses on streamlining students into areas in which they are already talented. So, the academically inclined end up at universities like the National University of Singapore, while others become experts in their craft, whether that be construction or plumbing. Everyone plays a role, everyone deserves respect and everyone can excel in something.

Singapore does this, in part, by relying on exams and organising classroom instruction around them. Every student takes an exam at the end of both primary and secondary schooling. According to their performance on the Primary School Leaving Examination (PLSE), taken around age eleven or twelve, the students are sorted into three streams: one for those with the highest scores, and two others for more average scorers. Even from here a child's future is not yet determined. Students take another exam, the O-Level exam, typically at age sixteen, the results of which determine their college options.

Thanks to these policies, some 90 per cent of students from Singapore's bottom socio-economic fifth today achieve some kind of post-secondary education, a number that dwarfs those posted by just about any other country on earth.[42] A Singaporean child born to parents in this bottom fifth of incomes has a 14 per cent chance of moving into the top fifth by the time they reach their early thirties – compared to only 8 per cent in the United States and 9 per cent in the United Kingdom.[43]

Singapore's successes speak for themselves. Any interaction with one of Singapore's many quick-witted and deceptively youthful diplomats in Washington or London is enough to remind you just how much the country's government has got right.

The stats back up this assertion as well. Singapore's education system constantly ranks atop the Organisation for Economic Co-operation and Development (OECD)'s Programme for International Student Assessment, a triennial test of fifteen-year-olds in dozens of countries in maths, reading and science. The assessment found that Singaporean students are some three years ahead of Americans in maths, for instance.[44] In 2020, the World Economic Forum ranked Singapore fourth in terms of education equality and eighth in terms of education access.[45]

Singapore's education system is imperfect, like everyone else's, with inequality and elitism persisting, as it does everywhere. But it is impossible to disagree with the *Economist*'s admittedly bold proclamation that '[e]ducation would be much better if more countries copied Singapore's homework'.[46]

* * *

With thousands cheering him, Prime Minister Goh sauntered onto the stage at Singapore's Kallang Theatre in August 2000. It was a sweltering day, as are most days in Singapore, and Goh was set to deliver the National Day speech, an annual address in which the city-state's leader discusses challenges and lays out future plans. Goh, somewhat uniquely, focused on the importance of meritocracy amid both global and regional challenges.

'These are exciting times,' he told the crowd. 'But they are also unsettling. Exciting, because of the vast opportunities that are emerging. Unsettling, because the changes sweeping the world will require major adjustments in our economy and society.'[47]

Goh was right, Asia was swept up in change. In Indonesia, the relative stability of a strongman, Suharto, had 'given way' to social uprising. In Malaysia, the opposition was threatening the long-time ruling party. And Taiwan's election of Chen Shui-bian had inflamed existing tensions between China and the self-ruled island.

But, more importantly, Goh emphasised the challenges and opportunities posed by rapid globalisation: China was preparing to enter the World Trade Organization; South Korea had reformed itself to become more competitive; Japan's economy, too, was improving.

Yet Southeast Asia was lagging behind, with the region 'slow to shake off the effects of the [1997–8 financial] crisis', as Goh noted. Most countries were struggling to make necessary structural reforms. But as Goh made clear, this was not the time to be complacent. 'Globalisation,' he declared, is 'driving many changes in the economic landscape. Wherever you are, and whatever you do, you now compete in the global arena, for skills, talent, investments and markets.'[48]

So, as Singapore's leaders tend to do, Goh doubled down on what had made the country great: meritocracy. 'We must not envy those who have made it rich,' he told the country. 'Rather, we must provide the opportunities for more to be like them. It means operating on the basis of meritocracy – that you can get ahead in life if you work hard, and regardless of your background.'[49]

But Goh did not advertise meritocracy as a means only to personal wealth. He, like Lee before him, believed meritocracy to be the secret source of Singapore's national success: the tool by which Singapore could fill its top-class civil service with the 'good people' that Lee deemed necessary for 'good government'.

He was right.

Today, while many of the most talented young people living in democratic countries look to banking or big business to reap the rewards of their educational success, Singapore has convinced at least some of these people to join their country's civil service, which is today among the world's best. It is Singapore that has figured out how to make the most of its own people.

* * *

Singapore begins recruiting talent early on by offering competitive undergraduate scholarships for students to attend top foreign universities like Oxford and Cambridge – but only if they commit to serve in the government for five to eight years upon their return.[50]

These Singaporeans are not vaguely co-opted into public service with little expectation of staying beyond some short period, as in some American programmes. Rather, they are assessed upon return, and if they meet the standards, they join the premier Administrative Service, where they are pushed and tested to become top public-sector leaders.[51] The best become Permanent Secretaries (heads of government ministries) or even cabinet ministers, if they eventually decide to enter politics.

This was the story of former diplomat and UN Security Council Chair Kishore Mahbubani, who came from a poor family and used a government scholarship to attend the National University of Singapore. Former Trade and Industry minister Lim Hng Kiang attended Harvard and Cambridge under similar auspices. Another Trade and Industry minister, Chan Chun Sing, used government scholarships to attend Cambridge and MIT.[52] Singapore, Mahbubani writes, has created a 'pipeline of talent into the civil service through the scholarship system'.[53]

And after bringing such talented people into public service, Singapore has figured out how to *keep them* there. Whereas American and European officials know they can leave the government and greatly increase their salaries in the private sector, Singapore incentivises public-sector work by paying people what they are worth.

Since the 1970s, the government has steadily increased the salaries of its civil servants to keep the state's talent.[54] Since 2000, the government has also offered performance-based benefits to all civil servants. By linking pay and performance, Singapore easily differentiates between its high- and low-performing staff, reinforcing the country's own meritocratic ethos.[55]

Because these civil servants are so well-paid, and because patronage and networking cannot really help you move up the ladder, corruption is extraordinarily rare. And because recruitment into and promotion within the civil service are nearly always strictly test-based, there is no real room for patronage – unlike in much of the West, where one good boss can elevate you and change your whole career. In London or Washington, one family connection to the right politician can set up your child's career; not so much in Singapore. With a system so test-based, it is difficult if not impossible to make your way through patronage and graft, rather than through skill. Nobody can honestly network their way through an exam.

Because civil servants have no reason to pursue graft, and because the government cracks down on corruption impartially, Singapore, in 2021, was ranked fifth globally – and first in Asia – in Transparency International's Corruption Perceptions Index.[56] Singapore has retained high-quality staff and minimised corruption by simply paying civil servants what they are worth.

In 2000, Lee said that Singapore 'will remain clean and honest only if honest, able men are willing to fight elections and assume office' and are 'paid a wage commensurate with what men of their ability and integrity are earning elsewhere'.[57] And so, it has.

* * *

After recruiting and retaining Singapore's best, the government manages to keep quality high by ruthlessly maintaining standards, rather than offering civil appointments for life.

The government frequently puts its administrative officers through performance evaluations in which they are ranked and subject to reassignment if they are performing below expectations. 'A significant number', in the words of scholar Kenneth Paul Tan, 'are mercilessly removed to make way for new officers.'[58] Seniority plays a limited role; twenty years of service mean little if those are not quality years.

Singapore has avoided stagnation by also constantly tweaking the civil service evaluation system to be more holistic and transparent. The government has refined and clarified what qualifies as 'leadership potential' while also helping civil servants identify their career goals in the short- to medium-term.[59] The prime minister at the time of writing, Lee Hsien Loong, has also sought more mid-career entrants from the private sector to boost experiential diversity in the civil service's top ranks.[60]

These efforts have largely succeeded. Singapore generally appoints civil servants without discriminating based on ethnicity, religion or gender. Selection is meritocratic, with personal connections playing little role. Promotion and tenure are not guaranteed but result from the officeholder's demonstrated strong performance.[61]

The World Bank now ranks Singapore in the 100th percentile of effective government. The United Nations, too, has praised

'Singapore's exemplary public service cadre' as 'one of the most disciplined bureaucracies in the world, because of its efficiency, low levels of corruption and a high standard of accountability'.[62]

Ultimately, those who reach Singapore's top rungs of government are those who not only have the on-paper qualities needed to impress, but also have a demonstrated and measurable track record of success. The same cannot be said of several democratic governments, which appoint too many officials based on their connections: because they met the right people, worked for the right campaign and demonstrated loyalty throughout. Others simply get hired because a parent knows the president.[63]

* * *

Singapore's Secrets

No system is perfect, and Singapore is no exception. As time passes and people get richer, any meritocracy risks decline. The Singaporean government is aware of this conundrum.

'Unlike the first generation of Singaporeans where students are mostly from humble backgrounds,' Minister of Education Ong Ye Kung admitted in 2018, 'the next generation is pushing off blocks from different starting points, and students from affluent families have a head start.'[64] And when certain people have a head start, the promise of meritocracy becomes diluted.

Singaporean officials understand that to preserve their meritocracy, the government must address children's needs earlier and earlier to prevent poorer children – and those without well-educated families – from falling behind before they can enter school. So, they've increased their outreach to lower-income families to level the playing field from the start. Singaporean officials are aware, too, that their civil service needs constant reform. Rather than rest on their laurels, these officials constantly tend to its roots to ensure that it continues to bear fruit.[65]

It is with this attitude that democracies can emulate Singapore's success to strengthen their systems and the allure of liberalism at large.

In fact, Singaporean universities decades ago emulated *American* higher education, remodelling the city-state's British-style academic programmes to offer students greater exposure to cross-disciplinary learning. Whereas critics suggest that Singapore produces uncreative thinkers attuned only to maths and sciences, the country has followed the US model to increasingly expose its students to the liberal arts. Ironically, on the other hand, the liberal arts are now a course of study increasingly available only to privileged Americans – who are less concerned about locking down high-paying jobs immediately after graduating than their poorer counterparts, who need more lucrative jobs than a liberal arts degree affords to make a dent in their outrageous amount of student debt.[66]

Singapore learned from us. Now it is our turn to learn from them.

Some democracies are already doing so. At summits of the world's education ministers, 'everyone listens very closely' to what Singapore has to say, according to Andreas Schleicher, head of the OECD's education assessment programme. The United Kingdom has even tried to adopt some elements of the 'Singapore model' by, in 2016, directing half of England's primary schools to follow the city-state's approach to teaching maths and science.[67]

But it is not just Singapore's textbooks that account for its success. It is the overall system of meritocracy, in which the best can rise – something that is not the case in the United Kingdom, United States and beyond. Democratic governments should therefore look to learn from Singapore by emulating the country's general commitment to meritocracy, rather than copying only its textbooks, because to restore both the functionality of and trust in democracies we need to draw from the best. And the best decidedly do not come only from elite households.

Like Singapore, we must start with our education system.

* * *

Democratic education systems are in various stages of disrepair. The European Union has not lived up to its promise of inclusive education.[68] South Korea has struggled to maintain equality of opportunity. The list goes on. But the American public education system is particularly bad.

American public schools are funded by property taxes, meaning that richer neighbourhoods will have better state-run education. And because Black (and other minority) Americans were prevented from living in these neighbourhoods for years, we are left with a stark gap in opportunity across not only class but racial lines.

As the scholar Linda Darling-Hammond wrote in the late 1990s, 'the U.S. educational system is one of the most unequal', with the wealthiest 10 per cent of US school districts spending nearly ten times more than the poorest 10 per cent.[69] By the mid-2010s, the situation had decidedly not improved, with low-poverty districts spending 15.6 per cent more per student than high-poverty districts do.[70] American schools are more segregated today than they were when the US Supreme Court ruled such segregation illegal with the landmark *Brown v. Board of Education* decision in 1954.[71]

Arlington, Virginia – where I live – sits just across the Potomac River from Washington, DC. Arlington is home to lobbyists and government contractors, many of whom commute to the capital for work. It's a nice place to live: a safe semi-suburb just around the corner from Washington that maintains the trappings of urban life while also offering pretty and spacious homes. And because Virginia allows school districts to fund themselves with local property taxes, the city's annual spending for public school students here is a strong USD 22,000 per student.

But just three hours away in Hampton City, Virginia – whose public school students are largely from low-income, minority households – the district spends only about USD 10,500 per student annually. That means that the children of Arlington are receiving *100 per cent* more investment than their counterparts in Hampton City. That statistic alone makes a mockery of America's promise of meritocracy.

Arlington's kids are no more talented than those in Hampton City; my neighbours are just starting on third base, while those in Hampton City are being asked to hit a home run.[72]

* * *

For all the United States' and United Kingdom's struggles, American and British universities remain the world's best. Yet those who get to attend them come overwhelmingly from elite families. Some of these students are certainly talented, but those without resources far too often fail to even have the chance of a university education.

One way to at least marginally fix this is by banning legacy admissions, the process by which the children of alumni are admitted to US universities explicitly because of these ties – and often their family's financial contributions to the school – even if the child is not genuinely qualified. I've seen this happen over and over again: the number of people I know who got into an Ivy League school despite being profoundly unqualified for those slots because their parents went there and donated to the school is truly troubling.

At Harvard, the acceptance rate for legacy students hovers around 30 per cent, dwarfing the overall acceptance rate of only 6 per cent.[73] The children of Harvard alumni also have the benefit of being wealthy: in 2021, nearly a third of legacy freshmen hailed from households making more than half a million dollars per year.[74]

The losers in these unequal systems will be our less privileged kids. But on a collective level, the loss will be ours, too. By failing to foster ingenuity, our countries will fall further and further behind at a moment when autocracies like China are looking to cement their power.

And of course, when these kids fall behind, their parents will blame their 'corrupt' governments. When these parents see the under-performing children of top financiers and politicians vaunted into top schools and jobs because of connections, these parents will rebel against the system that allowed for this to happen. They will look to the politician who speaks for them, and who condemns and promises to uproot the system. They will vote for the would-be dictator.

* * *

Beyond education, democracies must also look to Singapore to improve the way in which they staff their governments.

Whereas Singapore works hard to retain a strong civil service, democracies increasingly treat career government employees as marginal, singling them out as examples of wasteful spending.[75] But excellent civil and foreign services are key to strong governance. There is no way for democracies to compete with autocracies if our governments are not staffed by our most talented people.

Democracies around the world struggle with this issue, but the American civil service is particularly broken.[76] This is partially because promotion potential is limited and because it is difficult to remove an employee from the civil service, meaning that there are limited performance incentives. This all feeds into an American perception of civil servants – and, to some extent, diplomats – as lazy, incompetent and simply not worth the money.

Major publications like the *Atlantic* have deemed civil servants 'welfare queens', while Trump railed against the so-called 'deep state' and worked to lay off thousands of government employees.[77] Segments of both the left and the right increasingly view Washington, DC as a 'swamp' in which lazy government workers twiddle their thumbs while living off hard-earned American tax dollars. This view is not exactly correct, but 'the mere perception that incompetent federal employees operate with impunity creates fractures that divide agencies from their workforces, the legislative branch from the executive branch, managers from their employees and the American people from their government', as Eric Katz writes.[78] The result is an increasingly ineffective government.

Similar issues bedevil other democracies like France, Ireland and Spain.[79]

One way for these democracies to improve their governments is by using the Singapore model to make existing civil and foreign services far more merit-based. Just as Singapore stringently tests and examines its officials to ensure that they are performing adequately, so should democracies.

Democracies should also work to recruit a new generation of excellent civil servants.

With the exception of a few elite tracks, the overwhelming majority of Western, democratic elites pursue opportunities in the high-paying private sector. Just about nobody I know who went to Harvard, Yale, Princeton or Stanford looked around at all their vast opportunities and decided to become a civil servant, or even a career diplomat. The majority of them went to work somewhere like Goldman Sachs or McKinsey – which is great for them, but decidedly bad for America. Only around 7 per cent of Harvard graduates enter public service immediately after graduating. That number is deeply dispiriting, particularly when a famed inscription on one of Harvard Yard's gates specifically instructs graduates to 'depart to serve better thy country and thy kind,' quoting former Harvard president and philanthropist Charles William Eliot.[80]

There is nothing wrong or immoral about private sector work. I work in the private sector (as well as at a non-profit think-tank). There's no shame in that: the private sector makes the world go round. But if our democracies intend to keep pace with autocracies like China and Singapore, we must find ways to recruit a higher percentage of our best and brightest into the government – and keep them there.

One way is by offering a greater number of scholarships to high-performing students for both undergraduate and graduate education across a variety of fields with the expectation that, as in Singapore, they commit to work for the government for a significant period upon completing their education.[81]

Another is by paying them what they're worth, even though democratic leaders tend to believe this is impossible. As Goh told the crowd in 2000, while '[m]any Western leaders have told me in private that they envied our system of Ministers pay [. . .] they also said that if they tried to implement it in their own countries, they would be booted out'.[82] They would, not because their governments cannot afford to spend, but because Western publics consider their governments bureaucratic, inefficient and lazy – not exactly qualities deserving of higher pay.

But some Asian democracies have managed to create Singapore-like civil services.

Being a civil servant is one of the most sought-after jobs in South Korea because of stable working conditions and a strong work–life balance.[83] And while there is a perception that civil servants work less, nearly half a million South Koreans take the civil service exam every year.[84] Those who are accepted have greater job security than their private sector peers, are constantly tested and evaluated, and can access greater pay if they perform better.[85]

This system remains imperfect, with some 40 per cent of civil servants believing it to be unfair, but South Korea's civil service is leaps and bounds better than that of the United States, for instance.[86] There is merit in making government employment more meritocratic.

* * *

The United States faces particular challenges on this front. This is because when every new president comes into office, they are tasked with filling some *four thousand political appointments* – that is, finding four thousand politically aligned, well-connected people to serve in the government, all the way from cabinet level down to being a special assistant.

Many highly qualified individuals land these jobs. Specialised scholars and practitioners tend to fill State, Defense or National Security Council positions directly related to their areas of expertise. The same goes for positions at the Departments of Commerce, Transportation and so on. But far too often, competence takes a backseat to connections.

It is well known that President Trump stacked his government, from the Department of Defense to various ambassadorships around the world, with profoundly unqualified people. He made his children top advisors and let his son-in-law essentially run Middle East policy (and try to profit in the process).[87]

But for decades, the *quid pro quo* of 'support me, raise money for me, and I will find you a job' has been a profoundly bipartisan one.

Various US administrations have handed out plum posts to donors, also staffing the lower ranks of the administration with campaign staffers, donors and their children. Certainly, some of these people have the necessary credentials for these jobs; few of them are explicitly unqualified.

But as Walter Shaub, who served as director of the Office of Government Ethics from 2013 to 2017, has asked: 'How can these children of political appointees be the only people who are qualified for employment?'[88]

The United States does not need to get rid of all political appointments. Each president should be able to staff their government as they see fit.

Yet the United States could improve its broken system by converting many of these appointments into non-political career roles filled by those with clear expertise. Fewer political appointees would improve long-term US governance, as there would be continuity from administration to administration rather than jobs sitting open for a year or longer between presidents awaiting Senate confirmation.

Ratcheting down the number of political appointees would also limit friction between these appointees and career officials, possibly even improving the latter's performance. As the former Indian bureaucrat N. C. Saxena has written, 'nothing demoralises good public servants and destroys performance more than undue favouritism and unmerited patronage in recruitment and promotion' – which is precisely what civil servants see in the US political appointments process.[89]

When hiring for the remaining political appointments, administrations must make these postings public and accessible, rather than sharing them through only word of mouth. Right now, nearly every role is filled without ever being posted publicly.

America is exceptional, but this is one area in which we should be more like the rest of the world. From democracies like Denmark to autocracies like Singapore, when there are elections, maybe some few dozen jobs change – but not four thousand, to be filled by political allies and those with personal connections to the president.[90]

Improving the process of government staffing would surely improve government functionality, which would then improve people's trust in government. And when people trust the government, they are substantially less likely to vote for populists seeking to disrupt it.

* * *

The death of meritocracy is the death of democracy.

When our education systems enable only elites to rise, while our governments are run by stagnant civil services or by politically connected individuals, our governance becomes worse. And when people see their governments being staffed only by those with money and connections, they lose faith in that same government. How can people from Birmingham, Alabama, to Birmingham, England, believe in politicians' promises of change if these same politicians staff their governments with the same elite groups that Birmingham residents have no hope of entering? The answer, put simply, is that they cannot, and that they will look for disrupters: populists promising to reshape the system entirely.

To meet today's challenges, then, democracies desperately need to revitalise their meritocratic systems by improving their education systems – by accounting for the unequal starting points of children across the democratic world – and making sure their governments, like Singapore's, are truly staffed by the best. The result will be more effective governance, more trust in government and, more importantly, a lessened chance of autocracy at home.

2

Accountability

Takaaki Masui and Katsutoshi Ishibe were rich men.

Hailing from Japan, they worked for the Nissho Iwai Corporation, a well-known Japanese commodities company. But in the early 2000s, they wanted a new challenge, so they joined the company's Singaporean subsidiary, where they would sell a wide range of their goods to the city-state.

Their path was clear. They would make more money and live comfortably in Singapore before eventually returning to Japan. Nothing, it seemed, could go wrong.

But they were greedy.

In 2002, Ishibe approached Koh Pee Chiang – the sole proprietor of Chia Lee & Co., a company that distributed edible flour for Nissho – with a proposition. *Would Koh*, he asked, *be interested in a profit-sharing arrangement, even if it was unauthorised and probably illegal?* Koh was not given much of a choice: the Japanese pair told Koh that they would prevent him from selling edible flour at all unless he agreed to distribute their industrial lower-grade flour, used only in factory food production, and pay them nearly 85 per cent of the generated revenue.

Koh was not keen about the proposition. But he nonetheless agreed to distribute their industrial flour and share the profits – bribes, that is – as Ishibe and Masui asked. 'Koh,' prosecutors later said, 'was worried and nervous that if he did not agree to do this "favour", Ishibe would sell the edible flour to competing trading companies, which could put out Chia Lee of business.'[1] His options were to accept the bribes or experience financial ruin. In the end, Koh chose the bribes (even though he received a measly USD 3 out of the expected USD 23 profits per metric tonne of industrial flour, with Ishibe and Masui splitting the remaining profits equally).

Ishibe eventually returned to Japan. But the scheme continued without Nissho's knowledge. The transactions got more and more lucrative; Koh continued receiving only his USD 3 per sale.

The arrangement persisted until 2007, when Koh, with his company in financial distress, could no longer afford to pay the Japanese. The bribes had covered only his initial costs; they did not cover his additional costs as the industrial flour business grew. The global financial crisis, which began in November 2007, hit the flour industry particularly hard, only further hurting Koh's position. His company was on the verge of collapse.

Ishibe and Masui couldn't have cared less. They had already pocketed more than USD 2 million.

* * *

Nissho Iwai discovered the arrangement in 2009. By 2010, the firm had fired the two men. But there was no legal action. Company leadership seemed satisfied they were gone and did not see any benefit in bringing a legal case – or the public scrutiny that would go with it.

That all changed in late May 2018, when Singapore finally brought charges against the two men. After a thirteen-day trial, Judge Shaiffudin Saruwan found Ishibe and Masui guilty, sentencing them each to five years and six months in jail. He also ordered them to each pay a penalty of over USD 1 million. Failure to pay would result in an additional six months behind bars.

Ishibe and Masui appealed, and in 2020, Singapore's High Court cut their jail sentences down to just over three and a half years and reduced their fines to around USD 200,000.[2] Justice Chan Seng Onn wrote a harsh and lengthy judgment, saying that Ishibe and Masui had engaged in 'one of the most egregious cases of purely private sector corruption in Singapore'. There was, he added, 'a pressing public interest concern in discouraging the corrupt criminal conduct that has been displayed by the appellants'.[3] He explained that he reduced their sentences *not* because the crime was somehow less serious than initially thought, but because the original sentences, passed without much precedent to refer to, were excessive. Singapore did not have a sentencing framework for private sector corruption, because such corruption was so rare.[4]

The flour saga reflects one of Singapore's many strengths, even if these two men got off with somewhat lesser punishments. Unlike most autocracies, and even many weaker democracies, the country has a demonstrated commitment to the rule of law, and to prosecuting both public and private sector corruption when it emerges – which is not often. The result is increased public support for the government, which translates to more stable politics and thus stronger governance.

When, for instance, an assistant director of Singapore's renowned anti-graft watchdog misappropriated more than USD 1.34 million in public funds, the government jailed him for ten years.[5] When the manager of a town council took bribes from construction companies in exchange for advancing the business interests of the firms, the government sentenced him to forty months in prison.[6] And when the head of the Civil Defence Force accepted sexual favours from women seeking to influence government contracts, the government promptly removed him.[7]

The Singaporean government has a zero-tolerance approach to corruption and governmental incompetence. The rationale is multi-faceted.

First, strong prosecutions send a deterrent message. And because most corruption-related cases in Singapore involve the private sector trying to bribe the government, businesses have strengthened their anti-corruption protocols.[8] The government's commitment to holding the private sector accountable forces businesses to put their own houses in order, which in turn breeds more public support for the private sector, which is then seen to have more integrity.[9] This is something I've heard from more than a few folks working in or with Singapore: countering corruption is not only good for business, but necessary to do business in the city-state. Thus, Singapore creates a virtuous cycle.

Second, cracking down on corruption and incompetence helps boost public support for the ruling regime.

The People's Action Party (PAP) dominates politics, and has for decades, allowing for extremely limited political contestation. But this same government wins substantial public backing by making a real effort to hold officials accountable by ousting or demoting under-performing officials – even civil servants, as we saw in the last chapter – and responding doggedly to the rare corruption allegation.

Singaporeans do genuinely like the PAP, and not just because there's no real alternative.

* * *

Singapore's approach to corruption and incompetence is wise. The state's commitment to accountability generates public support for and belief in the government – even if problems persist – because this commitment shows that the government is trying to fix things. It is an approach mirrored by the governments of Vietnam and the United Arab Emirates, among others. And it stands in marked contrast to many democracies, specifically in the West, where people believe that their elected officials and private sector leaders get away with *everything*, from illegally trading stocks to brazenly breaking COVID-19 restrictions – and where such behaviour breeds distrust in government, weakening the very core of our democracies.

In sharp comparison to Singapore or Vietnam, public trust in the US government is at a near historic low, with only 2 per cent of people saying they trust Washington to do what is right 'just about always'.[10] That number only creeps up to 22 per cent when the proposition is softened to 'most of the time'.[11]

British support for government has also steadily declined in recent years, reaching the lowest level on record in 2021.[12] Almost two-thirds of Brits said that politicians were merely 'out for themselves', rather than serving to help their constituents.[13]

Some 46 per cent of French citizens believe that 'most politicians are corrupt'. Around 58 per cent say that elected officials do not care what ordinary people think.[14]

With numbers like these, democracies are clearly in trouble. Spend enough time in Washington and London, let alone in Lancaster or Wycombe, and you'll see the depth of our decay. Scepticism of and disdain for our leaders has become the norm in too many democracies around the world – in no small part because we have simply stopped punishing powerful people when they cross clearly defined legal lines. The result is a huge decline in support for the government, which ordinary people no longer believe can hold powerful people accountable. And the result of *that* is an increased propensity to vote for demagogues and would-be autocrats, who once in power severely undermine democracy's ability not only to work at home but to serve as a model for the rest of the world.

By recommitting to the principle of accountability, and recommitting to the rule of law, we can make everyone responsible for their actions, including the powerful – something that autocracies by definition cannot. This would allow our governments to regain the public legitimacy they need to take the bold action the twenty-first century demands, and to fend off autocracy at home. And because democratic institutions have the capability to be truly fair, our governments will be able to gain more legitimacy than any autocracy ever could – thereby once again allowing us to be a model abroad.

Most autocracies do not hold their leaders accountable; that is one of their main flaws. From Bishkek to Bissau, autocratic governments struggle precisely because they allow corruption to flourish while acting with little concern for their people's well-being. In non-democracies, non-accountability is the norm.

But some, like Singapore, Vietnam and the United Arab Emirates, have made an effort to handle corruption and poor governmental performance. Real problems remain on both fronts, yet the appearance of holding people accountable is enough to win the ruling regimes huge amounts of public support.

Autocracies have taken notice of the importance of accountability, if only in appearance. It's long past time for democracies to do the same, hopefully with more substantive results.

* * *

Autocratic Accountability?

Nguyen Xuan Son had everything going for him. Despite being born in war-torn Vietnam in 1962, living through the following decades of turmoil and then in a repressive communist regime, Son defied the odds to become a rich man.

In 2003, he held a senior position with the PetroVietnam Joinstock Finance Corporation, a subsidiary of PetroVietnam, the state-owned oil-and-gas giant. By 2007, he was the corporation's general director. Just a year later, in 2008, Son – then only in his mid-forties – became the chief executive of Ocean Bank, a joint stock bank partly owned by PetroVietnam. And in 2014 he became chairman of PetroVietnam itself.

He was a grand success, living a life of comfort completely unimaginable to his parents and grandparents. But Son just couldn't keep his hands clean.

In 2015, just about a year after taking over PetroVietnam, he was arrested. Vietnamese authorities alleged that he had committed massive amounts of fraud while running Ocean Bank. They said that Son, along with a former Ocean Bank chairman, had raised the interest rate above the one set by the central bank for nearly fifty thousand people, along with some four hundred companies and institutions – causing losses of USD 69 million.[15] Hanoi declared that Son was responsible for the loss of some 800 billion dong, around USD 37 million, that PetroVietnam and other shareholders had invested in Ocean Bank.[16] Ocean Bank ultimately accumulated losses worth USD 445 million and in April 2015 was forcibly taken over by Vietnam's central bank.

Several other troubling allegations began trickling out. Eventually, in 2017, Hanoi convicted Son of embezzling some USD 2 million and abusing his power to steal another USD 8.7 million from Ocean Bank.[17] The court sentenced him to death, while handing out a life sentence to Tham and convicting some other fifty defendants, most of whom were Ocean Bank executives.[18] Twelve of them received sentences of up to thirty years in prison; around thirty received suspended sentences of up to three years; the remaining five were sentenced to two years of re-education.[19]

Vietnam cracks down hard in cases like these, not only to deter future law-breaking, but also to satisfy a corruption-weary public. I've heard people around the country complain openly about paying bribes or simply about the supposedly corrupt elites in Hanoi. The Vietnamese public wants vengeance; the government reads the room and delivers.

In 2019, after the minister and deputy minister for information and communications were found to have taken some USD 3 million in bribes, the government handed down punishments that were unprecedented for officials this senior. Hanoi gave the former minister a life sentence, and his deputy a fourteen-year sentence.[20] In 2022, Vietnam then dismissed a deputy health minister after uncovering his involvement in a fake medicine trading ring.[21]

The list goes on, but the point is clear: when corruption is discovered, Vietnam tends to stamp it out not only aggressively, but publicly. These splashy trials, convictions and dismissals do deter corruption.[22] But they also represent an official response to its persistence. Punishments signal to the Vietnamese public that the government is taking action – satisfying the complaints of ordinary people, at least for a period.[23]

People want to trust their government; they need to see the corrupt held accountable. Vietnam delivers, at least on the surface.

* * *

In 2016, a steel plant accidentally released several deadly chemicals, including cyanide, off Vietnam's coast. Despite fears of government retribution, citizens around the country marched in protest, while others expressed their anger on social media.[24]

Hanoi hit back hard – not against the protestors, but against the steel plant. The government declared that the mill had used an unauthorised, dirtier production process, which caused the disaster. Authorities then dismissed several senior provincial and industry officials who were 'irresponsible and loosened their management and supervision on environment safety, leading to serious damage to the environment and local people'.[25] And in 2017, Hanoi fired the communist party boss of Ho Chi Minh City after alleging that he made 'serious mistakes' while heading PetroVietnam. The party said that he was responsible for a damaging lack of oversight, which led to financial losses.[26]

These cases are indicative of another way in which Hanoi holds officials accountable: by firing them for negligence, even if that negligence is not necessarily criminal. The rationale resembles that of the fight against corruption – incompetence, too, angers the public, which must be appeased with a proverbial head on a stake. Hanoi delivers to save its own skin.

This tandem approach to corruption and incompetence has won the Vietnamese government a huge amount of public support. The public believes that the party is making a real, substantial effort to resolve existing problems.[27] Because of this, and because the regime has delivered on quality-of-life improvements, data has shown for the better part of twenty years that most Vietnamese confidently back their central government.[28]

Vietnamese ruling party leader Nguyen Phu Trong and other top cadres clearly understand the connection between accountability and public support. This is part of the reason why officials like him have so aggressively promised to eliminate corruption, which he called a 'disease of people having power and [. . .] lots of money in their hands' in 2021.[29] 'The war to fight and prevent corruption will not stop,' Trong continued. The fight 'will not rest and have no restricted areas, no matter who it involves.'[30]

* * *

(United) Arab Accountability?

Abu Dhabi is literally built on sand. When gaps in the concrete sidewalk appear, one can see the infinite grains of desert below.

But cracks in the streets are rare, given that the United Arab Emirates (UAE), which rules this tiny eastern end of the Arabian

Peninsula, is not only one of the world's richest countries, but is also committed to excellence. Which is why this little speck of a country, like Singapore, was able to go from Third to First World in development terms in the space of a single generation.

Like Singapore, the UAE is a deceptively diverse country. It is a federation of statelets, each of which is different both culturally and economically. Dubai, for instance, has oil reserves that were only ever a fraction of Abu Dhabi's. But as a united group of emirates, the country followed a relatively simple recipe to success: it used oil profits to fund development and guarantee its people a high quality of life. From 1975 to 2019 the country's GDP jumped from USD 15 billion to 358 billion – an increase of around 2,280 per cent.[31] In this same period, life expectancy increased from sixty-five to seventy-eight, owing in no small part to government investment in social services.[32] And as the UAE looks to shift from an oil-based economy to a more diverse one, leaders have taken on Singapore's business-like approach to governing.

Both countries lack democratic accountability – neither one has free or fair elections. But both have nonetheless managed to ensure government accountability in a top-down manner inspired by the private sector. Top officials, like CEOs, hold the power; they keep their subordinates accountable to the overriding goal when the people, lacking the power of the ballot box, do not. And in the UAE, the goal is profit, because profit enables the government to provide the people with enough comfort to quell their potential democratic demands.[33]

UAE officials pursue this goal by following the concept of *Wali El-Amer*: responsible individuals should lead and others should follow. Bosses, like a parent, direct their subordinates, who in turn try to satisfy their bosses. And when this system works all the way up – satisfying everyone's bosses, including the president, who is focused on putting money in citizens' pockets

– it does function. The UAE is a hardened autocracy, but it is fairly accountable to its citizens.

* * *

The first way in which the UAE keeps itself accountable is by stamping out official corruption.

The country has cracked down hard on graft since at least the 1980s, and particularly since announcing itself on the global stage in the 1990s. By the early 2000s, the government was arresting officials – even senior officers – for graft and embezzlement.[34] This practice has only increased, with the UAE regularly imprisoning corrupt officials and expressing its commitment to rooting out corruption.[35]

The need to demonstrate accountability is why the president doubled down even further in August 2021, declaring that the UAE's Public Prosecution Office could now investigate top ministers and senior officials suspected of wrongdoing.[36] The decree also enabled the attorney general to bar officials from travelling abroad and freeze their money if necessary.[37]

As in Vietnam, these arrests and decrees serve to legitimate a profoundly undemocratic regime (and tend to veer into the political at times, with senior officials ousting their rivals on corruption charges). But unlike Vietnam – and like Singapore – the UAE's results seem to match their rhetoric. International watchdogs say that the UAE has steadily become less and less corrupt, so much so that by 2022 the country was less corrupt than countless democracies, including Taiwan, South Korea and the United States.[38]

The UAE still allows shady money to flow in and out of its borders, particularly with regard to Islamist terrorism. That much is indisputable.[39] But the country's leaders care less about what the world thinks about them and more about what their own people think – which is why the UAE government has worked to largely shield its public from corruption. Analysts in Washington and Brussels are right to express outrage about these terrorism-related financial flows, but the reality is that most UAE citizens do not care. They do not believe the institutions that matter to their lives are corrupt; they believe the government is moving against those corrupt officials who remain. The result is huge public support for the regime, even while the West complains.[40]

* * *

In July 2019, the UAE's top leaders announced a new plan. Over the coming months, they promised, the government would evaluate 600 government service centres across the country and – in a stunning show of accountability – declare the best and worst ones by 14 September. These leaders stayed true to their word. On 14 September, Sheikh Mohammed bin Rashid Al Maktoum, the country's vice president and prime minister, publicly highlighted the five best and worst centres, praising the Wasit Police Station in Sharjah while excoriating the Muhaisnah Preventive Medicine Center in Dubai.[41]

This move was pure political theatre. But it was incredibly smart and allowed the autocratic UAE government to demonstrate its commitment to competence in a transparent way. This is why the UAE then promised to evaluate all 600 centres every year. The results, Sheik Mohammed declared, would be released publicly.

Since 2008, the UAE has also steadily maintained and upgraded an electronic performance management system to enhance government decision-making processes.[42] Studies have found that the system – which was the first Arabic-language one in operation – has improved the efficiency and effectiveness of governmental operations.[43] Its mere existence also signals to the nation's public that the government takes these issues seriously.

Efforts like these reflect the top leadership's understanding that

76

committing to competence is key to the UAE's accountability, and thus to public support for the regime. This is why the government keeps ramping up efforts to improve government performance – and removing officials who are not up to snuff.

There is a reason why Sheikh Mohammed, the country's vice president and prime minister, keeps promising that his government will be competent and hard-working. To ensure it stays that way, he has said, 'Those who cannot keep up with us [. . .] may rest away from the government.'[44]

∗ ∗ ∗

Corruption and negligence both undermine the functionality of the state, but they also undermine faith in it, which is arguably more important for a non-democratic regime. If you don't have democratic elections that allow populations to blow off steam by voting, you risk allowing anger to fester until it erupts in a potentially destabilising moment of mass protest. This is precisely why Singapore, the UAE, Vietnam and other autocracies focus so strongly on these two prongs of accountability.

This focus seems to be paying off.

Singaporeans consistently say there is a low level of corruption in their country.[45] A 2021 poll found that an astounding 94.5 per cent of Singaporeans believe that either none or few individuals in state authorities are involved in corruption.[46] Over 80 per cent of Singaporeans express either 'a great deal' or 'quite a lot' of confidence in their government.[47] No other country in the world can report such a high level of public confidence in government.[48]

It should be clear, then, just how vital accountability is to building support for the state. To believe in their government, democratic or authoritarian, people must believe that their rulers are neither corrupt nor incompetent – that their government is working for them and working well. Remarkably, and despite Western wisdom that democracies are by nature more accountable, it is today in countries like Singapore, the UAE and Vietnam that people back their governments the most.

* * *

Our Unaccountable Democracies

It was 15 December 2020, and the world was in a shambles. A COVID-19 vaccine had just been discovered, and administered for the first time a week before, but the virus still took the lives of over 450 people in the United Kingdom that day, infecting another 18,000. London was under Tier 2 regulations that banned social events involving two or more people from different households.[49] 'Christmas', the *Guardian* solemnly declared, 'is on hold.'[50]

But twenty minutes from the newspaper's empty offices in King's Cross, Britain's leaders were in a more celebratory mood. Prime Minister Boris Johnson and his staff were meant to be taking part in a virtual holiday party, as nearly all of us did that December. He did take part in the virtual event, but did so in person, along with several of his staff members, thereby breaking his government's own rules. An image leaked later showed them in festive attire – one staffer donning tinsel, the other a Santa hat – and enjoying a half-empty bottle of bubbly. 'I can tell you,' he soon after proclaimed, 'that I certainly broke no rules.'[51]

One might forgive the prime minister for this minor slip-up. December 2020 was a difficult time for everyone; all of us needed some kind of release, and many of us broke COVID-19 regulations. But Johnson did so repeatedly and with impunity, until the scandal provoked public outrage much later (and helped bring about the end of his premiership).

While the country was in COVID-19 lockdown, he attended at least six illegal gatherings, more than a few of which he hosted at 10 Downing Street.[52] And when one of his top advisers, Dominic Cummings, travelled across the country during a lockdown despite experiencing COVID-19 symptoms, Johnson slapped down public outcry, defending Cummings for following his 'instincts'. Johnson declared that Cummings had 'acted responsibly, legally, and with integrity'.[53]

Johnson's COVID-19 travails do not amount to high crimes and misdemeanours. They are relatively minor scandals, even if they helped end his time in power. But Johnson's repeated refusal to follow the rules his own government set – and his willingness to defend colleagues who did the same – is unfortunate. His apparent belief that the rules apply only to *normal* people, not to him and those close to him, feeds British distrust of the government. It makes London resemble ever more closely a kind of 'shorthand for faraway people with no grasp of the nation's problems', as the scholar Adam Tooze has written.[54] It makes Scousers and southerners alike increasingly unwilling to believe in their leaders, and in democracy at all.

This attitude pops up across the Atlantic as well, where politicians also repeatedly flouted or ran quite close up against the harsh COVID-19 restrictions they imposed.

In November 2020, when California barred people in many counties from dining with people from other households – and warned people not to gather with their own families during the Thanksgiving holiday – governor Gavin Newsom attended a birthday party for his political advisor, a lobbyist, that comprised families from more than three households. To his credit, Newsom eventually apologised, unlike Johnson, saying: 'I need to preach and practice, not just preach and not practice.'[55]

But the message both he and Johnson sent is clear and is damaging for democratic societies based on the premise of equality under the law: 'There is one set of rules for normal people, another set for me and my friends, and we will not get punished for violating the ones you must follow.' That message will undermine people's faith not only in their leaders, but in democracy at large.

* * *

Tricks of Trading

I've known Tommy Tuberville's name for longer than I can remember. I grew up playing, watching and consuming everything related to American football. I still do – I won't miss a New York Jets game, even if my better instincts tell me I should. (The Jets have not won a title since 1969, when my father wasn't even five years old, and have been futile just about my whole life.)

To this day, I can remember specific moments from Tuberville's career. I remember him coaching Auburn University to an undefeated 13–0 season in 2004. I remember him at Auburn, tanned, slim and just beginning to grey, beating the University of Alabama – a national powerhouse – six consecutive times. I remember the customary victory bath of Gatorade dousing his orange jumpers and polos in celebration, seemingly over and over again. The guy was simply a born winner.

Tuberville would eventually leave Auburn, heading over to the University of Cincinnati, where he coached from 2013 to 2016. Never in my life, though, did I expect Tuberville to end up where he is today: the US Senate, long-known as the world's greatest deliberative body.

In 2020, he ran against and defeated the incumbent, the Democrat and former civil rights lawyer Doug Jones, to become a US senator from the state of Alabama. Upon entering office, Tuberville hardly wasted any time. Within weeks of being sworn in, he voted to overturn Joe Biden's legitimate victory. 'I have no regrets,' he later said.[56]

In the grand scheme of things, Tuberville has been in the US Congress for just about five minutes. Yet by early 2022, he had somehow managed to violate the STOCK Act – which prohibits Congressional representatives and employees from using any non-public information for personal benefit when trading stocks – over 130 times.[57] That means that in under two years in office, he failed on over 130 occasions to disclose trades, in which he was guided by private knowledge, worth nearly USD 1 million.

Tuberville has faced no apparent punishment, although he claims to have paid some minor fines for his late disclosure. The same goes for a swathe of other representatives from across the United States who racked up huge numbers of violations by constantly trading stocks while maintaining access to inside information.

Several other representatives are invested in the same companies that they are supposed to be regulating: some fifteen lawmakers on the House and Senate committees controlling US military policy had investments in top defence firms worth nearly USD 1 million in 2020.[58] As the COVID-19 pandemic raged, some seventy-five lawmakers bought and sold shares of the companies playing important roles in the US response. Forty-eight had invested in Johnson & Johnson. Forty-four held shares in Pfizer. Many of these lawmakers were among those who voted in 2020 and 2021 to authorise more than USD 10 billion to aid these companies' vaccine production.[59]

Clearly, something has gone wrong here. Lawmakers, Democratic or Republican, should not be allowed to invest in the same industries that they are supposed to be regulating, nor should they be allowed to make stock trades based on what is clearly inside information.

But this is only the tip of the American iceberg.

In recent decades, the United States has become less and less effective at enforcing the rule of law, allowing powerful people – in the government and private sector alike – to get off scot-free.

In late 2021, a US government watchdog found that at least thirteen top Trump officials had broken a law restricting partisan political activity by active federal employees. Secretary of State Mike Pompeo broke the law by using State Department resources to speak to the Republican National Committee from Jerusalem. Kellyanne Conway, a top Trump aide, broke the law by promoting Trump's re-election campaign during official interviews on Fox News.[60]

The list goes on, but not one of these officials faced punishment. As of writing (early fall 2022), neither has President Trump, who tried to overturn the 2020 election, obstructed justice at least ten times, tried to secure a bribe from Ukraine by threatening to withhold aid from the country unless its government found him dirt on Joe Biden, and violated campaign finance rules with alarming frequency. He even used USD 2.8 million in charitable donations from veterans for political purposes, which is plainly illegal.[61] (In September 2022, New York state filed a civil suit against Trump, three of his children and the Trump Organization that accuses them of fraud and misrepresentation.)

On paper, nobody in America – politician or otherwise – is above the law. But in practice, few Americans believe that to be true. Alarmingly, the same can be said about democracies around the world.

In the early 2000s, the Greek government spent huge amounts of money despite slowing economic growth, so when the global financial system crashed in 2007 and 2008, Greece's economy was left in pieces. The ensuing debt crisis has weighed on the country since – leaving the country's GDP per capita almost 50 per cent lower today than it was in 2008.[62] Nobody has been held accountable, which helps explain why less than 20 per cent of Greeks today have confidence in their national government.[63]

American and European bankers, meanwhile, were together responsible for this crisis; they took excessive risks and eventually burst the US housing bubble that they themselves had created. Yet almost nobody was ever punished on either side of the Atlantic, whether in Washington, Westminster or Berlin.[64] Those who were punished came overwhelmingly from Iceland, a democracy hit extraordinarily hard by the recession, and one where bad bankers go to prison – and where the central government enjoys a healthy amount of public support.[65]

Yet a lack of accountability continues to enable poor governance in too many democracies.

Spain was unable to handle COVID-19 despite relative societal consent precisely because of government failure. When the virus first arrived, people stayed at home and wore their masks, but the government squandered their sacrifice. Politicians did not strengthen Spain's public health system, nor did they make plans for school reopening or tracking the virus.[66] So when the country reopened in June 2020, the COVID-19 rate skyrocketed, plunging Spain into one of the world's most deadly outbreaks.[67]

Other politicians have been swept out of office for their poor handling of the virus – as with Trump in the United States – but no such thing happened in Spain, because the ruling government faces no electoral challenge. 'Our politicians,' writes the Spanish journalist David Jiménez, 'have little incentive to strive for excellence, because they know that Spaniards' loyalty to their parties rivals their loyalty to their favourite soccer teams.'[68]

This partisanship drives a lack of accountability, which, in turn, fuels a lack of confidence in the Spanish government. Spain now lacks accountability not only in relation to COVID-19, but seemingly *on everything*. Some 94 per cent of Spaniards believe corruption to be widespread.[69]

When you add the two together, the result is an ugly picture:

Spaniards, despite living in a democracy and getting to choose their leaders, have no confidence in those leaders, believing them to be both incompetent and corrupt – yet not held accountable for either failing. This helps explain why nearly 70 per cent of Spaniards are dissatisfied with how their democracy is working, and why a not-insignificant number of the population now supports Vox, a far-right, outsider, anti-establishment party with authoritarian tendencies.[70] It is a complete lack of accountability that feeds public distrust in Spain's democracy, which in turn feeds support for those who promise to do away with the establishment and would prefer to see many liberal protections swept away.

* * *

The list goes on and on, from East to West and everywhere in between, but the story is the same: government incompetence and corruption have resulted in failure and calamity, and seemingly nobody has been punished. It should really be no surprise, then, that many of the people living in democracies around the world don't believe in their governments, or even in democracy as a concept anymore.

Government performance and accountability matter. The ability to deliver on promises matters, as does the ability to prevent graft. This is why Singapore, the UAE and Vietnam hold their own country's officials accountable regarding both competence and corruption, despite refusing to hold even vaguely free or fair elections.

Their top leaders understand that to win public legitimacy, with or without elections, the government must be both corruption-free and effective. And while our democracies *do* hold fair elections and *do* allow people to hold officials accountable by voting them out, our leaders must hold themselves accountable to increase confidence in the government, and thus the government's ability to function.

Because if they don't, they will invite not only distrust in government, but also the rise of the autocrats looking to sweep them, and their democracies, into the dustbin of history.

* * *

Making Democracy Accountable Again

Park Geun-hye was a force of nature.

The daughter of South Korea's one-time dictator, Park Chung-hee, the younger Park arrived on the political scene in 1998, becoming an assemblywoman before quickly moving up the ranks to run for the presidency in 2007. She lost, but only narrowly, and she would not be deterred. By February 2013 she had successfully climbed the mountain to become South Korea's president. *Forbes* declared her one of the world's twenty-five most powerful women and the most powerful woman in Asia. In a piece highlighting just why voters loved her so much, the *New York Times* feted Park's 'unsoiled aura' and reported that 'her main appeal is not her policies, but her character'.[71]

The American paper of record has made better characterisations than when it praised Park.

Behind the scenes, she was engaged in a corruption scheme that was as brazen as it was bizarre. Since at least 2014, she had relied on a shadowy confidante – Choi Soon-sil, a friend of hers for forty years with no official government role – to advise her on just about everything. The pair would ultimately extort tens of millions of dollars from South Korean companies.[72]

Why, you might be wondering, *did these massive companies not speak up?* Because Park or her aides had made the requests directly, and the power of presidency has the power of compulsion. They feared that the Park administration would retaliate by drumming up tax or other investigations.[73]

When the scandal was made public, Park's approval rating plummeted to 4 per cent, marking an all-time low for any democratically elected South Korean leader.[74] Citizens took to the streets, demanding her resignation. Over 500,000 people gathered in Seoul in November 2016, holding a candlelight vigil and brandishing signs reading 'Resign'.

The country's government responded. By December, Park had been impeached. Far more than the required two-thirds of the 300-seat National Assembly voted for her ousting. And while the vote was secret, it was clear that almost half of the 128 lawmakers from Park's own party had voted to remove her.

In a lesser democracy, this scandal might have provoked serious unrest or a yearning for autocracy – for a strong hand to guide the troubled ship. But not in South Korea. Instead, people saw this result as an indication of hope for the system, proof that nobody, not even the president, is above the law. 'I'm not really worried about the future because the people are gathering,' said one protestor. 'I think our democracy has a bright future. We're getting better and better. Our democracy is developing.'[75]

In 2018, Park was initially sentenced to twenty-four years in prison (which was raised to thirty-three years after retrial, and then reduced in 2020 to twenty years). The sentencing may not have prompted joy, but it brought about something like relief and hope.

Yet in 2021, the South Korean government pardoned her, with President Moon Jae-in's office saying that she was in poor health. Moon had previously ruled out a pardon for his former rival, who bested him in the 2013 elections. He even used her corruption case as a means to secure the presidency for himself, promising throughout his 2017 campaign to root out corruption.[76] Both of these realities made Moon's decision to pardon her even harder for the Korean public to swallow.

Park's conviction and subsequent pardon may seem exceptional, but this story is a far-too-common one in South Korea. Park is one of *four* South Korean presidents to be convicted for bribery and the third to be pardoned.

Park's predecessor, Lee Myung-bak, was convicted of corruption in 2018 and sentenced to fifteen years in prison.[77] Prosecutors said that he accepted bribes from some of South Korea's largest firms and embezzled about 24 billion won, or around USD 20 million.

Decades before, in 1995, Roh Tae-woo – who served as president until 1993 – admitted in a stunning television address that he had amassed a USD 650 million slush fund while in office and left the post with USD 230 million in secret bank accounts.[78] Prosecutors later indicted him and former president Chun Doo-hwan, alleging both corruption and that they had masterminded the coup that brought them to power in 1979.[79] A court found them guilty in 1996. Both had their sentences commuted before being released from prison in December 1997.

Despite these scandals, South Korea remains a democracy, and a strong one at that. The country today ranks among the twenty freest countries in the world, above the United Kingdom, United States, Portugal, Japan and several other democracies.[80]

Yet people have limited confidence in their government. The public believes corruption is endemic. People regularly scrutinise politicians for their tight ties to the country's family-owned conglomerates, or *chaebol*, which control huge swathes of the economy.

The perception of corruption in South Korea is probably worse than the problem. But these high-profile scandals – and Seoul's constant willingness to pardon those convicted – have done serious harm. The prosecution of these corrupt presidents sends the right message, projecting a government promise of accountability; pardoning them does the opposite, and makes waste of prosecuting them in the first place.

The message being sent by these pardons, once again, is that there are two sets of rules: those for everyone and those for the elites. And when a message like that blares so loudly, for so long, it helps explain why people do not believe in their democratic governments and are increasingly looking for something else.

* * *

South Korea has at least half the accountability equation right. So too does France, which found former president Nicolas Sarkozy guilty of illegal campaign funding in 2021 and sentenced him to a year in prison, although he will likely avoid serving actual jail time.[81] Whereas the United States, United Kingdom and others often refuse to even *prosecute* powerful people, South Korea and France have done just that.

But in the end, even South Korea and France are letting the powerful off the hook, and ultimately sending the wrong message. Without accountability we cannot have democracy. If people do not believe that the rule of law applies to all, including those in power, the foundations of democracy will crumble. As the US founding father John Adams declared, democracies require 'a government of laws, and not of men'.

Perhaps surprisingly, Malaysia – a country not exactly known for its clean politics – seems to be living up to this adage. On 23 August 2022, the country's top court rejected former prime minister Najib Razak's appeal of his July 2020 conviction for multiple crimes including abuse of power, corruption and money laundering. Najib stole millions in US dollars from the Malaysian government's 1MDB development fund that he set up in 2009. He began his 12-year prison sentence hours after the high court upheld his conviction.[82]

Malaysia's political system is anything but free of graft; corruption remains an endemic problem, prompting anger from the country's citizens.[83] But confirming Najib's sentence, coupled with the king's refusal to issue a pardon (at least so far), is an important step in the right direction – for Malaysia, Asian democracies and democracies everywhere.

Yet too many democracies have become governments of the men and women that run them, not of laws. We seem to have two sets of laws: lenient for the powerful and stringent for everyone else. Singapore, the UAE and Vietnam's ability to hold up these democratic failings as examples of why their systems are better only makes it more embarrassing, and profoundly damaging to democracy itself.

What our democracies need is a return to the rule of law. We need to realise that holding everyone accountable is key to building trust in government, which itself is key to that same government's functionality.

And because democracies are inherently more free, open and equal than autocracies, our governments can hold people accountable in a way no autocracy ever could. Democracies can truly make the guilty and negligent reap the consequences of their failings – and they must do so, both for the health of our democracies at home and for our hopes of spreading democracy abroad.

* * *

Democracies must first expand open records laws in government at all levels, restricting information only when genuine national security secrets are at risk of being exposed. The United States promises such disclosures, but requests under the Freedom of Information Act often take years to be fulfilled and are hugely redacted, fulfilling the letter of the law but not its spirit – and making them useless unless you file a lawsuit to force government action.[84]

Europe is bedevilled by similar problems.

The public should know how many complaints have been made against court security officers or the value of penalty fares issued by private inspectors on the tube system. I've lived in London; I would have liked to have known that information, and more. Yet these are examples of freedom of information requests that the UK government denied because existing laws did not cover the organisations responsible for their disclosure.[85] There is no good reason for this: for people to believe in their government, they must be able to understand how it operates.

Second, democracies need to increase the transparency of money in politics.

A large part of the reason democratic citizens have such limited confidence in their government is because they believe their politicians' acquiescence has been bought by big corporations. The *Guardian* has proclaimed that 'big business controls government', while the *Atlantic* has declared that 'corporate lobbyists [have] conquered American democracy'.[86] Headlines like these may be overstating the case, but they are not altogether wrong, and they illustrate why people have such limited confidence in their government.

In the United States, some simple improvements might include passing the DISCLOSE Act, which would require full disclosure of all political spending and overhaul the country's Federal Election Commission, an institutional so dysfunctional that it can barely enforce the law.[87]

Another suggestion for democracies everywhere is to establish or improve existing institutions charged with rooting out corruption. The Labor-led Australian government, to its credit, has promised to create such an institution.[88] These institutions must be independent, staffed not by political allies or appointees, but by top-quality, committed public servants. There is nothing wrong with people spending money to support their preferred political causes, but ordinary citizens must know who is supporting which candidates, and that they are doing so legally.

Third, democracies must expand what counts as illegal corruption. There remains far too much activity among politicians that is legal but corrupt and serves only to undermine public confidence in democracy.[89] It remains legal in many democracies for politicians to accept financial contributions from individuals and groups and to in turn provide them with implicit benefits – such as weakening or strengthening certain regulations.[90] It remains legal for former bankers, serving as US Treasury staff, to participate in multi-dollar bailouts for their old firms.[91] It remains legal for just about anyone, including former top government officials, to become lobbyists for our adversaries, as former German chancellor Gerhard Schröder has done by lobbying for Russia.[92] And of course, it remains legal for US Congressional representatives to trade stocks even when they're privy to inside information.

Democracies should therefore expand their definitions of corruption to account for political *quid pro quos* and the participation of former private sector titans in government decisions directly related to their old colleagues. Sitting lawmakers should be forced to place their investments in blind trusts, not allowed to trade stocks; even if they believe they are trading legally, the appearance of corruption serves only to undermine public trust. To that end, we should also bar former government officials from lobbying for adversarial foreign governments and state-affiliated companies attached to them. Government agencies will accordingly need to produce a yearly list of 'adversaries' to clarify that lobbying, say, for Taiwan's inclusion in a trade pact is far different from lobbying for Chinese or Russian interests.

Fourth, democracies must enhance whistle-blower protections.

When people come forward to report wrongdoing, either in the government or the private sector, they are risking everything; they face personal and professional harm and must be protected. But whistle-blowers are vital: they exposed President Trump's immigration abuses and his blackmailing of Ukraine.[93] Whistle-blowers have also exposed corruption throughout Europe, yet most European citizens believe they cannot safely make such reports because they will face reprisals for speaking up.[94]

Australia, dubbed the world's 'most secretive democracy', has repeatedly investigated journalists and whistle-blowers in a more aggressive manner than just about any advanced democracy – even raiding reporters' homes.[95] The country's government also regularly issues suppression orders to keep court proceedings private and rejects public records requests. The result has been to weaken trust in the country's governance. As Johan Lidberg, a professor in Melbourne, put it, Australia is perhaps the only 'mature liberal democracy that pursues and hunts down whistle-blowers and tries to kill the messenger'.[96] August 2022 reports that former Australian prime minister Scott Morrison secretly made himself the head of several government ministries only further damaged Australian trust in government.[97]

Clearly, even the most advanced democracies desperately need robust legislation that will strengthen whistle-blower protections. Only by doing so – by legally barring retaliation and providing whistle-blowers with the right to seek justice through the courts if they do face retaliation – can democracies ensure that wrongdoing is reported.

This is not impossible. Japan has in recent years amended its own whistle-blower protections, requiring companies to punish employees who harass or demote whistle-blowers, as well as insisting they establish a contact point and put an official in charge of documenting whistle-blowing. Tokyo has set a strong example for other democracies around the world.

Fifth, democracies need to restore public confidence in the parts of government with which ordinary people most regularly interact by instituting public annual reviews of bureaucracy, as is practised in the UAE. But democracies can go a step further: because we are democracies, we can appoint apolitical, outside experts to review the functionality of institutions ranging from the US Department of Defense to the UK National Health Service, and everywhere in between.

And once leaders receive these results, they should publicise them, as the UAE does. This approach will certainly frustrate under-performing institutions and offices, but it will also incentivise them to perform better. Nothing pushes people like the fear of being embarrassed.

Sixth, and finally, democracies must prosecute powerful people who are clearly implicated in a crime. Trump should be prosecuted in court for his various brazen violations of US law. The bankers responsible for the 2008 crisis should have appeared in American and European courts for their wilful neglect. And if they were convicted, they should not have been pardoned without good reason.

Ensuring that these people face charges is key to restoring trust in democracy. And restoring trust is key to fending off autocracy's rise – by making clear that, unlike one-party states riven by favouritism and rivalry, we, as democracies, can and will hold everyone accountable.

* * *

All of these steps are premised on a basic notion that sunlight is the best disinfectant, as the former US Supreme Court Justice Louis Brandeis declared. In other words, that exposing the truth does generally improve the situation. Nowhere is that truer than in government and among the most powerful.

But sunlight is not only a disinfectant. It can also be a salve; its warmth – let's call it accountability – has the ability to restore trust in troubled democracies, and thus improve our democracies' very foundations, if only our leaders will let it. The result will be not only better democracy at home, but a better base from which our system can serve as a model everywhere.

The outlook for making these changes may seem dismal. But it is not impossible, as even American politics demonstrates. The seven Republican senators who voted to impeach Trump in January 2021 – Richard Burr, Bill Cassidy, Susan Collins, Lisa Murkowski, Mitt Romney, Ben Sasse and Pat Toomey – are a sign of hope. These senators are committed to the rule of law and, at its heart, liberalism: they want democracy to work. They can be allies in the push to ensure the greater accountability of our democratic systems, and to fend off the dictators both at home and abroad.

Ultimately, it is on us, the public, to demand more of our leaders. It is on us to appeal to our politicians' better natures and ensure that they hold *everyone* – even their colleagues, even their families, even their university friends – accountable. We must not just hope but demand that they listen. Democracy everywhere is at stake.

3

Trust

Vietnam was preparing for a party. It was January 2020, just days before the Lunar New Year – known as *Tet* in Vietnam – and families were planning for the holiday. Professionals in Ho Chi Minh City and Hanoi gathered their belongings, buying beer and *banh chung* to bring home. In villages, towns and cities throughout the nation, their families were eagerly waiting for them. Everyone was ready to celebrate. But the Vietnamese government was preparing for a crisis.

On 23 January, Vietnam detected its first case of COVID-19 in a man who had travelled from the Chinese city of Wuhan to visit his son in Ho Chi Minh City, formerly known as Saigon.[1] Authorities did not know exactly what they were dealing with or how best to manage it; they were still referring to COVID-19 as a mysterious new pneumonia. But they nonetheless knew they had to act. They knew that even a mild spread of the virus would easily overwhelm Vietnam's relatively poor medical system.

So, they chose prevention and containment, believing that the public would trust the government enough to comply with lockdowns throughout the country, even if doing so caused economic distress. On 3 January – the same day that China reported a mysterious cluster of pneumonia cases to the World Health Organization – the Vietnamese Ministry of Health announced plans to increase disease control measures on the country's land border with China.[2] By late January, Vietnam's then-prime minister Nguyen Xuan Phuc had banned flights to and from Wuhan and other parts of China where the virus was spreading. By 1 February, Vietnam had banned all flights to and from China. The government even forced people to celebrate a toned-down *Tet*, with travel restrictions preventing many from seeing their families.

All the while, Hanoi was quietly preparing its next steps, foreseeing that things would get worse. The government closed schools for the *Tet* holiday and did not open them again until mid-May. Authorities then embarked on a huge and labour-intensive contact-tracing operation, conscripting medical students, retired doctors and nurses to join the fight.[3] And when the government told people to stay home, they did – largely because they trusted the government, but also to avoid official retribution in this one-party state. Trust was crucial to Vietnam's approach; without it, none of this would have been possible.[4]

By mid-April 2020, Vietnam had recorded fewer than three hundred COVID-19 cases and no deaths – at a time when the United Kingdom was recording over five thousand cases and one thousand deaths daily. Vietnam then managed to carry out a successful vaccination campaign, giving at least one dose to 75 per cent of its population by early December 2021. At the time, this was a better vaccination rate than in the United States, Estonia, Latvia and several other democracies.

Vietnam had seemingly got it right; they contained the virus because people trusted the government, while the opposite happened in the West and in some democracies elsewhere. Guy Thwaites, an infectious disease doctor, explained that Vietnam 'adopted a zero-tolerance approach to get rid of the virus. Basic measures were implemented, but it wasn't easy.' But he added, 'When people trust the government, people do what the government says.'[5]

* * *

Modern Vietnam is nothing if not a paradox. It is presided over by a nominally communist regime, under whose leadership the country has experienced rapid economic growth sustained for decades – precisely by integrating itself into the capitalist global economy. Its existence is predicated on military defeats of two of the same powers, the United States and China, on whom Hanoi relies economically today (to say nothing of Vietnam's strong security ties with the United States, or amicable relationship with France). It is a country whose locals welcome Westerners with open arms, despite our complex history. 'The past is the past,' I remember one shopkeeper in the country's undeveloped centre telling me as we watched Vietnam's national soccer team compete in a pan-Asian tournament a few years ago. 'We're focused on the future.'

Yet Vietnam still has a GDP per capita of only around USD 2,800 – a number nearly fifteen times less than that of the United Kingdom and twenty-three times less than that of the United States. How, then, did Vietnam manage to keep COVID-19 under control while the virus decimated rich democracies around the world, at least until the appearance of the Omicron variant?

The answer is another paradox: despite being a one-party, repressive authoritarian state, Vietnam enjoys a level of public trust that no democracy can rival. People from Ho Chi Minh City to Hanoi and just about everywhere in between will tell you – as they've told me – that they trust their government because their government works, and that they increasingly don't see the appeal of our 'messy' democracy. The numbers back up my anecdotes: in 2020, a staggering 93 per cent of Vietnamese reported either 'quite a lot' or 'a great deal' of confidence in the government.[6] No democratic nation reports numbers even close to those.

Like everywhere else, people in Vietnam still regularly criticise their government. They complain about pollution, corruption and the state's perceived weak approach to China, of which most Vietnamese have a strongly negative view.[7]

Once COVID-19 took hold, however, the Vietnamese government understood the importance of public trust and invested in improving it. Hanoi understands that without elections, the need to win public trust is more important than in an electoral democracy – because without elections, there is no way for people to demonstrate their trust in the government, and thus for the government to assess whether it actually enjoys trust on a national scale.

Hanoi knows that without trust, there is no truth; that without truth, the people will not listen; and that without their cooperation, nothing can be done.

So, as the pandemic spread and the global crisis ballooned, Vietnam embarked on what scholars have called 'a deliberate policy of trust creation'.[8] This policy hinged first and foremost on transparent government decision-making. The Vietnamese government went to great pains to inform the public of what it was doing, and why. Ministers held daily television briefings, while the government flooded people's phones with text messages. As part of this transparency effort, the government very plainly stated that it was going to 'sacrifice short-term economic interests to better protect people's health and lives', as Prime Minister Phuc said.[9] Leaders trusted the public with this difficult truth; the public appreciated that honesty and rewarded their government by trusting them in turn.

The government coupled its commitment to transparency with an effective COVID-19 leader – the young, widely respected deputy prime minister, Vu Duc Dam – and a smart communications strategy that tapped into Vietnam's past. Anti-COVID-19 posters borrowed from Vietnam War-era iconography; officials painted the disease as just one more struggle in Vietnam's millennia of resistance against China, France and the United States. Right before the government issued its national lockdown on 30 March 2020, Communist Party General Secretary Nguyen Phu Trong told the public: 'For the sake of the whole nation of Vietnam, let us work together, unanimously surmounting all difficulties and challenges to overcome the COVID-19 pandemic.' This was a call with unmistakable war-time echoes, and it resonated.[10]

By being honest about both the threat and the costs of COVID-19 and the coming response – and by making symbolic connections with Vietnam's history – the government managed to build a huge reservoir of public trust. Many Vietnamese citizens, even pro-democracy bloggers prone to criticising the government, realised that the government's information was true, and that, as far as the pandemic was concerned, Hanoi really did mean well. The government already enjoyed high levels of trust among its populace, but officials' management of the pandemic bolstered this further, creating a virtuous cycle that produced a population even more willing to cooperate with COVID-19 restrictions.

Hanoi's policy of trust creation is a large part of the reason Vietnam was able to hold off the worst of COVID-19 for so long. People trusted the government, so they believed its dire warnings – about just how bad things could get if they didn't cooperate – and in turn cooperated with official directives. And because they did so in aggregate, Vietnam managed to weather the COVID-19 storm better than just about anyone else.

Trust enabled the cooperation that made Hanoi's pandemic policy work.

Indeed, trust makes possible the cooperation that is so vital to any country's functioning. But the breakdown of that trust prevents public cooperation, resulting at times in calamity.

Even in Vietnam, it was when the government lost the people's trust on the pandemic – thanks to a lack of transparency and mixed messages that tainted the government's previously clear communication – that COVID-19 numbers spiked.[11] Things got bad only when people lost trust and stopped cooperating as willingly with the government, which in turn found itself with limited political space in which to manoeuvre.

And even then, Vietnam's trust numbers remained far better than in any Western democracy; its hospitalisation and death numbers remained far lower. By any measure, Vietnam's COVID-19 policy was a resounding success – thanks, in no small part, to trust.

* * *

Losing Faith

Democracies around the world – but particularly in the West – are experiencing a crisis of trust. People do not trust their neighbours. They do not trust the media. And they certainly do not trust their governments.

I've heard this sentiment in conversations around the world – from taxi drivers in my hometown of New York City, from barbecue vendors throughout the American south, from football fanatics in Liverpool and London, and from street vendors from Kota Kinabalu to Jerusalem. Their gripes are similar: *the government is corrupt*; *the government is ineffective*; *our politicians don't care about us.* And so, they say, *we want something new.*

This was true even before the pandemic. In 2019, only 35 and 41 per cent of Americans trusted their government to handle domestic and international problems, respectively.[12] In that same year, only 19 per cent of people in the United Kingdom said that they trusted politicians to tell them the truth; just 42 per cent trusted the government to 'do what is right'.[13]

Many of the most striking demonstrations of government mistrust have been the rise of populist movements with autocratic tendencies: Trump's election, the Brexit vote, and the rise in far-right parties from Hungary to Spain – all have occurred in the West. The conversations I've had with Orbán voters, who ardently believed he would oust the 'corrupt politicians' they distrusted and create a better Hungary, are lodged in my brain precisely because they remind me deeply of similar conversations I've had with people in our own democracies: Trump voters in Tennessee, Brexiteers at Goodison Park and frustrated families in Seoul. Orbán's ability to mobilise distrust in government – and wield that distrust into a parliamentary super-majority – is a warning for democracies around the world of what happens when you lose your people's trust.

The emergence of these anti-establishment leaders and movements is possible only because so many people do not trust the establishments that have governed their countries for decades. If the Hungarian and American publics trusted their governments, Orbán and Trump could never have been elected; the same goes for the Brexit vote. When people do not trust their government, they are far more willing to vote for leaders and movements that rail against this same government's purported misgovernance and promise something new. Without trust, democracy is at risk.

Yet democracies beyond the West are experiencing their own crises of trust, too. In 2019, around 40 per cent of Japanese reported trust in their government; about 30 per cent of South Africans and Brazilians said the same.[14] It is no coincidence that South Africa is in a constant cycle of political crisis, nor that Brazil in late 2018 elected the right-wing populist Jair Bolsonaro – who expresses contempt for democracy and admiration for autocracy – in that same year. Distrust can doom democracy. (Japan's politics are more predictable, but in 2022 that country experienced its first political assassination in decades.)

It should worry us, then, that the most trusted governments are autocracies.

In 2019, nearly 90 per cent of Chinese reported trust in their government; some 80 per cent of UAE citizens said the same, as did almost 70 per cent of Singaporeans.[15] And when you speak to a Singaporean, even one who does not particularly like their government, they will tell you that they trust their government a hell of a lot more than they do those of the United States, Europe or Japan.

Singaporean 'distrust' looks more like annoyance than genuine discontent.

Many people living under these non-democratic governments believe that their governments are working well, and that their personal futures are bright. It's tempting to wonder if these results are skewed by fear – after all, people in non-democracies may worry about government retribution if they express opposition – but many of these studies controlled for that factor. Autocracies' ability to exert substantial control over the media, and thus control the narrative that reaches their own people, tends to boost public trust in these governments as well. Regardless, the numbers are impressive.

Remarkably, COVID-19 augmented this divergence: throughout the pandemic's first eighteen months or so, autocracies saw trust in government improve.

Survey after survey shows that Chinese citizens trusted their government more as the pandemic dragged on – until the Omicron variant emerged and China maintained its 'zero-COVID' policy. Chinese trust in national government hit 98 per cent after authorities controlled the initial outbreak in early 2020.[16] China may have let COVID-19 escape, but the government did, for a long period, prevent severe outbreaks without extreme economic repercussions; it is thus not hard to understand why 72 and 82 per cent of Chinese citizens still trusted their government in 2020 and 2021, respectively.[17] A similar trend is evident in the UAE, Singapore and other relatively well-governed autocracies.[18]

Yet the pandemic fuelled distrust throughout the democratic world. From 2021 to 2022, trust in government fell in the Netherlands, Canada, Australia, Italy, Germany, South Korea, the United Kingdom, the United States and Japan. Of those countries, the Netherlands, Canada and Australia were the only ones where more than 50 per cent of people expressed trust in the government.[19] That means, then, that only three of these leading democracies enjoy the trust of most of their population.

Democratic citizens are not supposed to be this distrustful of their government. We choose our leaders. We hold our governments accountable at the ballot box, regularly voting out those who do not perform – unlike in China or Vietnam, where stagnant elites can remain in power for decades. We have the right to criticise our governments on social media and in newspaper columns, unlike people in the UAE or Saudi Arabia. Why, then, are people in democracies so distrustful of their governments? What went wrong?

The answer is surprisingly simple: people are disappointed.

In the 1990s, countries around the world experienced strong economic growth. People in many countries, particularly rich ones, felt this growth in their wallet, enjoyed greater material well-being and credited the government with at least boosting this period of success. Critically, their governments were still offering strong social safety nets and a sense of security. People believed and trusted that their governments would deliver a high quality of life for them – and an even higher quality of life for their children.[20]

They expected these trends to continue, but the course of recent history has left them disappointed. In contrast to their peers in Singapore or Shenzhen, people from Wilmington to Wycombe no longer believe that their children will have better lives than they did. They believe that things are getting worse; they lose sleep over their children's future. They do not trust their governments because they do not believe that government institutions can deliver.[21]

That is a staggering democratic failure, particularly when the citizens of several autocracies believe the opposite. And it is a failure that leaves fertile ground for the rise of autocracy at home.

* * *

American trust in government hit an all-time recorded high in 1964. Circumstances helped. The Vietnam War had not yet started in earnest; Lyndon B. Johnson was president, and still benefiting from the sympathy earned after JFK's assassination the previous year; and, most important of all, the economy was booming.

Writing in 1965, officials from the US Department of Commerce said that 'the year of 1964 was one of strong expansion in the American economy', noting that 1964 marked the 'establishment of numerous records', not only in production and sales but also in employee compensation, employment and living standards.[22] It was also the 'fourth consecutive year of upturn'.[23]

Racism, homophobia and misogyny prevented *everyone* from enjoying this period of American success. But life in America was good for most: a staggering 77 per cent of Americans – Black and white, gay and straight, male and female – trusted their government.[24]

Within a couple of decades, Watergate and the Vietnam War, coupled with economic malaise, would bring this number down to the thirties and even the low twenties, at times. President Ronald Reagan's relatively short-term economic success bumped this number back up to the low forties; President George H. W. Bush's skilful management of the Cold War's end saw this number creep up to 46 per cent, the highest level of public trust reached since before Watergate. But Bush also oversaw the early years of the 'Great Moderation', in which volatile US economic performance – of huge growth followed by drastic drops – was replaced by decent growth, low inflation and short, if modest, recessions. It wasn't all so bad, but Americans wanted better; they had become accustomed to better in those previous peaks, even if the worse generally followed with valleys soon after. Which is why Bill Clinton defeated Bush by campaigning on the slogan 'It's the economy, stupid'.[25]

Clinton's presidency offers perhaps the clearest illustration of how economic success fuels trust in government. When he took office, trust in government was near what was then an all-time low, hovering around 22 per cent. The next eight years saw robust economic growth and record job creation and surpluses, while unemployment and core inflation were at their lowest levels in more than thirty years.[26] The American system was, in fact, working. And Americans rewarded their president: when Clinton left office, 44 per cent of Americans trusted the government – the highest in nearly a decade, despite the Lewinsky scandal. This means that on the back of huge economic success, Clinton managed in eight years to double the percentage of Americans who trusted the government, despite facing an embarrassing impeachment scandal.

Yet it was under President George W. Bush that the United States recorded its highest level of trust in government since Watergate. Just weeks after the September 11 attacks, this number rose to 60 per cent – clearly the result of a 'rally around the flag' effect. People felt vulnerable; they wanted a strong leader, and Bush fitted the bill well enough, for a time. But his poor record, namely his instigation of two wars and enabling of the 2008 financial collapse, left US levels of trust in a shockingly poor position. By the time Barack Obama took office in 2009, only 23 per cent of Americans trusted the government. That number has not risen above 26 per cent in the decade and a half since.[27]

This link – between economic success and trust in government – is evident also in Japan, where people's trust in their government began to rise from 2012 onwards, as the economy steadily recovered from the financial crisis.[28] A similar story played out, too, in the Czech Republic, where trust in government rose from just 17 per cent in 2012 to 44 per cent in 2015, on the back of 7 per cent growth in GDP per capita.[29] Connections like this are evident across the democratic world.

This link is evident in autocracies, too. People in China have trusted their government for years not because the government is transparent – which it is not – but because officials have largely delivered on their promises to raise the standard of living. The same can be said for the governments of the UAE, Singapore, Vietnam and others. These governments made substantial promises; for most, they delivered. People consider these governments legitimate because they perform.

Just think about it for a second. If your government, democratic or otherwise, increased your country's GDP per capita by nearly 2,400 per cent from 1980 and raised the standard of living to levels previously thought impossible, as China has, wouldn't you place at least some trust in that regime?[30] And if your government did not deliver on this front – if your wealth did not grow and your standard of living did not improve, all while the elites got richer and richer – would you really continue to trust the government, even if it did wear a kinder, more democratic face?

Probably not, as the democratic crisis of trust is showing.

In 2022, huge majorities of people in leading democracies said that they and their families would not be better off in five years' time. In Japan, only 15 per cent believed they would. Eighteen per cent said the same in France, as did 22 per cent of people in Germany. Several democracies – including Japan, France, Germany, Italy, the Netherlands, Canada and the United States – recorded all-time low economic confidence in 2022. In each of these countries, trust in government fell from 2021 levels. In some countries it did so precipitously: Germany saw trust drop by 12 percentage points.[31]

The main democratic exceptions are Switzerland and the Scandinavian countries, which enjoy levels of public trust ranging from 68 to 84 per cent – in some cases, double the levels of trust seen in leading democracies such as the United States and Japan.[32] Trust in these countries stems from governmental willingness to provide for their people. Not only do the Nordic countries and Switzerland maintain safety at home, but they also offer universal access to comprehensive 'cradle-to-grave' public services and welfare benefits (which while imperfect remain vital). Alongside open societies and well-functioning systems of democratic governance that hold people accountable – thereby stamping out corruption – this provision of basic human security instils public confidence in the government.

Whereas the United States, United Kingdom and others struggle to offer adequate public services and increase the average citizen's welfare, the Nordic countries appear to have done just that and have been rewarded with high levels of public support.[33]

Trust hinges on performance, and to a somewhat lesser extent, transparency. For people to trust their governments, these governments must have a recent track record of success and remain open about their actions, which far too many democracies decidedly do not.

'The way to make people trust-worthy is to trust them,' Ernest Hemingway once wrote. Democratic citizens *did* once trust their governments – but after years of governmental failures, these same citizens have realised that they made a mistake. And once it was seen to be misplaced, that trust evaporated.

* * *

Why Trust Matters – and How to Get It Back

The countries with the highest levels of trust in government are those, like Vietnam, that performed the best during the COVID-19 pandemic.

This should come as no surprise. Generalised trust is necessary to create a collective belief in what is true – which is particularly vital when people are trying to determine whether a new virus is truly a threat. High levels of trust also underpin state capacity. Trust is associated with higher vaccination rates and compliance with government regulations.[34]

A divergence in trust helps explain why, when huge majorities of citizens in autocracies China and Vietnam lined up to get their jab and stayed at home when asked, countless Americans and Canadians and others throughout the democratic world refused to get their shots and protested, even violently, against well-meaning COVID-19 restrictions.

Trust is no longer a privilege of democracy. The most successful autocracies – like China, Singapore, Vietnam and several Gulf States – all enjoy higher levels of trust than nearly every democratic country. On paper, it doesn't seem like authoritarian regimes should be entitled to any trust at all. But people's confidence is the result of perceived good governance, and of governmental efforts to keep that trust once it has been established. It is the result of careful policy-making and of delivering on promises.

It is troubling, to say the least, that repressive systems are enjoying greater trust than their free-world counterparts. Trust is the building block of effective governance, and especially of good governance within democracies. When people do not trust their government, they will not listen to, support or even engage with it. In democracies, this means that people will not vote. And when people in Muscle Shoals, Leeds and Gangwon are so disconnected from their governments in Washington, Westminster and Seoul that they don't vote, the government will not provide for them effectively – because officials are not mind-readers; they cannot serve a population from which they have grown distant. So, when people don't trust their government and thus opt out of civic participation, the result is a 'mistrust loop' in which a distrustful public is disengaged, resulting in a government even more disconnected from the public.[35] This, in turn, leads only to the further deterioration of trust, which prompts people to look for solutions in new places and people – including in populists with authoritarian tendencies.

Several other problems also emerge when trust declines. People comply less with rules and regulations. They commit more crimes, whether in the streets of Manhattan or Miaoli. And when crime is not addressed by the state, distrust deepens even further.[36]

People who do not trust their government also become more risk-averse, delaying investment, innovation and employment decisions to err on the side of conservatism.[37] This blunts democracies' innovative spirit. People who do not trust their government are also less willing to pay taxes – vital to important redistributive programmes such as welfare and food assistance that blunt inequity. Their dissent therefore makes government less effective, thereby fomenting only more distrust of not only the government, but of society at large.[38]

Predictably, as public trust in the United States declined after the Kennedy and Johnson presidencies, politicians sceptical of both the establishment and active government gained more and more influence in US politics. As these politicians entered the country's halls of power, they produced less active public policy – weakened safety nets and financial regulations, for starters. This more inactive policy created less and less effective government, which only further augmented public distrust, and nourished the rise of would-be dictators who feed on this distrust.[39] Thus the cycle of distrust became vicious, helping produce a less responsive government that made people's yearnings for something different, perhaps even autocracy, all the more salient.

With trust, you can do just about anything. Without it, you're in trouble.

* * *

The Trust Crisis

It took little more than a month of COVID-19 lockdowns for Americans throughout the country to begin rejecting 'stay at home' orders. Protestors stormed the capitols of states as diverse as California, Wisconsin and Washington, saying that the restrictions violated their freedom, and that the new virus was simply not as bad as the government was saying. Waving Trump flags and American flags, and bearing posters claiming 'our rights are essential', they rebutted government and experts' claims, preferring to take matters – and risk – into their own hands. 'We are adults,' declared one Oklahoma organiser. 'We assume personal responsibility for the decisions that we make.'[40]

'They're telling people: we're going to take your civil liberties away and put you out of work but, by the way, we're not really sure about any of these numbers,' said an anti-lockdown protestor in Michigan.[41] 'The models were wrong,' echoed more than a few signs in Idaho, reflecting protestors' beliefs that the elites running the country were lying to them.[42]

Anti-lockdown protests popped up also in democracies around the world, in places as different as Berlin, Bangalore and Busan. People in democracies around the world did not trust their governments to tell the truth, let alone trust them to do what is best – which is why people in these cities, among countless others in liberal societies, took to the streets to protest against government restrictions. They preferred to take matters into their own hands and reopen economic activity, even at the risk of COVID-19 infection, than trust the government and keep everything closed. Many said they had no choice: they needed to work to make ends meet because government assistance was not enough.

Of course, the content of these demands – that the economy be open not only for leisure activities, but more importantly, so that they could work and feed their families – shows that democratic governments around the world did not do enough to support their people before or during this crisis. If the government had told everyone to go home and promised to keep the funds flowing, and if the people had trusted them to keep that promise, then perhaps citizens wouldn't have taken to the streets.

* * *

Countries around the world eventually lifted restrictions on the back of COVID-19 vaccinations. But again, the lack of trust struck a heavy blow: because people in democracies did not trust their governments, more than a few refused to get vaccinated, slowing the speed with which their countries could get back to some form of normal.

In the United States, poorer and less educated people of all races – those most likely to believe that the government has left them behind – were the most likely to refuse vaccination.[43] People simply refused to get the jab or at least were sceptical about doing so. *The government*, they said, *has lied to and hurt me for years, why is this vaccine any different?*

In the United States, race played a troubling role in this regard: Black Americans were half as likely to get vaccinated as their white counterparts in the early months of the vaccine roll-out. Many Black Americans pointed to past racist US medical practices, like the notorious Tuskegee experiments, as reason to distrust the government.[44] By October 2021, only 28 per cent of Black residents in my own New York City were vaccinated, compared to 52 per cent of the city's white population. Black New Yorkers flooded social media with reasons, but their rationale ultimately came down to one factor: they did not trust the government with their health.[45]

This resistance only hardened after the United States suspended use of the Johnson & Johnson vaccine following the discovery of a rare link to blood clots in women. 'It reaffirmed my hesitance, it reaffirmed everything,' said one Black New Yorker, a graduate student, adding: 'It just shows Black lives don't matter. You can test that on us just like you tested syphilis on us.'[46] A Black Lives Matter leader summed up these concerns with a pithy question: 'Since when,' he asked, 'does America give anything good to Black people first?'[47]

Vaccine hesitancy – or out-and-out resistance – is neither a specifically Black nor American problem.

When authorities began rolling out the vaccines in the spring of 2021, under half of South Koreans and Japanese citizens said they trusted these inoculations.[48] The Koreans least likely to get vaccinated were conservative younger people who distrusted the government – those same Koreans who expressed the most dissatisfaction with their economic status.[49] The Japanese least likely to get vaccinated were young people who distrusted the government.[50] As in South Korea, this group is the least satisfied with the state of their country, and thus with their government's performance.[51]

To varying extents, these countries eventually managed to vaccinate enough people to reopen with relatively low death rates, even if cases (but not deaths) eventually spiked because of the Omicron variant. But time was wasted, and not-insignificant numbers of people – like NBA star Kyrie Irving – have *still* refused to get their shots because they actively distrust their government.

Put bluntly, people died because democratic governments failed to secure the trust of their people, and without that trust, they were not able to secure people's cooperation in well-intentioned solutions, like staying at home and getting vaccinated.

Around the world, distrust meant death.

* * *

COVID-19 has been a horrible crisis, but it will not be the last one the world sees. And it might not even be the worst of its kind. There is a non-zero chance of an even worse pandemic occurring – imagine something with Ebola's death rate and COVID-19's transmissibility. Without re-establishing public trust, democracies will not be able to handle such a crisis.

But you don't need to indulge in hypotheticals to see the price of low public trust. Already, a lack of trust has severely undermined countries' ability to take meaningful action on climate over the last few decades. Data shows that a lack of trust in institutions has blunted the public's perception of climate change, thereby undermining their willingness to support behaviours or policies to address the threat.[52] If you do not believe the government in general, which, for years, most democratic citizens have not (and do not today), of course you will doubt these same elites when they tell you action is needed to address climate change.[53]

The result of this distrust was limited, piecemeal action that was far from sufficient.

Without trust in government, there was for decades little agreement on the truth – that the crisis was a crisis – and there was little collective action as a result. The 2015 Paris Accords were a step in the right direction, but they were years late and nowhere near enough. It did not help that the United States, helmed by a leader in Donald Trump who came to power by riding a wave of distrust in the establishment, removed itself from the pact in 2020.

Current US President Joe Biden has returned the United States to the Paris pact and pushed important climate legislation, but his government – like many democratic ones around the world – continues to struggle to make more meaningful progress on the climate challenge. This is in no small part because Americans still do not trust their government and with limited trust in this government, leaders, both presidents and legislators, have little political space in which to operate and deliver solutions.

Leaders everywhere have struggled (and are still struggling) to enact key climate policies – ones that may cause economic disruptions – precisely because they have so little public trust to fall back on. The huge public uproar Biden would face if he, for example, announced plans to even halve emissions by 2030 makes such action impossible.[54]

The lack of trust our insufficient approach to the climate crisis demonstrates will also blunt democracies' ability to handle slow-moving crises, such as the automation of work and the ageing of our populations.[55] When people do not trust the government, officials will struggle mightily to make necessary if unpopular decisions that may carry economic consequences.

Perhaps most worrying is the effect our trust deficit will have on democracies' ability to mobilise in the face of war with, say, China or Russia. Even if such conflict remains unlikely – although considerably more likely since the Russian invasion of Ukraine – it is worth considering the trouble democracies would be in if we had to face these or other adversaries in a potential kinetic conflict. China and Russia can compel their people to fight with the threat of violence; most democracies cannot. We will instead need people to volunteer or to at least comply with a citizen draft. Yet it is just about impossible to imagine that Americans, Brits, Germans or even Japanese would happily sign up or even allow themselves to be drafted into a military force to take on Russia or China.

Why would they? If you don't trust your government, you won't trust national leaders to decide what's a threat, who's an adversary and who needs to be fought. Following US disasters in Vietnam, Iraq and Afghanistan – on which Americans believe our leaders misled us – it is ludicrous to suggest that the United States could reintroduce forced conscription without public pushback.

Certain democracies on the frontlines of authoritarian aggression are exceptions. South Korea and Taiwan require all men to serve in the military; Israel requires both men and women alike to serve. People in these countries certainly would band together if their country was threatened, as in Israel in 1967 and 1973, even if they have lost trust in their respective governments.

But these are exceptions, not the rule. The reality is that if China invaded Taiwan, or Russia invaded Estonia or Latvia, it is extraordinarily difficult to imagine that the United States, France or Japan could willingly mobilise enough people to fight these authoritarian powers. People no longer trust the authorities that would be calling them to fight, particularly on behalf of some faraway foreign friend.

Trust is always important, but in times of crisis, whether a war, a pandemic or some other yet unimagined scenario, it is vital. Without it, we – and our liberal international order – could crumble.

* * *

Rebuilding

I can't count the number of times somebody – somebody patriotic and active in their community – has told me that while they don't trust their government, they do, in fact, love their country. It's a common refrain I've heard from Uber drivers in Memphis and fishermen in Malaysia. *I don't like my government*, they say, listing off their leaders' faults, corruption and inaction chief among them. But after pausing, and taking a second, they add: *I do love my country*. More often than not they have a national flag somewhere nearby, whether adorning the backside of their pickup truck or hanging outside their home.

If you travel around the democratic world and have conversations with people around you, you will hear some version of this refrain.

This evident lack of trust is troubling, but there is a silver lining. The comment's last bit indicates that despite what may look like a sorry state of affairs, all is not lost: people may not trust their leaders but they do believe in the *potential* of trusting them – they believe in the possibility of rebuilding trust. They believe, that is, in their countries, if not in their governments or systems of governance. They believe in Britain or America or Japan even if they don't believe in democracy right now.

Some 84 per cent of Americans say that the level of confidence they and their compatriots have in the federal government can be improved.[56] Illustrating something similar is the fact that in the United Kingdom, trust in the national government rose during the country's first COVID-19 lockdown.[57] Remarkably, from January to May 2020 – when the COVID-19 pandemic truly took hold – several democracies saw huge increases in government trust: by twenty-four points in the United Kingdom, twenty points in Canada, nineteen points in Germany, thirteen points in France and twelve points in Mexico.[58] When people needed their governments, and their governments delivered, citizens learned to trust their leaders once again.

These numbers eventually fell back to earth, primarily because national governments failed to control the pandemic, mismanaged their vaccine roll-outs, or became embroiled in other scandals and problems. But what the era of COVID-19 should teach us is that trust in government is not static: it is not lost, it can be won back, although governments will have to earn it.

Democracies have a window to save themselves. We don't know how long it will last. But right now, with the world having largely recovered from the worst of the pandemic, we have a moment – one that may yet prove fleeting – to reverse the steady slide in trust and restore the functionality of governments and society. Doing so will improve the state of our democracies at home, making us more able to model success for would-be democrats abroad.

To get there, we will need to take bold action, action that at times may prove uncomfortable for those in power but that will benefit them, their constituents and their countries – not to mention democracies everywhere.

* * *

Americans do not trust their government because it has for years failed to achieve meaningful reforms at home, whether of the healthcare system or of national infrastructure. They think that their government is sclerotic, hyper-polarised and rigid. The Senate, once considered the world's 'greatest deliberative body', is now thought of as one where people simply vote on party lines and obstruct progress – rather than band together to enact change.

The Japanese are similarly frustrated. While they believe in democracy as a concept, they do not believe in their democracy, considering their system to be inattentive and ineffective.[59] They complain about the government's inability to address economic sluggishness and inequality, and to wean the country off fossil fuels, which became prohibitively expensive in the wake of the Russian invasion of Ukraine. Something similar can be said for the citizens of democracies around the world, with dissatisfaction remaining highest in the West.[60]

More than anything, people want a functional government, even if it is helmed by a leader who does not share their political preferences. The most important way to restore trust in government is simple: the government must do things, big things, and advertise those successes loudly and widely. Trust works like the old adage about justice – governments must follow through on their promises, and, crucially, be seen to follow through.

The irony is that many distrusted democratic governments are not as ineffective as they may seem; they're just bad at publicising their own achievements. So, while journalists and activists like to point out how useless the US Congress is, the reality – as the writers

Matt Yglesias and Simon Bazelon have noted – is that Congress gets quite a lot done, just not on the highest-profile issues.

This 'Secret Congress', as they put it, has in recent years delivered truly important legislation, like the Drinking Water and Wastewater Infrastructure Act of 2021, which passed in May of that year and appropriated USD 175 billion to upgrade public water systems across the country. Another success was the Veterans' Access to Care through Choice, Accountability, and Transparency Act of 2014, which was spearheaded by the democratic socialist Bernie Sanders and staunch conservative John McCain.[61] The Senate has in recent years also overwhelmingly passed bills to help farmers profit from climate action and overhaul the United States Postal Service. These are not headline-grabbing items, but they are ones that will impact the everyday lives of many Americans.[62]

Democrats and Republicans might be deadlocked on voting rights, abortion and a whole host of other issues, but Congress is clearly more productive than most Americans think.

Similarly, recent South Korean National Assemblies – one of which was dubbed the 'least productive in history' – have managed to pass budgets and fund the government without controversy, something that is not a given in many democracies (like the United States and Israel).[63] The European Union may have declined moderately in legislative productivity over the last decade, but it too has managed to pass important laws.[64] Something similar is true of the legislatures of Austria, the Netherlands, the United Kingdom and other Western democracies. There is little evidence to support the notion that democratic legislatures have become substantially less productive in recent years.[65]

Our much-maligned institutions do seem to be getting at least some parts of the job of governing done. Why doesn't the public think so?

Because both media and politicians alike have incentives to highlight failure. For the media, failure generally brings in more viewers than success; images of failure confirm viewers' existing negative opinions and keep them coming back to their channel of choice. This is particularly true in places like the United States and India, where the media is highly partisan, with many commentators more interested in convincing people of a political opinion than presenting information and letting citizens make their own decisions.

Democratic politicians around the world have increasingly run negative campaigns largely for the same reasons. The American Democrats, British Tories and South Korean conservatives have all won elections in the last few years by highlighting the things their rivals have failed to do, or have done poorly, rather than those that their own party has got right. They may have won their elections, but their victories hardly improved their public's trust in government. Trust in government has declined since both Biden and Johnson took office.[66] (There is no such data yet for South Korean President Yoon Suk-yeol.)

Negative campaigns may deliver short-term victories, but politicians would be better served if they ran on a platform of successes rather than mudslinging. Their countries certainly would be better off.

One simple way to improve trust in government, then, is for politicians, writers and activists to focus more on their victories. They need not frame these victories as partisan wins, but as governance wins for everyone. Postal service reform is not a Democrat or Republican victory, but a genuine victory for everybody who uses the service. Politicians, writers and activists should say just that, rather than push the polarised politics that sell subscriptions and drive donations. Hyper-partisan campaigning might work in the short-term, but it does not in the long-term, either for one's party or for one's polity.

Positive discourse is, to put it mildly, not something with which democratic politicians appear acquainted in this moment. But if leaders intend to leave a real mark – if they intend to improve their

countries rather than simply boost their own political positions –
they should learn to speak in positive terms. They should talk about
just how good at their jobs they really are.

* * *

Another way to demonstrate government effectiveness is to partner
with the private sector. This suggestion may seem curious, given
loud disdain for bankers and big business on both sides of the
Atlantic, as well as in democracies elsewhere. But the polling is clear:
most people trust the private sector more than they trust their
government – even if fringe politicians and activists are less sanguine.

From 2019 to 2020, business was tied for the most publicly
trusted institution across twenty-seven of the world's leading countries, most of which are democracies. In 2021, business became the
only trusted institution, with majorities of people around the world
distrusting NGOs, the government and the media.[67] (Business was
also the only institution that majorities considered both ethical and
competent.) Trust in business increased in 2022 from the preceding
year in thirteen of the eighteen surveyed democracies, including the
United Kingdom, France, Spain, Germany, the United States, Canada,
Italy, Australia and the Netherlands. The only democracies where
less than 50 per cent of people trusted business were South Korea
and Japan, at 47 and 46 per cent, respectively.[68]

Americans prefer the private sector so much that when they receive
high-quality public services, many mistakenly believe these services
are privately provided. They believe the government to be so incompetent that they simply cannot fathom functional public-sector action.[69]

Why do people trust business, even if they are sceptical or even
critical of capitalism? Because they consider the private sector
dynamic and productive, in contrast to their rigid and ineffectual
governments. Whereas SpaceX literally reaches for the stars or

Apple creates the world of tomorrow, governments from Downing Street to the White House look as if they are stuck in the world of yesterday. The active private sector offers the aspirational promise of a better life, whereas tired governments remind people of what they've lost, and how cloudy their futures appear. Like it or not, people trust Pfizer more than they trust the US Congress. They trust Amazon more than they trust the Taoiseach. They trust Tim Cook more than they do Rishi Sunak.

Governments should accordingly invest in principled public–private partnerships in which each party is committed to shared goals.[70] When partnerships are based on this shared understanding and strong coordination, they tend to produce huge successes, such as Australia's upgrade of the Ballina Bypass highway, which was completed in 1996 by the government – along with four private firms – seven months ahead of schedule and for USD 100 million less than estimated.[71] Other examples of such successful public–private partnerships abound, from Japanese railways to German housing.[72]

Perhaps the most successful public–private partnership in recent years is the development of COVID-19 vaccines. The Trump administration's 'Operation Warp Speed' sped up the development of several vaccine candidates by funding them with USD 10 billion from the US Congress. The operation worked largely because it followed the model of successful US mobilisation during the Second World War, when Washington leaned on the absolute best of private industry – on its 'energy and productivity', per historian Arthur Herman – while providing government oversight from start to finish. The US government guided the operation but did 'not micromanage the private economy's efforts'.[73] The German government took a similar approach to funding Pfizer's successful COVID-19 vaccine.[74]

Still, companies are not in the business of fixing societal problems; they are in the business of making money. But if the government works with the private sector to harmonise these goals, with both sides putting into action meaningful plans and highlighting them publicly, the result would be not only better governance but a huge lift in public trust. People trust the private sector more than they trust the government, and they want action. As a pair, private and public leaders can surely deliver.

* * *

People will not trust a government they think is corrupt. One way to combat this perception – along with accountability, discussed in a previous chapter – is to make the government more transparent.

Chief among government decisions that need to be more transparent are those around spending. People need to know where their tax dollars are going, and why. Only then will they trust the government to make wise decisions with their money, rather than express anger when tax season comes around. There are several common-sense steps that democratic governments around the world can take on this front.

First, they should post government spending online, for all to see. Some governments do this to varying extents, but, too often, the data they post is unreadable to the average citizen. Budgets should be posted in simple, readable language, along with a host of graphics, to ensure that people know what is going on. Knowledge will breed trust.

Second, governments should publicise the spending of interest groups, both non-profit and lobbying groups alike. Lobbying may not be as significant a problem everywhere as it is in the United States, but all democracies could certainly benefit from increased transparency on this front.[75] Former British prime minister David Cameron said over a decade ago that lobbying – defined as the 'far-too-cosy relationship between politics and money' – was 'the next big scandal waiting to happen'.[76]

He's not wrong.

People around the democratic world today increasingly believe that their politicians are bought and paid for; if it is known who is supporting politicians financially, then our leaders will have much more of an incentive to demonstrate their independence, which could improve government functionality and therefore trust.

These public disclosures must be user-friendly. Such a disclosure platform should, as US Congressman Ro Khanna has suggested, 'standardize and streamline campaign finance data' and 'include data on campaign contributions and independent expenditures from all sources'.[77]

Third, governments around the world should work to make more 'private' documents available to the public, particularly on sensitive issues like national security, which are far too often hidden behind a veil of secrecy that augments the public's belief in a nefarious 'deep state' looking out for their own interests, rather than those of the public.

Former top US national security official Nancy Soderberg helped make this clear years ago. In 2011, US President Barack Obama chose her to serve as chair of the Public Interest Declassification Board (PIDB), a Congressional advisory committee designed to promote public access to US national security decisions. In 2012, the PIDB published a report calling for the complete overhaul of the government classification system, with Soderberg declaring the system 'outdated and incapable of dealing adequately with the large volumes of classified information generated in an era of digital communications and information systems'.[78] Other leaders, like Senator Ron Wyden and top Biden administration official Avril Haines, have publicly made clear that the system is still broken.[79] It is paper-based and cannot keep up with the digital work. Its failures undermine US trust in government. It must be reformed immediately.

The European Union has taken positive steps on this front. This is because Brussels understands how important transparency is to the European Union – an institution people are prone to distrust because it is run not only by elites, but by foreign elites at that. This is why the Union has passed various laws requiring disclosure of information on policymaking and spending.[80]

But even these efforts have fallen behind the times, with the Union's rulebook on transparency now over twenty years old.[81] Neither the European Commission nor the European Council archive WhatsApp messages, even though these messages are a key source of member communications.[82] (The United States already bans bankers from using this and similar apps, which otherwise could allow traders to skirt record-keeping requirements.[83]) Advocates say that the body's transparency rules have fallen short, while data platforms designed to make transparency effective are unusable and unstable.[84]

Věra Jourová, a Czech politician and vice president of the European Commission for Values and Transparency, has proposed an overhaul of the law.[85] Yet various European efforts to reform transparency rules have gone nowhere, hitting several roadblocks in recent years. It does not seem to be much of a priority today.

The need for transparency is just as pressing in other parts of the world, too. Japan demonstrated a lack of transparency during the COVID-19 pandemic, failing to communicate with and prompting anger from its citizens.[86] Far afield, in Mexico, transparency exists in name, but not at all in reality – as is the case in many developing democracies.[87]

The push for transparency may seem curious or even naïve, given the panoply of problems facing democracies around the world. But effective problem-solving will require trust, and to instil trust our governments must be more accessible. They will have to make themselves vulnerable, in terms of both donors and decisions, if they truly want their countries to succeed.

People have a right to know what is happening in their governments. They *deserve* to know. And they will only trust their governments once they do.

* * *

People will not trust a government they think is racist or otherwise biased.

In the United States in particular, a history of racism has seriously undermined the government's ability to connect with and serve minority communities, particularly Black Americans. By early 2019, about halfway through the Trump presidency, just 9 per cent of Black Americans trusted the government.[88] And while that number has improved substantially since, it has not risen above 37 per cent.[89]

This lack of trust clearly hurt the US COVID-19 vaccine roll-out. Black Americans were among the least likely to get vaccinated of any racial group. Only 57 per cent had received at least one COVID-19 dose by March 2022.[90]

This was predictable given that study after study shows Black Americans to be mistreated by the healthcare system. Black women, for instance, are systematically under-treated for pain.[91] With data like this, it makes sense why a majority of Black Americans do not trust the system, even when it comes to ending a pandemic.[92]

Racism has also severely damaged Black Americans' view of their country's justice and political systems. A staggering 61 per cent have very little or no trust in the US criminal justice system, while just 11 per cent have very much or a lot of trust.[93] The percentage of white Americans who trust the police more than doubles the percentage of Black Americans who say the same.[94] Again, with numbers like these, it is obvious why Black Americans are hesitant about listening to or even engaging with the police, the criminal justice system and the government more broadly.

It is not hard to understand why many Black Americans don't even vote for the government when they consider this same government to be both racist and ineffective. They think the government is a lost cause.

America's history with race and racism is in many ways unique; the American understanding of race is not the proper lens through which to view the rest of the world. But other countries are experiencing similar trust deficits among their own minority communities, with whom these states have their own complex histories.

Scholars have shown that in countries where ethnic minorities perceive power to be distributed unequally, these same minorities trust the government less.[95] This is true in countries as diverse as Belgium, Croatia, the Czech Republic, Denmark, India, Norway, Slovakia and Slovenia, along with Taiwan.[96] In the United Kingdom, ethnic minorities were less likely than white people to trust government scientists and public health officials during the COVID-19 pandemic.[97] In Israel, Arab citizens have for years trusted state institutions and officials less than their Jewish counterparts.[98] Indian Hindus and Sikhs trust their government nearly 95 per cent more than other Indian citizens, namely Muslims.[99] And throughout Europe, Muslims – particularly Muslims who believe they are discriminated against – have less trust in their respective governments than members of the non-Muslim majority.[100]

South Korea offers a particularly telling anecdote.

Parts of Seoul may seem progressive enough for the visiting tourist, reminding them of New York's West Village or London's Soho, but South Korea remains marked by an anti-LGBTQ streak. Even the country's most recent progressive president, Moon Jae-in, opposed gay marriage. The government has long refused to pass anti-discrimination laws to protect LGBTQ South Koreans. LGBTQ South Koreans have rewarded this failure with a staggering lack of trust in the government.[101] This lack of trust has already had material, negative impacts.

In May 2020, the South Korean government tried to trace the spread of COVID-19 following an outbreak in the LGBTQ-popular Itaewon neighbourhood. But many LGBTQ South Koreans refused to get tested, fearing what the government might do with their information – including, crucially, their status as an LGBTQ person. 'The government claims it will protect our identities,' said Kim Yu-jin, a dance teacher. 'But if they can't even protect our human rights, how can we trust them?'[102]

The American, South Korean and other examples all reflect the same basic truth: minorities – ethnic, sexual and otherwise – will not trust their government, and will thus not comply with their government's rules or provide the government with necessary information, if they feel that leaders are biased against and thus not serving them. There is a vital need for democratic governments to not only address the underlying problems of discrimination, but – and especially in times of crisis – to engage these communities to build trust with them.

One way to do this is for government officials and institutions to partner with trusted community organisations. The NAACP, the United States' oldest civil rights organisation, did this during the pandemic, hosting meetings with high-level Black figures, including Marcella Nunez-Smith, a Yale physician who was named co-chair of Joe Biden's coronavirus advisory board, and National Institutes of Health researcher Kizzmekia Corbett, who had been on the frontlines of vaccine development. The results were predictably positive.

'I was about 70 per cent sure that I was not going to take it. [. . .] I know about Tuskegee. I know about those women they sterilised,' said Yvonne Robinson Horton, a Black woman and retired teacher in her seventies. 'I'm from Bolton, Miss[issippi], we have a strong mistrust of government, to say the least, like many Black people do. [. . .] We were taught that.'[103]

What seems to have changed Horton's mind was the presence of and comments from Corbett – an esteemed Black woman who was unwaveringly pro-vaccine. 'She was so compassionate about it that I began to listen to what she and other people said,' Horton said. 'I'm trying to take all that information in and process it, but I really think now that I'm leaning more toward taking it than not.'[104]

More such partnerships could be hugely useful in countries around the globe. Westminster and Berlin would be well served by engaging with ethnic and religious minority groups to facilitate government trust, as would Seoul by connecting to South Korea's LGBTQ community.

While this may seem like a difficult proposition for, say, religious conservatives regarding LGBTQ communities, these same conservatives should recognise that failure endangers not only the directly affected community but, as COVID-19 in South Korea demonstrates, those around them, too. A minority group's distrust doesn't hurt only their community, it hurts everyone.

* * *

There is one more key way to improve minority trust in government – and one that is particularly salient in the United States. There is a need, put simply, to address voter disenfranchisement and improve minority access to the ballot.

Since the mid-1800s, white politicians have fought to prevent Black Americans from voting, using violent intimidation or, more commonly today, legislation. Since a 2013 Supreme Court ruling struck down much of the Voting Rights Act, there has been no federal oversight of jurisdictions' voting changes. With the leash off, states have pursued more and more regressive laws. In 2020 alone, lawmakers across the fifty states introduced over three hundred and sixty bills with provisions that restrict voting access.[105] In 2021, after Trump's defeat, that number spiked to 440.[106]

These changes are not written to clearly single out Black Americans more than others, but they do. When politicians in the American South implement voter ID laws – requiring people to present their physical identification, which many Black Americans do not have, to vote – after Black voter turnout spikes and delivers Democratic victory, the motives are clear. The effects are clear, too: most people who are economically disadvantaged, as some Black Americans are, do not have passports; many don't have the money to get one, let alone take the foreign trips for which it is necessary. This is also true of many domestic IDs required to vote in certain states, like a driver's licence. When the US state of Georgia first instituted a voter ID law, some 25 per cent of Black Georgians did not own a car or have the licence that would go with one.[107]

Other countries do not have the same histories as the United States, but other governments have taken brazen steps to restrict critical populations from voting.

In Hungary, as Prime Minister Orbán has consolidated his rule, he has made voting more difficult for Hungarian migrants living in Western Europe – who are more liberal-minded and likely to oppose his Fidesz party – but far easier for those ethnic Hungarians, including some who were previously not even citizens, living in countries like Romania and Slovakia that are in Hungary's backyard.[108] These ethnic Hungarians in the near abroad have proven themselves more supportive of Orbán's nationalist, anti-immigrant rhetoric; as ethnic minorities in their own countries, they fear losing Hungary's 'national culture' perhaps more than the average Hungarian in Hungary.[109]

Orbán accordingly increased outreach to these Hungarians in Central and Eastern Europe, granting many of them citizenship

– even though most had never resided in Hungary. The Orbán government also declared that Hungarians living abroad who do not have a Hungarian address, which is normal for ethnic Hungarians living in neighbouring states, are allowed to mail in their votes, while Hungarians who have at any point maintained their addresses in Hungary – as most of those who move to Western Europe have – must go to polling stations overseen by Hungary's National Polling Office.[110] This was essentially step one in an effort to disenfranchise liberal-leaning Hungarians living in places like Berlin or Paris. Step two was the Hungarian government's decision to provide far fewer polling offices than were needed in these Western European countries, preventing many Hungarians living there from voting, frustrating them and augmenting their distrust in the Orbán government.[111]

Orbán has crafted an electoral system that discourages many critics from voting while simultaneously selecting certain pro-Fidesz Hungarian nationals for citizenship. He has created a built-in electoral advantage – one not so dissimilar from what many far-right US Republicans would like to see throughout their own country. Ostensibly democratic governments in Greece, Italy and Poland have tried to do something similar.[112]

Part of the solution, in the American case, is to pass the 'John Lewis Voting Act.' The legislation would restore the 'Voting Rights Act' and reinstate the federal government's authority by once again requiring states with histories of voter discrimination to get approval from the Department of Justice or a federal court before enacting voting changes.[113] Yet Senator Lisa Murkowski was the only Republican to vote in favour of the bill in 2021.[114]

I understand why her conservative colleagues, believing in limited government, do not want to restore such broad federal oversight. But if they are serious about restoring trust in the American government – and thus America's influence abroad

– they need to offer a legitimate alternative that will allow all Americans to vote.

The European Union, for its part, must punish governments that seek to restrict access to the ballot, as Hungary and others have. So far, Brussels has shown a staggering fecklessness when dealing with leaders like Orbán, allowing him to increasingly cement an autocracy in the heart of Europe.[115] Governments like these need to understand the cost of dismantling or undermining democracy. The European Union expresses 'concern' all the time, but on issues like this it is far too frequently subdued.

Voter access is key to any democracy's functionality. When politicians select their own constituencies, it is no surprise that those outside this constituency will have far less trust in these same politicians. But when people can vote in meaningful contests, they will feel responsible for and connected to their governments – even if their preferred politicians are not elected. When people know that their voices are being heard, particularly at the ballot box, they may be more willing to trust the government. And that trust is something our democracies desperately need.

* * *

This chapter aims to make two things abundantly clear.

First, trust is vital to state and societal functionality, particularly in democracies. For a democracy to be successful, people need to trust the government; if they don't, they will become more likely to vote into power those demagogues seeking to shake the system to its core.

And second, democratic countries around the world are experiencing a trust crisis. Our institutions have failed people for far too long and now, people no longer trust their leaders.

Troublingly, several autocracies, for all their repressive measures, are outdoing democracies when it comes to public trust. They've earned that trust, even from many citizens who disagree with their ideals, by following through on important measures that improve quality of life for the people and by making sure that their ability to deliver gets noticed. Democracies, on the other hand, seem to have slipped into a downward spiral of incompetence, transparency failures and voter disengagement that disastrously erodes trust in the government – thereby weakening our democracies by laying the groundwork for autocracy, the rise of which at home makes it just about impossible for us to contest authoritarians abroad.

But we are not doomed. As this chapter shows, there are many steps democracies can take to restore this vital trust – from publicising successes to partnering with business and engaging with the disenfranchised. It helps our case that people want to trust their leaders, even if they don't trust them right now. They want to believe in the possibility of improvement, and the ability of the government to deliver it. Now, our leaders need to act – and plant the seeds of trust in that fertile ground. There is no time to waste if we want not only to fend off autocracy in our backyards but also to reap the harvest of a better future everywhere.

4

Long-Term Thinking

Gustave was known for his tremendous energy and quick temper. He was born in 1910 in the swamps of New Orleans and grew up there, far from the halls of American power. But he never did share his hometown's languid personality.

He was too energetic even for college. He attended Tulane University for only a brief period, but he had better places to be – and better things to do. So, he dropped out, and set off on his path. He would become what one US bigwig later called 'the great American success story, coming out of his beloved New Orleans to make his way in the big city'.[1]

This big city was New York, where Gustave moved in 1928 for a low-level job at the brokerage firm Newborg & Co. It was a small position, one without much clout or compensation. After toiling there for five years, Gustave 'Gus' Levy – still without a college degree and still only in his early twenties – leapt at another opportunity, taking a job at Goldman Sachs as a trader on the foreign bond desk.

Despite Goldman's grandiosity today, this, too, was a small job, and one Levy took at a precarious moment. Following the Great Depression, commodity prices had fallen and production had slowed, prompting lenders to retreat. Stocks had lost nearly 90 per cent of their value.[2] It didn't help that one of Goldman Sachs' funds had failed in the 1929 stock market crash because people believed the firm to have engaged in share price manipulation and insider trading.[3]

So, when Levy joined Goldman Sachs, the firm was hardly the behemoth it is today. The foreign bond desk he joined was a one-man department; he earned a salary of USD 27.50 a week. This is about USD 600 per week in 2022 dollars – 40 per cent less than the average US worker makes per week today.[4]

But Gus was good at his job. So good that Goldman named him a partner in 1945. It was at this point that he began forging Goldman's new era. He transformed the firm's approach to risk management, laying the blueprints for what would eventually become its Securities Division. He also overhauled the firm's sales and trading function by popularising the use of block trades – huge, privately negotiated security futures.

Block trades, put simply, are when firms like Goldman purchase large amounts of stock, usually more than ten thousand shares, in one fell swoop directly from issuers at a previously agreed-upon price. The buyer takes on the risk of eventually selling these stocks, hopefully at a higher price.[5] As institutional investors – like mutual and pension funds – came on the scene in the mid-twentieth century, Goldman's willingness to carry out these huge purchases was a valuable service.[6]

Before block trades, any firm trying to sell such substantial amounts of stock would have to break up these shares into smaller pieces that the market could absorb without damaging the share price; selling everything in one moment on the public market would drive the price downward, as there would be far more supply than demand.[7] By agreeing to purchase all of these stocks at once, Goldman facilitated faster, simpler and more profitable sales.

Goldman was taking on substantial risk, even if the firm often raked in profits from the fees. All the risk was in buying. But Levy was willing to bet that he would eventually be able to sell these stocks at a higher price than the one at which he purchased them.[8] More often than not, he was right – so much so that by the late 1960s, Levy's trading was producing half of Goldman's profits.[9]

In 1968, after he executed a record-breaking block trade with Alcan Aluminum worth USD 26.5 million (around USD 225 million today), *Finance* magazine declared him 'The Biggest Man on the Block'.[10] And finally, in 1969 he received the title he had long wanted: everyone who mattered knew him as 'Mr Wall Street'.[11]

* * *

It is hard to understate the impact Levy had on Goldman, and on investment banking more widely. When he arrived at the firm in 1933, Wall Street was essentially just a 'bunch of undercapitalised private partnerships', according to historian William Cohan. The way these firms made money 'was taking companies public, raising debt for them, raising equity for them, advising them on merger and acquisition deals, and advising them on how to manage their money. There was very little trading. Very little risk for them.'[12]

This kind of business was plainly client-driven. If you burned bridges with a client because of short-term greed and subsequently lost them, you weren't just losing tomorrow's business – you were losing the next hundred years of their business. You had little choice but to treat your clients right.[13]

It was, however, on the trading side of the business that Levy made his name, *not* from the part that took businesses public. And because he was so successful, he changed both the firm and Wall Street – and not necessarily for the better.

As reflected by the risk of block trading, Levy's success made Wall Street firms more and more comfortable operating less and less as advisory institutions and more as casinos. They increasingly made bets on the future, believing that the stocks they purchased *en masse* now would be worth more later. The focus was no longer on the clients, but on future profits.

When asked in the early 1970s why Goldman was so successful, and why it stood out among other Wall Street firms, Levy gave a simple answer. 'At Goldman Sachs, we're greedy,' he said. 'But we're long-term greedy.'

Yet as trading became more and more popular, Goldman and other banks became more and more focused on immediate profits, rather than the long-term ones that Levy preferred. Many traders today do not focus on clients at all; instead, they are placing bets – educated but risky ones – in the hopes of making as much money as soon as possible. It was these 'bets' that helped inflate the housing bubble that crashed the global economy in 2008.[14]

Long gone are the days of Levy's 'long-term greed'. Instead, Wall Street now pursues short-term (or quarterly) capitalism to return profits to their shareholders as quickly as possible. This short-termism may be good for Wall Street, but it's bad for just about everyone else – as the 2008 financial crash made obvious.[15]

When you focus only on today, not on tomorrow – let alone on next year – you are bound to eventually fail and bring people, innocent and otherwise, down with you. So, despite Goldman's eventual shift, Levy's commitment to 'long-term greed' remains wise and relevant today.

Several companies have taken this lesson to heart. Amazon's Jeff Bezos has made clear his commitment to 'plant[ing] seeds that take seven years to bear fruit', with the company investing in initially loss-making ventures that are now hugely profitable. Kindle, Amazon Web Services and Amazon Prime are just a few examples. 'If we needed to see meaningful financial results in two to three years,' he said, 'some of the most meaningful things we've done we would never have even started.'[16]

Apple, arguably the world's most innovative company, has similarly made clear its commitment to long-term greed. Short-term stock market performance has 'little to no effect' on Apple's ability to innovate, according to CEO Tim Cook. 'Why,' he added, 'would you ever measure a business on 90 days when its investments are long-term?'[17]

Stories of such strategic thinking abound throughout the private sector. Companies around the world have for decades understood the importance of focusing on the long-term, rather than becoming mired in the potential losses of the current quarter. The best CEOs are busy thinking not about today's problems, but about tomorrow's profits – which is why so many of them use five- or ten-year plans to make those profits a reality. Companies operating with a true long-term mindset consistently outperform their industry peers across almost every financial measure.[18]

Some governments take a similar approach.

China's five-year plans were long mocked throughout the West, but they have increasingly proved their worth, if only as aspirational guidelines. They are not so different from the type of strategic plan that a top US corporation might create.[19] Saudi Arabia, too, has taken a proactive approach to the future, introducing the Vision 2030 strategy specifically to reduce the country's reliance on oil and boost private sector investment.[20]

Some democratic governments have taken some similar steps. Several European governments have produced long-term industrial policies. Britain has its Plan for Growth, the Integrated Review and proposed plans to invest in infrastructure in the north of Britain as part of the Levelling Up agenda – even if politics tends to get in the way of these plans. The European Union has put together a whole host of aggressive industrial plans to create competitive advantages where none currently exists, such as on semiconductors, the small, complex microchips that are necessary to the functioning of cell phones, home appliances and modern weaponry. The EU has also pushed forward with its own Green New Deal. And of course, a huge number of governments from around the world also committed to the Paris Climate Agreement.

Many democratic politicians are indeed offering long-term plans on issues like climate change or energy security. Much of the West remains focused on industrial policy for the long-term, even if these policies have taken a bit of a different name. But while plenty of focus goes into long-term thinking on these fronts, on other issues like maintaining the social safety net and even parts of foreign policy, democratic politics suffers from a bad case of short-termism. The result has been to weaken democracies' ability to address existential issues like climate, which has only further fed the impulse for non-democratic action – such as so-called 'eco-fascism'.

Reasonable people can debate how successful democracies are at thinking about the long-term and putting these plans into action. But it should be apparent to everyone that we need to do more of this thinking, particularly as autocracies like China not only devise plans for the future but mobilise and allocate the resources necessary to make their visions a reality. Some leaders in the West are rightfully ringing the alarm bell because our homes are on fire, but far too often it seems like nobody is listening because they're too focused on short-term interests: on winning the next election or maintaining support from donors who oppose putting out the fire.

It does often seem like democratic governments are incapable of thinking beyond the next election. It seems as if our system of governance is simply less capable at dealing with these challenges: neither Joe Biden nor Fumio Kishida can wave a wand and phase out fossil fuels by 2025, whereas an authoritarian leader can, in theory (if not in reality). What this means is that we tend to appear inept in the face of long-term challenges, even if there are exceptions – and even though democracy is a form of governance better equipped to deal with long-term challenges, if staffed with the right politicians. Effectively addressing these challenges would make democracies more responsive to their people, politically stronger at home, richer and therefore better able to combat autocracies abroad, not to mention serve as a better model for countries everywhere.

At this difficult moment, what we need are leaders who are committed to the future – and not just the immediate one. We would be better off if we developed and acted on five- or ten-year plans, as our best private sector companies do. And yes, we would be better off if our leaders were 'long-term greedy', not for profits, but for the flourishing of their people and for democracy.

Autocracy's Plans

Not so long ago, nobody cared about China's five-year plans. They seemed more like a joke than a strategy. Washington and Westminster mocked them; even Seoul and Tokyo couldn't be bothered take them seriously.

Why? Because these plans are a relic of the country's Maoist institutions, which are themselves echoes of the Soviet Union's Stalinist setup. In both contexts, the centralised plans were so poor and the economic systems they were meant to guide functioned so badly that foreigners paid little attention to each new announcement of ambitious long-term goals that wouldn't be realised.

During China's Maoist period, officials used these plans to lie about the productivity of their country's economy, seeking only to please their superiors. They regularly produced false numbers when production targets did not meet those set by the government, which they rarely did.[21] Factory managers knew they would be fired for failure if they reported the true numbers; so, they lied.

Such centralised planning, with its lack of flexibility around regional differences and blindness to real economic behaviour, squandered resources and left huge swathes of China impoverished.[22] Foreign observers thus viewed China's five-year plans with derision, believing them to be evidence of Beijing's backward thinking.[23] China, they thought, was following the Soviet Union's well-trodden path of centralised mistakes. And like Moscow, Beijing would fail.

But since China began opening its economy in the 1980s, foreign observers have paid ever more attention to these five-year plans – because as China changed, so did these blueprints. As China became more and more capitalist, Beijing turned the five-year plans from dogmatic, quota-laden communist paperwork into aspirational documents that aim to set out the path for China's future. No longer are these plans just rigid agendas; instead, they are manifestos about how top officials want to lead their country.[24] Nor are they any longer restricted to economics; instead, they give space to issues like education, the environment and even 'the modern cultural industry system' – things like television, film and games.[25]

So when China's top officials gathered in Beijing's Great Hall of the People in March 2021, listening to the Communist Party (CCP)'s top leadership unveil a detailed plan for their country's next five years, foreign observers listened carefully, too.[26] That year's plan, the fourteenth since the CCP took over in 1949, set a clear path for China: building the country into a self-reliant technological powerhouse, accelerating green development, achieving quality economic growth and, of course, elevating China's leadership role on the global stage.

Newspapers covered it breathlessly. The *New York Times* declared that China had 'sent a forceful message [. . .] advancing the top leader Xi Jinping's sweeping agenda for the country's economic and political ascent'.[27] Columnists debated whether the plan signalled massive confidence, or deep insecurity.[28] Think tanks translated the plan word for word, trying to understand what, exactly, China envisioned for the future.[29] Businesses did the same, searching the stilted language for clues to thinking about one of the world's most important markets.[30] Even the White House responded by outlining sweeping plans to secure critical products for America, near-shoring the production of certain goods or at least shifting production from China to friendlier nations.[31]

China was planning for the future, seemingly dictating the pace of competition – and whether they took a sunny or a stormy view of China's plans, the world's democracies were just reacting. Beijing was galloping ahead; Washington, Brussels and Tokyo were just beginning to try to chase the Chinese down.

* * *

It was 2016, and Mohammed bin Salman, better known as MBS, was on the ascent. At only thirty-one years old, he had already become Saudi Arabia's deputy crown prince, brutally outmanoeuvring his rivals to get there. All the while, he had worked diligently to craft a particular perception of himself abroad: as a moderniser who was revamping Saudi society, known for its conservatism and oil-reliant economy, into something fit for the twenty-first century.[32]

He had his work cut out for him. Saudi Arabia was (and to some extent, is) stagnant, repressive and socially stuck in a previous era. Its progress was also hindered by short-term thinking – by elites mired in their own rivalries and sustained only by the country's oil wealth.[33] The prominent Saudi economist Abdulhamid al-Amri put it simply: the lack of a comprehensive vision, he said, 'led to the waste of trillions of riyals, the spread of monopolies, corruption, unemployment, poverty and the delay of development projects.'[34]

So, in April 2016, MBS unveiled a long-term plan for change, one that he promised would shepherd the country into life in a low-oil-price world. 'We will not allow our country ever to be at the mercy of commodity price volatility or external markets,' the prince told journalists.[35] Instead, with his plan – Vision 2030 – Saudi Arabia would attract even more foreign investment, all while relaxing (at least a little) its ultra-conservative social policies, such as the ban on women driving. The plan was slack on details. But it was a start.

'Laying out a vision is the first step on a road of a million miles,' the economist said. '[T]he implementation remains.'[36] MBS aimed higher; how could he not when he was promising his people a new Saudi Arabia? 'The vision is not a dream,' he said. 'It's a reality that will come true.'[37]

Yet since he was elevated to crown prince in 2017, MBS's own bloody choices have taken Saudi Arabia off course. That year, he rounded up hundreds of members of his own family and other wealthy Saudis, imprisoning them in Riyadh's Ritz-Carlton hotel and holding them on charges of corruption.[38] He then impulsively ordered the brutal and disturbing assassination of Jamal Khashoggi, a critical *Washington Post* journalist, in 2018.[39] MBS also master-minded Saudi Arabia's disastrous bombing campaign in Yemen, which has killed countless civilians and escalated a diplomatic crisis with Qatar.

All these missteps have rightfully angered the West, whose leaders still hold out hope that MBS will not become king and have started giving him the cold shoulder (except for when they need his oil). The frustration is justified. MBS looks like a rogue leader, one from whom most democratic leaders will want to distance themselves.

Yet for all his very evident flaws, MBS has quietly focused on Vision 2030 – and expressed frustration that the rest of the world has not acknowledged how well it is going. 'Saudi Arabia is a G20 country,' he told journalists from the *Atlantic*, bristling at the international focus on blunders such as the Khashoggi murder. 'You can see our position five years ago: it was almost twenty,' he added, alluding to global GDP rankings. 'Today, we are almost seventeen.'[40] He pointed out the country's strong non-oil economic growth and growing foreign investment, along with limited social reform. 'If we were having this interview in 2016, you would say I'm making assumptions,' he added. 'But we did it. You can see it now with your eyes.'[41]

Even critical foreign observers can't help but agree, at least to a degree. Pro-democracy Western think tanks admit that the vision has produced some 'noteworthy achievements to date', including 'fiscal stabilization and macroeconomic management, the development of capital markets and the banking system, the digitisation of government services, and social reforms'.[42]

Vision 2030 – much like the leader who masterminded it – is anything but perfect. The plan, also like its leader, was hugely ambitious. But Vision 2030 lacked details from the start and has suffered as a result. Efforts to create jobs and transform the private sector into a positive sector are running into headwinds, thanks in part to entrenched Saudi special interests.[43]

Still, as in China, the country is well served by having grappled with and identified its problems. Saudi leaders – namely MBS – have identified what is wrong with the country and what is needed to fix it. That alone is a positive step.

* * *

Xi and MBS do not hold the keys to a better future. Far from it.

Authoritarian regimes – no matter how well they are run – are, by their very nature, unstable, unwieldy and difficult to manage.[44] Just because these two men have made ambitious promises for the future of their respective nations does not mean that they will achieve them. Just as Chinese President Xi Jinping acts impulsively, placing his country on a confrontational path with the West, so too does MBS remain power-hungry and ruthless. Both men's countries, and their respective visions, will suffer from their centralisation of power, and from their poor instincts and willingness to lash out. Their respective top-down approaches limit their respective ability to make real, positive change.

143

With leaders like these – and with top-down systems that quash the feedback mechanisms needed to improve governance – it is not hard to see why autocracies like China and Saudi Arabia will face challenges in both the short- and long-term.

But their focus on the future should not be overlooked. At a time when democratic citizens and observers abroad believe that democratic leaders cannot think beyond the next election cycle and have accordingly lost trust in their government (and in some cases, their system), it is notable that Xi and MBS speak about the world of tomorrow and are taking steps towards creating that world. No wonder there is an increasingly popular view that democracies are just too complicated to handle difficult, long-term problems like climate change, whereas China and Saudi Arabia – with their top-down regimes that allow for decisive action – can solve these problems.[45]

That view is wrong. Full stop.

It was China's authoritarian system that failed to handle COVID-19's emergence, and then imposed a Draconian containment strategy that left the country's economy in a weakened state. This is not a system that will be able to meaningfully address long-term problems such as climate change. The same goes for Saudi Arabia; as much as MBS has promised to facilitate the green transition, he is going to rely on oil revenue for as long as he can, precisely because it allows him to fund the patronage system that has long kept his family in power. Neither man has an acceptable solution.

So while authoritarians may promise and even pass policies that seem geared to address long-term problems like climate change, the actual implementation of these outcomes almost always fails, in no small part because autocracies lack the civil society activism that is inherent to democracies and needed to make this implementation work.[46] The result, in just about all cases, is policy that is worse than in democracies.[47] Autocrats may claim to deliver for their people, particularly on long-term problems, but more often than not, they deliver mainly for themselves.

Indeed, there is no convincing evidence that autocracies are better at addressing long-term problems than democracies. In fact, it is democracies' civil society activism that has driven much of our climate action – which is one of the reasons why autocracies, lacking this activism, are behind on this matter. A disruptive public does push democratic governments to act on the long-term problems.

But the perception that democracies cannot focus on the future is real and damaging, both at home and abroad.[48] The value of long-term thinking is clear; the private sector successes of Amazon and Apple testify to that reality. These companies are responsive to their shareholders in a way democratic governments are not to their publics. The result of this divergence in effectiveness is happy shareholders and disgruntled democratic publics.

What our democracies need, then, are leaders who think about our future – policymakers who act not just for the current quarter, but for the long-term.

* * *

Losing Focus

Franklin Delano Roosevelt had a problem and a plan. The US economy was struggling, the Great Depression having left people's lives and whole sectors in tatters. But he had an idea – one that might not work immediately, but that would work in the long-term.

And so, he managed to put into place the famed New Deal, which fundamentally reshaped the US and Western approach more generally to governance, radically changing people's relationships to their government. Under FDR, the United States government enacted countless programmes designed specifically to reform and repair the country's economy, not only for the days in which he served, but for the future, too.

Washington exhibited similar long-term thinking at the end of the Second World War, opting to send huge amounts of money to a dilapidated Europe – including to former enemies like Germany – to rebuild the continent. Conservatives criticised the massive government spending; critics on the left said that it was too hostile towards the Soviet Union. But Harry Truman, the president who enacted the Marshall Plan, made it happen nonetheless. In so doing, he demonstrated true long-term thinking. 'The seeds of totalitarian regimes are nurtured by misery and want. They spread and grow in the evil soil of poverty and strife,' he said, explaining to the American public that sending money to Europe now would prevent another war tomorrow. 'They reach their full growth when the hope of a people for a better life has died. We must keep that hope alive.'[49]

European democracies have had their own long-term successes, too.

Following the Second World War, the United Kingdom wisely created its own welfare state – making permanent the notion that the government should support its citizens in their time of need.[50] Throughout his nearly two decades in office in the 1980s and 1990s, German chancellor Helmut Kohl's ability to focus on the long-term allowed him to eventually achieve German unification.

Long-term thinking is not foreign to our democracies. Democracy does not prevent leaders from making smart and necessary bets on the future – even when facing opposition in the short-term. There is a fine tradition of doing exactly that for today's leaders to draw on.

But today's democracies increasingly appear incapable of looking beyond the next election cycle to address existential and long-term problems, both at home and abroad. Around the world, we appear to be losing focus on tomorrow by only thinking about today.

* * *

By the time an American House Representative takes office, they have less than two years before their next election. They have just about a year in office before they have to begin campaigning yet again. They must start fundraising from day one.

What's the easiest way to stay in office? To avoid rocking the boat. As the Republican Eric Cantor put it just months after losing his seat, too many of his former colleagues are not 'willing to go home to constituents and explain to them the reason you need to affect a change – to essentially reduce the fear of that change so that it is less than the fear of the status quo'.[51] It is much easier to focus on the easy thing in front of you, rather than complicated issues posing problems down the line.

American politicians are anything but alone on this front.

While in office, former British prime minister Boris Johnson repeatedly reshuffled his cabinet, not for any real cause, but simply because moving cabinet members would theoretically 'refresh' Downing Street's thinking or give voters the impression that he was acting. In so doing, he incentivised short-termism: he instilled in his ministers the need to demonstrate clear successes now lest they be sacked, rather than take on big projects that could work towards solving the country's lingering problems.[52]

The Japanese government, meanwhile, continues to spend huge amounts of money, making the country more reliant on public spending while ballooning its debt to an unimaginable size and doing little to mitigate the problems this debt promises.[53]

Italian policymakers have similarly long lacked a far-sighted focus, instead demagoguing and making unreasonable promises

– without the financial means behind them to satisfy voters, who have punished the country's governing parties in every election since 1994.[54]

Israeli politics are so polarised and short-term focused that the country went three years without being able to pass a budget, doing so only in 2021.[55]

And, of course, former German chancellor Angela Merkel exhibited a lack of long-term thinking throughout the late-2000s financial crisis, when she refused to consider a pan-European financial stimulus anywhere near the size of those enacted by the United States or China.[56] Merkel probably knew, deep down, that a huge stimulus package was exactly what the doctor ordered. The world's top financial minds knew and said as much. But she also knew that German citizens were tired of purportedly paying for the continent's southern economic mistakes – and that forcing Germans to do so would carry huge political risk.

After the capitalist West Germany and formerly communist East Germany merged into one, in the early 1990s, citizens in the west allowed their government to pour huge amounts of money into the east. The new unified German government sent nearly USD 2 trillion to its poorer territory, but with little practical benefit.[57] The eastern part of the country remains poorer and less developed to this day.

Germans were willing, if somewhat begrudgingly, to pay this price for their actual national brethren. Almost two decades later, they were decidedly not willing to do the same for foreigners. Poll after poll showed that while Germany could certainly do more to revive Europe's economy, Germans did not want to. Thanks to their experience in the 1990s, Germans did not believe that stimulus alone could put the region back on track.

Merkel read the room. She knew that German citizens would never forgive her if she agreed to give their tax money to Greece or Italy or Portugal – countries that, as far as Germans were concerned, got themselves into this mess and should get themselves out of it.[58] So rather than spend to jumpstart a sinking economy, as both China and the United States did, Europe's leaders, none more than Germany, refused to do anything of the sort. They instead fell back on the tired axioms of austerity, which only worsened the crisis for those already bearing its brunt, and eventually plunged the continent back into recession.

* * *

Our inability to think in the long-term is having meaningful, negative impacts, and not just on the future; the effects can be felt today. Democratic governments around the world are failing to take the necessary steps – painful as they may be – to address the existential problems we face, leaving us looking impotent.

Leaders are not investing the political and actual capital needed to build strong healthcare systems or coordinate mechanisms in case a new pandemic arises. Far too many politicians are trying simply to move on and forget the crisis, but it is essential that they prepare for the next one.

The Biden administration has wisely requested some USD 65 billion from Congress for pandemic preparedness, but this is hardly enough. Those billions are down payment, rather than the house we need.[59] Something similar is true of democracies in Europe and elsewhere, which simply have not done enough to fix what went wrong the first time, when COVID-19 emerged.[60]

Just about every democratic government has been similarly slow to address climate change. The United States has struggled because a large swathe of its politicians – and public – simply do not believe climate change is real, and because a small number of companies that contribute to the lion's share of carbon emissions are unwilling to make the necessary changes until they absolutely have to, or until

149

the market allows them to do so profitably.[61] Europe has unveiled ambitious plans, but the continent's execution has so far fallen short of what scientists say is necessary. The same can be said of democracies in Asia and beyond. Just about everyone is falling behind, even when this is the one issue on which we cannot afford to compromise.

One example from my own New York City makes this troublingly clear. After a freak hurricane struck the city a decade ago, local politicians promised to prevent such a weather event from seriously harming New Yorkers ever again. Yet New York leaders still have not devised plans to protect lower Manhattan from rising sea levels.[62] And in early 2022, an Antarctic ice shelf the size of New York City collapsed, demonstrating with brutally ominous imagery just how horrific the coming effects of climate change will be.[63]

'Our kids and grandkids will judge us on one issue above all others,' Gerald Butts, the former principal secretary to Canadian Prime Minister Justin Trudeau and a former colleague of mine at Eurasia Group, has said.[64] Let's hope they're not underwater first.

* * *

Democratic short-termism has a clear geopolitical impact, too.

Romania, for instance, essentially does not have its own long-term national security strategy – other than on paper – because policymakers have not properly invested in making one real. Rather than develop their own plans, Romanian leaders have basically outsourced such planning to NATO and the European Union. Bucharest vaguely sends its views – particularly on Moldova, the Black Sea and energy security – to Brussels. The Romanians hope that these views make their way into NATO and EU plans, which they then accept as their own. But if local concerns are not uploaded effectively, which they generally are not, Romania is essentially lost, since the country is not as powerful as Poland or the Baltic nations, which can freelance and pursue their security interests independently.

So, while Romania spent years trying to get NATO to take serious control of the Black Sea and prevent it from becoming a 'Russian lake', the bloc never did. Bucharest is now helpless unless it can convince NATO, the European Union or the United States to do something. Bringing the Europeans and Americans on board has consistently been easier said than done.

Yet the Romanians continue to outsource their long-term security policy – which is one reason why, when Russia invaded Ukraine, Bucharest immediately fretted that it would end up more vulnerable. And it is one reason why Romania essentially has no idea how it would respond to potential Russian adventurism in Moldova.[65]

Some may say that Romania is failing to develop these long-term plans because it is an underdeveloped country and a relatively new democracy. But the reality is that leading democracies such as the United States also tend to let short-term politics cloud strategic thinking as well.

The United States, for instance, cannot even sign trade deals – particularly with Asia, the world's most dynamic region – because many legislators have come to oppose free trade, despite its evident economic benefits. This opposition is more emotional than it is logical. But the result is a US Congress in which a traditional free trade agreement, which requires Congressional approval, is essentially a non-starter.[66] Without the ability to offer such agreements, the United States has fallen behind while competitors like China – and allies like Australia and the United Kingdom – pursue their own trade deals, particularly in Asia. As China increasingly asserts and cements its influence in that part of the world, which is the most economically dynamic, it is a shame that Washington cannot offer the region a truly compelling alternative. It is a shame, too, that

Americans will not benefit from the economic gains that free trade can bring if managed properly.

Even President Biden's new Indo-Pacific Economic Framework, while ambitiously named and likely to have *some* positive impact, is not a trade deal; it may raise labour, tech privacy and other standards among its 14 members, but the Framework does not offer Asia access to the huge US market. The Framework offers limited tangible benefits to Asia.

'You Americans talk about free trade, but you offer us nothing' is a complaint I hear over and over again from Asian officials in Washington and throughout the region. 'So,' the diplomats say, 'you leave us with no choice: when China offers *real* trade deals, we're not going to say "no".'

* * *

Democratic political systems have recently not been good at accepting costs today to prevent crises later. This is not because something is wrong with democracy itself. As this chapter makes clear, democracies have in decades past invested substantially in long-term problems, both at home and abroad, with huge success. The New Deal and Marshall Plan are the most obvious examples. These plans succeeded only because US leaders were brave and willing to stand up to a domestic backlash and say, for instance, why it was so important for Americans to throw huge amounts of money at a dilapidated Europe. (It certainly helped that these leaders enjoyed more public trust than just about any democratic leader does today, demonstrating again the importance of building trust.)

Democracy may provide politicians with reasons to shy away from such plans and focus on the day-to-day, but the reality is that the best democratic leaders have always waded through the mud of today to build the oasis of tomorrow.

The problem today is not democracy itself. The problem is the politics within our democratic systems – that leaders around the democratic world are too willing to respond to short-term incentives and ignore our shared future, focusing instead on their own political and personal gains.

Troublingly, too many leaders seem to be making decisions not on practical merits, but with the next election in mind. And with every election that passes, our governments seem to become less and less able to handle the long-term challenges we face – and more and more prone to self-defeating short-termism. With each election, our democracies look less effective, making democracy appear unattractive, both at home and abroad.

* * *

Being Brave

The margins were thin. It was 2010, and then-president Obama was trying to pass his landmark healthcare legislation, dubbed 'Obamacare'. He needed all the votes he could get. The Democrats held comfortable majorities in both the House of Representatives and the Senate, but even liberals were sceptical of Obamacare.

They were sceptical, not so much of the bill's substance, but because they feared political consequences. They were right to worry. Obamacare was a decidedly long-term bill. Its main benefits were hypothetical, future ones that would not be evident by the upcoming 2010 mid-term elections, which were just eight months away. And if the government committed huge amounts of money to a long-term, major reform effort like this – and did not produce immediate results at a time when many Americans were struggling following the 2008 financial crisis – the party that had passed it, the Democrats, would almost surely face retribution at the ballot box.

Everybody knew this. The consequences were plain, which is why almost three dozen Democrats running in competitive races to keep their seats voted against making the bill into law.

Tom Perriello had every reason to be one of them. He represented Virginia's fifth district, a rural one situated in the state's south and centre. Parts of the district may be less than two and a half hours from Washington, DC, but these farms, towns and voters might as well be a world away from the capital's cocktail parties.

Until Perriello's narrow 2008 victory, in which he won by 0.2 percentage points, Republicans had held the district for six terms (twelve years). This was not a district in which it would be easy to sell Obamacare, an effort that Republicans branded as wasteful spending – a notion with which much of the public, still reeling from the financial crisis and still being told to tighten their belts, agreed.

But Perriello believed in the legislation. He had travelled the district; he knew that Americans in Virginia and around the country needed healthcare coverage, and that Obamacare would provide it to them, even if the legislation was imperfect. And so, on 21 March, he voted for it.

The backlash began almost immediately. On 22 March, right-wing organisers urged anti-Obamacare campaigners to 'drop by' Perriello's house to give a 'personal touch' to the expression of their views.[67] By 25 March, the gas line at the home of Perriello's brother had been cut in what police said was a deliberate act.[68] (The vandal thought the house was where the congressman lived.)

Predictably, Perriello lost his seat in November. His opponent, the Republican state Senator Robert Hurt, criticised Perriello's willingness to increase taxes and spend money. He defeated Perriello by over four percentage points.

Perriello had every right to be disappointed. He was a young man, in his mid-thirties, who had just lost a plum job – one that he could have held for life – seemingly because of a single, bold vote.

But he didn't mope. Nor did he express regret. In fact, he did the opposite. Losing his seat, he later said, was 'much less important' than giving tens of millions of Americans healthcare coverage.[69]

He was right. Obamacare, for all its flaws, did save lives. And for all its flaws, it did make the US government more effective, and it probably did improve some people's views of democracy. It was undoubtedly worth the cost of Perriello's seat.

* * *

Our problem is not that voters are fickle and demand unreasonable things. Our problem is that too many elected officials – unlike Perriello – are too cowardly to vote boldly and deliver on their promises. And while a change in voting laws or term limits has been floated as a popular solution, neither reform would likely push these politicians to focus on the long-term. Hardly anyone looking at the US Senate, which gives senators six-year terms, could reasonably say that this relatively long-term length has produced bolder and more long-term-minded public servants.

We don't need new electoral laws. What we need is a new approach to governance. We need a new political consensus to address the long-term challenges we face. And we need new political leaders who are willing to make long-term decisions that may lead to their own ousting. Courage that produces good policy and poor electoral results is better – for the country, if not for a politician personally – than weakness that produces poor policy and lets that same politician keep their seat.

A strong first step towards institutionalising this new approach would be requiring democratic governments, whether in Washington, Seoul or beyond, to develop five- or ten-year plans, like top US private sector players do. We should then require governments to produce reports reflecting their progress or lack thereof on these goals – to put their achievements on the scoreboard. Leaders can augment these efforts by bringing in outside experts to review governmental progress. If a non-partisan group of outside experts, ones who do not stand to gain financially from the advice they give, reviews government action and assesses their progress towards long-term goals or lack thereof, this will further incentivise governments to think and act with the long-term in mind. The results of these scorecards need to be public and widely covered by not only niche but national media.

The US Quadrennial Defense Review, replaced in 2018 by the National Defense Strategy, is a good starting point. This document requires that US military planners set a course for their operations by analysing their objectives and describing potential threats. The document is public and receives constructive criticism and scrutiny from policymakers and academics alike. But it rarely garners much attention beyond the policy-minded *intelligentsia* in Washington.

Most democracies around the world have similar defence strategies. Yet far too few of them have national economic strategies, national healthcare strategies or national human capital strategies. Very few have national goal-setting documents like China's plans or Saudi Arabia's vision. The closest thing that the United States has is probably the US federal budget, but even the budget often fails to clearly demonstrate the president's agenda.[70]

There is no good reason for democratic legislatures not to advance legislation that requires agencies beyond the military to define their long-term focuses, and then requires the executive to compile these reports into a national agenda. By keeping score, we can prevent short-termism.

Leaders must also encourage the drafters of these documents to be bold and imaginative in their descriptions of future threats. By being more open-minded in their forecasts, officials can better combat seemingly far-fetched problems – such as the COVID-19 pandemic that seemingly popped up out of nowhere – rather than flying by the seat of their pants when the surprise arrives. We can better plan for the long-term if we ask, 'What if?' when building our strategies, rather than 'What now?' when problems emerge.[71]

Having such an agenda and list of potential problems on paper won't fix everything. But it would be a good start.

* * *

Another important step would be for politicians across the spectrum to begin highlighting the long-term benefits of their policies, rather than giving into seductive short-term impulses. This is particularly important when sharing political content on the internet, which generally worsens everyone's short-term impulses – and tends to highlight short-term shortcomings while hiding long-term benefits.[72]

So, when Japanese policymakers make the case for immigration reform or when Americans make the case for improved social spending, they should spend real time and effort communicating these long-term benefits. They'll need to be up front with the costs if there are any: politicians need to treat their people like the adults they are, as we discussed in the chapter on trust, because people are often willing to bear short-term costs if they believe there will be long-term benefits. This is precisely how Truman justified the Marshall Plan. He successfully convinced the public that by spending USD 80 per capita, they could prevent another costly war in Europe. The investment was very clearly worth it; nobody serious would go back in time and reverse the Marshall Plan.

Similar honest communication is needed today. Obviously, politicians should not make dramatic, incorrect claims to advance their agendas – or simply lie to their people, as many Republicans did about the 2020 election, resulting in an armed insurrection at the US Capitol. Leaders need to be honest about their actual policies, too.

The Biden administration's claim that its eminently worthwhile Build Back Better agenda cost 'zero dollars' and added 'zero dollars to the national debt' served only to undermine support for this same agenda – because the claim is somewhat misleading.[73] It would have been more effective for Biden to say: 'Look, this agenda may add some amount of money to the US debt, but in the long-term it will improve people's lives and American productivity, so much so that we'll eventually make it all back.' This forthright communication of the long-term benefits has a better chance of winning over voters, and thus their representatives, than bravado that is not entirely backed up by facts.

Of course, everybody has a different definition of what a long-term benefit is. Some people will not see more immigrants as good, even if increased immigration would boost GDP and provide necessary tax revenue. Leaders need to recognise this reality and work even harder to sell their long-term plans. They'll need to better explain why something matters in the long-term, and why it is worth making sacrifices in the short-term to get there.

They won't always be successful, but they stand a better chance if they are honest. People want to believe in their government. Their leaders should let them.

* * *

Leaders often let us down, though, so more power should be placed in the hands of the people.

As discussed in previous chapters, governments need to double-down on voter access. We cannot have functional democracies – and free societies – if a huge swathe of voters do not or cannot participate in elections. Yet voter turnout has declined over the last two decades in places as diverse as the United Kingdom and South Korea.[74]

One way is to delegate more power to the local level. Whereas representatives in Washington or Tokyo are prone to focus on the short-term because they, personally, are doing alright in life and are comfortable in their jobs, people affected by long-term inaction are generally more willing to make what are the right decisions for them and their communities. The more politically engaged that people are, the more likely their communities are to do the thinking required to address long-term risks. Study after study shows that citizens' assemblies – in which people vote on specific questions – have improved long-term thinking in democracies around the world.[75]

To be successful, these assemblies need to focus on simple issues. By focusing on a specific question like 'Should we open a power plant next door?' or 'Should we give Amazon a tax break to come here?' and opening up the discussion to public debate, these assemblies can produce longer-term thinking than that shown by national leaders. True deliberation – something that many of our legislatures have lacked in recent years – among a diverse group of people (something most of our legislatures are not) can truly enhance willingness to make sacrifices for future generations, thereby improving long-term policy outcomes.[76]

This should not come as a huge surprise. Ordinary people deliberating in these settings are not worried about appeasing voters or lobbyists. Citizen assembly participants may be selfish – as we all are – but studies show that their selfishness often channels itself into long-term rather than short-term greed.[77]

National leaders would improve their countries' long-term thinking by putting certain decisions back in the hands of citizens because communities often know what's better for them than do those in their far-off halls of power. More often than presidents and prime ministers would like to admit, they do not know always what is best for Birmingham, Osaka or Dresden. There is, after all, a reason why when nations fall, cities remain.

* * *

In the end, what we need more than anything is bravery, which may require a new crop of politicians, ones willing to put their people first. For all my talk of reform, democracies will be able to focus on the long-term only if everybody is a bit braver. Ordinary citizens need to stop tuning out their politicians and instead pressure them to think beyond tomorrow – and beyond their own lives – and look to the lives of their children and grandchildren. Our leaders will have to show the bravery needed to listen if we are to restore government functionality and thus trust in democracy. Ultimately, we will need to be brave to make plans for the long-term, which will allow us to beat back autocracy at home and set the standard for democratic governance everywhere.

None of this is easy. But we've done it before. Democratic citizens, both ordinary civilians and politicians, have throughout history sacrificed in the moment for long-term gain – which is one of the reasons why democracies have been so powerful for so long. Our ability to meet these challenges head-on has long been key to our success. There is no structural reason why we cannot do the same today. We just need the courage to try.

5

Safety Net

Unlike the rest of Europe and much of the world beyond in 1918, Denmark was not in ruins. The flames of destruction had marched through the continent, reducing cities and families to rubble, but the Danes managed to maintain a neutral position throughout the First World War. The country avoided calamity. After the armistice, Denmark found itself with mostly functional infrastructure and a generation of able-bodied young men – assets that many nations had lost in the war.

The country proceeded to enjoy economic development at a level that many others around the world could not have imagined, all while Germany, the United Kingdom and several other nations struggled to rebuild themselves.

Denmark's economy relied on agriculture, which employed somewhere around a third of the country's workforce and accounted for some 20 per cent of its total GDP.[1] Much of this farming was done cooperatively.[2] Industrialisation and dairy production soon picked up, too, with huge majorities of Danish farmers joining cooperative dairies and slaughterhouses.[3]

Denmark quickly got rich, at least compared to the rest of Europe. But workers were not feeling the benefits. The national GDP was growing; people's wages were not. So, the workers made their voices heard: in 1924, the Social Democrats won their first election and formed a working-class government with the Radical Liberals. By 1929, the Social Democrats had cemented their power.

This was a critical moment. Denmark's unemployment rate was high, approaching 15 per cent.[4] (By way of comparison, the US rate peaked at 10 per cent during the 2008 global financial crisis.[5]) The Great Depression negatively impacted some 40 per cent of Denmark's organised industrial workers.[6] And in 1932, Britain established a system of preferential tariffs for members of the Commonwealth, seriously undermining Denmark, which was (and remains) reliant on foreign trade – but not part of the Commonwealth.

The Social Democrats sprang into action. Their government devalued the Danish currency and froze existing wage agreements. More importantly, in 1933 they convinced the Left, a moderate party, to support the establishment of a modern welfare state. And because the crisis was so bad, there was political consensus to act. The government passed huge reforms comprising pensions, health insurance, unemployment, accident insurance and farming subsidies.[7]

People were hurting; Denmark responded.

Denmark was not as lucky in the Second World War as it had been in the First. This time around, Nazi Germany refused Denmark's claims of neutrality; German troops crossed the border in 1940 and occupied Denmark until 1945, after which elections were held and a new Left-led government was formed.

Yet Denmark's safety net survived and soon after the war expanded.

When the Social Democrats came back into power in the 1950s, they introduced the concept of the 'welfare state', believing that it was the state's job to improve housing and the economy, and ensure people's security.[8] As the Cold War set in, dividing the world between a communist East and a capitalist West, Denmark's left-wing government identified their country with the latter. This pragmatic decision allowed the Social Democrats to avoid ideological debates that could have compromised the existing welfare system. The Social Democrats wisely walked back their talk of socialising and planning the economy as it became clear from the Soviet experience that such moves would fail.[9]

Perhaps paradoxically, it was this moderation that allowed the government to complete the Danish safety net's creation.[10] As Denmark rapidly industrialised, the country integrated itself into the global capitalist economy: its exports to the world brought foreign money into the country, which in turn fuelled a boom in domestic consumption, leading to substantial economic growth through the 1960s.[11] This growth then enabled the Democrats to further solidify the Danish safety net. Capitalism allowed Denmark to create its social support system.

And while young left-wing activists would dominate the headlines of the 1970s, protesting in favour of a socialist state rather than their social democratic one, for most Danes, and for the Danish government, life went on as normal.[12] It actually got better. As the scholar Klaus Petersen has written, 'Bigger and bigger houses were built, more cars filled the roads. There was more of everything.'[13] There were more social services, too. With more money, the government built more hospitals and schools, including kindergartens, because more women were working than before.[14]

Denmark was not perfect. No country ever is. But with peace, safety, a high level of trust in government and a poverty rate in the 1990s of under 1 per cent – while the rate in the United States hovered around 13 per cent – things were working well.[15]

* * *

Denmark today is not so different from the country it was then, at least when it comes to government spending. Despite facing various challenges, from the 2008 financial crisis to the COVID-19 pandemic, the country has maintained its vast social safety net. In fact, public spending accounts for more than half of Denmark's GDP – a stunning number at which more free-market-minded thinkers may recoil.

Yet the system seems to work.

Danes are more likely to have jobs than Americans and often earn substantially more. In fact, Denmark – contrary to what much economic theory predicts – has a substantially higher rate of labour force participation than lower-tax countries like Germany, Japan, the United Kingdom and the United States.[16] People in Denmark live longer, too.[17]

So while far-right commentators on both sides of the Atlantic like to agitate and exaggerate about the horrors of Danish socialism, in reality the country remains pretty much a model democratic society: one that is effective, deliberative, open and enjoys the rule of law.[18] It continues to win approbation from thinkers as diverse as the conservative Francis Fukuyama – who famously equated creating a stable, peaceful and prosperous nation with 'getting to Denmark' – and the democratic socialist US Senator Bernie Sanders, who has said that the United States should build a welfare state more like the one run by Copenhagen.[19] The more centre-left Democrat Pete Buttigieg praised Denmark, too, going even as far as to say, 'The number one place to live out the American Dream right now is Denmark.'[20]

This is all well and good. The system does, as I said, work. But Denmark's safety net is now running into its own problems.

Denmark's government continues to provide free healthcare and an overall high quality of services, but people have for decades expressed frustration with this and other public systems. They now say that these services are too slow and not effective enough.[21] And as the Nobel Prize-winning economist James J. Heckman has shown, despite having a strong safety net, Denmark has surprisingly poor social mobility.[22] In fact, Denmark and the United States have about the same level of educational mobility – despite the Nordic country's far more generous welfare state.[23] As Ida Auken, a Social Democratic Party member of the Danish parliament, writes: 'If your parents have no or little education, chances are high that you will end up at the same level yourself, even in Denmark'.[24] Denmark's poverty levels have increased in recent years, too.[25]

What's gone wrong?

Technology, COVID-19 and a whole host of factors have fundamentally changed the economies of countries everywhere, with labour markets looking little like they did when much of the democratic world designed their welfare states some sixty or seventy years ago. And Denmark is no exception.

The welfare state's designers, there and elsewhere, created policies for a world in which populations were young and relatively homogeneous thanks to limited immigration, and in which people remained in the same, stable job for decades.[26] This is a far cry from today, in which democratic countries are ageing rapidly and accepting huge numbers of immigrants, and whose economies are increasingly flexible and gig-heavy. The Danish safety net – like lesser safety nets elsewhere – was created for a world that simply does not exist anymore.

* * *

Still, Denmark's safety net remains one of the world's best. That much is inarguable. It is more comprehensive than those provided by countries like the United States, United Kingdom or South Korea.

Denmark's struggles should therefore alert us to the seriousness of the problem we now face. If Denmark, a top performer among us, is having problems, it should be apparent that democratic safety nets everywhere are in desperate need of an update.

As these nets sag under the weight of our new world, people will become less supportive of their governments; they will then become less supportive of democracy generally, yearning instead for the idealised strongman who will deliver practical benefits for them as soon as possible. The situation will only worsen if these nets snap.

Updating the social safety net is therefore not only good domestic policy – how can countries succeed if their people cannot pay their bills or access quality healthcare? – but imperative to meeting the autocratic challenge abroad, too.

The costs of falling behind on this front are plain to see. Democracies' struggle to keep people fed, housed and even *alive* during the pandemic has cast doubt on the viability of the democratic system. There's a reason why trust in democracies, including the United States and United Kingdom, plunged in 2021, when COVID-19 raged despite widespread vaccination, and when people were struggling to make ends meet without adequate government support. This lack of trust risks feeding the autocratic impulse at home and making us – and our system – look inadequate abroad.

If countries like Singapore and Saudi Arabia continue to provide for their people while democracies seemingly force their citizens to fight for scraps, authoritarian governance will become more and more popular. People in democracies need to believe their system is best; increasingly, they don't, because their systems are under-performing.

Failing to revamp our safety nets for the twenty-first century is irresponsible foreign policy, too: if we cannot satisfy our own people, we cannot advance our strategic goals – and the moral imperative of democracy's spread – abroad.

All of this is and should be a cause for concern. But words will only take us so far. It must be a cause for action, too. Beating back the would-be dictators at home requires that we tend to our people; it requires that they know their system is working, and that it can withstand the future's challenges. It is only by doing so that we can tend to the geopolitical garden abroad – because the average American,

Brit, Korean or other democratic citizen is a part of the collective engine that has powered and must continue to power democracy's spread. If democracies cannot succeed in the twenty-first century, then we will see would-be autocrats rise even further in our politics; the allure of our political system will suffer accordingly. If people cannot succeed because our states are not offering them enough support, we can hardly hope to defeat the dictators, whether at home or abroad.

* * *

Protecting Our People

In March 2020, COVID-19 infection rates were exploding across the United States. The government was telling Americans to stay at home. Businesses were shuttering, sometimes for good. As a natural consequence, they were firing people.

In April 2020, American workers lost more than 20 million jobs, bringing the unemployment rate up to 14.8 per cent – the highest number ever recorded.[27] By December 2020, more than ten million people were still unemployed.[28] All told, COVID-19's first 18 months or so created an economic downturn worse than at any period since the Second World War. The crisis left a huge number of Americans reliant on what can at best be described as a patchwork social safety net.[29] And because the US safety net is so under-resourced, many people were left to fend for themselves.[30]

But this was a time of crisis, so the government took swift action. The US Congress provided some USD 5 trillion in federal aid that included expanded unemployment insurance, nutrition support and direct cash payments.[31]

These aid offers were full of holes, particularly regarding income loss and for those lacking access to health insurance.[32]

Racial and gender disparities persisted. Studies nonetheless show that this spending lifted tens of millions of Americans above the poverty line in a time of truly unprecedented insecurity.[33]

Yet in September 2021, the US government began shrinking its COVID-era safety net. Nearly ten million people lost their expanded unemployment benefits. A federal ban on evictions expired, although 'for millions of people nothing ha[d] changed from a year and a half ago', as one union leader said.[34] Congress did not agree. So, policymakers moved to return the American social safety net to its unacceptable state of 'normal', in which untold numbers of people are left to fend for themselves on the streets.

In early 2022, the government then ratcheted back its expanded child tax credit – which offered around USD 300 per month to parents per qualifying child, depending on their age. The credit had cut child poverty by some 30 per cent.[35]

Think about that for a moment. During a global pandemic that disrupted economic activity and dragged down growth everywhere, the United States managed to reduce child poverty by nearly a third because the virus prompted policymakers to send money to families in need. Unfortunately, the US Congress did not see this as enough of a benefit to continue the programme. Republicans' unwillingness to cement the expanded credit forced policymakers to reverse course, plunging some four million American children back into the poverty from which they had just emerged.[36]

The United States cannot maintain crisis policies all the time. But it is undeniable that Washington needs to do more to support its people, far too many of whom are struggling to make ends meet. Because when people – above all children – struggle, so too will the nation, not to mention democracy at large.

* * *

The United States curtailed its child tax credit and other aid programmes too early, but at least Washington threw workers a direct if temporary lifeline by widely expanding unemployment benefits. Governments throughout Europe took a different tack: they tried to stop companies from firing employees by offering wage subsidies and restrictions.[37] The goal was essentially to stop the crisis before it happened. If companies did not fire their employees, the thinking went, then these employees would not need government support.

This logically makes sense. But such an approach neglects self-employed or temporary workers, who comprise an increasing share of the labour force.

Europe did not entirely forget these workers, who range from your favourite bakery's owner to your Uber driver. But when the continent's governments did offer them direct payments, this assistance was generally less than what was offered to full-time employees.[38] In the end, Europe essentially left its self-employed and temporary workers hanging out to dry. Some 14 per cent of the EU's workforce was self-employed, compared with only 6 per cent in the United States.[39]

'A lifetime's worth of work collapsed before me,' said one Italian who had to close all her restaurants in March 2020 and received little support from the government.[40] A German hotel worker employed on temporary contracts faced an even bleaker future when the virus ravaged the tourism sector, and she lost her source of income, finding herself without government support in a charity-run shelter. 'To begin with, you have hope,' she said. 'But it does start to die at some point.'[41]

Something similar happened in Japan.

Non-regular workers – essentially, those without traditional full-time jobs – comprise about 40 per cent of Japan's workforce.[42] Some 30,000 of them lost their jobs in the pandemic's first eight months.

Huge numbers applied for welfare cheques until they could find new jobs, but the government often rejected them, even if they had paid unemployment insurance premiums, because officials deemed them to have left their job voluntarily.

This is a quirk in the Japanese system. When workplaces closed, operators offered the employees worse jobs with less pay. When workers declined, the government declared that they were technically leaving their jobs of their own free will and were thus not eligible for unemployment benefits. Employers generally provide the materials that the state uses to determine whether someone resigned voluntarily, only further stacking the deck against non-regular workers.[43]

The experience of one forty-two-year-old Japanese woman who bounced around non-regular jobs for twenty years, barely keeping herself afloat and not amassing any savings, before losing her job due to COVID-19, is instructive and worth quoting at length. The *Mainichi Shimbun* newspaper describes her interactions with the Japanese state:

> She thought she qualified for the loan, but the public servant who talked to her was curt and dismissive, saying they didn't think she had lost her previous job due to the virus and that, in any case, her situation didn't sound as bad as other people who had applied for the loan. After all, she would start a new part-time job in two weeks. Couldn't she get by until then? The job eventually fell through. The woman left the office empty-handed, embarrassed that she had asked for help.[44]

Japanese newspapers reported several cases like these, in which the state turned away or otherwise discouraged potential welfare recipients.[45] This mishandling of welfare cases – along with general confusion around the system – left substantial numbers of non-regular workers without income or benefits. In Japan, there is also a somewhat stronger stigma of being a welfare recipient than elsewhere in the advanced world; this stigma made many people reluctant to seek help, which worsened things further.[46]

'There are a lot of adults who can't eat,' said one worker who lost his job.[47] 'People who were already struggling were confronted with the coronavirus,' echoed an advocate for Japan's unemployed. 'They were on a tightrope and the rope just snapped.'[48] And nobody was there to mend it.

Initially, the story in South Korea was much the same. Yet in that country, the self-employed account for a staggering 25 per cent of total employees – a much higher number than most first-rate economies.[49]

But most self-employed South Koreans, more than four million, are not gig workers. They run their own businesses, perhaps a *tteokbokki* stand or construction company, often without any employees; others operate as independent contractors for larger firms.[50] Many of them are therefore unable to sign up for national social and labour accident insurance because employers subside this insurance. The self-employed often find this coverage too expensive to be worth the cost.[51]

When COVID-19 hit, South Korea's self-employed were at risk. And while South Korea had expanded the Employment Insurance Scheme (EIS) – its main safety net – following the 1998 Asian financial crisis, this expansion did not include the self-employed. Most of the self-employed were not eligible for public assistance as asset holders.[52]

To Seoul's credit, the government did eventually allow some non-regular workers, such as delivery drivers, to receive EIS benefits in 2022.[53] A government commission did eventually admit the system's failure, reporting that South Korea's labour laws and social security systems relied on an overly 'strict dichotomy between wage labour and self-employment'.[54] The government was stunned to find that technological advances and COVID-19 had 'mass-produced laborers belonging to the lowest income percentile' – something that the private sector and others have known for years.[55]

Yet the government offered inadequate support.

Throughout the pandemic's first two years, the government agency in charge of overseeing the self-employment economy had given out only hundreds of dollars. When the government finally gave a lump sum of USD 2,500 to every small business owner in early 2022, this was seen as not only a political move ahead of the March elections, but a grossly insufficient one.[56]

In the end, almost 40 per cent of self-employed workers considered closing their businesses.[57] Almost a third of self-employed workers reported severe depression.[58] Hundreds, finding themselves unable to afford their rent during the pandemic, committed suicide.[59]

So, the National Self-Employment Emergency Task Force took to the streets. In January 2022, they gathered in front of the National Assembly in Seoul to commemorate those who had committed suicide and call for reform. They used candles to write out 'HELP' on the ground, even as freezing snow poured down. 'It would be good,' they said, 'if you listen to our cry.'[60]

* * *

The reality, then, is that though the US social safety net is an object of derision in rich democracies around the world, Europe and Asia's safety nets did not perform so much better than America's when COVID-19 hit. Democratic governments around the world were a step behind – and the pandemic showed us just how far. Our leaders have not adapted our social safety nets to reality, particularly that of the 'gig economy', whose non-regular workers tend to fall outside the bounds of the welfare state built decades ago. The fact that so many people in rich democracies were one pay cheque from destitution is troubling on its own. There is no reason for democratic citizens of rich countries to live like this. '

People around the world have long looked to us as models. But during the pandemic, democracies couldn't keep our people off the streets. We couldn't even keep many people alive. Why would anyone, in our own democracies or otherwise, want a system like that? Why would anyone think democracy could work in new places if it isn't working where it began?

* * *

Autocracy's Aid

In a region still marked by poverty and under-effective governments, Singaporeans live long, healthy and generally happy lives, not just by Southeast Asian standards, but by global ones. The average Singaporean lives around eighty-four years – longer than citizens of every democratic country except Japan. Singapore's infant mortality rate is 2 per 1,000, better than almost every democracy.[61] (Singapore and several democracies, mostly Nordic ones, have the world's lowest infant mortality rates.[62])

And Singapore does all of this by spending less than democracies do.

The United States spends a staggering 17 per cent of its GDP on healthcare per year. Most advanced economies – like Australia, Germany, Japan and others – spend around 10–11 per cent of their respective GDP on healthcare. Singapore spends less than half of that, at just 4 per cent, while managing similar, if not better, rates of economic growth.[63]

Singapore outperforms us despite paying less not only by

173

preventing people from falling into poverty in the first place, but by building a proactive substantial safety net oriented around pensions, healthcare and housing.[64]

Notably, the country's pension system is contribution-based, meaning that Singaporeans and their employers pay into their own personal accounts, rather than paying it forward to the current generation of elders – as in the United States – in hopes that the generation that follows you will do the same. This provides people with substantially more security than in many democracies, where you pay into a system without knowing exactly where those funds are going.

The government has also created a unique healthcare system that aims to provide everyone with coverage. The government runs and pays for much of the medical system, forces people to save and then use a certain amount of their salary for health expenses and provides coverage for catastrophic care. This is not single-payer healthcare in the classic sense where everyone sees the same doctors and cannot control their care; it is a system in which people explicitly choose their own path of care, with money they are forced to save by the government. Those who fall through the cracks are still covered by systems like Medifund.[65]

Then there is Singapore's exceptional public housing system. I'll never forget staying in a Singaporean government-owned apartment block – one that while relatively grey and unattractive on the outside, inside contained all the trappings of modernity, and even luxury. It was a lovely apartment, owned by a successful couple, but not a rich one. The amenities worked, space was ample, the neighbourhood was safe and the couple was happy. It felt nothing less than a world away from the council houses of London or projects of upper Manhattan.

This is because the Singaporean Housing Development Board (HDB) uniquely both builds and sells homes – and around 80 per cent of the country lives in an HDB-built house or apartment. A staggering 88.9 per cent of Singaporean households own their home, with many having purchased it from the government.[66] (Just 65 per cent of Americans, 63 per cent of Brits, along with around 65 per cent of Canadians and 61 per cent of Japanese, own their homes.[67]) Luxury penthouses in Singapore might sell for USD 54 million, but the government has made sure that just about everyone can afford a home.[68]

This approach would be just about impossible to replicate around the democratic world; running the housing market requires far too much state control than is acceptable. But Singapore has succeeded in 'creating a nation of homeowners' and avoiding 'the growth of slums and the incidence of homelessness that plague many other capitalist countries', as the scholar Ron Haskins has written.[69] This success only feeds the notion that it is Singapore, not the democratic world, that has the answer to our problems.

Taken as a whole, Singapore's social safety net produces a coherent coverage plan in a way few democratic governments' own systems do. The city-state's system means that people are not at risk of losing everything – their retirement, their health and their homes – when they lose their job or otherwise misstep. It means that one wrong decision in a Singaporean's life does not mean utter disaster. And it is a shame that the same cannot be said in much of the democratic world.

* * *

Singapore is almost always an exception in just about every respect. It is a tiny country ruled by perhaps the most benevolent authoritarian government to ever exist. It benefited massively from the strong leadership of one man, Lee Kuan Yew, who built the country out of nothing and exercised a huge amount of power to keep its trajectory going in the right direction.

Yet the city-state is certainly not the only authoritarian country providing its people with strong social support. The Gulf States – like the United Arab Emirates and Saudi Arabia – garner legitimacy from the public by providing free or highly subsidised healthcare and housing, along with cash payments.[70] That's part of the trade-off: people give up their freedom in exchange for comfortable, state-supported lives.

Hong Kong, like Singapore, was never democratic, but the city is now increasingly becoming a Chinese province – a rich one, sure, but one with authoritarian governance. Some folks have left as China takes over, but many Hong Kongers and expats are not fleeing, attesting to the relative strength of that city's safety net and overall quality of life, even as its governance declines. Hong Kongers, on average, live to be eighty-five – more than the average Briton, Korean or Swede.

What the relative pliability of those living in these richer autocracies suggests is that people around the world are more willing to trade freedom for material gain than democrats in the West might like to think. This is why it is such a victory for autocracy that Hong Kong, Singapore and the UAE have higher life expectancies than the United States.[71] US life expectancy actually dropped by the sharpest margin in 100 years from 2020 to 2021, with the average American living just 77 years.[72]

But many of the world's best social safety nets are in democracies.

The Nordic countries outperform just about all of the world's rich autocracies on this front.[73] So too, to some extent, does New Zealand, which recently reformed its already-strong healthcare system and raised its benefit rates during the pandemic, particularly for families.[74] The island country – whose government provides housing to those in need, supports the unemployed, and sends funds to both young and single parents – today maintains an average life expectancy of eighty-two.[75]

The list of democracies with strong safety nets is relatively long, compared to a pretty small list of wealthy autocracies. But there is no reason to think it will be that way forever. Rich autocracies like Singapore and Saudi Arabia are constantly tweaking their systems, and developing autocracies are looking to these countries for guidance – because Singapore and Saudi Arabia demonstrate that an undemocratic regime can stay in power for decades on end by satiating people with strong social benefits.[76] COVID-19's exposure of so many democracies' safety nets as inadequate does not help matters.[77]

The autocrat's bet is not only that democracies are falling behind, but that providing quality services at home will quell people's democratic demands. Their wager is that people would prefer to live comfortably in a country like Singapore than deal with complications of life in a messy democracy like the United States. As much as we in rich democratic countries may like to think that people are intrinsically supportive of freedom, anchoring policy on that belief would be naïve. It would be misguided, to say the least, for us to let our social safety nets decay simply because they are currently better than those of many of our rivals.

While betting against democracy is never a good idea, betting against people's willingness to trade freedom for material gain would be similarly unwise. If rich autocracies provide better for their people than rich democracies, liberals will struggle to convince people both at home and abroad of the superiority of our system. Democracy cannot win if it cannot provide.

* * *

The Realm of the Possible

'I love Denmark,' Hillary Clinton declared, confronting Bernie Sanders, the self-declared socialist vying for the Democratic Party's presidential nomination. 'But we are not Denmark,' she added, speaking to millions of Americans through the cameras trained on her at the first Democratic debate of the 2016 presidential campaign in Las Vegas, Nevada – a city not exactly known for its regulatory spirit. 'We are,' she said defiantly, 'the United States of America.'

Clinton's comment prompted an outpouring of anger from the American political left. *Why*, they asked, *should we not become Denmark?* They pointed out that whereas America has wealth inequality and spends too much on the military, Denmark has seemingly solved both problems. They said that Clinton's statement reflected an American unwillingness to learn from other countries.[78] They accused Clinton of being a Grade-A American exceptionalist – and they wielded this term as a slur, taking for granted that it's wrong to believe in America's exceptional nature.

But Clinton had a point. America is not Denmark; Denmark's system will almost surely never be plausible in the United States, for a whole host of sociological reasons, including Americans' historical distrust of government and aversion to paying high taxes. It's just about impossible to imagine a return to the Second World War–era reality in which the US tax rate exceeded 50 per cent without a drastic crisis – and the most recent drastic crisis, a global pandemic coupled with a major European war, wasn't anywhere near enough.[79]

Her observation does not imply that the United States and other countries cannot learn from Denmark. Quite the opposite. She did recognise that Copenhagen's prioritisation of individual well-being is something that Washington – and Tokyo and Madrid – could emulate, even if the policy specifics might differ. While social media posts tended to clip her video after her declarative 'We are the United States of America,' she did allude to learning from Denmark. '[I]t's our job,' she said, 'to rein in the excesses of capitalism so that it doesn't run amok and doesn't cause the kind of inequities we're seeing in our economic system.' These are hardly the words of a hard-headed politician unwilling to consider her own country's problems.

The reality, as she noted, is that every democratic country will need to find a social safety net that works for them. Everybody may want to 'get to Denmark', as Fukuyama describes it, but most democracies do not have societies that will allow their governments to exactly duplicate the Danish system. This is not a cause for despair. It simply reflects the rough-and-tumble reality of the world – which should encourage democratic reformers everywhere to reject utopianism and do what is possible, where it is possible. Different countries will have different paths to prosperity.

The solutions that follow, then, are decidedly in the realm of the possible. The goal is not to tear out existing social safety nets root and branch, but to ensure they are strong enough to withstand the twenty-first century's vicious winds.

* * *

Before the pandemic hit, the world's labour force seemed to be in good shape. A higher share of people were employed than at any point in the last twenty years. But much of the growth in employment was in part-time jobs. By early 2020, one out of every four workers in the world's richest countries were temporary workers or self-employed as, say, an Uber driver or contractor.[80]

In a sense, this was a good thing. When labour markets are flexible, people are, too: workers can find employment that better fits their schedules and desires, often finding new opportunities that they might have been unable to obtain before. Business can then reap the benefits, such as scaling up quickly by relying on freelancers or simply maintaining a lower cost; without full-time workers, you don't need to set up healthcare programmes or human resources departments.

So, while the outgrowth of part-time work, known as the 'gig economy', has many critics, it exists for a reason. It exists because everybody – companies, workers and customers – benefits to some extent (even if surveys show that most freelance and temporary workers would prefer full-time employment).[81]

But somebody must provide the benefits to part-time workers that employers are not. These people cannot be forgotten, particularly as they comprise more and more of our workforces and increasingly work full-time without having the same status.

Yet our safety nets were failing to catch them even before COVID-19. This is because our safety nets were created mainly to cover those who had fallen on hard times and lost work, not a solid 25 per cent of the labour force. Our safety nets were not meant to prop up people working full-time hours without the benefits of a full-time job. COVID-19 was a shock to an already outdated system.

Many governments took temporary steps during the pandemic to fill these gaps. Washington, for instance, began offering unemployment insurance to freelancers and contractors for the first time.[82]

Rolling back these changes – as some governments already have – is a mistake, with the global gig economy sure to expand.[83] Failing to reform our safety nets to catch the workers whose labour provides profit would be a drastic error, not only for these workers and the democracies they inhabit, but for democrats everywhere, and for the world we want to create.

This gig economy has fundamentally reshaped the nature and form of our economies. The previous economic model – in which people worked for the same few companies for their whole lives, securing benefits through that firm (and being entitled to government benefits if they lost their job) – is rapidly disintegrating.

Democracies across the board have no choice, then, but to upgrade their safety nets for the twenty-first century. They must make non-regular workers eligible for retirement, sick leave and unemployment compensation, and lower the cost of the premiums they must pay for such coverage.[84]

This is a universal message about a universal problem. From America to Europe to Asia, gig workers were essentially uncovered when the pandemic started. Some of this was a result of simple government oversight – of safety net systems being stuck in a previous century. But in Japan, South Korea and elsewhere, the system is so onerous and non-worker-friendly that gig economy workers who clearly qualified for aid were not able to secure it. A swathe of reforms will be needed to fix these systems to ensure they provide for everyone, not only in times of crisis, but all the time, because without providing for them, they will not support democracy at home, let alone become ambassadors for democracy abroad.

We can't and shouldn't all become Denmark. But we can all look out for our people.

* * *

One key reform would be to make non-regular workers eligible for high-quality health insurance that travels with them from job to job. Many democratic governments do, of course, already allow this. Freelancers in Taiwan are covered by its national health insurance.[85] Even a foreign freelancer can access Taiwanese health insurance after living on the island for six months.[86] Something similar is true in parts of Germany as well.[87]

It is decidedly not true of the United States. That means that when I was more or less a freelancer, cobbling together writing and think-tank jobs, it would have been easier for me – if I was not on my parents' insurance – to access high-quality healthcare in countries thousands of miles away than in my own neighbourhood. The same is true for any part-time American teacher or contractor who is over twenty-six and has aged out of their parents' care (if their parents covered them to begin with).

Freelance workers not having access to quality health insurance is unacceptable for the richest country in the history of the world.[88] Obamacare improved the situation somewhat, but Republicans' efforts to undermine the bill have sent premiums higher and higher in recent years, all while pushing more and more doctors to become 'concierges' – more expensive doctors who accept fewer kinds of insurance (if at all), and whom people on Obamacare cannot afford. I can tell you from personal experience that trying to navigate the American healthcare system *with* quality health insurance is a hassle; without good insurance, almost surely provided by your full-time job, it is a nightmare.

But when people lack access to good insurance – or any insurance – they do not seek the medical care that they probably should. This leads to higher mortality rates, which is not only disturbing but bad for the country.[89] The financial costs of not having a functional healthcare system are higher than spending the money to have one that works.[90]

Providing greater coverage does not require full-fledged universal healthcare, as in the Nordic system. Such a system could undermine the competitive attitude that makes the United States one of the world's leaders in medical innovation and the undisputed global champion in terms of scientific advancement.[91] If the system is universal, and there are no (or limited) profits to be made, then there is no financial incentive for companies to spend money on the research that produces innovations that save lives.

This problem is admittedly American, but the future of the US healthcare system will have an outsized impact on the world, too. Danes today can outsource medical innovation to the United States; Americans don't have the same luxury. If Washington was to institute universal healthcare that regulated out the spirit of competitive capitalism, the world would suffer from the lack of American innovation. Not everybody can be Denmark.

It is also difficult to imagine that any American universal healthcare system would not be plagued by the same issues that plague universal systems abroad.[92] Currently, US doctors detect cancer earlier than their counterparts in the United Kingdom because the US system allows people to see a doctor and get surgery sooner, whereas the socialised UK system is slower. While care is cheaper in the United Kingdom – free, if received through the NHS rather than a private provider – cancer is generally discovered later, when it's more aggressive, leading to higher mortality rates.[93] A universal healthcare system is not a one-size-fits-all solution for every society.

Instead of adopting full-fledged universal healthcare, the United States should move immediately to provide a minimum baseline amount of coverage for everyone, particularly for gig workers. A key starting point would be universal catastrophic coverage (UCC) – meaning that nobody goes broke when they break their leg or have a stroke and need months of recovery. UCC would fill the gap between the poorest people, who get government insurance, and people who are too 'rich' to qualify for such insurance but are nonetheless one accident away from financial ruin. There are millions of people who fall into the latter category.[94]

This is not complete universal healthcare. It does not guarantee widespread health provision. Nor does it undermine the market incentives that have made the United States so great at medical innovation. But it does ensure that people do not die because they cannot afford healthcare, or that they are not left homeless because of an accident. It is a political compromise that the US Congress and other more conservative legislatures in nations beginning to examine the question of healthcare could potentially pass and then build upon.

And it is one that would save American lives while keeping our innovative spirits alive – to the world's everlasting benefit.

* * *

A second reform would be to make safety net systems more worker-friendly.

This will look different in every country, but the broadest solution would be to reclassify gig workers and self-employed people as employees, thereby entitling them to the same benefits as normal workers. Some in the European Union are trying to do just this – a move that would give four million people the right to a minimum wage, safety protections, paid leave and unemployment benefits. Companies like Uber could challenge the reclassification, but the onus would be on them to prove that no employment relationship exists.[95] It remains to be seen if Europe can make this policy a reality; still, the continent's effort is one example of how broadening the definition of who is an 'employee' can serve to update the safety net for the twenty-first century.

There are several other less sweeping yet similarly meaningful reforms that governments can enact in the meantime.

Japan should audit its safety net operations to ensure that public servants are not simply dismissing those who ask for help and are eligible, which happens at a distressingly regular rate. The country should also listen to both workers and employers when determining if workers left jobs voluntarily, which would disqualify them from receiving unemployment benefits. Far too often the government takes the side of the employers, who at times say that workers left voluntarily when they did not. Listening to the workers themselves would be a significant step forward.

South Korea should look to lower the cost of national social and labour accident insurance for self-employed and other non-regular workers. Doing so will not only increase coverage – preventing the bad outcomes we saw when COVID-19 hit – but also possibly increase entrepreneurship. When people are less skittish about striking out on their own for fear of not being able to afford insurance, they are less likely to innovate and produce the businesses of tomorrow. Ensuring that South Korean entrepreneurs can afford this insurance is one way to ensure also that these innovations continue.

The United States will need to support gig workers by taking a whole host of steps. Washington must provide safety protections and overtime rights to gig workers, as well as unemployment benefits – not on a temporary status, but permanently. If this requires classifying them as employees, so be it, although firms may push back. Yet even companies like Uber that rely on gig workers have signalled their willingness to meet in the middle by offering workers some of the benefits typically provided through full-time employment.[96] The path to an improved social safety net may be an uphill battle, but it is not impossible.

* * *

One additional and deceptively simple solution is to streamline and digitise the benefit application process.

When individuals, gig and full-time workers alike, lose their jobs, they far too often find themselves facing a labyrinthine set of applications through which they must navigate like Theseus. But many people do not have the luxury of time: they cannot waste precious hours poring over onerous applications only to be turned away by a public servant for having filled out some small part wrongly, meaning they must circle back to step one. When you're worrying about how you're going to pay for your next meal, or for your next month of rent, you're not going to take the time to fill out several complicated forms, let alone do so correctly. Just securing and keeping food assistance in the United States requires people to fill out piles of paperwork and make multiple visits to government offices, which is why some 25 per cent of those eligible do not receive these benefits.[97]

Simon Tung shut down his Manhattan bakery when COVID-19 hit; he then filed for unemployment online, but the government said he needed to call to give the state more information. He called hundreds and hundreds of times, rarely getting through: the phones were too jammed, with the government having not hired enough people to handle the increased demand. When he got through, he heard only a pre-recorded statement telling him that the system was overwhelmed, and that he should call back later. He finally received his first direct deposit from New York – only to find out that the state had given him zero dollars. 'It got to a point where it went from anxiety to frustration to defeat, and you're just laughing at everything,' he said.[98]

Many would say this is a uniquely American problem. They'd be wrong.

Homeless people in Japan fail to secure welfare because government officials are 'unresponsive to their questions about the byzantine process and elaborate rules'.[99] Officials subsequently disqualify them for some infraction or missing piece of paperwork.[100] Many homeless people simply just give up on their applications.[101]

Applicants for several kinds of state support in the United Kingdom complain, too, about onerous application processes and confusing rules. Just the process of applying causes a substantial spike in stress for people with families and little money.[102] Several UK organisations blame these onerous application processes for limited assistance uptake throughout the country.[103] Similar mechanisms are at play, too, in the welfare systems of both advanced and developing democracies alike, including Germany and South Africa.[104]

In comparison, the US stimulus payments – of USD 1,200, 600, and then 1,400 – distributed during the pandemic were so popular because they were simple and easy.[105] You did not have to complete any onerous application, nor did you have to comply with insulting bureaucratic requirements. You didn't have to talk to anyone. Yet the money did make a difference.

The lesson is clear: benefits will reach the people they're supposed to when the process to secure them is simple and obvious.

Key to any reform of the safety net, then, is streamlining and digitising the application process. When somebody applies for one benefit – say, unemployment – they should be simultaneously considered for all benefits for which they may be eligible, such as Medicaid, childcare and energy assistance. When there are lower administrative burdens for securing assistance, people are more likely to complete the necessary applications and receive the benefits for which they are eligible.[106]

Some entrepreneurs and US states have begun taking the steps to make this a reality.

The design studio, Civilla, has worked with benefit applicants and the Michigan Department of Health and Human Services to combine five benefit applications into one.[107] A Georgetown University report found that the new application was 80 per cent shorter and took the government half the time to process.[108] Importantly, the application is available in a mobile phone-friendly format that allows people who may not own a computer to manage their benefits, upload documents and receive text notifications. A Michigan Department of Health and Human Services leader called this new application 'some of the best work I've done in my 35 years of public service'.[109] GovTech magazine declared the system 'a blue-print for lasting and effective government change'.[110]

Yet governments continue to under-invest in updates like these that consider users' preferences and are built for the world of today

– not yesterday. Stories like Simon Tung's, sadly, remain more common than those of certain benefit recipients in Michigan.

* * *

Immigration, it must be said, poses a broad and serious challenge to the existing social safety net. More properly stated, domestic reactions to immigration pose a challenge to the safety net.

In the 1990s, US President Bill Clinton limited illegal immigrants' access to certain benefits. Sweden has more recently cut paid parental leave for new immigrants. Even Denmark has limited non-European migrants' access to benefits, particularly for unemployment and children's expenses, since the early 2000s.[111]

Why? Because, as studies show, people are simply less willing to offer benefits to people who don't look like them.[112] Swedes are less willing to support the Bulgarians than they are the Dutch (who are also ethnically Nordic).[113] Europeans across the continent simultaneously support more benefits for 'natives' while limiting access to migrants.[114] Some Japanese similarly suggest that immigrants would drain the country's welfare institutions (while many Japanese also oppose immigration for fears that immigrants would lead to the 'irrevocable loss of Japanese culture', a separate issue addressed in Chapter 8).[115]

Motivations may differ slightly, but the policy results are similar: less assistance for immigrants, and thus a general shrinking of the safety net.

These short-sighted policies set immigrants up for failure. This is evident in the case of Southeast Asian refugees in the United States – to whom Washington initially provided little support when they arrived in the late 1970s, resettling them in poor urban neighbourhoods like parts of the Bronx without much financial assistance. Today, some Southeast Asian immigrant communities have poverty rates around 26 per cent – higher than among Black Americans.[116] Failing to offer immigrants at least some welfare undermines their ability to succeed and depresses the amount of tax revenue they may be able to provide the state down the line.

Yet more immigrants are fleeing the global south for the north. This trend promises to continue as climate change worsens, forcing people to leave places like Bangladesh and Vietnam, where large areas will be too hot if they're not underwater. The safety nets democracies built decades ago were not made for this world of mass migration.

There is no quick fix for this; changing societal attitudes is no easy task. But an important first step would be for democracies to highlight the actual economic benefits of migration. Data shows over and over again that migrants contribute more in taxes than they cost in public services, whether in Europe or the United States or elsewhere.[117]

It may seem deceptively simple, but one way to shift public opinion is for responsible public officials to make these stats clear. Liberals tend to make the case for immigration in moral terms, but they would be better served by using practical ones. At a moment when democratic citizens are feeling the pinch in their pockets, people don't want to hear nice stories about how they absolutely must accept the poor and weary for moral reasons; they want to hear about how these people can benefit their economies, and thus themselves.

This issue will become more and more pressing as democracies across the world continue to age, making immigrants fundamental to these countries' futures. Without immigrants – as I'll discuss later – these governments will not be able to pay their elderly people's social benefits, let alone thrive and innovate for the future. And without including legal immigrants in the safety net, rich Western countries will become less appealing destinations.

Such a reputation decline has already happened across the Gulf States, particularly in Qatar – where reports of exploitation and deaths of legal migrant workers, who are explicitly not granted many basic rights, let alone access to a meaningful safety net, have become commonplace.[118] This is why many migrant workers, from places like Bangladesh and Nepal, are increasingly willing to take lesser-paying jobs in their native lands rather than move to the Gulf.[119] It's evidently better to live safely at home with less than to make a bit more abroad at risk of injury or death.

Democratic governments may struggle to convince their publics of the need to provide legal immigrants with access to at least some parts of the social safety net. But we must get started before it's too late – lest we drive away talent from abroad. The failure to do so will only cost us later.

* * *

Reasonable people can disagree on the size of the social safety net, and how much reform various countries can afford right now. But I hope leaders from across the political spectrum will agree that reforming our social safety nets is vital to democracies' economic and geopolitical success – and key, in particular, to meeting the challenge posed today by autocracies like China.

This isn't a cryptic argument for socialism. To succeed, our democracies need capitalism. The West, Japan, South Korea and countless other success stories owe their wealth and power and allure to capitalism, albeit in different forms. No socialist or mercantilist economy could ever truly challenge us. Of course, it is uber-capitalist China, communist in name only, that poses the grandest challenge to the West today.

Yet it is still liberal capitalism – that is, capitalism with democracy – that produces the world's best innovations. The world's best vaccines come from the West. The best technology comes from the United States and democratic Asia: places like Japan and Taiwan. The world needs liberal capitalism for the innovation it produces. We cannot rely on the Chinese, Saudi or Singaporean versions of capitalism to produce the innovations that organise our world. We need the animal spirits of our liberal capitalism.

But capitalism cannot survive without a reformed social safety net. Voters won't let it. If people do not feel supported – or if they feel like they are nothing but cogs in the machine, neglected by their state while the rich get richer – they will vote for economically regressive nationalist leaders, on the left and the right, who promise short-term fixes without any kind of long-term vision. More than a few of these leaders will have authoritarian tendencies. Their short-term fixes may make people feel good in the moment, but they will hamper the competitive spirits that have for centuries fuelled democracies' victories, not to mention weaken our democracies, and our ability to advance our model abroad.

Our democracies need capitalism and capitalism needs a reformed social safety net.

* * *

William Beveridge, the architect of the British safety net and former director of the London School of Economics (LSE), knew this to be true. Writing in early 1942, he put forward the plan that would result in the British safety net with an eye towards securing capitalism, not supplanting it with some form of socialism or reliance on the state. He knew, as *The Economist* put it, that 'by insuring people against some risks of creative destruction, welfare states would bolster democratic support for free markets'.[120]

Yet democratic support for both the welfare state and capitalism has declined in recent years owing to the under-performance of the former and the ill-managed version of the latter.[121] People increasingly believe their safety nets to be bloated and inefficient, meaning that they'd be better off keeping their money in their own pockets.

This may very well be true.

But the size of the net is less important than its design. The problem today is that the net is designed for a world that no longer exists, meaning that billions of dollars are being wasted on an outdated system.

Reforming the safety net for the twenty-first century should therefore be a goal behind which both the left and right can rally. The left can highlight the coverage such reforms will provide for the needy, while the right can highlight the amount of money these reforms will ultimately save or generate. Both sides can highlight how vital these reforms are to beating back our competitors abroad.

The costs of failure are clear.

In democracies around the world, people are already revolting against the status quo. They are angry with their governments' failures and are rejecting the establishment. They are voting for people like Trump and Marine Le Pen, for movements like Brexit, and taking to the streets – sometimes violently – to express their displeasure.

Continued failure to support them with strong safety nets will lead to only more disruptions. More disruptions will weaken democracies around the world. And if democracies cannot even get their own homes in order, they will not be able to put forward their system as a model. A reformed safety net, one fit for the world in which we live today, is the foundation stone of the strong shelter we promise to provide. As Minouche Shafik, the current director of the LSE, has said: 'The political turmoil we observe in many countries is only a foretaste of what awaits us if we do not rethink what we owe each other.'[122]

What awaits us is the rise of populist authoritarians around the democratic world, and a weakening of the democratic model. Without an improved social safety net, what awaits us are more autocrats, fewer democrats, and above all, less freedom.

6

Human Capital

The boy's family didn't think he would have the chance to attend college. How could they have? He was born in September 1964 in the Chinese city of Hangzhou at a time when the average Chinese citizen had less money than the average Liberian or Cambodian.[1] China was a grindingly poor country ruled by the economically illiterate Mao Zedong. There was no reason to hope that the boy would become anything more than a local merchant, at best.

It did not help matters that soon after the boy was born, Mao began conjuring up the Cultural Revolution from his retreat on Hangzhou's West Lake. In 1966, Mao unleashed the revolution with the stated goal of purging supposed evils, such as capitalism and traditional elements of Chinese society, from the country, and to impose real communism. Radical youths rampaged across the country, obliterating 'the Four Olds' that he said were holding China back: old ideas, old culture, old habits and old customs. They stormed through Hangzhou and demolished the city's cultural sites and antiquities, plastering locals' Buddhist temples with signs that read 'destroy the old world' and 'establish a new world'.[2]

Yet Hangzhou would play a central role in shaping China's brighter future. It was here, once again on West Lake, that Chinese premier Zhou Enlai brought US President Richard Nixon in 1972 to finalise the Shanghai Communiqué in which both leaders promised to work for the 'normalisation' of relations, and to expand 'people-to-people contacts'. It was the start of a new era.

Not only had the staunchly anti-communist Nixon reached out to the world's secondmost powerful communist country, but capitalists themselves began to flood into China. English speakers, the 'people' of the promised 'people-to-people' contact, made their way even to Hangzhou. The city's Hangzhou International Hotel became their de facto home. It quickly became one of the boy's favourite places.

Most mornings, for nine years, the boy – now an attentive adolescent – went to the hotel to give Western visitors tours of the area he knew so well. Money might have been a motive, but English was more important to him. The boy – whom one tourist would name Jack, deeming it easier to pronounce than his Chinese name, Yun – wanted to practise the visitors' language, one that offered the promises of the rich West. He was curious: he wanted to learn about the world from which his parents and grandparents had previously been cut off. The name Jack stuck.

* * *

By the mid-1980s, Jack was living in a completely different world. Mao was gone, having been replaced by the more pragmatic Deng Xiaoping. China was opening to the world. Its economy had become increasingly capitalist. And there were, finally, opportunities for people like Jack – children of non-elites – to attend what were increasingly strong universities.

Jack graduated from Hangzhou Teacher's Institute in 1988 with a Bachelor of Arts in English. After bouncing around odd jobs throughout the late 1980s and early 1990s, in 1994 he managed to start his first company, the Haibo Translation Agency. A natural step, the company leaned on his strength for languages to offer translation and interpretation. In early 1995, Jack then travelled to the United States on behalf of the municipal government and, for the first time, came face to face with the internet. He was surprised to find out that it held no information about China. And he realised China's lacking presence represented a monumental business opportunity. He and his friend promptly created an admittedly 'ugly' website about China: chinapages.com. He did all this despite still not owning a computer himself. Within three hours of China Pages' launch, investors had reached out wanting to invest in it.

People wanted to learn more about China, so Jack and his friend built China Pages into something of a directory of Chinese companies looking for foreign customers. The business continued growing. In April 1995, Jack and his friend opened China Pages' first office and soon after registered the domain chinapages.com in the United States. Within three years, the company made the equivalent of USD 800,000.

But this new China had not evolved as much as Jack might have hoped. In 1996, China Pages was pressured into forming a joint venture with Hangzhou Telecom, a state-owned firm that wanted to control China's internet presence. This deal put the Chinese government firmly in charge. Jack accepted the government's power and moved to Beijing to work at Infoshare, an internet advertising agency run by China's Ministry of Commerce. But he quickly grew tired of state-owned sector work; he lasted just fourteen months.

Firmly determined to run his own company, he returned to Hangzhou. With the help of American friends, he started building websites for other Chinese companies. On 21 February 1999, he launched the website that would make him famous. Gathered with seventeen friends in his second-floor lakeside apartment, he spoke at length about his personal ambitions, but also about how much China, as a nation, needed a great start-up. His new company, Alibaba, would fill this gap.

Alibaba was built on a simple premise: helping Chinese businesses find customers overseas. If an American or Japanese retailer wanted to purchase silk-woven scarves from China, they could turn to Alibaba.com. And if a Chinese producer wanted to export these same scarves to the United Kingdom, they could advertise on the site. Alibaba would connect China with the world. And it would make Ma Yun, better known today by the name that tourist gave him as a teenager – Jack Ma – fabulously wealthy and famous.

Jack Ma, the boy who grew up in a country still reeling from the Cultural Revolution, is today one of the world's wealthiest men, having accumulated a net worth of some USD 30.5 billion. Alibaba, his great start-up, hosts one of the world's largest consumer-to-consumer and business-to-consumer websites. It owns some 50 per cent of all retail e-commerce sales in China.

All of this is more remarkable when you consider that Ma's parents grew up without access to foreign technology or expertise, and, broadly speaking, without access even to foreign ideas.

Just over a generation ago, only a select, elite group of Chinese had the privilege to attend college – and Ma's parents were not included. Many of these elites would go to prestigious schools abroad, particularly in the West. Upon returning to China, fancy degrees in hand, they would take jobs overseeing under-educated workers who provided the cheap labour that turned China into the world's factory, fuelling the country's rapid economic growth.

This was the social system that allowed China's economy to thrive, at least for a period. And it was self-perpetuating: the elites passed on their wealth and privilege to their children, while the lower classes stayed the lower classes, even as their quality of life increased. If you were not an elite, you almost certainly were not finishing high school, let alone college.

In 1990, only 27 per cent of Chinese aged sixteen to eighteen were in school; that number was even lower, under 7 per cent, for those aged nineteen to twenty-two.[3] Even by 1996, only one in six Chinese seventeen-year-olds had graduated from high school.[4] The United States has not seen such low educational attainment rates since 1919.[5]

But as China became richer and more educated, people like Jack Ma found themselves with opportunities of which their parents had never dreamed. As an increasingly powerful country – one where more and more people were expected not only to produce things, but to design them, too – China needed more educated workers. With government support and foreign investment, the number of Chinese completing high school and attending college steadily grew. By 2013, three in five young Chinese graduated from high school.[6]

This was an improvement, sure, but it was far from enough. The three-in-five proportion matched the United States' performance of only the mid-1950s.[7]

In China, college was still too expensive for too many. Recognising the problem, the Chinese government invested in education – so much so that by 2013, China was spending upwards of USD 250 billion per year to build new universities, to reform the outdated education system that prioritised memorisation over critical thinking and debate, and to provide students with scholarships. Some scholarships helped people study in China. Others enabled graduate students to study abroad, in fields like engineering and science, where the West remains superior.[8]

The goal of these efforts was simple: to become a richer and more powerful country by creating a more educated public to compete with those of the West. The effort largely worked, at least so far. Corporations used to go to China for raw labour, but now, as one management consultant told the *New York Times* a few years ago, 'they are going to China for brains'.[9]

* * *

China's education system remains riddled with problems. Rural education is weak: a staggering 70 per cent of working-age Chinese do not have high school diplomas.[10] Education across the board still emphasises rigid learning systems, which tend to limit the development of students' creative skills.[11] There is a clear and persistent gap between what the Chinese government wants China to look like versus what the country looks like.

But Beijing's monumental investment in human capital – in the population's knowledge, skills, abilities and experience – was a meaningful push in the right direction.[12]

The numbers speak for themselves. The share of China's labour force having at least senior-level high school education increased from about 6 per cent in 1980 to over 28 per cent in 2015.[13] The proportion of Chinese in the labour force with a college education increased from only 1 per cent in 1980 to about 13 per cent in 2015.[14] Higher demand for education – and growing financial returns from being educated – clearly helped drive this growth, as did the 'aggressive' government policies that allowed for more slots in public schools.[15]

The result has been to produce not only magnates like Jack Ma, but an educated workforce comprising top-class computer programmers and architects. China has come further than imaginable from that previous era, when lower-middle-class parents could hope for little for their children. By 2006, even those in the lower class were not only thinking about but planning for more.

'My son is three years old,' one disabled migrant worker told a journalist. 'No matter what, we want him to get some education when he gets older. I don't want him to go out to work somewhere else. I have high hopes for my son.'[16]

* * *

International investors today pour money into China, aiming to profit off the back of this educated workforce. Policymakers and commentators across the democratic world now worry that this new generation of educated Chinese could rapidly usher in a world in which Chinese workers are superior to their counterparts in leading democracies like the United States, Germany and Japan.[17]

These fears are not unfounded.

The West and China now compete as much for political pre-eminence as they do for technological pre-eminence. Both sides understand this to be true; both sides understand that winning the future requires winning the technological battle. Washington, London, Tokyo and Beijing all understand that developing and owning both current and future innovations will be key to developing their own economies – and to ensuring that the future world order is more favourable to their interests, and more consistent with their own values.

Faster semiconductor production or artificial intelligence advancements will help countries, whether China or the United States, to do more frictionless business. That will speed up and boost their economies; that success, in turn, will allow countries to better spread their geopolitical influence, both by spending more on international efforts and by more softly advancing their governance system as a model abroad. Such innovations will be vital to winning future military confrontations as well: semiconductors alone are key to lasers, rockets and a whole host of military technology.

Taiwan, a key member of the free world, currently dominates semiconductor production, being home to over 90 per cent of the world's advanced chips. The fact that a democracy owns this technology, and that the chief executive of the world's leading chip firm – the Taiwan Semiconductor Manufacturing Company (TSMC) – studied and got his start in the United States, another democracy, is not a coincidence.[18] There is a reason why Taiwan has innovated to produce the best semiconductors, rather than the richer Asian polities of Hong Kong or Singapore (or even China, so far).

Yet the West and its allies are at risk of losing our edge. China has already developed advanced unmanned weapons systems described as 'autonomous' (自主) or 'intelligentised' (智能化) – weapons systems that could very well challenge democracies' top technology.[19]

Thus the battle for technological supremacy – which will be won *only* by investing substantially and effectively in human capital – is in many ways a microcosm of the governance battle in which we're currently engaged.

China understands the importance of these advancements. 'Scientific and technological innovation has become the main battlefield of the international strategic game,' Xi said in May 2021, adding: 'The competition around the commanding heights of science and technology is unprecedentedly fierce.'[20] Just months later, he added: 'Talent is a strategic resource to achieve national revitalisation and win the initiative in international competition.'[21]

Much of the democratic world gets it, too. Biden said in July 2021 that 'as we compete for the future of the twenty-first century with China [. . .] we have to stay on top of the cutting-edge developments of science and technology'.[22] There is a relative bipartisan consensus on this issue, not only in the United States but throughout the democratic world. Everybody seems to know that winning this battle will be key not only to sustaining democracy at home, but to protecting and advancing it abroad.

Yet while both sides are aware of the stakes, it increasingly seems that only one side is turning words into reality. One side, led by China, seems to see spending on education and research to produce these innovations existentially important, while the other side – democracies – tends to see such investment as frivolous spending to come only after other more politically-sensitive priorities are satisfied. While China spends and spends, investing in education as well as in research and development (R&D), the West and its partners have fallen behind or, at best, stagnated.

US federal spending on research and development as a percentage of GDP has steadily decreased since the 1970s.[23] Federal spending on elementary and secondary education has remained just about the same since 2005.[24] And while the United States remains a top spender on education compared to other countries, the results are not matching the investment: the money is not producing better-performing students.[25] Something similar is true too of democracies like France, Japan and the United Kingdom.[26]

Still, the West remains ahead of autocracies on the human capital front – mainly because we've had something like a hundred-year head start.[27] Across just about every measure, Americans, Germans and others still outperform China and other autocracies in terms of educational attainment, innovation and technological strength. Even while democracies seem sclerotic and perhaps underfunded, we are, for the time being, producing more innovative and high-skilled people than their autocratic competitors.

Some of these issues are inevitable – a one-party state will struggle to produce the same amount of innovation as a democracy can, given that innovation relies on free-flowing discussion and an open society (which autocracies do not have). Others are the result of China shooting itself in the foot. Under Xi's 'common prosperity' drive, Beijing has cracked down not only on the technology and real estate sectors, but also on education and entertainment, as well as on purported societal problems like 'effeminate' men. This spectre of state control has undermined and will continue to undermine China's ability to reap the benefits of massive investments in human capital.

China faces other structural issues, too. Income and regional inequality are growing. Environmental degradation is worsening. And the country has in recent years faced domestic shortages of raw materials, agricultural production and energy resources.[28] Perhaps most worryingly for Beijing, China is facing a population decline of nearly 50 per cent by 2100, fuelled by the previous 'one-child' policy and a falling birth rate (which China cannot rectify with immigration as democracies across the West can).[29]

But the struggles of autocracies must not induce complacency in the democratic world. While autocracies have many problems, they also have advantages – chief among them being a government willing to spend massive amounts of money to strengthen their workforces, and to fund the development of technologies like semiconductors, robotics, 5G telecommunications and biotechnology.

Americans, Brits, Japanese and other democratic citizens will not simply continue dominating these spaces because they have for years. To do so, our governments need to make serious reforms and investments. Failure will result in economic pain and the weakening of our democratic system's legitimacy, both at home and abroad.

It's not just about spending money. It's about spending that money well, not to satisfy individual politicians' concerns or line their pockets, but to uplift the citizenry and create the next generation of innovators. It is people, educated, analytical, creative, who will man the most vital lines of defence in our battle with the would-be dictators at home and the actual dictators abroad.

* * *

Investing in Democracy

Throughout history, it is rich countries that have reached the future first, the Irish journalist Eamonn Fingleton has written.[30] It is these countries that spent the most money on human capital, even if that concept didn't exist yet, and produced many of the innovations on which their world was built.

The ancient Mesopotamians invented simple things like the wheel, writing and bricks.[31] Ancient Egypt invented paper and coloured ink; ancient China created the concept of a meritocratic civil service exam.[32] None of these societies was anywhere near democratic, but they nonetheless produced innovations that decided for centuries what the world would look like. These authoritarian countries led everyone else into the future they designed.

For the last hundred years or so, democracies have been at the forefront of innovation because they've spent the most on human capital. The United States and its partners simply spent enough money to create the best schools and invest more in R&D. In turn, people in democracies produced cutting-edge innovations: everything from the Google search engine to modern aircraft carriers. These innovations made the lives of democratic citizens better, which boosted faith in democracy at home and abroad; they also made democracies more practically powerful abroad.

But democratic spending on these fronts has stagnated, and in some cases declined. Such complacency has helped usher in our current moment of instability – a moment when autocracies, namely China, are spending ever more on human capital development and are producing innovations that increasingly rival ours. No wonder commentators and lawmakers around the democratic world fear that it is China and its partners who will set the trends for the future and establish the rules to its road.[33]

The fifth-generation mobile network, 5G, is a perfect example. It operates at a faster speed, which not only boosts the speed of commerce but has national security implications, too.[34] The previous transition, from 3G to 4G, enabled mobile computing that was previously thought impossible, allowing for the creation of applications like Google Maps and Uber, which were birthed in democracies.[35] 5G will similarly enable not only trivial advances, like quicker movie downloads, but improved military intelligence, surveillance and reconnaissance systems.[36]

Whether competition with autocracies is peaceful or violent, developing technology like 5G is clearly key to victory – to advancing our economic growth, our military capacity, our power abroad and the attractiveness of our democratic model.

But we're being outraced.

The Chinese government has already spent USD 50 billion to expand its 5G network and plans to spend another USD 150 billion by 2025.[37] By way of comparison, in 2022 the US Department of Defense spent only around USD 600 million on the technology.[38] And while Congressional leaders recently passed a bill to better compete with China on this front, that legislation authorised less than USD 1.5 billion for 5G networks.[39]

We're largely being outperformed, too.

South Korea and Norway may have the world's two fastest 5G systems – at over 400 megabits per second – but many of the next top performers include autocracies like Saudi Arabia, the United Arab Emirates, Kuwait, Thailand and China.[40] US, British and German 5G download speeds are slower than in all those countries. A Chinese 5G user in Beijing or Shanghai can download a file about three times as quickly as an American in New York or Los Angeles.[41] China also offers 5G in more cities than any other country – and at a much higher speed than the United States, its only close competitor in terms of coverage.[42]

China's advancement has sped up commerce at home, boosting the country's economy. It has allowed Beijing to advance geopolitical goals. China controls around 30 per cent of the world's 5G infrastructure and has sold such technology to countries like Russia, Saudi Arabia and South Africa, all of which are already using it to deliver 5G services.[43] No US firms sell 5G infrastructure abroad.

Certain democracies and other US partners have refused to use Chinese 5G, citing security concerns. But China is winning the global 5G race, particularly in the developing world, the majority of which remains run by authoritarians. Globally, autocracies outnumber democracies; the number of people willing to use Chinese 5G thus far outpaces those prone to boycott it.

The ramifications of losing the 5G race are hard to understate. Not only could China use its 5G carriers to spy on users, but by controlling most of this technology worldwide, Beijing will essentially be able to set its standards in its favour, without any regard for privacy or human rights. China could also use 5G to speed ahead in advances like artificial intelligence and self-driving cars.[44] A 2018 US National Security Council memo put it simply, stating that China 'has achieved a dominant position in the manufacture and operation of network infrastructure' and that the United States is 'losing'. Chinese domination of 5G, the report added, will see China 'win politically, economically, and militarily'.[45]

* * *

5G is not the only front on which we're falling behind thanks to our under-investment in human capital.

China now produces somewhere around 22 per cent of the world's advanced technology – a staggering increase from just 4 per cent in 1995. The United States, by way of comparison, has in that period seen its market share fall from 24 per cent to just around 22.5 per cent. Industry players now warn that Beijing is threatening Washington's competitive advantage. The more ground China gains in these industries, the more the United States and its partners will lose.[46]

Data now suggests that by 2030 China will outpace the United States in producing semiconductors.[47] Without these chips, our world will cease to function.

These projections seem dire. But democracies have not yet lost the race. It is not too late for democracies to double down and invest in the human capital – the scientists, manufacturers and others

– who make 5G and semiconductor innovation possible. It is not too late for democracies to strengthen themselves and their model by investing in our people. China, Singapore and the Gulf States' ramping up of their own investment on these and other fronts should be motivation enough.

It is long past time that we make human capital a national priority and invest in ourselves – in democracy and in all we have to offer.

* * *

The Age of American Innovation

Samuel was the fifth son in a British farming family of eight. He came of age in the late 1770s, a period when England was at war with colonial America – and, remarkably, lost.

When Samuel Slater's father died, his life forever changed. Slater's family, unable to make ends meet, indentured him to Jedediah Strutt, who ran the Derbyshire cotton mill. Strutt trained his apprentice well. By twenty-one, Slater knew the ins and outs of cotton-spinning. He began to realise that he could use his knowledge to make money, not necessarily at home, but in the New World. In 1789, having memorised all he could, he departed for New York.

Around the same time, the American industrialist Moses Brown, along with his son-in-law and cousin, had purchased an Arkwright water frame – the same one that Slater had mastered back in Derbyshire. But the Americans did not know how to use it.

Slater did.

He knew that for the frame to work, workers had to consider the variance of fibre lengths. He understood, too, how to operate Arkwright's other machines. Sensing an opportunity for someone with his specific skills – someone with his specific human capital

– he reached out. He wrote to them, promising to make the Arkwright work, saying: 'If I do not make a good yarn [. . .] I will have nothing for my services but will throw the whole of what I have attempted over the bridge.'[48]

By 1790, Brown had signed Slater to a contract, with the Englishman promising to produce English-style designs using technology that seemingly nobody else on that side of the Atlantic could operate. Slater also adjusted the British technology, better fitting it to American needs. By December, their shop was operational; by 1791 it was profitable. And in 1793, the pair opened North America's first water-powered cotton-spinning mill, in Pawtucket, Rhode Island.

Slater, thinking bigger and bolder, began instructing his workers, teaching them to become skilled mechanics. He would eventually own over a dozen mills in Rhode Island, Connecticut, Massachusetts and New Hampshire, around which he developed tenant farms and company towns. All the while, more and more people followed Slater's lead, building their own mills. Other, even bolder thinkers, such as Francis Cabot Lowell, traded duplication for innovation, improving upon Slater's factory system to make it more productive, and more profitable.

Slater's story marks the unlikely beginning of the American industrial revolution. It was the beginning, too, of a new era of human capital development: the Fourth Industrial Revolution, known as Industry 4.0.[49]

This new chapter is the one in which economies shifted from being resource-based to production-based. No longer did people simply eat what they produced and sold the rest, but they went to work in factories, where they used their hands and brains to make things. These products sped up human exchange and gave rise to contemporary capitalism, in which people specialise in what they are best at and purchase other necessities. No longer did everyone have to grow their own food to survive. Instead, they worked for someone or for a company, specialised in a few skills, and helped produce ever more efficient technology, including fuel engines, light-bulbs and the telegraph.

This was the beginning of the age of human capital – the age in which people are valued for what they can produce not only in their own homes and on their own land, but in concert with others, and for their knowledge as well. It was this age in which democracy flourished and spread around the world, because with human capital came wealth, and with wealth – at least in some places – came the legitimacy needed to establish and maintain democracy.

This is precisely what happened after the Second World War in Japan, where the US-backed government invested huge amounts of money in education, ultimately fuelling unprecedented economic growth that did not rely on cheap labour or abundant natural resources, of which Japan has none. Instead, armed with US funds, Japan invested in its people: in building the human capital needed to compete in an ever-more-connected world. Successive Japanese governments turned their people into a resource. 'It is education,' wrote the Japanese scholar Ryōji Itō, 'that plays the leading role in improving the quality of man.'[50]

Japan's story is a tried and true one of human capital achievements fuelling economic growth. Just as Slater's mill-spinners became the backbone of American growth, so too did Japan's electronics producers.

Similar stories have played out around the world.

From the early 1960s to the late 1990s, Asian economies like Singapore, South Korea and Hong Kong invested heavily, creating well-educated and skilled labour forces, which fuelled rising incomes and even greater growth.[51] These three countries, and Japan, are today among the best at mobilising their citizens' potential.[52] They are now some of the world's most advanced economies, while two of them (Japan and South Korea) are leading democracies – which is remarkable in the grand scheme of history, given that many observers in the 1960s believed them to have less potential than many other developing economies.[53]

But their stories are not particularly exceptional.

Vietnam, whose economy has grown at a faster rate than any of its neighbours for years, ranks in the top forty globally for human capital – and has relied on its skilled labourers to win high-tech manufacturing jobs from companies like Apple that are relocating from China.[54] Even Bangladesh and Sri Lanka, countries further down the economic development scale, continue to make progress; they saw their economies grow by 21 and 16 per cent, respectively, from 1981 to 2010 because of human capital development.[55]

None of this should come as a surprise. We know that improving a country's human capital is one of the most important factors, if not the key factor, to its economic growth.[56] We know that the increased duration of schooling by one year leads to an estimated 6 per cent increase in GDP per capita.[57] We know that better human capital leads to both increased production and innovation – both of which fuel economic growth, and accordingly better allow countries to compete with their foreign adversaries.[58]

We know, too, that countries do and will fall behind and lose the trust of their people if they do not invest in their people. And we know that in a democracy, losing trust will mean the loss of legitimacy – which will mean the decline of democracy at home and the weakening of our system's attractiveness abroad.

Yet democracies are not doing enough. Canada, Norway, Spain, the United Kingdom and several other rich democracies invest less than 2 per cent of their GDP in research and development.[59] Russia spends more on R&D by this measure than does India. Singapore spends nearly twice as much as do Spain and Italy.[60] And while it is democracies – like Israel, Japan and South Korea – that still spend the most, the trend is broadly in the wrong direction; too many democracies are stagnating.[61]

Australia, Canada, New Zealand and the United Kingdom's per capita R&D spending has barely increased since 1996.[62] All of these countries spend less today than do China and Singapore.[63] New Zealand's spending hovers today around a meagre 1.4 per cent of GDP. Wellington spends less today than both Beijing and Singapore – not to mention less than Abu Dhabi.[64] India has essentially not increased its R&D spending since 1996 and today spends less than each of these autocracies.[65] Yet even New Zealand's limited R&D spending more than doubles that of India.

Since 2011, on the other hand, the United Arab Emirates has just about tripled such spending.[66] Over the last two decades or so, China has almost doubled its per capita R&D spending, also becoming the second-largest spender on R&D in raw terms, behind only the United States. And while the United States focuses much of its spending on applied and basic research, China spends upwards of 80 per cent on experimental research.[67]

The competition is for the future; Beijing and the world's most powerful autocracies are acting like it. These investments seem to be paying off.[68]

In 2021, the World Intellectual Property Organization ranked China fourth in its Knowledge and Technology outputs – just one spot behind the United States.[69] In that same year, it was Chinese scholars, not Americans (as was previously the norm), who published most of the world's peer-reviewed papers.[70] American articles have for years been of a higher quality, comprising most of the world's most-cited articles; in 2019, Chinese research ranked as about high – and maybe higher – than US scientific studies.[71]

R&D spending is not the full equation. That measure does not account for spending on higher education. But China is directing billions towards education, too, particularly when it comes to science and technology.[72]

Since 2000, China has increased its education spending as a percentage of GDP by some 75 per cent.[73] The country today spends some 3.5 per cent of its GDP on education, about the same as the United States – and more than democracies like Austria, Germany, Italy and even Japan.[74] Data shows that China spends around the same amount (a little more, by some measures) of its GDP on education as does the average OECD country.[75]

Education spending is an imperfect measure because spending does not always correlate to increased performance, as in the United States, where high spending has not produced better students. But China's performance *is* improving.

In 2000, US universities awarded twice as many STEM (Science, Technology, Engineering and Mathematics) doctorates (18,829) than Chinese universities did (9,038). By 2010, China had more STEM doctorates. Over the last decade or so, China has widened the gap – so much so that in 2019, Chinese universities produced 49,498 PhDs in STEM fields, while US universities produced 33,759. Projections suggest that by 2025, China will annually produce nearly twice as many STEM PhD graduates as those in the United States.[76]

This gap is evident at a more basic level as well: children.

The OECD's Programme for International Student Assessment, which measures fifteen-year-olds' abilities, reported in 2018 that Chinese students had the highest average score in each of maths, science and reading, followed by Singapore, Macao and Hong Kong – none of which is a democracy and the last two of which are under China's control.[77] Even Russian students, who are not exactly considered top global performers, posted better average scores across these three measures than did their democratic counterparts in Lithuania, Italy, Croatia, Chile and Uruguay.[78]

It is worth noting, too, that the OECD also oddly excluded authoritarian Vietnam because its students performed inconceivably well given the country's relatively low level of economic development, saying: 'Vietnam cannot be validly reported on the same PISA scale as performance in other countries'. But the results were largely consistent with Vietnam's strong performance at the international maths-science Olympiad, suggesting that Vietnam is doing something right as well.[79]

These results should concern us. They make plain that even if many democratic governments spend more on education in both raw and per capita terms than autocracies do, something has gone awry. It should be apparent that our systems are not working as well as they should – and that this decline has fed distrust in our governments and our system of government itself, offering an opportunity to wannabe autocrats at home and for existing dictators abroad. It should be apparent, too, that our self-confidence, our foolhardy belief in democracy's everlasting victory, has left us complacent at a moment when our rivals are not only investing more, but performing better, too.

The good news is that democracies are armed with the knowledge to design the future we want. We know how to build human capital, and build it back better. We just need to get our act together.

* * *

Asleep at the Wheel

American ingenuity like that of Samuel Slater has driven the global economy for the better part of the last two hundred and fifty years. Thomas Edison created the lightbulb. Alexander Graham Bell created the cell phone's predecessor before 1900.[80] Johnson & Johnson created the world's first modern disposable contact lens. Americans created the stealth bomber plane, Wi-Fi, the iPhone and some of the most effective COVID-19 vaccines.

It is impossible to imagine what our world would look like today without American ingenuity. It is frightening to imagine what our world will look like tomorrow without it. Innovation – particularly American innovation – is an engine of economic growth every-where; it is also a means for addressing problems of both today and tomorrow.[81]

But where does innovation come from? Is innovation simply the result of the American spirit? Or is there something in US institutions that fuels innovation?

The answer is some combination of all the above. American culture tolerates a unique combination of risk, failure and seemingly crazy ideas. The American drive for innovation is, it seems, directly tied to the country's frontier-conquering past: Americans, more than other people, don't just look at the horizon but look beyond it – we look for ways to seize whatever the newest frontier might be and make it ours.[82]

This is not to say that Americans are the only people who can innovate. Democracies from Sweden to South Korea and beyond innovate across a range of fields.[83] And they do so at a higher rate than autocracies – even if the autocrats are catching up.

But America has long been exceptional on the innovation front, even if that is somewhat less the case than it was in the nineteenth and twentieth centuries.[84] Both then and today, a unique combination of our culture, laws and general approach to business has fuelled the American drive to innovate. There is a reason why the United States, despite having just 5 per cent of the global population, has produced almost 50 per cent of Nobel laureates in the sciences (chemistry, physics, medicine and economics) over the last hundred years and over 70 per cent of those in economics.[85]

Democracies around the world will not be able to exactly

replicate the American spirit on this front. Nor should they necessarily try; every country is different – every country has different histories, presents and futures. They will need to find a path forward that works for them. But there are some shared lessons that democrats can take from both the American and other models if they want to continue producing the world's best innovations – that is, if democracies want to own the future.

* * *

To our advantage, acting on these ambitions is far more difficult without democracy. Without freedom, there is no way for people to challenge existing limits; respect for the individual – the most vital principle of liberalism – is key to innovation. And liberalism, coupled with something unique in the American spirit, has produced unprecedented levels of innovation.

But adequate credit must be given to something else, too: money.

America's truly innovative period didn't start until the mid-twentieth century. In the 1930s, the United States was little more than an adopter of foreign technology, as Samuel Slater and his colleagues had been.[86]

The Second World War changed this. Facing an existential threat in the Axis, the US government allocated huge sums of money to corporations, explicitly encouraging them to spend more and more on research and development. And when American veterans returned home, the government – through the G.I. Bill – granted them scholarships, allowing them to attend colleges and acquire skills that they never would have had otherwise. Some eight million Americans took advantage.[87]

The result? A whole host of leaders, from President Gerald Ford to civil rights activist Medgar Evers to Jerome Kohlberg, who founded KKR – a company that revolutionised the financial investment industry.[88] 'The GIs were appreciated, and more than that, the country realised that education was important to the country,' Kohlberg said later. 'And that education paid for itself ten-fold, if not more.'[89]

Just over a decade later, Washington found itself facing another existential challenge in the communist Soviet Union. Moscow was seemingly racing ahead of Washington, as evidenced most plainly by its 1957 launch of the Sputnik satellite.

But the United States was not simply going to sit back and let the Soviets surpass us. Soon after Sputnik took flight, President Dwight Eisenhower promised to spend USD 5.2 billion (USD 53 billion in 2022 dollars) on missile research alone.[90] This was not enough; Congress would later insist on even more money, which Washington used to create NASA, and to pass the 1958 National Defense Education Act to subsidise science, technology, engineering and maths education. That legislation alone pumped one billion US dollars (USD 10 billion in 2022 dollars) into grants and scholarships.[91]

Sputnik also spurred Eisenhower to invest in R&D by spending big on agencies including the Defense Advanced Research Projects Agency (DARPA). DARPA funding would help innovators create technologies like the internet, Global Positioning Systems (GPS) and the virtual assistants that would become Siri – all of which not only made life easier and economic exchange more seamless, but also made America more powerful.[92]

These efforts were huge human capital investments, even if policymakers weren't using that term. Such spending evinced Washington's awareness that beating the Soviets required America to develop the skills and knowledge it needed to own the future. Which it did: US human capital investment played a substantial role in democracy's defeat of the Soviet dictators and their allies.

Yet the funding surge did not last.

In 1964, federal spending accounted for nearly 70 per cent of total R&D funding.[93] By 1975, that number had dropped to just about 50 per cent.[94] By 1999, it was down to under 30 per cent.[95] Today, federal spending accounts for only about 20 per cent of all R&D funding.[96]

Spending as a percentage of GDP paints a clearer picture. In 1965, US R&D spending comprised around 2 per cent of GDP. Today, it is only around 0.5 per cent.[97]

What happened?

First, America's apparent victory in the space race and its eventual defeat in Vietnam altered Washington's priorities. Politicians focused on other, more politically salient areas; the 1970s' oil crisis further hampered the US economy, prompting the government to tighten its belt. And ironically, once the Cold War ended – with the West coming out on top, thanks in no small part to these US human capital investments – politicians wrongly deemed such investment a waste of taxpayer funds.[98] The emergence of a new crop of politicians who believed that the private sector and free markets must, without government assistance, be the principal drivers of innovation did not help matters. (Of course, these politicians rode discontent into power – discontent that would not have existed if American democracy was delivering for all.)

Without such investment, US human capital performance has plummeted: US human capital today ranks in the mid-thirties globally, trailing countries like Latvia, Lithuania, Iceland and Poland.[99] Americans' trust in the US government and democracy generally has fallen alongside the United States' decline in these rankings.

When any country's human capital declines, so too does its ability to innovate. Which is part of the reason why US innovations have in recent years been limited to certain fields like information technology and finance; no longer is our inventive spirit leading the world across the board.[100] And it is not only Americans who will suffer.

* * *

Democratic leaders may be confident in their societies' innovative capabilities, but throughout history it is not only or even mainly democracies that have produced innovations – but rich countries, democratic and authoritarian alike.[101]

Certainly, democracies have an advantage. But history suggests that China, Singapore and the UAE very well could emerge to produce at least some meaningful innovations. They could even surpass the United States and its democratic partners if we don't act. China has already produced many meaningful innovations; democrats should not be so naïve as to assume that autocracies will not innovate more heavily than the United States and its partners over the next fifty years.

Relatively rich autocracies seem to have an advantage because they can throw money at the wall of human capital and hope that something will stick. Whereas politicians in Washington and Westminster haggle over government funding, leaders in Beijing, Riyadh and Singapore can simply direct money where they believe it needs to go – whether that be R&D or science and technology education. If autocracies get richer, they could very well begin to have levels of human capital surpassing those in democracies.

Some already have. Singapore is already ranked the best country in the world in terms of human capital development.[102]

How does Singapore do it? Unsurprisingly, again, the answer is education – not just basic education for children and young adults, but a comprehensive system that supports skill development for workers across key industries.[103] The government plans to spend even more money on education, with annual expenditures set to soon reach over S$1 billion (around USD 730 million).[104]

The leaders of the tiny city-state understand that without a high level of human capital, both the state and the government are doomed. This is true, too, of a whole host of governments of small countries, such as Bahrain and the UAE, which are investing ever more in human capital, particularly related to technology.[105]

Such spending is wise, not only for economic growth but also for regime strength. History shows that human capital investment helps autocratic governments stay in power.[106] Such investment boosts people's skills, allowing them to achieve more in life and become richer. This wealth essentially satiates their yearning for freedom, at least for a period.

Money can be a hell of a drug – one that can, in a certain time and place, dull one's desire for more freedom, more democracy, whatever. Singapore's huge investment in human capital is therefore as much aspirational as it is self-preservational.

So, too, is China's human capital spending. Beijing believes such investment will not only fuel economic growth at home, thereby boosting the Communist Party's grip on power, but also aid Chinese geopolitical goals abroad.

These investments are already paying off. The quantity and quality of science and technology graduates in China is rapidly rising.[107] Armed with these graduates, the Chinese government funnels huge funds of money to the development of technologies like semiconductors and robotics.[108] The government leaves many rural Chinese behind, but China's investments have produced great human capital gains, and can equally clearly continue to produce many more.[109] As the American journalist Rebecca Fannin writes, Beijing 'is creating a tech universe that is a counterweight to the long dominance of the United States'.[110]

Of the world's top fifty most innovative companies, China now claims seven.[111] China is today the world's eleventh most innovative country, ahead of democracies like Japan, Canada and Australia.[112]

China's performance is particularly striking given that the country still ranks just seventy-seventh globally in GDP per capita.[113] That means that China – which is effectively still a middle-income country in terms of GDP per capita, being poorer on this front than Guyana, Belarus, Kazakhstan and even American Samoa – has nonetheless turned itself into one of the world's leading innovators.[114] Beijing has done this by spending substantially on human capital. There is every reason to assume that China will only spend more, and have more success on this front, if it can continue getting richer.

Still, China faces huge problems on this and other initiatives – problems that show why autocracy itself is not prone to produce better governance than does democracy. Some of China's companies and sectors are extremely innovative, but most are not. Some people are highly educated and reaping the rewards, but most are not. And while some Chinese science and technology graduates want to serve the Communist Party, many, if not most of them, want to leave and emigrate to bastions of freedom in the West.

The smartest people, the ones more likely to innovate, are often the most curious. Curiosity cannot be sustained within the strictest of autocracies, which China under President and Communist Party General Secretary Xi Jinping increasingly appears to be. Reaping the true rewards of human capital investment does, still, require more freedom than China offers. It is no small thing that democracies have that going for us.

* * *

Taking Action

Democracies and autocracies alike are facing an uncertain future. With more automation, more workers will find themselves without jobs. Climate change will drive further disruptions, with hurricanes and pandemics breaking the flow of normal life. The overall shift in labour market dynamics has left and will leave many workers in precarious positions. Unlike a generation ago, when many employees worked at the same company for their entire career, workers today are expected to jump around – something that young people like, but that middle-aged workers find disorienting.

Countries everywhere will need populations with the skills, knowledge and experience to handle this increasingly digital and uncertain world.[115] If democracies intend to own the future, they will need to continue producing economic growth and ensuring that the benefits reach their people. Neglecting human capital will lead to stagnant growth, which will produce unrest at home; this unrest will see populist would-be autocrats gain more political power.

If we are beset by unrest at home and cannot offer other countries a path to prosperity, democracy will no longer be a model. The authoritarian capitalism of China or Singapore will instead become preferable.

Which means, put bluntly, that democracies will have to spend money to win the human capital race. But unlike autocracies, democracies do not have the capability – or political space – to throw money at the wall. We cannot rashly spend money on ineffective projects, and then expect taxpayers to fork over more of their hard-earned cash. Democracy cannot, does not and should not work that way. With the right leaders, this seeming hindrance to investment actually *benefits* democracies by curbing wasteful spending. Billions spent on failed efforts will weaken people's faith in that government and drive the officials responsible out of office.

Leaders understand that and do generally look to invest well. Democracy does protect better against waste.

In our troubling moment, democratic voters are particularly attuned to any signs of government waste. Voters want to see improvement in the short-term; politicians need citizens to see such improvements, or voters will stop putting in power those who demand their money. This means that democracies should spend carefully on specific, proven programmes with a high potential of success, rather than on ambitious over-the-horizon projects. Big, flashy plans are nice, but substantive, relatively uncontroversial investments are better.

Such investments will come in different forms in different democracies, but I have a few suggestions.

First, democracies must offer more undergraduate and graduate scholarships for students seeking to develop skills critical to future innovation, namely in science and technology. If someone has evident talent, with the marks to prove it, they should be able to study for an engineering or mathematics PhD without worrying about the cost.

Too often, though, degrees are reserved for the rich – for those who can, essentially, afford to not make money during the prime money-making years of their lives.[116] Expecting people to study for degrees that, at worst, cost tens of thousands of dollars or, at best, allow one to just about break even is fundamentally unreasonable. I know more than a few extremely bright people around the democratic world who passed up on – or gave up on – pursuing such studies because they could not afford them.[117] This fact alone shows that democratic governments don't seem to take human capital development seriously.

So, too, does our limited investment in vocational and trade schools, which remain under-supported, even as Europe, the United States, Japan and South Korea experience skill shortages.[118] We simply do not have the people needed to fill the blue-collar jobs that make our economy function.[119]

Institutions like the US Bureau of Labor Statistics believe that blue-collar occupations – like wind turbine service technicians and solar panel installers – will comprise a growing number of US job openings through 2030.[120] Yet in democracies everywhere, people are incentivised to seek a BA or BSc rather than a degree that would give them more practical skills. We need more people willing to build our phones and laptops, rather than those whose jobs rely on them. We need more semiconductor factory workers than we do brand managers. And we should be increasingly funding and prioritising the schools – vocational and trade institutions – that will allow people to fill these roles, make meaningful money and live good lives in the process.

Despite what you might hear in our capital cities, many people are already clamouring for these types of schools. Studies show that people across Europe would prefer increased funding for vocational education than for higher education and early childhood education.[121] Americans are more open to vocational education, too.[122] (Japanese and South Koreans are generally less open to it for a variety of cultural reasons, but that does not change the reality of the labour crisis they're facing.)

Shifting to vocational education is about funding, but it is about culture, too. Educators across the democratic world need to highlight the benefits of vocational education for students for whom it might be the right option. And parents will need to make clear to their children that becoming a solar panel installer is not an embarrassing career choice, but a smart one. Restoring the functionality of our vocational schools is just as important as restoring the virtues of working with your hands.

* * *

Second, democracies should learn from Singapore to provide constant skills training for all workers. The need is obvious, given that most workers will require some type of education or skills training beyond high school.[123]

In Singapore, the government takes a minuscule amount of company money – no more than S$11.25 (about USD 8.13) per employee per month – and turns it into financing for employee training. Employers can access these funds by claiming some 90 per cent of the subsidy for their employees' skill development. Employers are therefore financially incentivised to send their employees to these training programmes, because this is the only way they can secure at least some benefit from the levy they have no choice but to pay.[124]

The government created this mechanism in 1979 and has revised it since, specifically because employers were not spending enough money on training, leaving policymakers worried that the country's workforce would fall behind.[125] This mechanism has been successful, particularly in improving the human capital of small- and medium-sized enterprises, which generally invest less in skill development than larger firms due to financial limitations.[126]

The mechanism helped Singapore vastly improve its skills within a single generation.[127] With improved skill comes an improved economy, more tangible power and a more attractive system abroad.

Implementing something like this in our democracies may seem like a pipedream, but there are some promising, if convoluted, examples. Local governments from Ontario, Canada, to Texas in the United States offer various forms of skill development. But accessing them requires folks to fill out complicated applications – an onerous, time-consuming business that people in need of skill development probably won't do.[128] Whereas Singapore's system incentivises constant re-training, many of those in democracies incentivise inaction.

The process must be simpler.

There are some positive movements on this front, too. Some local governments offer businesses tax incentives for training investments, including a few US states.[129] But data suggests a steady decline in the amount US employers are investing in their workforce.[130] This is in large part because employers expect their workers to leave in short order – given new labour market dynamics – and are accordingly less willing to invest in their development.[131]

There is a clear gap, then, between governmental goals for human capital development and the private sector's interest in profits. So, whether democracies choose to impose a Singapore-type levy or offer companies that invest in building their human capital some kind of tax break (like the popular US R&D tax credit), our governments must take the first step instead of expecting the private sector to act. Building human capital is often not always an executive's long-term priority, let alone a short-term one in our world of pandemics and supply chain disruptions.[132]

Industry can make a huge positive difference, but it may need a push – or a hand – from its government.

* * *

Third, democratic governments should support the innovative, human capital-focused companies that the political scientist (and my former colleague) Ian Bremmer has called 'national champions'.[133]

These are companies willing not only to invest in their workforce and the future, but also to align themselves with the priorities of their home governments, whether they be in Beijing or Brussels. Yet while China compels companies like Huawei or Tencent to back Beijing's priorities, firms in the United States and other democracies gravitate towards the model for financial reasons. They believe that aligning with their governments, and supporting their practical and values-based priorities, not only fulfils some patriotic duty but also promises better balance sheets. This is why Microsoft is willing to increasingly police the digital space on behalf of the United States and allied democracies, and even to provide cloud-computing infrastructure to the US government (and why Amazon is also offering the US government this infrastructure[134]).

Washington, to its credit, is already directing huge sums of money to companies willing to train and hire workers to produce semiconductors in the United States.[135] In August 2022, President Biden signed into law a landmark legislation that will see the United States invest USD 52 billion in semiconductor production alone.

This is a good and important start. But US and allied discussions about human capital investment generally reflect a somewhat limited sense of what we consider national goals.

Semiconductor production is such an obvious one because these chips literally make our world work. But as the world becomes more complicated, democracies would be wise to expand this definition to include information-sharing platforms prone to spreading disinformation or those developing artificial intelligence innovations with possible military usages.

The point here is simple. Our democracies have free markets. Our governments cannot require companies to further national goals by investing in human capital. Nor should we. But we should incentivise such alignment, and reward those who do – because their investments strengthen our economies, our democracies at home and our system abroad.

And we should be willing to expand the definition of 'national' if a company in, say, Japan or South Korea is working on cutting-edge technology, wants US or European funds to hire and train more workers (ideally from the potential investing nation), and can ensure that such technology will not go to adversaries. In such a case, Washington and Brussels should consider providing them with funds.

The United States has already done this with regard to semiconductors. The aforementioned legislation will provide aligned semiconductor companies – American ones, but also foreign ones like Taiwan's TSMC and South Korea's Samsung – with significant subsidies as long as they restrict their investment in adversarial nations like China.

This approach reflects the growing American understanding of the need to support not only 'national champions', but firms that are better described as 'champions of democracy': companies more interested in aligning broadly with countries committed to the liberal order than with any one country. Democracies everywhere should reward such decisions in the name of human capital development.

∗ ∗ ∗

Fourth, democracies around the world should look to recruit more foreign talent.

Following years of rising anti-immigration sentiment and COVID-19-related border closures, foreign enrolments in democratic countries' science and technology programmes have fallen.[136] This is true particularly in the United States and Europe, which remain more attractive destinations for foreign students than Japan and South Korea (whose best students still often want to go to the West).[137]

The human capital benefits of migration are apparent. Immigrants founded top US companies like Google, Intel and Pfizer. First- or second-generation immigrants founded nearly half of all Fortune 500 companies.[138] It was a German-based couple – the husband being Turkish, the wife being the daughter of Turkish immigrants – who created the German company BioNTech, that teamed up with Pfizer to produce extremely effective COVID-19 vaccines.[139] There is a clear correlation between the migration of highly skilled individuals and innovation, including the development of more 'complex technologies', in the countries that host them.[140]

Democracies today should open their arms to skilled immigrants, particularly those working in science and technology – and those interested in trading their autocratic passport for a democratic one. We should be looking to attract Chinese scientists who are highly educated but uninterested in serving the Communist Party's goals. The same goes for dissident scientists from countries like Russia and Saudi Arabia.

Accepting them is not only the right thing to do morally, it is vital from a strategic perspective, too. It is hard to overstate the soft power victory democracies can quietly declare when autocracies' best and brightest flee their countries – even as their leaders proclaim the West's downfall – for our democratic shores, messy as we may be.

* * *

Democracies remain ahead in the human capital race. And we retain an advantage that autocracies do not have: transparent legal systems, intellectual property protections and liquid capital markets.

Autocracies, even the best of them, cannot provide this. One-party states imply the ever-present hand of government, which hangs over industry like a guillotine, leading many firms and people in these countries to avoid risk – the same risk that produces cutting-edge technology – for fear of retribution. This is not a conducive environment for innovation.

For all of democracy's struggles, we still have and can strengthen the systems that China and other autocracies cannot. By doing so, we can ensure that we make the most of our investments in human capital, that these investments boost our economy and strengthen our democracy systems both within our borders and beyond – that we stride even further ahead of the autocracies looking to chase us down.[141]

We can win the race. We *must* win the race. To do so, our leaders need to invest in the people who make innovation possible – they'll need, that is, to invest in us.

7

Infrastructure

Less than fifty years ago, Shenzhen was nothing more than a tiny village of a few thousand. Most residents were fishermen, relying on China's pristine Pearl River Delta to make a living; they pulled as many catfish and perch out of its waters as they could every day. The more fish they caught, the better their families would be fed.

Shenzhen is less than fifteen miles from the glittering towers of Hong Kong, but until the 1980s it might as well have been a world away. While much of Shenzhen relied on subsistence fishing to survive, Hong Kongers made their names as players in an international business centre. Millions of dollars flowed in and out of the then-British city daily; Shenzhen had no modern economy of which to speak. In 1979, Shenzhen's total GDP was a mere 196 million yuan – less than USD 3 million.[1] In that same year, *The China Syndrome*, the Jane Fonda-led US movie about a nuclear accident in China, grossed over USD 35 million.[2] That means that a mediocre American film about China was worth over eleven times more than Shenzhen.

But Deng Xiaoping, China's first post-Mao leader, saw Shenzhen's potential. When he opened China to controlled capitalism and foreign investment, he looked to Shenzhen. He gave the city China's first Special Economic Zone.

These zones, better known as SEZs, were laboratories of capitalism, portals to the West: they were areas in which China attracted foreign capital by offering tax breaks, lighter regulations and, most importantly, cheap Chinese labour. In return, China received not only revenue but also the transfer of both technology and skills.

Deng opened the first SEZ, in Shenzhen, in 1979. Companies flocked there. In 1981, Pepsi-Cola became the first American corporation to set up production at the zone, producing 4.8 million cases of bottled and soft drinks a year.[3] Pepsi chose the city because of the SEZ – the 'abundant cheap land and labor', as the *New York Times* reported – but also because of the city's proximity to Hong Kong.[4]

Yet while money flowed from Hong Kong to Shenzhen, the road between the two consisted of little more than fields and small outposts patrolling the border.[5] Goods moved from one side of the border to the other only by dirt roads, on which peasants lugged all they could carry by truck or water buffalo.[6] Other Chinese roads to Hong Kong were similarly rudimentary. The roads from Canton (today Guangzhou) to Hong Kong were so primitive that industrial cargo could move only by rail, boat or air.[7] Shenzhen itself had barely any infrastructure.[8]

The two cities still seemed like worlds, or at least decades, apart. Hong Kong was the future; Shenzhen was the past.

Without adequate infrastructure, there could be no modern commerce in Shenzhen. And while China's leadership was still not quite attuned to capitalism's complexities and didn't necessarily understand or prioritise this issue, investors abroad did.

Gordon Wu, a Princeton-educated Hong Kong businessman, came up with the idea of a superhighway to connect Guangzhou with Shenzhen. He had huge investments in Guangdong Province, where Guangzhou is; he knew better than most the business that could happen with improved infrastructure. He could provide some funds for the highway, but he would need government support. The highway, he promised, would let people get from Guangzhou to Shenzhen (and vice versa) within an hour. It would take only ninety minutes to get from Guangzhou to Hong Kong. This would give people – and China – even more opportunities to get rich.[9]

China's leadership agreed.

By 1982, the government began planning the highway, which estimates said would cost around USD 400 million (nearly USD 1.2 billion today).[10] This was a huge investment for any country, not to mention what was still a lower-income one. But China's leaders had come to understand the vital role infrastructure would play in their country's continued development. They knew that to get rich, they had to lay the physical groundwork necessary for capitalism to take root.

Construction began in 1987 and was completed in 1993. The road became operational on 1 July 1997. As he promised, it did promote commerce; the road may have cost USD 1 billion, but it paved the way for billions more in commerce between Guangdong and cities like Shenzhen and Hong Kong in subsequent years.[11]

This road was just one of Shenzhen's steps into the future. As the city began to get wealthier, its officials learned the lesson of infrastructure's importance from building the road and began to invest more in large-scale development and construction. This investment fuelled urban development, which in turn fuelled economic growth. This growth attracted even more foreign investment, which officials then used to build roads and telecommunications at rapid speed.[12]

This positive cycle of development continued through the early 2000s. As Shenzhen became more modern, more connected with Hong Kong and the rest of the world, foreign investment came calling. Local labour followed, motivated by the opportunity to get their own hands on that money.[13]

The cycle made Guangdong Province governor, Huang Huahau, quite the man about town.

Upon becoming governor in 2003, Huang became someone with whom everybody – particularly foreigners – wanted a meeting. The province's rapid development had brought him inconceivably far from his earlier life, the one in which he spent eight years of his mid-twenties and early thirties mining coal. Thanks to his position in the new Guangdong, foreigners needed to know Huang if they wanted to invest in the rising cities of Shenzhen or Guangzhou.

As if to make that point obvious, Huang attracted a swathe of industry titans for a three-day business conference he hosted in 2003. Among the attendees were the chairman and chief executive of the American International Group, the chairman and chief executive of the Eastman Kodak Company and the chief financial officer of the BP Group.[14] It was an attendance list that 'a state governor in the United States could only dream of', as the *New York Times'* Keith Bradsher wrote.[15] It truly was quite the 'who's who' of foreigners looking to make money in China – and in cities like Shenzhen specifically. With Huang in power, the funds continued to pour in; international business was thrilled to take advantage of the region's developing infrastructure and workforce.

Armed with funds from this success, Shenzhen officials doubled down. They established a modern traffic network. They improved public facilities, bolstering sewage treatment and reducing ambient noise levels.[16] When Shenzhen had to adjust its approach in 2012 because of soaring land costs, the city pivoted to improve new infrastructure for emerging industries like biochemicals and internet-related sectors.[17] Shenzhen's high-tech industry then grew rapidly, as did the financial services sector. In tandem, and on the back of these necessary infrastructure investments, the city became a key link in the global supply chain. Logistics and e-commerce thrived.

The city has since moved only higher up the global supply chain, thanks to growing talent and investment in innovative institutions. Shenzhen has continued spending on infrastructure, building a smart city – one reliant on state-of-the-art information-sharing and big data systems.[18] Officials have also built an increasingly green city, one that conserves water and energy.[19]

In 2018, Shenzhen officially emerged from Hong Kong's shadow, surpassing the once-British city's GDP for the first time.[20]

Shenzhen's story is simple: officials made the city an attractive investment centre not only by offering tax breaks, but by laying the literal groundwork needed to facilitate commerce and attract talent.

Shenzhen is today the world's eighth most competitive city.[21] Its subway length is in the top ten internationally. The Shenzhen Port can handle around 25.2 million twenty-foot equivalent unit (TEU) containers per year, making it one of the world's largest ports, behind only Singapore, along with Shanghai and Ningbo – both of which are also in China.[22]

No city has grown more in the last forty years than Shenzhen, surpassing all other mega-cities by a wide margin.[23] It now has a population of at least 14 million – a 63,536 per cent growth from its pre-1979 total of around 22,000.

Shenzhen and surrounding Guangdong now produce most of the world's consumer appliances. The area is increasingly known as the 'Silicon Valley of China', hosting homegrown tech giants like Tencent.[24] This industry has given Shenzhen a GDP of somewhere around 2.7 trillion yuan, or USD 455 billion.[25] That makes Shenzhen – which many older millennials will remember as a tiny fishing village, if they remember its past at all – one of the world's twenty richest cities.[26] It is richer than each of Toronto, Taipei, Atlanta, Madrid, Munich, Sydney and Berlin.[27]

No wonder people increasingly speak of 'Shenzhen Speed' and the 'Shenzhen Miracle'.[28] The city seems to be moving towards the future at lightspeed, like Star Wars' *Millennium Falcon*, while its democratic counterparts remain firmly rooted in the present – or even the past.

* * *

Just about any American, Brit or German who travels to China returns with stories about the country's high-tech infrastructure.

Whenever I've spoken to a friend about their time in Beijing, Shanghai or Shenzhen, they regale me with stories about the country's high-speed railways, giant stadiums and sleek airports. They are captivated by just how well things seem to work, and by how advanced it all is. 'I spent a month in Shenzhen as a visiting professor,' one American academic wrote recently. 'It felt like I had travelled to the twenty-second century.'[29]

When these Westerners claim to have seen the twenty-second century in China, they come home wondering why their own countries are stuck resolutely in the twentieth. They wonder why Britain, or France, or the United States looks so outdated. Why have their own governments been so incapable of building what the Chinese have?[30]

On the other hand, any Chinese person visiting the West – the United States in particular – will tell you how shocked they are by declining infrastructure. Even European and Japanese visitors to the United States will tell you how floored they are that the richest country in the history of the world has such shoddy infrastructure. It's not just a perception; American infrastructure is genuinely among the worst in the developed world.[31]

Amtrak trains that travel about a hundred miles between Wilmington, Delaware and Washington take more than ninety minutes; it takes just sixty-five minutes to go around the same distance on a bullet train between Shanghai and Hangzhou.[32] The Amtrak train I've taken more times than I can count from Washington, DC to see family in New York City is more often delayed for one reason or another – whether heat or simple congestion – than it is not. Internet and cell phone services are stunningly poor in rural parts of the United States, and patchy even in urban areas. As made infamous by Flint, Michigan, some parts of the American drinking-water supply – again, in the richest country in history – contain dangerous levels of lead. And in August 2022, the water system in Jackson, Mississippi then failed, leaving people without water to flush their toilets or fight fires. The city even temporarily ran out of bottled water.[33]

Despite all of this, before Biden's 2022 bill, federal infrastructure investment was at the lowest level in forty years measured both relative to GDP and as a share of federal spending.[34]

Estimates now suggest that American households could lose out on as much as USD 3,300 annually from 2020 to 2039 if infrastructure is not revitalised.[35] Those losses will exacerbate stagnation and lead to a lower national growth trajectory – which will fuel further distrust in government and set the stage for populists, thereby weakening not only our democracy at home, but what remains of our democratic model abroad.[36]

As is a theme, this problem is anything but unique to the United States.

Outdated, energy-inefficient infrastructure is costing British households around GBP 500 per year (USD 585) and forcing small- and medium-sized businesses to pay an extra 18–25 per cent in energy costs.[37] Germany's 'creaking' infrastructure – the result of the government spending less as a percentage of GDP on infrastructure for years than just about any major economy – has forced closures of motorways, railways and even canals, all of which impedes commerce and slows economic growth.[38] Existing Australian infrastructure cannot account for population growth in the country's major cities; the cost of road congestion is on track to rise to some AUS 38 billion (USD 26 billion) by 2031.[39] Public transport crowding could increase fivefold by 2034, costing more than AUS 800 million (USD 558 million) a year.[40]

These numbers will stack up. Under-investing in infrastructure will eventually cost households and businesses – and governments – everywhere. Disruptions will reduce efficiency and slow economic growth in the long term. Necessary emergency repairs will do the same, also requiring vast expenditures. The result will be frustration with democracy, which will inevitably see the self-destructive rise of populists and would-be dictators around the world.

It would be one thing if this spending was wasteful and would never pay itself back in future benefits. But the World Bank has found that OECD member countries would save money in the long-term by repairing their own infrastructure: every one US dollar spent on road maintenance is just as effective as USD 1.50 in new investment.[41] Saving our infrastructure is genuinely an investment that would essentially pay for itself.[42]

The problem is that politics and bureaucratic inefficiency continue to stand in the way. As leaders haggle over their own priorities, everything decays.

It is no surprise, then, that many in the West exhibit China envy – a yearning to build things like Beijing does. Sometimes, this manifests as nostalgia: a desire to build the way we used to. Former US president Donald Trump, no friend of China, wasn't immune to both sentiments. 'They have bridges that are so incredible,' he proclaimed at a 2016 rally.[43] 'Make America Great Again' was his powerful electoral slogan, with, for our purposes, an emphasis on the first word.

And while Trump is given to simplism, it's understandable why he's attracted to China's infrastructure. Not only is infrastructure a tool for politicians hoping to win over their people, it is a legitimate economic driver, too. Its construction employs huge numbers of people and boosts economies; its completion facilitates even greater and more efficient commerce, thereby effectively paying for itself down the line. Failure leads to stagnation and undermines our democracies' ability to deliver.

US President Joe Biden seems to understand this. By invoking China's accomplishments, he has justified his over USD 1 trillion infrastructure investment as a cost the US needs to pay to 'outcompete China'.[44] But the state of democratic disrepair – particularly

American disrepair – could not help but overshadow Biden's efforts. In January 2022, hours before he was set to speak in Pittsburgh about the need for more US infrastructure spending, a major car bridge in the city collapsed. Ten people were injured; buses and cars were left stranded, forcing rescue crews to scale 150 feet of hillside to deliver care.[45]

The collapse 'left a mass of concrete rubble and twisted metal as a visual metaphor for America's crumbling infrastructure', wrote the *Guardian*'s Ed Pilkington.[46] 'It would be hard,' he noted, 'to imagine a more dramatic way to illustrate the need for investment.'[47]

Despite the unfortunate coincidence in Pittsburgh, Biden's approach is the right one: democracies – particularly in the West – do need to invest in infrastructure to compete in the twenty-first century. We have taken some positive steps, as with Biden's infrastructure plan. But what we've done so far is not enough.[48] We clearly need to go further to ensure we're building not only the infrastructure of today – bridges and the like – but the infrastructure of tomorrow, too.

We must realise that infrastructure is not just transport; in our modern world, infrastructure also includes digital infrastructure, particularly broadband and digital payment systems. The pandemic, which increased internet reliance, has made this all the clearer.[49] Studies have even shown that access to high-speed internet reduced US COVID-19 deaths: a mere 1 per cent increase in access across the country reduced mortality by nearly 20 per cent per 100,000 people.[50] In urban areas, a 1 per cent increase reduced deaths by a staggering 36 deaths per 100,000, holding all else constant.[51] Access to the internet was literally a matter of life and death.

Tackling social inequalities and laying the groundwork for the course of democracy's future will require us to invest in all these forms of infrastructure, not just bridges and tunnels, and not just in times of crisis.

Not only does infrastructure investment fuel economic growth at home, which in turn boosts a country's tax revenue (and its ability to spend on national goals), successful infrastructure spending also boosts the investing country's prestige. It is a massive problem for democracies everywhere if the world is looking towards Shanghai, Singapore or Dubai as examples of the infrastructure they want – rather than to New York, London or Seoul. It makes us look not only weak, but unattractive. So, too, does the political unrest that is inevitable when democratic infrastructure decays, and when people get sick of that decline.

* * *

Shenzhen is one shining example of Chinese construction, but Beijing builds abroad as well, largely through the Belt and Road Initiative (BRI). This effort, on which China has already spent some USD 200 billion, has aided the construction of everything from Malaysian roads to Nigerian railways.[52] The BRI has succeeded not just in building China's geopolitical influence by helping advance Beijing's standards across these and other sectors, but also in advancing China's governance model. China is today most of the world's development partner of choice.

Being outcompeted on the infrastructure front is not just a domestic democratic challenge, it is a national security concern, too. If we do not build roads, bridges and internet cables for the future, we risk being overtaken by China, Singapore, the Gulf States and others not only at home – slowing our economies and decreasing our global power – but abroad, too, as these authoritarian countries' models gain only more and more purchase. There are short-term and long-term costs of failing to invest in our infrastructure, both at home and abroad. We will have to spend to defeat the dictators, here and there.

When developing countries align themselves with China, they do so not so much out of authoritarian solidarity, but largely in hopes that China will send them educated engineers and businesspeople to fill in significant infrastructural and other developmental gaps. Much to Malaysian, Nigerian and other disappointment, Chinese state-run and state-aligned companies contracted to build BRI projects tend to hire Chinese workers who would otherwise be unemployed in China.[53]

Hiring these young men allows China to tamp domestic unemployment concerns. But these workers tend to make the news for all the wrong reasons – such as calling Kenyans 'monkeys' or establishing a foothold in Latin American narco-trafficking. They also frequently build less-than-quality projects.[54]

This is because the BRI is more of a marketing campaign than it is a highly coordinated investment plan. Despite sensationalist media coverage in the West, Chinese policymakers have surprisingly little control of the state-owned enterprises and asset managers that build these projects.[55] Such projects often lack quality because, while they are built faster – in line with local asks – they are not subject to the same 'red tape' as democratic investments are, particularly when these investments are in countries with governance issues.

So, while China may be able to rapidly build a USD 12 million-dollar bridge in Kenya, the bridge will be prone to collapsing – as happened in 2017, just days after the Kenyan president lauded its construction.[56]

Stories like these are surprisingly common, particularly in Africa. Rains have washed away part of a Chinese-built road in Zambia, while Angolan officials had to shutter a Chinese-built hospital when bricks started to fall from its walls, prompting fears of collapse.[57] And in June 2019, a Chinese-owned unfinished building in the Cambodian city of Sihanoukville – a Chinese gambling hub – collapsed, killing nearly 30 Cambodians and prompting a wave of anti-Chinese sentiment on Chinese social media.[58]

It does not help matters that many BRI projects are tied to corrupt local officials and are subsequently left unfinished when these officials have siphoned off enough funds. The BRI story is now increasingly one of half-finished and unused buildings.

More crucially, stories like these are fairly common within China as well. Once again, there is a substantial gap between what China wants to be and what it is. Because of the country's lacking transparency and rule of law – a problem known to bedevil just about every autocracy – there is limited oversight of construction, which in turn enables dangerously shoddy projects to be built.

China may be able to rapidly construct quarantine hotels – as in 2020 in response to COVID-19 – but it should surprise nobody when one of those same hotels collapses, as in the city of Fujian.[59] It is also no surprise when a Chinese expressway collapses, as in 2021, or when a residential building simply descends into rubble, killing fifty-three people, as in 2022.[60]

Stories like these are common in autocracies around the world, even rich ones. The gleaming towers of Qatar and Saudi Arabia may stand tall, but buildings collapse in those countries all the time, often killing the migrants who work for wages and at standards no advanced democracy would consider acceptable.[61] Neither Russia nor Turkey nor Iran perform any better. None of these countries maintains effective checks and balances; the result is that infrastructure, while perhaps built speedily, is often shoddy at best.

Democracies have these problems, too, albeit to a lesser extent. A fire consumed London's Grenfell Tower in 2017, while a Miami apartment building collapsed in 2021 – both horrors the result of lacking oversight.[62] These problems are real, and we, as democracies, need to grapple with them.

Yet it nonetheless remains inarguable that autocracies are not more likely to produce good infrastructure or good governance at large than democracies are. Advanced democracies maintain better oversight and in turn can build better infrastructure than do autocracies such as China or the Gulf States. That is why so many countries – despite having all the BRI opportunities one could ask for – still want infrastructure investment from Australia, Japan, the United States and other democracies.[63] It is because, for all our faults, we tend to build better infrastructure, if at a slower pace. And that better infrastructure serves not only our people, but people abroad – pushing both to see our model as preferable to what's being offered by Beijing and Dubai.

* * *

Autocracy's Investments

It was the spring of 2020, and COVID-19 was rampaging around the world, with no vaccine in sight. Much of the world shut down for fear of the virus, leading to huge economic costs. In the first quarter of 2020, the global economy contracted by 3.4 per cent – or by USD 189 billion.[64] China's economy shrunk by 9.8 per cent, France's by 5.3 per cent, Germany's by 2.2 per cent and the United States' by 1.3 per cent.[65]

Everybody was in trouble.

Most countries responded with fiscal stimulus. Trump consented to an aid package, Biden then pushed his infrastructure plan through Congress. Germany's EUR 130 billion (USD 145 billion) stimulus featured tens of billions for infrastructure.[66] South Korea offered a USD 200 billion stimulus package, including support for public infrastructure.[67]

For rich countries that could afford it, this crisis – like others before it – was an opportunity to spend big and fix lingering problems, such as declining infrastructure.

China also took advantage, promising to spend USD 500 billion. This is a big number, but substantially less than the country's 2008 stimulus, owing to China's slowing economic growth and demographic issues. But China focused these funds, yet again, on infrastructure.

Local governments were told they could issue up to 3.75 trillion yuan (USD 527 million) in special bonds, which they could use to build 5G networks, railways, airports and other infrastructure projects.[68] That was a huge increase from the 2.15 trillion yuan (USD 325 million) they were allowed to issue the year prior.[69]

Countries everywhere focus on infrastructure during times of crisis, not only because infrastructure employs people who may have lost their jobs, but because it is a necessary building block for economic success. China has long spent more on this front than just about anyone.

From 1992 to 2011, China dedicated an eye-popping average of 8.5 per cent of GDP to infrastructure annually, investing in projects like the massive Jinggang'ao Expressway – which stretches some 1,400 miles and is among the world's most significant freight corridors, facilitating billions in business – as well as in social and digital infrastructure.[70] By way of comparison, Biden's USD 1 trillion 2021 infrastructure bill brought annual US infrastructure spending up to only 1.25 per cent of GDP.[71] Remarkably, US infrastructure-spending under the New Deal from 1933 to 1937, of around 1.36 per cent of GDP, was about six times less per capita than China's 1992–2011 spending.[72] China today spends more on infrastructure than the United States and Europe do, combined.

At times, though, China's spending is ill-advised. The country's economy is slowing, and thanks to the government's massive 2008 and 2020 stimulus spending, its public debt has ballooned, soaring by 100 per cent of GDP since 2008 to around 250 per cent of GDP.

Many of China's infrastructure projects are genuinely wasteful. Beijing mobilises construction workers to build things during times of crisis, only to have them knock down the same projects when the next crisis strikes. There are constant reports of 'white elephant' projects that burden the financial system with loans that won't be repaid. China has more than a few 'ghost cities' filled with skyscrapers and luxury apartments – but nobody to live in them. Even in major cities like Kunming, officials have found themselves needing to demolish buildings that were built during infrastructure drives but sat unused.[73]

As the pandemic dragged on, though, China seemed to be learning this lesson: money cannot be thrown at all infrastructure but must be directed at projects that the country needs. This is why in April 2022 – with China sticking to its 'Zero-COVID' policy and Xi leaning on his country's 50 million construction workers once more – Beijing embarked on a more targeted spending spree.

At the central government's demand, local governments put together lists of 'major projects' that the capital expected them to see through. This planned investment amounted to some 14.8 trillion yuan (USD 2.3 trillion).[74] That is more than double the spending in the Biden infrastructure package that the US Congress approved in 2021.[75]

But China has already built much of the modern infrastructure it needs, at least in areas where the government is focused. So, while the West tries to repair our declining infrastructure – our railways and roads – China has focused on something different. Only 30 per cent of China's 2022 'major projects' were of traditional infrastructure; more than half were those that would support the manufacturing and service industries, like industrial parks and technology incubators.[76] The focus is no longer on the goods that China was once known for: clothes or sneakers. Now, the focus is on high-tech goods that the entire world *needs*, like semiconductors, electric vehicles and batteries.[77]

China is serious about owning the future, both within its borders and beyond. While we try to fix the infrastructure of yesterday, China is building tomorrow.

* * *

Something similar is happening in several other autocracies around the world.

Singapore has promised to issue new bonds worth nearly USD 70 billion to finance major long-term infrastructure projects over the next fifteen years.[78] These projects include not only the infrastructure classics – such as new subway lines – but tidal walls to protect the city-state against rising sea levels. Singapore also plans to issue bonds for climate-related infrastructure.[79]

The United Arab Emirates has approved stimulus programmes worth nearly USD 80 million, including major funding for renewable energy, manufacturing and the digital sector.[80] The government then approved budgets setting aside billions for infrastructure, including for the digital economy.[81]

It is no coincidence that both Singapore and the UAE have ranked for years as having some of the world's highest-quality infrastructure, particularly in digital terms.[82] Both rank ahead of democracies like Canada, France and Switzerland.[83] China comes in fourth – ahead of not only these three, but Germany as well, along with countless other rich and generally well-governed democracies.[84]

Clearly these autocracies are doing something right: they are providing for their people and winning popular support, which boosts their models abroad. And while some might say the UAE and Singapore are unique, China's success indicates that size does not prevent countries from advancing into the future if they prioritise it. Size only holds us back if we let it.

* * *

Asia's Advances

Before people visited Singapore and Shanghai claiming to have seen the future, they went to Tokyo. They marvelled at the city's skyline, dotted by dozens of skyscrapers and backed by Mount Fuji to the West. They compared the city's ultra-fast subway systems and clean streets to their own slow metros and dirty streets in Washington or Paris. More than anything, they walked around Tokyo in awe, simply happy to be there, to be in a place so different yet also so advanced. 'It's a sort of fairyland, beckoning to adventure,' wrote the *New York Times*' Harold C. Schonberg, adding, pointedly: 'More than any city in the world, Tokyo on the surface of things appears American, except that everything works.'[85]

It really was like walking around in the future.

People were stunned by how far the country had come in just forty years or so from its post–Second World War dilapidation, when some 40 per cent of its infrastructure was destroyed.

From the start of the American occupation of Japan, both the Japanese and Americans recognised how important infrastructure was. During the six-year occupation – from 1946 to 1952 – the United States invested around USD 2 billion (USD 22 billion today) in rebuilding Japan. Some 40 per cent of these funds, or around USD 10 billion in 2022 dollars, went to economic infrastructure: power, transportation and communication.[86] By 1952, Japan found itself with much of the infrastructure it needed to prosper in the twentieth century; it had the economic infrastructure that would enable the Japanese miracle.[87]

The Japanese wisely doubled down on these building blocks. When Hayato Ikeda took office as prime minister in 1960, he outlined the so-called 'Doubling Plan', under which, he said, Japan would see its GDP double within a decade. He rapidly expanded government investment in key infrastructure projects such as highways, railways, airports and dams, as well as in the communications sector.[88]

To accomplish his goal, Ikeda needed the Japanese economy to grow by a staggering 7.8 per cent per year. At the time, the West considered it a success to post annual growth of around 2, 3 or 4 per cent. Ikeda's plan seemed more ludicrous than ambitious.

But his rhetoric somehow managed to live up to reality. Beginning in 1960, his country's economy grew *10 per cent* annually – meaning that the economy doubled in less than seven years.[89]

Along the way, Japan unveiled the Meishin Expressway that first connected Osaka and Kyoto before expanding to Kobe and Nagoya; Japan also produced the Tokaido bullet train, which ran on the world's first high-speed railway.[90]

That train operated at a speed of 130 miles (210 kilometres) an hour upon opening in 1964.[91] With trains that speed, the trip between London and Liverpool would take only sixty-nine minutes, yet today, that trip takes a British commuter around two hours. In 2019, it took me closer to three hours. An unexplained 'error' forced us to leave the train somewhere closer to Alton than to Anfield, and to then take a bus the rest of the way. Japan, on the other hand, has improved its Tokaido train to run at speeds closer to 177 miles per hour – meaning that it could make the London to Liverpool trip in less than an hour.

The list of Ikeda's projects goes on and on. Not only did officials see these efforts as vital building blocks for the future, but they made Japan more than twice as rich in 1970 as it had been in 1960. His 'doubling plan' worked.

Japan's infrastructure spending did not stop with him. Instead, as Japan moved up the global economic ladder, its leaders continued to invest huge amounts of money in infrastructure, seeing better roads and bridges and trains as a continued mechanism of economic growth.[92]

But some Japanese investment drives were marred by poorly thought-out projects – the so-called 'bridges going to nowhere': a term that came to describe wasteful projects built in remote parts of the country with little hope of boosting economic activity. The massive Hamada Marine Bridge, completed in 1999, may look nice, but it serves a city of only 61,000 residents and was certainly not worth the cost. Neither were the city's new highway, sports centre, ski resort and aquarium.[93]

The lesson to take from Japan's infrastructure experience 'is that public works get the best results when they create something useful for the future', as the Japanese academic Toshihiro Ihori has noted, because when projects are useful, they serve the people and boost a democracy's legitimacy.[94]

Japan has somewhat learned this lesson. In responding to the 2008 financial crash, leaders generally applied this 'future use' clause to the revitalisation of existing, decaying infrastructure. Japan's future generations did, in fact, need better roads and tunnels. People did appreciate these tune-ups. There was much less waste this time around.

When COVID-19 hit, the Japanese government spent on infrastructure, but of a different kind: green innovation, digital innovation, public health infrastructure and even the country's endowment fund to help strengthen its semiconductor supply chains.[95] 'We have,' proclaimed then-prime minister Yoshihide Suga, 'new measures [. . .] to achieve new growth in green and digital areas, so as to protect people's lives and livelihood.'[96]

* * *

Reasonable people can debate the wisdom of spending such huge amounts of money when your public debt is already the largest in the world, when your people are ageing and when you are unwilling to accept immigrants to fund your government in the future – all of which is true in Japan.

Yet it is impossible to do anything but marvel at Japan's top-tier infrastructure. It is still ranked among the world's best.[97] Despite what some leaders in Beijing or Dubai might say, Japan's successes prove that liberalism does not preclude democracies from laying the groundwork needed to compete in the twenty-first century and beyond.

Japan's infrastructure is not perfect, nor will it remain so good forever if left untouched. Japan's infrastructure is decaying in some parts of the country. Ageing bridges and tunnels will require fixing.

But the goal for democracies like Japan must no longer be maintenance in the moment. We can no longer simply patch up these faults if we are to keep our democracies strong and spread our model abroad. We need bold spending on the infrastructure of the future, because with the right investments, people might once again travel to Tokyo and Toronto and proclaim to have seen the future *there* – in the bridges and towers and internet speed of democracies – rather than in Shanghai or Dubai.

* * *

Why Infrastructure Matters

The Chinese, Japanese and Singaporean experiences make clear that infrastructure spending spurs economic growth. What these examples make less clear is that democracies cannot afford to ignore infrastructure – because doing so leads to stagnant economies, which fuels distrust in democracy, thereby weakening our systems at home and harshly handicapping our ability to promote democracy anywhere.

The connection between infrastructure and economics is clear and persistent throughout history: creating modern infrastructure – the physical framework of an economy – improves the functionality and growth potential of that same economy, while failing to do so leads societies to fall behind.

Areas in the Roman empire with greater road density, for instance, were also those with greater settlement formation, meaning more economic activity. These same areas were then the ones with more modern roads and economic activity in the early twenty-first century.[98]

Why?

Because the initial investment in infrastructure had a gravitational effect, drawing in more commerce and more people for years, with each wave seemingly bringing even more people to follow. It was the Romans who built the first major roads into Londinium (contemporary London) and Lutetia (contemporary Paris). And it was these roads that brought people and money into these cities, allowing London and Paris to become the centres of commerce, culture and democracy that they are today.

A similar connection between infrastructure and economic activity persists contemporarily.

The non-partisan US Congressional Budget Office (CBO) says that if the United States reallocated USD 500 billion of existing funds for infrastructure projects, US real GDP would rise steadily up to 2038, and essentially persist at that level to 2051.[99] (If the government spent USD 500 billion of new funds on infrastructure – rather than repurposing funds, as in the first scenario – the CBO predicts that the effect would be more short-lived but still positive.[100])

The International Monetary Fund says that a one percentage point increase in infrastructure investment relative to GDP would lead to average long-term output gains of between 1 and 2.5 per cent.[101] The Scottish government's Chief Economist Directorate says that sustained public investment in infrastructure would boost growth.[102] The OECD has found that all but one of its members would see positive returns in terms of long-term growth and labour productivity if they increased infrastructure investment.[103] (Japan is the notable exception: its generally strong infrastructure means that the remaining gains are somewhat marginal; it also has an extraordinarily high level of debt and an ageing population – problems that no Western government faces to the same extent.)

This positive effect is even more pronounced in developing countries, which often have basic infrastructure that needs updating for the modern world. In cases like these, the marginal benefit of investing in infrastructure is the highest.[104] Building upon an existing but not fully mature network allows productivity jumps seemingly overnight, leading to rapid economic growth.

This is essentially what happened in China, Japan, Taiwan and South Korea over the last forty to fifty years; they had some infrastructure, and just needed funds to improve it for the modern world following years of conflict.[105] All four of those places developed rapidly, based at least in part on strong infrastructure investment. Three of them became democracies in no small part because of this economic growth.

There are several developing democracies that are on the cusp of such advancements. Indonesia, the world's fourth-largest country in terms of population, needs significant investment in its roads, ports, airports, railways, water and power plants.[106] The Indonesian economy is today so weak because its economy is highly inefficient.[107] The same is true, too, of developing democracies like India, the Philippines and Mexico.[108]

These are all countries with large and growing populations. They all have some basic infrastructure but would all clearly benefit from more. Such investment would feed productivity, which in turn could allow for even more effective governments – not only improving people's quality of life, but boosting their confidence in democracy, too. It would be a win for one of democracy's core tenets: its ability to provide a roadmap to the good life.

* * *

The mechanism at work here is simple: better roads, bridges and internet connections facilitate faster supply chains, while run-down infrastructure makes it hard for goods and services to move from one place to the next.[109] Better economic performance leads to more trust in government, which makes democracy work even better; lagging economies, on the other hand, allow for the rise of destabilising politics.

If democracies are to build the infrastructure necessary for liberal governance to survive in the modern world, this equation must include digital infrastructure. If your country does not adapt to the digital world – by installing smart grid applications and improving cyber-security to facilitate a faster flow of online business and commerce – your economy's growth potential will suffer, as will your democracy's functionality.

And while infrastructure spending may take years to yield economic results, even on the digital front, everybody from investment bankers to the most spending-resistant politicians understands the need to invest.[110] People everywhere understand that building new infrastructure and improving what exists will not only have the short-term benefit of putting people to work, but will also improve productivity and a country's potential for economic growth in the long-term, giving that country a better chance of preserving and strengthening democracy.

By demonstrating our ability to do things – and, more importantly, by building the digital roads of the future and defining their rules

– democracies will deliver better on their promises, thereby promoting trust in government and even better democratic governance. Doing so will make democracies and our model more attractive.

Autocracies can spend as well, but our open systems and strong regulatory institutions give us the upper hand in literally building the future. Despite China's spending, people everywhere do generally prefer Western, Japanese and South Korean infrastructure, if given the choice. There is a reason why countries throughout the developing world continue to clamour for democratic-built infrastructure, even while China makes seemingly endless offers to build roads and railways in Nairobi, Naypyidaw and beyond.

Infrastructure is the literal road not only to prosperity at home, but to competing abroad, both physically and reputationally. Rotten roads, on the other hand, will surely stop us in our tracks.

* * *

No Rest for the Weary

Some democratic countries cannot afford to invest as much as others. Indonesia's coffers are smaller than those in Washington or London. Japan is facing such a demographic and debt challenge that pouring huge amounts of money into infrastructure projects will weigh on growth moving forward.

But many governments, particularly those in the West, can afford to invest greatly in infrastructure. While our birth-rates are declining – engendering fears of a Japan-like demographic disaster – we can (and must, as the next chapter explains) increase our populations through immigration, as many countries already have.[111] With this increased taxpayer base, governments will find themselves with the money to spend on infrastructure spending to spur growth not only in times of crisis, but in the long-term, too.

Some countries might still need the basic brass tacks that make up a nation's infrastructure: more bridges and roads. The United States certainly does.[112] US public transit systems need about USD 176 billion in work right now – and will need some USD 100 billion more in funding by 2030.[113] Europe, too, is falling behind in terms of infrastructure spending, leaving behind huge gaps in digital sectors and urban transport, for starters.[114]

Yet even as these and other democracies look to fix what is breaking, they also need to build the infrastructure they don't have yet. They need to build the infrastructure of tomorrow, from high-speed internet connectivity to digital grid applications.

We have the tools and in many cases the finances to write the future we want. But we cannot just throw money at the problem. No, we will need targeted, intelligent and future-focused investments to ensure that our systems work in the long-term, and that we win tomorrow.

* * *

Perhaps the most vital investment will be in internet connectivity.

Democracies around the world will not be able to keep up with autocracies like China, the Gulf States and Singapore if so many of our people do not have access to high-speed internet. Without such connectivity, Americans, Brits and others won't be able to participate in the digital economy, or even produce the innovations that democracies need to claim the future.[115] They will also be more likely to feel disconnected from their countries' government and business elites, thereby producing even more distrust in these systems and a higher propensity for populism. With such connectivity, meanwhile, democratic citizens – no matter whether in urban centres or in rural villages – can innovate and truly become part of their country's democratic communities.

Being connected to high-speed internet at a low cost is indeed a fundamental accelerant, allowing creative thinkers to innovate the world over, with examples abounding from Red Wing, Minnesota, to Karnataka, India.[116] High-speed connections enable manufacturing by connecting people to open-source maker spaces.[117] No wonder studies have shown that high-speed internet access fuels economic growth.[118]

Yet far too many parts of democracies lag behind. Only 60 per cent of rural EU households have high-speed internet access, for instance, compared to the Union's total average of 86 per cent.[119] Only 41 per cent of rural adults in the United States have access to high-speed internet.[120]

Part of the problem is the scandalous cost of high-speed internet. The monthly cost of such access is USD 66 in the United States, USD 64 in Canada, USD 42 in the United Kingdom and USD 41 in Japan.[121] By way of comparison, the monthly cost is only USD 14 in China.

Prices are so high in many democracies because the largest internet providers have little economic incentive to serve rural communities, given their smaller populations. As a result, they can (and often do) jack up prices to turn a profit. Former US FCC chair Tom Wheeler once recalled meeting a rural internet service provider executive who told him that his company charged so much simply 'because I can'.[122]

The free market is vital to economic growth and raising living standards. But it cannot solve every problem. The reason so many Americans, Europeans and others do not have high-speed internet access is because of the high cost of laying the necessary cables across sparsely populated land.[123] On the other hand, it is precisely because the government has stepped in to provide such internet where the private sector will not that South Korea leads the world in terms of internet access. Some 90 per cent of South Koreans have such access; they also pay less than half of what Americans do.[124]

Specific solutions to this problem will be different for every democracy, but the general answer is at least some government action. Governments would do well to subsidise high-speed internet provision in rural areas. And when the necessary cables are laid and people can purchase internet access if they want (and can afford) to, governments should offer subsidies, tax breaks and other incentives to get people to sign up.

* * *

Democracies also need to invest in a broader array of digital infrastructure, such as modernised electric grids and smart cities.[125] Just like roads and airports, all these improvements will produce financial returns in the tens of billions. And these returns, if they do truly trickle down, will put more money in people's pockets and produce more trust in democracy, thus strengthening our system of governance.

Such investments must be targeted based on national need, but some options include funding IT system modernisation for local governments.[126] Imagine how much better our government bureaucracies would be if they had the high-tech that Silicon Valley uses on a day-to-day basis. Imagine how many more people would trust their democratic governments if their bureaucracies worked as they should in the modern world.

Governments must also invest in communication network improvements like 5G and Wi-Fi 6. And because governments do not always have the capacity to build such infrastructure themselves, they should partner with the private sector. The additional benefit is that people trust the private sector more than they trust the government.[127]

In doing all of this, governments will need to prevent systems from being fragmented and thus inefficient – a problem across Europe. Investment is good, but money does not solve problems alone.[128] So, when one city or branch of government decides to invest in 5G or IT modernisation, they should work with other facets of that same government to share best practices and ensure that their new systems will connect effectively to those already installed at the national level.

* * *

Many democracies are already starting to invest in digital infrastructure, creating hybrid digital–physical projects. Even seemingly mundane pieces of our infrastructure, like water utilities and dams, have become increasingly digitised, relying on smart technologies.[129] This is a positive development.

But these hybrid infrastructures do not have the cyber-security required. And our adversaries have taken notice.

In 2013, Iranian state-sponsored hackers penetrated the Bowman Avenue Dam – located in the quiet suburban village of Rye Brook, New York. The dam's main purpose is simply to prevent a small creek from flooding basements and ground floors in homes downstream.[130] Yet Iran tried to take the dam offline, probably as something of a test run for a more disruptive effort. American investigators were dismayed because the attempt indicated that Iran could seize control of US computer-operated infrastructure – such as a hydroelectric generator or some key element of the nation's power grid.[131]

Other countries are vulnerable, too.

In 2020, Iranian hackers infiltrated an Israeli water-pumping station and tampered with equipment. Pumps stopped working; officials scrambled to provide millions of people with water.[132] Experts warned that the hackers were trying to poison water supplies.[133] These developments ushered in a new era of covert warfare, according to the head of Israel's National Cyber Directorate, who warned 'cyber winter is coming'.[134]

It very well may be. And if Iran, a relatively poor country, can hack America and Israel, imagine the damage China or another more well-resourced adversary could do.

What this troubling situation should make clear is that as democracies digitise their infrastructure, they cannot skimp on cyber-security. For every dam or water utility that we connect to the cloud, we should make sure that we are resourcing government offices working on developing solutions for tomorrow.[135] As more and more facets of the government, from our healthcare to social security systems, become more digitised, these solutions become more vital.[136] Data breaches in places like Germany have already undermined health and other systems and slowed down their operations, leading in some cases to death – which, of course, undermines people's trust in these same systems.[137]

Some solutions already exist. For example, with hackers increasingly trying to 'phish' into our systems, several governments have wisely adopted multi-factor authentication.[138] Also key to this effort is training government workers to understand how to use these systems – which will require time and money.

But governments do not produce the best solutions to complex problems like these; the government did not create the internet (although government funding did fuel the innovators who did). These solutions will instead come from a new generation of cyber-security professionals – in whom governments must invest more – and from liaising with both the private sector and academia.[139] Governments must therefore not try to improve cyber-security in a vacuum; they must work with the professionals to make us all safer.

If they don't, we'll all be at risk. Previous attacks are a warning: failing to protect our increasingly digital critical infrastructure will result in death, not to mention even more democratic distrust in basic institutions.[140] Hackers of a previous era may have only wanted money; today, they want to cause chaos. And we're not prepared for them.

* * *

This chapter does not offer an exhaustive list of solutions. But I hope readers will walk away understanding the nature of the problem, and with some ideas about how to fix it. We, democratic citizens of the world, are at risk of falling behind; those of us lucky enough to visit somewhere like Singapore or Shanghai understand that leading autocracies are spending to create the physical and digital world they want – and that we need as well.

Failing to invest in our existing infrastructure and the infrastructure we'll need for the future will undermine our countries' economic growth, in turn undermining our own governments' functionality and therefore trust not only in these governments but in democracy at large. This decline will see our power and allure atrophy on the international stage. People around the world will not want to emulate the United States, Europe or Japan if our infrastructure falls further into disrepair and self-defeating populists claim power all while the seemingly steady hands of authoritarians in China and Singapore jump into the twenty-second century some seventy years in advance.

We know what's gone wrong, we know what the risks of inaction are, we know at least some of the action that's needed to prevent this gloomy future from coming about. Now, our policymakers just must take a few steps in the right direction. And we'll need to vote them out and replace them if they don't. We hardly have time to waste.

8

Immigration

In the 1970s, the dominant tone of life in Moscow was one of greyness. Soviet authorities brutally imposed this malaise on the city's people, attacking the *intelligentsia* whenever the Soviet Union's best and brightest veered too far from the party line.[1] The city's most creative people had been beaten into submission; their future in the Soviet world of cinderblocks and planned economics was bleak, and they knew it.

Mikhail and Eugenia were members of this small circle of intelligentsia, but they were a relative exception. They kept their heads down and towed the line. They didn't necessarily approve of the government's decisions, but they knew better than to question them. When anti-Semitism reared its ugly head against the couple, both Jews, they took it. And because both had PhDs and important jobs – him at the agency responsible for central economic planning, her at the Soviet Oil and Gas Institute – they lived lives of relative comfort.

Just about every other Muscovite crammed generations of multiple families into tiny communal apartments. The couple shared their tiny, three-room apartment – 350 square feet in all – with just their son and Mikhail's mother. While institutional anti-Semitism had prevented them from studying certain subjects and securing certain jobs, they were nonetheless as happy as one could be in the Soviet Union.

By the early 1970s, things were beginning to change. Mikhail was starting to understand just how unfair the Soviet system was, and how limited life was within the Union. He was realising that raising children there meant dooming them to a life not only of mediocrity, but of captivity. It was when Mikhail attended a 1977 mathematics conference in Warsaw, Poland that the dam finally broke.

For the first time in his thirty years of life, he had the chance to engage and talk freely with colleagues from the United States, England and Germany. He discovered, contrary to Moscow's propaganda, that these Westerners 'were not monsters', but mathematicians striving for much the same solutions as he was.[2] Upon returning to Moscow, Mikhail had made up his mind.

'We cannot stay here any more,' he told his wife, mother and four-year-old son.[3]

Despite the perils of applying for an exit visa – being shunned by Soviet society as traitors and unable to find work, yet also not being granted the visa and thus not allowed to leave – the couple moved forward with their plans. They lost their jobs. For the next eight months, they worked temporary contracts and waited, hoping that their request would come through. Eventually, and against the odds, it did. Someone in the bureaucracy looked out for them; or maybe it was an oversight. Either way, in May 1979, they left the country. They were some of the last Jews allowed to do so until the Gorbachev era.

Eugenia would later give a simple explanation of their decision to leave. Mikhail 'said he wouldn't stay, now that he had seen what life could be about'. He had seen lands of opportunity, and simply couldn't forget their promise. Yet as much as Mikhail was thinking about his own professional future, for Eugenia – who had been less sanguine about the idea from the get-go – the decision came down to their now six-year-old son.

She knew it wouldn't be easy to uproot their lives as adults. She knew it would be even harder on their boy. But in the long-term, moving – and moving to America specifically – would offer him more opportunity than it would cause pain. Their son would be able to experience life in all its glory and take advantage of all it had to offer, rather than spend his years toiling away in the repressive grey-ness of the Soviet Union.

In the end, for Eugenia, the decision to leave was straightforward. She would trade the Soviet cinderblocks, all she had ever known, for America's promises of milk and honey. And she would do it for her son.

'It was,' she later said, '80/20 about Sergey.'[4]

* * *

The family's first stop was in Vienna, Austria, where they met offi-cials from the Hebrew Immigrant Aid Society, an organisation that ferried thousands of Jews from behind the Iron Curtain into the free world. From there, they journeyed to the Parisian suburbs, where Mikhail's informal PhD advisor – a fellow Jew who had emigrated from the Soviet Union just one year earlier – had arranged a tempo-rary research position for him.

Once more, the family was in limbo. To be sure, limbo in Paris was better than limbo in Moscow, but again, they were waiting for visas, this time from the United States. Mikhail's advisor was trying to get Mikhail a teaching job at the University of Maryland, but things were slow. So, they stayed in Paris for several months. The city was fine, but they were intent on moving to the United States, where there were more Jews, particularly more Jews of Soviet extraction, not to mention a job waiting for Mikhail.

Once again, the visas came through, as did Mikhail's job. And so, on 25 October, the family arrived at New York's John F. Kennedy airport, where they were greeted by friends from Moscow.[5]

The family settled in a lower-middle-class neighbourhood not so far from the University of Maryland in College Park, where Mikhail was teaching. With a USD 2,000 loan from the local Jewish commu-nity, they bought their first piece of the American dream: a 1973

Ford Maverick. They enrolled Sergey at a Montessori school – institutions that generally encourage freedom in children, rather than forcing a curriculum upon them.[6]

Mikhail and Eugenia settled in quickly, but Sergey couldn't quite get comfortable. He didn't speak much English. And the English he did speak came out in a heavy Russian accent. He was awkward. It was clear to everybody around him that although he was a boy in America, he was not yet an *American* boy. He was one from a part of the world they simultaneously mocked and feared.

Sergey's first year in America was difficult. But he pressed on, steadily making his way through the Montessori school, whose unique educational method he appreciated.[7] Before long, he truly began to hit his stride; those around him began to understand what he could become.

From the Montessori school he went to Eleanor Roosevelt, a large Maryland public high school. It was around this time that he returned to Russia as a sixteen-year-old as part of a maths exchange run by his father. Mikhail decided to bring the family along, in no small part so Sergey could see the country he had fled for the first time since leaving. On the second day of the trip, Sergey took his father aside after visiting a sanatorium near Moscow, looked him in the eye, and told him simply: 'Thank you for taking us all out of Russia.'[8]

Sergey excelled in high school, finishing in three years and earning so many college credits that he completed his college course at the University of Maryland in three years as well, all while being top of his class. He won a scholarship to attend Stanford, where he planned to follow his parents' lead and get his PhD.

But history had different plans.

In the spring of 1995, just two years into his doctorate, he met Larry Page, a computer science student from the University of Michigan. Like Sergey, Larry came from highly intelligent Jewish parents; like Sergey, Larry was brash and obnoxious. They got on well. They began working together, trying to figure out how, exactly, they could leverage a relatively new invention – the World Wide Web – to find information as quickly as possible.

By 1996, they had realised that just as academics' citations measured a paper's value, so too do the internet's 'citations': links. Linking to a page was essentially a citation of it – more than a testament to its mere existence, it represented a vote of confidence in its importance and reliability. Leaning on Sergey's maths expertise, the two men created the 'PageRank' algorithm to rank the results based on this linking behaviour.[9] They launched their search engine, the world's most powerful to date, on Stanford's private network in August 1996.

At the time, the internet did not operate like this; people did not search for content but read what the Yahoo! or AOL portals presented to them. Sergey and Larry believed in their search engine, nonetheless. They knew that people would eventually come to appreciate the ability to sift through huge amounts of information and retrieve what they needed within seconds. They knew that their search engine – 'Google' – would change the world.

* * *

The two men initially struggled for investment. They shopped the venture around for USD 1 million, but nobody was interested. Nobody quite got it – that is, except for Andy Bechtolsheim, the billionaire founder of SUN Microsystems and yet another Jewish immigrant from Europe.

Having emigrated from Germany in the late 1970s, initially to pursue his own PhD at Stanford, Bechtolsheim knew what talent and drive looked like. He was willing to take a chance on two young men. And so, after seeing a quick demonstration in 1998, Bechtolsheim invested USD 100,000 in Google.

In 2001, the pair recruited former SUN CTO Eric Schmidt to run Google, and to provide what Sergey called 'adult supervision'.[10] Then, in 2002, Yahoo! tried to buy Google, offering USD 3 billion – 3,000 times more than the one million Sergey and Larry had tried to secure just four years earlier. But they were already thinking bigger. So, they turned down the deal, believing Google to be worth USD 5 billion, at least.[11]

They were right.

* * *

In the years that followed, Google would launch new product after new product, each one more successful than the last: Google News, the content aggregation service that fundamentally reshaped not just how people everywhere consumed news, but also how media companies distributed it; Gmail, which offered users more storage and more advanced search capabilities than any competitors; and Google Maps, which was more intuitive and simply better than contemporary competitors.[12]

By this time, Google had gone public. Sergey and Larry had turned their idea – and Bechtolsheim's investment – into a company worth USD 27 billion.[13]

But as the best businesses and governments do, Google refused to rest on its laurels; instead, its leaders looked for more ways to improve, such as by purchasing YouTube, launching the Chrome browser and rolling out Chromecast.[14]

Today, Google's market cap is over USD 2 trillion. Its parent company, Alphabet, was created in 2015 and manages several technology companies, including Google and many of its subsidiaries. Alphabet – mostly because of Google – is now one of the world's richest companies.[15] Google is central to the lives of billions of people, not only in the United States, but around the world.

Yet the company has not forgotten its roots. Google has invested nearly USD 40 billion in the United States over the last five years, including nearly ten billion in 2022 alone.[16] The whole world may benefit from Google's innovation, but it evidently pays to be American – to have a government and culture that fosters and hosts these innovations, and to ultimately reap its benefits.

* * *

What this story and chapter make clear are the benefits of immigration and the need for advanced democracies to accept more people from abroad. They may not all be Sergey Brin, but most immigrants are law-abiding taxpayers who make positive contributions to society. Their tax revenues and consumption will play a vital role as our countries rapidly age. Without immigrants, democracies face an economic disaster – a disaster that will see support for ruling governments weaken, bringing about the rise of even more regressive populists who undermine our power and allure everywhere.

The main points of this chapter are simple.

First, immigrants are a net economic benefit to their host countries in terms of taxation, GDP growth and innovation. Second, democracies in the West – along with Japan, Taiwan and South Korea – are experiencing demographic distress, and immigrants are the only reasonable solution. Third, much to our advantage, most would-be émigrés everywhere still want to move to democracies, not to China, Russia or Saudi Arabia. Fourth, democracies must fix their immigration systems, which range from broken (as in the United States) to hopelessly onerous (Australia). Fifth, and finally: if we don't bring in more immigrants, we will just about seal our decline by setting the stage for more distrust and weakened democracies at home, which will render us increasingly impotent abroad.

We must, put simply, do more to bring people here, not only because of the moral imperative, but because we need them. It is glaringly obvious.

To defeat the dictators both at home and abroad, we need strong economies; such economies are possible only with adequate numbers of people, which we simply do not – and will not – have thanks to declining birth-rates. If we intend to keep our own economies and democracies afloat at home and fund the governance projects needed to set the global standard, not to mention fund our geopolitical efforts abroad, we will have to accept more immigrants.

The fact that immigrants are an economic, social and cultural benefit regardless of demographics is an added, similarly important point. So, too, is the fact that by accepting more immigrants, we can highlight the differences between us and autocracies: people still want to come to our shores, much more than they want to move to China or Russia. There is a reason why authoritarian leaders from Cambodia to Jordan and everywhere in between send their children to study in the West, mostly in the United States and the United Kingdom – because something about our system is better and, deep down, even the dictators seem to know it.

Defeating autocracy, then, hinges in no small part on opening our doors to immigrants, not only because of our own declining birth-rates, but because of the innovative spirit and willingness to work that migrants bring to our democracies, and the symbolic importance of accepting them.

What we need now are leaders willing to look opportunity in the eye and act accordingly.

* * *

Benefits and Backlash

The cliché is well-worn: America is a country of immigrants. And it's true. Many of our best and brightest, from Alexander Hamilton to Sergey Brin to AIDS researcher David Ho, were not born in this country, coming here either fleeing persecution or in search of opportunity.[17] Countless others are the children, grandchildren or at least great-grandchildren of immigrants (as I am).[18] The American dream centres on immigration.

The country's original sins – of slavery and violence against the Native Americans – certainly colour this perception. It is necessary to remember that many Black Americans are the descendants of people *who did not want to come* to the United States and were forcibly brought there to work in hellish conditions. They were not immigrants, they were forced labourers carried across the Atlantic. Their stories are part of the American story and must not be forgotten.

With slavery's end, the United States began to more fully live up to its promise – including to immigrants. Over the last hundred and fifty years or so, the United States has built itself up with dreamers from Asia, Africa, Europe and beyond. This is something of an aberration in the history of state-building: most countries are built around centuries-old ethnically homogenous societies, as in France or Japan. Yet there is no American wealth without immigrants. There is, in fact, no America.

This remains true today.

Immigrants everywhere tend to be highly entrepreneurial; those who come to the United States are 80 per cent more likely to launch a new business than their native counterparts.[19] Immigrant-founded businesses in the United States create 42 per cent more jobs than do native-born-founded firms, relative to population.[20]

This is not surprising: people willing to leave behind their own countries for an unknown life are clearly the same people willing to take risks, which is key to innovation and entrepreneurship. But the United States has long out-innovated our competitors and partners, seemingly indicating that something else cultural is at play – likely a unique US tolerance for failure and a risk-prone business culture, along with our willingness to attract and accept immigrants.

Immigrants on aggregate produce a substantial economic benefit to the United States. They add somewhere around USD 2 trillion to the country's GDP annually, and around USD 460 billion in taxes.[21] Even refugees, people who generally arrive from impoverished countries with little more than the clothes on their backs, pay USD 21,000 more in taxes than they receive in benefits during their first twenty years in the country.[22] After paying their taxes, immigrants – refugees and economic migrants alike – accumulate over one trillion in spending power annually, allowing them to consume goods at a level vital to the increasingly consumption-based US economy.[23]

Modest increases to US immigration, which slowed under the Trump administration and during the COVID-19 pandemic, would pay off handsomely.[24] Accepting 50 per cent more immigrants would add some USD 1,300 per capita (about USD 428 billion in raw numbers) to the US GDP every year up to 2050. That number spikes to USD 93,200 – around USD 82 trillion in raw numbers – if immigration numbers were doubled.[25]

* * *

Brits may not know it, but they owe the MINI car – perhaps the icon of British 1960s culture – to Greece.[26] The car was an invention of the Greek-born asylum-seeker Sir Alec Issigonis. It was also the Belarus-born Michael Marks who, after arriving in the 1880s, teamed up with Thomas Spencer to create the omnipresent store, Marks & Spencer.[27] And it is immigrants and the children of immigrants who make up the majority of England's world-class national football team.

Tottenham forward and England captain Harry Kane's father is from Ireland, Arsenal midfielder Bukayo Saka's parents are Nigerian and Chelsea winger Raheem Sterling was born in Jamaica. In fact, half of the twenty-six-man squad that England sent to the 2021 European Championships could have chosen to represent another nation.[28] But they didn't. They chose England, and England benefited.

The benefits of such choices are evident in the private sector, too. Some 50 per cent of the United Kingdom's fastest-growing businesses have at least one foreign-born co-founder, despite just 14 per cent of UK residents being foreign-born.[29] About a quarter of the country's top earners are migrants, meaning that while the popular perception is of immigrants living off state benefits, many immigrants actually pay more tax.[30]

The British government has also found that immigrants, on average, contribute more to the public purse than native-born Britons do.[31] Immigrants from other parts of Europe contribute some USD 95,000 to the government over his or her lifetime, around USD 3,000 more annually than the average British-born adult.[32] Non-European migrants make a positive lifetime contribution of around USD 35,000 per person. Other studies suggest that from the mid-1990s to early 2010s, immigrants from outside the European Union made a net financial contribution of around USD 6.3 billion to the UK government – meaning that despite incendiary headlines, they paid about 3 per cent more into the system than they took out.[33]

Studies similarly show that immigrants from the European Union add some 0.2 per cent to German GDP annually, while the 2010s surge in Syrian and other Middle Eastern migrants boosted German employment rates.[34] Immigration contributes USD billions to Canada's GDP every year.[35] The Australian government has found that by 2050, each individual migrant will on average be contributing 10 per cent more to Australia's economy than existing residents.[36]

New Zealand's government has said that migrants add USD 1.9 billion to the economy annually.[37] Even Japanese researchers have found that increasing annual immigrant flows is a necessity that will 'dramatically improve the welfare of current and future generations'.[38]

I could go on and on, but the point should be quite clear: immigrants are a net positive to democracies – particularly when native-born populations are ageing, as is true across the West and in countries like Japan and South Korea.

While the evidence is clear, the politics are anything but.

All around the democratic world, politicians campaign against immigration, calling migrants everything from leeches who survive only because of state funds to outright criminals.

So, at the same moment that scholars, policymakers and bureaucrats are telling anyone who will listen that advanced democracies need more immigrants, why are the leaders of these same democracies rallying against immigration?

It's not because politicians don't understand the social science. Many of them do. It's because many of our leaders are prioritising certain narrow political constituencies (or because they themselves are xenophobic).

Politicians understand that, whether in the southern United States or northern Hungary, native-born citizens are worried about losing their own culture, and thus their sense of identity. For some, it's even their sense of being. And politicians understand that by leaning into rather than combatting these fears – which are generally not held by the majority of the population, but by powerful minorities in certain key electoral areas – they can secure the votes needed to win office. (Some politicians also understand the power of the vitriolic, anti-immigrant white nationalism.)

The political scientist Ivan Krastev has made this point about Eastern Europe, noting that as educated Hungarians, Bulgarians and others moved West, to Berlin or Paris – and as Muslim migrants made their way towards Europe – the older people left behind began to worry about what was coming next.[39] They began to worry that they were being replaced by migrants, that because non-Hungarians and non-Bulgarians were coming to Hungary and Bulgaria, while younger Hungarians and Bulgarians moved to the West, 'their national cultures were under the threat of vanishing', as Krastev put it.[40] Anti-immigration politicians like Hungary's Viktor Orbán recognised this sentiment and capitalised on it all the way into power.

Something similar is happening around the democratic world, where younger, educated people tend to leave behind their home-towns for urban centres. There is a very real fear among native-born citizens, particularly older folks in rural areas from the United States to Japan, that everything they know – and everything their ancestors built – is at risk of disappearing. The most politically salient case against immigration is social: it's tapping into people's concerns about a changing world and telling them about all the problems that change will bring, rather than highlighting the economic benefits that same change promises.

Of course, these fears are often informed by existing racial preju-dice. But it is not unreasonable for a Hungarian or Pole who saw their country effectively subsumed into the Soviet Union for years to worry about the dissolution of their unique national culture. As much as global elites may like to describe themselves as 'citizens of the world', they would do well to remember that most people still prioritise their nationalities, ethnicities and cultures – they want to see their traditions live on and are sympathetic to politicians who promise to protect their culture.

But native birth-rates are falling and have been for a long while. The reality is that countries everywhere have and will become more diverse, even if everyone were to put up walls now. This diversity may scare some, but it is quite clearly an opportunity. Diversity carries a whole host of economic and social benefits, even if the politics are tricky. More immigrants will be the 'ammo' we need to defeat the dictators.

Not only do immigrants tend to innovate and start businesses, such as Google, they also serve as a powerful reminder of what makes democracy so special and such a notable thing for which to strive. There is a reason why Sergey Brin created Google in the United States, not in the Soviet Union. There is a reason why so many leading American, British, German and other doctors and scientists came from somewhere else or are the children of those who did. There is a reason why Brin was so 'glad' his father took him out of Russia.

The reason is that people, particularly the smartest people, still prefer to live in democracies, messy as our politics may be. For most, an open society remains preferable to a closed one.

Autocracies still have not figured out how to fix this problem. Indeed, there is no autocracy in which Sergey Brin's story would have been possible. It could have only happened in a democracy – which is why the brightest Chinese, Saudis and even Singaporeans still want to study in the West, or in places like Australia and Japan. It is why many of them want to move here, and why an insignificant minority of them do.

Welcoming them – and seeing them succeed in our boardrooms, labs and legislatures – is a reminder not only of immigration's tangible benefits, but also of how immigrants demonstrate democracy's superiority. Every immigrant testifies to democracy's strengths and autocracy's flaws. They will fuel our economic and political rejuvenation, if we let them.

* * *

Democracies' Demographic Distress

Much of the discussion about immigration centres around Western politicians like Donald Trump and Marine Le Pen. But it is Asian democracies – namely Japan and South Korea – that are most in need of immigrants as their populations rapidly age, even as their politicians are among the most opposed to such migration.

Japan already has the highest proportion of elderly people anywhere in the world and does not have the fertility rates to change that.[41] Currently, the rate is about 1.3, meaning that every woman is having around one child – an 'ultra-low' rate compared to nearly all societies in human history.[42] It is far below the threshold of 2.1 per cent that demographers say is necessary to maintain a functional demographic balance.

Let's think about this issue in real terms. Today, there are some 127 million people living in Japan. That number is expected to drop to 114 million by 2030 and below 100 million by 2049.[43] The drop in the working-age population will be even starker, declining from 81 million today to only 67 million by 2030.[44] By 2036, a staggering one in three people will likely be elderly.[45] No society has ever been successful with demographics like that.

South Korea, though, now has the world's lowest fertility rate, dropping in 2021 to a meagre 0.81; on average, South Korean women have fewer than one child in their life.[46] This situation is largely the result of the country's professional culture, which generally holds motherhood against women, and financial constraints: huge numbers of South Korean women simply do not believe they can afford to have children.

But ageing populations will place huge pressures on the Japanese and South Korean labour forces and budgets. Already, employers in Japan are struggling to find Japanese people to fill jobs.[47] The country's health expenditure reached nearly 11 per cent of GDP in 2018 and will exceed 12 per cent by 2030.[48] (The OECD average is closer to 9 per cent.[49]) As their populations decline, so will Japan's and South Korea's tax bases, making it even harder to provide the ever-more elderly population with proper care.

This shrinking population has already driven up Japan's public debt to the highest in the world, raising questions about how, exactly, the country will pay for social services moving forward. Debt like this tends to weigh on economic growth and precede a crash – which is why it's no surprise that the International Monetary Fund believes Japan's economic growth will decline by an average 0.8 per cent annually through to the late 2050s due to demographics alone.[50]

If current trends persist, South Korea will also by 2050 find itself spending so much on healthcare for older people that net government debt will be over 130 per cent of the country's GDP.[51] (Its existing debt is only around 43 per cent of GDP, compared to 126 per cent in the United States and 117 per cent in France, for instance.) The country's annual GDP growth rate is expected to drop to around between 1 and 1.5 per cent by 2050, down substantially from the 3.3 per cent it averaged in the 2010s – not to mention the average 4.83 per cent annual growth posted during the 2000s, despite the 2008–9 financial crisis.[52] Demographic decline could alone knock 0.4 per cent off the country's GDP growth annually up to and including 2060.[53]

Yet both countries refuse to accept enough immigrants to remedy these demographic troubles. In 2018, the last year before the COVID-19 pandemic began, South Korea accepted just 70,000 new immigrants on a long-term or permanent basis.[54] Japan accepted only around 115,000.[55] That amounts to about 0.13 and 0.05 per cent of their total populations, respectively.

By way of comparison, in 2018, the United States accepted 1.1 million new immigrants – a relatively low number for us due to

Trump administration policies. But 1.1 million immigrants still amount to around 0.3 per cent of our population.[56] That means that in an off year, the United States accepted 56 per cent more immigrants per capita than did South Korea, and 83 per cent more than Japan did.

Several other countries, including not-so-immigrant-friendly ones, dwarf Asia's leading democracies on this front as well. In 2018, Austria accepted 85 per cent more long-term immigrants per capita than did South Korea, and 94 per cent more immigrants per capita than Japan – even with the immigration-sceptical Sebastian Kurz running the country.[57] Hungary, which is regularly lambasted for its anti-immigrant policies and rhetoric, accepted 67 per cent more long-term immigration per capita than did South Korea, and 87 per cent more than Japan did in 2018.[58] Apparently, Viktor Orbán better understood the economic importance of immigration or at least prioritised it more than did Shinzo Abe or Moon Jae-in.

The issue here is not that Japanese and South Korean leaders do not understand the need for immigration. They get it. But they're arguably more sensitive to domestic politics on the issue than politicians across the West are.

History has made Japan and South Korea highly homogeneous countries; this homogeneity has produced societies sceptical of diversity, leading Tokyo and Seoul to long block immigration even from other parts of Asia, let alone further afield.[59] These countries also do not have the land borders with other states that produce substantial migrant flows, as the United States and European nations do, meaning that they have long insulated themselves from incoming migration. It does not help that life is difficult for many migrants in Japan and South Korea, owing in large part to those countries' homogeneous cultures.[60]

This homogeneity may at times allow Japan and South Korea to sidestep some of the complex politics around race and identity, but a lack of ethnic diversity will not serve them well in the long run – because it will keep people, much-needed people, away.

These countries' limited bureaucratic focus plays a role, too. Governments in the West have long facilitated huge waves of migration, if quietly, when being led by anti-immigrant politicians, but Japan and South Korea have no such history. In the West, even if a Trump or Kurz takes office, the bureaucracy – boosted by a cultural proclivity towards accepting at least some immigrants – chugs along, continuing to bring more and more people to their countries. Japan and South Korea, on the other hand, have only recently become attractive destinations. Not only do they not yet have cultures of accepting immigrants, they don't have active bureaucracies either.

The result of all this history, politics and policy is a self-destructive immigration policy, particularly at a moment when birth-rates are declining due mainly to economic pressures. Both countries, along with Taiwan, need more people; the natives aren't producing them fast enough. There is – as Tokyo, Seoul and, to a lesser extent, Taipei must realise – only one other place from which they can come: abroad.

Policymakers are increasingly aware of this problem.[61] Seoul, for instance, admitted in 2021 that 'amid the rapidly declining birth rate, the government needs to undertake fundamental changes to its relevant policies'.[62]

But these 'policies' do not yet seriously include immigration. Rather than boost their populations by accepting immigrants from around the world – who are keen to come to these countries – politicians are trying and failing to convince natives to have more children.[63] Successive Japanese and South Korean governments have offered a range of financial incentives for couples to have children, but as is a trend throughout advanced economies, more people are choosing to remain single or get married later in life. And if they have children, they choose to usually have only one child.

Most young people in these countries – and in the West – are not conceptually opposed to having children. Many of them want to be parents. But they don't believe it's practical. They're worried about their wages, and about the world into which they may be bringing children, particularly about what increasingly looks like an impending climate disaster.[64] But above all, it is financial pressures that have left a whole generation in these democracies sceptical and unable to afford children.[65] Sexism in the corporate world only makes matters worse – women regularly report losing their jobs or opportunities within their companies because they decided to have children.[66] These realities produce powerful disincentives against becoming a parent, and particularly a mother.

Limited government financial incentives to have children have not bucked this curve.[67] The problems are too deep-seated for any government to solve in time to avert the coming demographic crisis.

'It would have been nice to have children and start a family, but after a lot of soul-searching, I decided against it,' as one South Korean woman in her late thirties put it. 'It's a shame, because I love kids, but they're luxuries I can't afford.'[68]

* * *

These Asian democracies are a glimpse into the West's future. Today, not a single European Union country maintains the desired 2.1 per cent fertility rate needed for a stable population, according to demographers. Neither do Canada (1.4), the United States (1.6) or the United Kingdom (1.6).[69] The European Union's average is a paltry 1.5; the OECD average is 1.6.[70] Even countries with well-regarded social safety nets – ones that *should* alleviate the financial pressures felt by would-be parents – lag behind the desired number. Both

Denmark and Sweden maintain a fertility rate of only 1.7; Finland's is only 1.4.[71]

What gives? Why are people in the richest, most advanced countries – democracies at that – refusing to have children? The answer, as in East Asia, is both economic and social.

There are positive incentives, such as increased wages, for women to delay motherhood, or to refuse it entirely. There are also financial pressures that make couples want to have fewer children than they might have done fifty years ago. Cuts to the social welfare state play a negative role, too.

Social changes – in gender roles, for instance – are relevant as well, but their impact should not be overstated.

Despite vast improvements in gender equality, which led to more women in the workforce, polls over the last decade have shown that Americans and Europeans, particularly women, want more children than they have.[72] Most women on both sides of the Atlantic say the ideal family size for them is two or more children, even while the average in their countries is far below that.[73] Somewhere around 90 per cent of both men and women in the European Union would prefer to have families with two or more children, despite the Union's average being less than two.[74] Over 95 per cent of American women said their ideal was either two children (52 per cent) or three or more (44 per cent), yet the average American woman has fewer than two children.[75]

When, in 2018, the *New York Times* asked young Americans – aged twenty to forty-five – about their family plans, 25 per cent said they had or expected to have fewer children than they wanted. Why, might you ask? A staggering 64 per cent said it was because childcare is too expensive, 49 per cent said it was because they were worried about the economy and 39 per cent said they simply did not have enough paid family leave.[76] (These numbers add up to over 100 per cent because respondents could choose multiple reasons for having or expecting to have fewer children.)

So, despite manifest social changes and media focus on them, the issue is decidedly not people choosing to stay childless because of feminism or gay rights or anything else. The problem is that many people cannot afford to have children or would have to drastically change their lifestyle to do so. Social factors are clearly less important than economic ones.

The point here is obvious: Americans, Europeans, Asians and citizens of rich democracies the world over are having fewer children because wages are not keeping up with the cost of living and child-rearing – making it incredibly difficult for people to save enough money to raise children, who are prohibitively expensive.[77]

The mechanism here is fixable. If democracies take steps towards improving their people's economic outlook – through at least some of the steps offered in this book – it's reasonable to assume that people will have more children. Studies show that when people have more money in their pockets, and feel more optimistic about the future, they are likely to have more children, even as social mores shift.[78]

But those changes will take time. And they are far from guaranteed. Which means that democracies need something of a stopgap measure as our native-born populations fall, promising to plunge us into demographic decline and economic malaise. If we are to get back to a place of stable financial footing for a broader swathe of the population, we must accept more immigrants. Simple as that.

* * *

Demographics are not the only reason to accept immigrants. A magical increase in our birth-rates would not be a reason to shutter our doors.

Study after study shows that new arrivals – regardless of their adopted country's demographic picture – have a positive impact on the economy, both by working low-wage jobs and by fostering innovation in the long-run. There is a clear net positive to 'refreshing' one's market, politics and culture with new arrivals from elsewhere. And those benefits manifest far beyond Pakistani paratha or Ethiopian injera.

It is worth noting, too, that while the richest corners of the world – the West and Northeast Asia – are experiencing declining birth rates, populations are booming across the rest of the globe. By 2050, a staggering 80 per cent or so of the world's population will live in Asia and Africa.[79] This population growth, particularly in Africa, will provide huge opportunities for economic growth, but it will also weigh on the world's environment. Nobody knows exactly how we can feed ten billion people, particularly in developing countries and as climate change drastically reshapes our world.[80]

Some have advanced the argument that declining birth-rates in the West and Northeast Asia are a good thing, because that means fewer mouths to feed.[81] Proponents of that position fail to grapple with the problems that stem from population decline – economic stagnation, for starters, which will imperil democracies' agendas both at home and abroad and prevent us from adequately feeding our own people.

Yet this decline is largely baked in, as is the developing world's demographic growth. Democratic governments need to wake up to this reality and develop plans to deal with it, to save not only their own skins, but also those of people who will be born in parts of countries like Bangladesh or Niger that could soon become too hot for any human to inhabit. There is a clear moral imperative for rich democracies to begin preparing for the influx of these people – particularly given that our industrialisation drove much of the climate change for which these poorer publics will now pay. It is the least we can do.

* * *

Autocracy's Fatal Flaw?

Despite autocracy's advances, people everywhere still want to live in democracies. For all the advancements of, say, China or Saudi Arabia, autocracies' best and brightest do, still, look for opportunity in the West, or in democracies like Australia and Japan.

But why? Why would you leave Shanghai, for instance, if you had made it into China's upper echelon?

Well, imagine being a young elite in China. Imagine having achieved everything that was expected of you as a young child and having secured a spot in a top-tier secondary school, which vaulted you into one of your country's top universities, maybe Tsinghua or Peking. Imagine having perhaps studied abroad, maybe in London or New Haven, and having tasted democracy. Imagine having returned home, to Shanghai or Beijing, having secured what seems like a global career – one of creativity and free movement – at a major foreign or domestic Chinese company. Imagine waking up one day and realising that you are effectively trapped within your own borders thanks to draconian COVID-19 policies, and that you are being ruled by what increasingly looks like a party of one in Beijing. Imagine having worked so hard only to find out that when the rubber meets the road, you remain, as a citizen of China, a cog in a machine directed by the whims of a brutal dictator. Imagine watching the cosmopolitan life of which you dreamed slowly slip away, only to be replaced by the visceral greyness of dictatorship. And imagine that this is the only life you could hope to pass on to your children.

A not-insignificant number of China's young people are experiencing this reality. As the pandemic dragged on – and as China's restrictions remained increasingly stringent, even into the fall of 2022 – more young middle-class or rich Chinese began thinking about ways to leave. They began speaking online of 'run philosophy'

(润学), a code for emigration.[82] In April 2022 alone, searches for 'immigration' increased more than fourfold on WeChat, the Chinese social media app. Users of Weibo, which is something like a Chinese version of Twitter, posted nearly eighty thousand times with the 'run' character in March and April.[83] All the while, more people in China's growing middle class were reaching out to immigration lawyers.[84] Immigration consultants say that enquiries about leaving China surged, even doubling by some estimates.[85]

'It's like an alarm bell has gone off,' said Miranda Wang, a young Chinese video-producer who moved to Shanghai after studying in Britain. She told journalists that Shanghai once felt not so different from London, but after two years of COVID-19, and after a two-month lockdown, she understood the differences and began researching ways to leave. The mirage of China had given way to reality. 'Now we realize, Shanghai is still China's Shanghai,' she added.

'No matter how much money, education or international access you have, you cannot escape the authorities.'[86]

* * *

COVID-19 may have exacerbated Chinese fantasies of flight, but the underlying yearning has been simmering for years. Immigration out of China has actually increased every year since 1985, by some measures.[87] In 2012 alone, nearly some 1.5 million people – or 0.11 per cent of the Chinese population – left the country, according to the World Bank.[88]

Many of those leaving were China's wealthiest; their most popular destinations were not rich autocracies, but democracies like New Zealand, Canada, Australia and the United States.[89] The wave of moneyed migration was significant enough that in November 2011, the state-run *People's Daily* newspaper even published an opinion article titled 'We Should Make It Harder for the Wealthy to Emigrate'.[90]

This pressure campaign failed.

By 2017, the number of people emigrating rose to 1.7 million.[91] A third of the country's millionaires said they wanted to leave, with the United States being their favoured destination.[92] In fact, since 2017, China's net migration rate – the number of incoming immigrants minus the number of emigrants – has worsened every year, reaching −0.254 per 1,000 people in 2022.[93] That means that China lost somewhere around 355,000 people in 2022 alone. (By way of comparison, the United States, Germany and the United Kingdom all posted positive net migration rates between 2.7 and 2.8.[94])

Remarkably, China's net migration rate has worsened every year since 2013. This was the year in which Xi Jinping became China's president and began replacing the country's traditional policymaking-by-consensus process to seize more power, subsequently steering China onto a more confrontational and inward-looking path – all while the country's world-beating economic growth slowed.

Economic growth and good governance can keep people from emigrating, even in an autocracy. A decline in both will send them for the fences, particularly in an authoritarian country. In China's case, it already has.

* * *

There is no worse advertisement for your system of government than when you seize people's passports or otherwise restrict their foreign travel to keep them from emigrating. This is a practice of a failing autocracy – of the late-stage Soviet Union or North Korea.

It is hardly indicative of state success, then, that in 2021 the Chinese government announced that it would not renew or issue most ordinary passports, except those for business, study abroad or emergencies.[95] It's not a great sign either that the number of passports the government issued in the first half of 2021 was a mere 2 per cent of the same period in 2019.[96] It's an even worse sign that authorities in at least one Chinese city went so far as to confiscate people's passports to prevent them from leaving.

And it's perhaps the worst sign that in May 2022 – amid the lockdowns and surging attempts to flee – China's immigration administration said that it would 'strictly restrict nonessential exit activities by Chinese citizens'.[97] Beijing said the decision was pandemic-related (to reduce imported infections) but more than a few Chinese social media users suspected that the measures were really about preventing emigration, and the brain drain that would go along with it.[98] (It is likewise not a great sign for the United States that a record number of Americans say they would emigrate abroad given the chance.[99])

But why is Beijing so concerned about emigration? Why wouldn't the Communist Party be *pleased* about seemingly unpatriotic people leaving? Why wouldn't Xi allow the critically minded to flee, resulting in a more pliant and 'patriotic' population?

The answer is simple: demographics.

China's one-child policy was integral to its short-term economic rise – because people had fewer children, parents had to spend less on children per capita, in turn boosting savings, investment and spending and thus economic growth.[100] But the policy is now coming to bite Beijing in the behind.[101] It has baked in a mid-twenty-first-century population decline of at least 100 million people.[102] Fewer Chinese people means less domestic consumption, and thus slower economic growth.[103]

Chinese citizens' contemporary collective decision to not have as many children – for similar reasons as their counterparts elsewhere – only exacerbates matters. Children are either too expensive, a burden (particularly for unwed mothers, who still face discrimination in China), or a drag on personal and professional development, or some combination of the three, among other issues.[104]

China's contemporary numbers are now worsening much faster than those of many other countries. Japan may have long been the poster child for fertility issues, but China's birth rate fell behind Japan's in 2021.[105] In fact, since 1990, China's fertility rate has fallen by almost 50 per cent, from around 2.25 – over two children per woman – to around 1.3.[106] No other country has posted such a drastic decline.[107]

And, unlike democracies, particularly Western ones, China struggles to attract immigrants as an answer.

China's immigration trends are actually moving in the opposite direction. Beijing knows as much, which is part of the reason why Chinese leaders have tried to woo foreigners – both rich immigrants from the West (often of Chinese ethnicity) and students from China-friendly developing countries in Asia, Latin America and across Africa.[108] But students are not permanent residents; nor are many rich Australians or Brits planning to relocate to China permanently, even if they are ethnically Chinese. Neither are the Cambodians nor Nigerians given scholarships to study in China. The citizens of developing countries who study in China do so in order to return home and lead their own countries; China is their waystation, not their home.

* * *

China is not the only autocracy struggling to maintain population growth.

Even relatively well-off autocracies – those in the upper third of global GDP per capita – are struggling. Russia's net migration rate is hovering around 0.7 per 1,000; that number will continue to decline amid decreasing native Russian births and the vast numbers of Russian men fleeing government conscription into fighting the war in Ukraine.[109] Thailand's is only 0.28, down from nearly 0.5 in 2014, when the ruling military ousted the democratic government in a coup.[110] Kazakhstan's is around −0.2.[111]

Some of the richest autocracies – those like Qatar and Saudi Arabia that have relatively strong net migration rates – have also continued posting declines in net migration every year for the last decade, if not longer.[112] Hong Kong's net migration rate has declined by 70 per cent since China took control of the city in 1997. That number will now surely fall further, owing to both the city's stringent COVID-19 restrictions and China's crackdowns.[113] From June 2021 to June 2022 alone, Hong Kong's population dropped by some 121,500 people, or 1.6 per cent of the population – the largest third straight year of decline and the largest decline in at least 60 years.[114]

Even idealised Singapore, the richest autocracy per capita, is having some limited problems.[115] The city-state continues to post a net migration rate of 4.6, higher than that of the United States, the United Kingdom and others, but this rate has fallen by 85 per cent since 2008.

Nonetheless, Singapore is certainly in a better position than most. It is probably the best-governed autocracy the world has ever seen. It will not face a demographic crisis like that of China, Russia or some of the Gulf States precisely because it is so well-governed – because it remains a relatively attractive destination for people the world over, and can get more people to move there with certain incentives, such as low taxes, a generally high quality of life and internationally renowned schools. There is a reason why many Americans, Brits and others happily move to Singapore, at least for a period.

But with the possible exception of Singapore, autocracies do not pull on the world's heartstrings like democracy and the West do. There is a reason why, when most people in developing countries think of success and wealth, they still think of America or Europe. There is a reason why – despite the vast amount of funds China and Russia have poured into Asia and Africa – emigrants there still prefer the West.[116] There is a reason why even after Trump dented America's image, the United States remains the top desired destination for potential migrants worldwide.[117] There is a reason why potential migrants' other most preferred destinations are all democracies, too.[118]

And that reason is the promise of the good life: of the freedom and wealth that only democracy can deliver, and that autocracies still cannot. China, Singapore, the Gulf States and others can lay claim to the future all they want, but the weary people of this world – those fleeing home only because home, as the Somali-British poet, Warsan Shire, has written, 'is the mouth of a shark' and the 'barrel of a gun' – give lie to these dreams.[119] It is always those facing the most desperate straits who are most likely to speak the truth. And in their most dire moments, those brave people fleeing the jaws of poverty and violence continue, against all odds, to choose us. They continue to choose democracy.

Their choice should remind us that democracies are a profound oddity not only in the course of human history, but today, when there are more autocracies in the world than there are democracies. Their choice should remind us of how lucky we are as citizens of democracy. It should remind us not only of the need to fight for democracy, but also to stand up to those xenophobes who would prefer that we put up walls and keep out immigrants – not only because of economics, but because these immigrants are the best ambassadors for democracy.

Every immigrant demonstrates all that we can offer, and all that autocracies cannot.

We would do well, then, to not look so harshly on those who are willing to sacrifice everything to become members of our exceptional societies – and to remember that they can help save our democracies. We must stand up for those who are willing to sacrifice to come to our shores.

People everywhere will drop everything to become democrats; for our benefit, and for theirs, we must find ways to let them.

* * *

Opening Our Doors

Borders are necessary to define the state. And it is states – and states alone – that can protect the rights for which liberal democrats have fought so hard. Only states can protect the right to the good life within their borders. A world without borders is a world of anarchy in which states have essentially no control.[120] A harmonious borderless world of free movement is a fantasy.

There is quite clearly a common-sense position in between the two ends of the spectrum: somewhere between those on the left arguing for what are essentially open borders and those on the right firmly opposed to any immigration.

So far, this chapter has made clear democracies' competitive advantage on immigration. People want to come to us and once here, they are disproportionately likely to make a positive impact not only economically, but symbolically. Immigrants are nothing less than a necessity. And while we maintain our borders, we should be doing far more to bring them in – all while sticking to that common-sense position.

* * *

Western democracies have long been a relative haven for immigration. That is why even the Trump-era United States and Kurz-era Austria accepted more than double the immigrants per capita than Japan and South Korea did.

But with anti-immigrant sentiment seemingly rising everywhere, politicians must stand up and make the economic case for immigration, along with the social one. We may like to think that our national brethren are altruistic, but the reality is that when the going gets tough, people are likely to look out for themselves and their 'tribe'. Which means that in a world facing manifest challenges, from inflation to inequality, leaders would be wise to explain the economic benefits of immigration, rather than just the values-based case. Ordinary people need to understand that immigration helps their country's economy, and that they themselves will likely feel the effects.

The data are quite clear. As our fertility rates decline, immigrants will help countries meet their social spending obligations, such as social security, they will do vital jobs that natives do not want, they will help us maintain economic growth and, as the data shows, some of them will develop the innovations democracies need to win the future.[121]

Key to facilitating more migration is making this economic case. Arguments that we must accept immigrants because it is the 'right thing to do' will only go so far when people are struggling to make ends meet at home.[122]

People can be forgiven for wondering why their leaders are so focused on immigrants when their own constituents are struggling.

A basic suggestion for pro-immigration leaders is to speak more about the tangible benefits immigrants bring. Focus your messaging less on terms like 'justice' and 'dignity' – which may win plaudits in Washington and Berlin, but ring hollow for most – and more on economics.[123] Most people are not well versed in migration theory, but just about everyone is worried about the economy and about the impact decisions made in the halls of power will have on their wallets.

Politicians therefore need to explain in simple terms to the farmer or bank teller that, no, the refugee from Syria is not going to take their job, but will pay more in taxes to the state than they receive in benefits. They may even be an innovator, or parent of a child who creates something great, but they need not be. Their very presence here, their pursuit of ordinary life and business ventures, stimulates the economy in and of itself and demonstrates the superiority of our democratic system.

Some people are simply racist and will not want to accept anyone who does not look like them. But most people are not; polls show that most people are not opposed to all, or even most, immigration in principle.[124] Yet many nonetheless believe immigrants to be a drag on the economy, and therefore on their own ability to make ends meet.

That's the typical gripe against immigration: it's about self-interest, not hatred of others. Convincing these people – the winnable moderates – of immigration's economic benefits is vital.[125] Prioritising moral and social concerns is thus a sure-fire way to lose them and, ultimately, lose elections.

But the only way to increase immigration numbers is to win elections. Particularly following the inflation struggles of the last two years, money is people's most important problem. Pro-immigration advocates need to speak and act more like it.

* * *

In addition to reframing the immigration debate, pro-immigration leaders must fix their broken immigration systems.

This is particularly true in the United States, which has failed to reform immigration policy since the 1990s. Its existing system is too restrictive, limiting the number of people based on nationality and even skill. There is even a limit on those with 'extraordinary ability'. Children of temporary workers who grow up here are forced to leave at twenty-one if they do not get permanent residency. The United States also issues no temporary visas to year-round workers who do not have college degrees.[126]

Just about all of this is bad policy.

Several other democracies are similarly struggling to produce immigration systems for the twenty-first century.

Japan's system is so onerous – and tolerant of worker abuse – that it hinders both low- and high-skilled workers from coming.[127] French immigration policy focuses not on attracting people, but on explicitly keeping them away.[128] Australia's overly harsh policy, which allows for years-long detention of asylum-seekers, has a similar effect.[129] (Singapore, on the other hand, is moving to liberalise its own immigration system, including allowing foreigners earning a minimum of S$30,000, around USD 21,000, per month to secure a five-year work visa.[130])

Let me restate, just for clarity: democracies must maintain their borders; we cannot and should not accept everyone looking to move. But at a moment when it is so apparent that immigrants boost our economies and demonstrate democracies' strengths, it should be similarly apparent that we desperately need to reform our systems. We should allow people to emigrate legally by updating our systems for the twenty-first century and beyond. A failure to do so will only leave us, native-born citizens, bearing the brunt down the line.

* * *

Democracies can only choose their immigrants to a certain extent. More frequently, people choose democracies, making the perilous trip here from their homelands, which are often rife with violence and corruption. These people tend to arrive as refugees claiming asylum, a status that, if granted, makes it illegal for them to be deported (assuming they become citizens, which many don't due to the US government's poor communication – a problem about which I've written elsewhere).[131]

Too often, refugees are discussed as a burden. Media reports highlight all the negative things about refugees, claiming that they are a drain on the welfare state or that they are taking jobs from the native-born population. Neither of those things is true, as the data shows.

But there are real cultural concerns. There is no question that a fifty-five-year-old Syrian refugee from Aleppo almost certainly does not have the same progressive views on LGBTQ people or Jews as a Berlin-born teenager. Polls show as much: a 2017 study reported that 54 per cent of Iraqi refugees and 52 per cent of Syrian refugees in Germany agreed with the statement: 'Jews have too much influence in the world.'[132] One academic in Germany, Antje Röder, found that Muslim immigrants in Europe are less accepting of homosexuality than their native-born counterparts.[133]

I am a gay Jewish man; clearly, I think these concerns are real and should be grappled with. But they should not be overstated.

We should do background checks to prevent literal terrorists from entering our countries – just about everyone agrees on that point – but we don't need all our citizens, refugees or not, to think the way elites deem 'correct'. Democracies survive because they tolerate peaceful differences of opinion, even on sensitive issues like these.

It's worth noting, too, that people often change their minds upon moving to and living in a new place. Röder, the German academic, found that Muslim migrant opposition to homosexuality 'weakens with longer stay', while Muslim immigrants' children are signifi-cantly more supportive of homosexuality than their parents.[134]

Children of one foreign-born parent and one local are actually more accepting of homosexuality than the average native, suggesting that people willing to inter-marry across ethnic lines – immigrants included – tend to hold more progressive views on LGBTQ people, which they pass on to their children.[135]

Cultural concerns must not stymie refugee resettlement. On the contrary, we should look to make the most of such resettlement to solve labour shortages for which there are no local solutions, with the expectation that cultural differences may persist, at least for one generation.

Denmark has demonstrated how this should work.

When several municipalities there realised they did not have enough people to work in lower-paying jobs, they turned to recently arrived refugees.[136] The municipality matched refugees with these open roles and trained them. The result was a 5 to 6 per cent increase in their employment after one year, and a 10 per cent increase after two years.[137] And of course, when refugees (or immigrants) have jobs, they have more money, and thus contribute more taxes and spend more – meaning that investing in their job training will benefit both the state and the economy.

Critical to Denmark's approach is that it was decidedly not skills-based. Efforts to bring high-skilled immigrants are important, but Denmark's approach demonstrates the benefits of accepting just about anyone ready to work. Denmark's policy was not an admission policy but one of integration.

The small American city of Utica, in the rust belt of upstate New York, did something similar. After years of depopulation owing to the disappearance of manufacturing and industrial jobs, the city revitalised itself by accepting waves of immigrants, particularly from the Balkans and Southeast Asia. Several non-profit organisations supported the effort with job training and language classes, with English skills being vital to employment.[138]

I attended college some twenty-five minutes away from Utica and spent more nights than I can count wolfing Vietnamese food at Pho Mekong or Cambodian cuisine at Sunny restaurant. The proprietors are lovely people looking simply to share a bit of their homeland with their new neighbourhoods, provide for their families and live in peace. They're chatty, the food is excellent.

Seeing their shops full of not only other college kids and migrants, but also older white people who have long called the region home – and very well may have voted for Donald Trump – is to me a moving *tableau vivant* of the American dream in all its splendour and peculiarity. It doesn't hurt that the city has seen substantial economic growth over the last few decades.[139]

The lesson from both Denmark and Utica is that countries facing labour shortages in lower-paying fields – in which locals often refuse to work – can fix the problem by accepting more immigrants, even 'unskilled' ones. Fixing that problem would make our governments and economies more receptive and more functional. The result would be improved faith in our countries, and in our democracies.

Just about everyone has some kind of labour problem right now. Japan and the United Kingdom are suffering from critical shortages of agricultural workers.[140] The United States has far more jobs in the transportation, social assistance, and accommodation and food sectors than we have people to work in them.[141] Even tiny Estonia does not have enough manufacturing workers to accelerate economic growth.[142]

Each of these countries, along with countless others, could quite clearly benefit from a Denmark-style immigration job-training programme or Utica-type resettlement process. This is particularly true in more rural parts of these countries, which are suffering from demographic decline far more rapidly than urban centres. These are the same areas more likely to have older populations who support anti-immigration politicians – which is why, when pushing such solutions, politicians need to tell their constituents that yes, they may look different, but the immigrant who will collect the rubbish or drive your bus is a net positive.

People want to live in democracies; most are ready to work. We just need to give them the opportunity, both for our benefit and for theirs.

* * *

Democracies are facing labour shortages in higher-skilled industries as well.

The United States has nowhere near enough computer-related workers: for every seven postings for such jobs, there was only one unemployed worker.[143] The United Kingdom does not have enough people to staff the National Health Service.[144] That country's skilled workforce is on track to be 250,000 less than needed to just meet demand in 2030.[145] Even Japan reports far fewer skilled workers than the country needs.[146]

The good news is that there are more highly skilled people around the world than ever before.[147] Democracies should look to attract them not only by offering benefits (scholarships, and so forth) but also by simplifying our immigration systems, specifically by offering would-be emigrants a sense of stability.

Currently, too many job-specific immigration programmes provide only temporary respite; they decidedly do *not* promise long-term residence, whether as a citizen or as a legal non-citizen resident.

One example is the US H-1B visa which, while intended for highly-skilled foreigners, is a specifically 'non-immigrant' visa, meaning that visa holders are explicitly allowed to stay in the United States only temporarily.[148] They must constantly renew their visa every time it is set to expire. After six years, most H-1B holders must leave the United States for a year before reapplying (if they do not qualify for an exception allowing an extension).[149]

This is bad policy. It makes little sense for a US company to hire someone on such a precarious visa and train them for years only to see them return to their home country. It would be far better to offer H-1B visa holders a path to citizenship after six years in the country, assuming they steer clear of criminal behaviour.

Sending a qualified data scientist or engineer back to China or Russia after six years in the United States makes no sense; keeping them here makes all the sense in the world.

Every democracy has different immigration regulations, but many do have problems like those exemplified by the H-1B visa: an onerous process, an unclear system and an overall complex set of restrictions that makes the high-skill immigration route more of a hassle than it is worth.

Several democracies, to their credit, have taken an increasingly positive approach to high-skilled immigration. Following former British prime minister Theresa May's shambolic decision to cap the number of skilled immigrants arriving monthly, the United Kingdom revised its skilled worker visa to allow people to work in the country for five years and to apply to settle permanently there after that.[150] Japan, too, has begun offering skilled worker visas with no time limit.[151] (This move seems like a response to skilled workers ranking Japan the last place in Asia they would want to live.[152])

More such reforms are clearly needed throughout the democratic world. Data shows that many publics support high-skilled immigration, suggesting that politicians will be pushing on an open door.[153] Our leaders just need to realise that reality and crack the gate a bit.

* * *

Moving Forward

Immigration is a charged issue. There is no way around that. Some people want no immigrants, others want only skilled immigrants and a loud minority says that any immigration restrictions are racist and beyond the pale.

The emotional nature of this issue often manages to obscure the data relevant to any reasoned discussion about immigration. It is those facts on which this chapter has leaned to make a few key points. And it is those facts that form the backbone of my argument.

I hope that this chapter makes clear the positive democratic case for more immigration: that immigrants serve to boost our economies and make our governments more functional, all of which has the potential to improve domestic trust in democracy – thereby giving our governments more political space with which to combat autocracy abroad, while also making the case for why our system is better at home.

If that is not convincing enough, consider that economists believe allowing more people to move from low-productivity poor countries to high-productivity rich countries would increase global GDP by trillions of dollars.[154] The benefits are real, and they will be felt by many.

These benefits will help democracies take on the challenges posed by autocracies like China and Russia: more money in people's pockets will fend off autocracy's rise at home; more money will also allow our governments to dedicate more resources to advancing our efforts abroad. The symbolism of successful immigrants continuing to choose us, rather than autocracies, will only further demonstrate democracy's superiority and boost our soft power efforts the world over.

This is a case not for open borders but for smart borders – for borders that allow the movement of both refugees fleeing persecution and a certain number of economic immigrants looking to make more money and live a better life. Their drive for success, and their willingness to work for it, have long been what make democracies great. It is immigrants who can help keep our democracies together at home. And it is their drive to flee autocracies that weakens authoritarian governments across the world, both practically and symbolically; you can hardly hope to stay in power or rewrite the international system's rules if your best people are fleeing to your rivals.

Our willingness to continue accepting these people, truck drivers and technology professionals alike, will ensure our greatness not just for my generation, but for those set to come beyond us. It is immigrants who will help us defeat the dictators, not only today, but tomorrow, too.

Conclusion
Whose World?

China has seized Taiwan. It was a grinding war, with heavy losses on both sides. But after eighteen months of gruelling attacks, including a horrific siege of Taipei, China prevailed.

The West and its allies provided Taiwan with money and military material, but we refused to fight a war on the island's behalf. We refused to even send forces to the island, no matter how much the Taiwanese – who had bet not only on their democracy, but on our democracies' support – pleaded for it. Our publics, particularly the American public, were too scarred by Afghanistan and Iraq, not to mention frustrated with a lagging economy at home, to fight another foreign war in a far-off land. Our people saw, too, what happened in Ukraine – that our weapons allowed Kyiv to fight off Moscow long enough, and that when Russia offered a ceasefire lopsided in its own favour, the West pushed Ukraine to accept it – and thought something similar was good enough in Taiwan. The island could make some compromises with Beijing and remain nominally independent.

We certainly weren't going to war on their behalf. We had enough problems of our own at home to deal with. And so, we gave them some weapons to boost their campaign, but we refused to fight.

There was simply no public support for sending troops.

The US president, struggling at home amid rising inequality, unrest and outright authoritarianism in statehouses around the country – all of which made America less powerful than at any point since the Second World War – couldn't muster a domestic coalition, let alone an international one, to fight for Taiwan. NATO was so divided by an authoritarian and China-aligned Turkey that it couldn't meaningfully come to Taiwan's defence. Hungary, China's closest partner in Europe, played a similar spoiler role within the EU. Russia, bolstered by Beijing's support following its own setback in Ukraine, came to China's support. Much of the developing world, itself now economically and politically attached to China, held its collective breath, refusing to support Taipei for fear of retribution from Beijing.

And so, outmatched by China's overwhelming military might, Taiwan fell.

The island is now just another Chinese province – one in which the Communist Party reigns, in which free speech is not tolerated, and where human rights are not respected. The island's former democratic leadership has fled to the West, where they continue to make their case heard. But Taiwan's cause has become something like that of Tibet: on the minds of a select few activists and academics, but without any forward momentum in anyone's halls of power. The democratic-minded *intelligentsia* still advocates for Taiwan in places like Washington, London and Tokyo, but no democratic government makes a serious case for liberating the island. How could they when they've already lost?

With its seizure of Taiwan, China now controls the flow of innovation and key goods like semiconductors, which everyone needs not only for basic technology like computers but for military material, too. China – including its newest province of Taiwan – now controls the island's vital semiconductor industry and produces around 95 per cent of these chips, and nearly all the most vital ones.[1] China also leads the world in green energy innovation and has secured a near-complete monopoly of rare earths, which people everywhere need to enable their electronic devices to function.

Democracies did not stand up for Taiwan because they simply could not afford to.

The leaders of democracies everywhere can no longer meaning-fully challenge China because the world now revolves around Beijing; China knows as much, and wields this centrality to its advantage. Beijing's closest partners – in Africa, Asia and beyond – benefit, their loyalty and pliant approach to China finally paying off. Beijing's erstwhile rivals, in the West and beyond, have no such privilege. They now must beg for the green tech they need to combat climate change and the semiconductors they need to make their economies literally work.

Challenging Beijing is no longer worth it. New Zealand's tough approach to China fades; Australia's own harder policy slowly gives away; Japan and South Korea follow; then Europe; and finally, the United States.

How could these defences not fall, when standing up to China would result in severe economic disruptions at home, and when these democracies – having continued to under-perform in their own deliverance of public goods and services – are experiencing such a continued public backlash that they cannot afford such disruptions? The US president, German chancellor and Japanese prime minister can hardly afford yet another disruption as their populations age, their innovation lags, their inequality persists and people remain dissatisfied with democracy. Any disruption risks their ousting and these politicians, having worked their whole lives for this moment, can't have *that*.

So, they don't challenge China. They give up on Taiwan. They don't do anything to help the Uyghurs or Tibetans, who continue to live under brutal repression. They don't stop Beijing from simply seizing parts of its neighbours, whether from India and Bhutan or in the South China Sea. They simply accept Beijing's economic bullying and use of forced labour as a part of our world.

Looking at all of this, China-sceptical countries in Asia – whether Vietnam or the Philippines – make the decision that they would be better off kowtowing to Beijing than believing in Washington or Tokyo. The US-led rules-based order in Asia thus gives way and is replaced by a similarly connected but now Sino-centric order that prizes power and Chinese interests over all else. The rest of the world soon follows.

We try to remedy the situation, but the die has been cast. Our troubled domestic politics, the natural result of long-unaddressed grievances (themselves the result of inaction), allow only for piece-meal efforts; they're hardly enough. When the rubber hits the road, we cower. We don't stand up to China, and China wins. Welcome to a world of second-class status.

* * *

This world in which China wins is not a world in which only China wins. It is a world in which China-aligned governments – from Cambodia to Djibouti – gain pre-eminence and power, too. It is a world in which Russia, humbled by its stalemate (or eventual loss) in Ukraine, has found a path back to global power by becoming China's leading lieutenant. Moscow may play second-fiddle to Beijing in exchange for support, but Russia is now more powerful than it has been in decades and continues to disrupt democratic politics, particularly within its nearby European neighbours.

China's partners become more powerful because of their rela-tionships with Beijing. Innovation now flows through them first, rather than through the West and its partners. They become the countries that reach the future first: the ones with the knowledge to craft the world in their image, whether it be artificial intelligence or future internet innovations. And they do: they create a world of standards without meaningful labour, environmental, privacy and human rights protections. Other countries, ones that previously sat on the fence between China and the West, promptly align with

Beijing, seeing where their bread will be buttered for the foreseeable future.

This is a world in which would-be autocrats gain power within democracies, too.

Because if autocracies already run the world, voters' thinking will go, whether that be in the United States, France or South Korea, *then why shouldn't a strongman rule in my country? It worked for China and its partners,* they'll think. *Authoritarians run these countries, which run the world. Why wouldn't it work for us?*

And so, once-democratic electorates put China-friendly autocrats into power; these autocrats then do away with the checks and balances critical to democracy and align themselves with China, the world's foremost power. The era of democratic world leadership, which now looks like a blip in the vastness of humanity's mostly authoritarian history, ends with a whimper.

* * *

This world could very well exist by the end of this century, if not sooner.

China already has something close to a monopoly of rare earths.[2] Australia, the United States and others are now just beginning to build rare earth refineries, which will not be functional until 2025 at the earliest.[3]

Even without seizing Taiwan, China in 2020 recorded nearly USD 40 billion in semiconductor sales – surpassing Taiwan and coming just behind Japan and the European Union.[4] China is also the world's leading solar panel manufacturer, with about 80 per cent of that good's global supply chain running through the country (including through Xinjiang, where China has conscripted ethnic and religious minorities into forced labour).[5]

This dominance, coupled with China's general economic power

and the relative attractiveness of its model, already makes countries everywhere hesitant to criticise Beijing. A Sino-centric order does not yet exist in full, but it certainly exists in part.

There are, for instance, almost no Muslim countries willing to criticise China's crackdowns in Xinjiang. Former Pakistani prime minister Imran Khan said he 'accept[ed] the Chinese version' of what is going on in Xinjiang; his government then aided Beijing by deporting some sixty Uyghurs back to face persecution in China.[6] Saudi Arabia has done the same.[7] These and countless other Muslim nations are willing to sacrifice their persecuted brethren to ensure close ties with Beijing. The costs of alienating China are already too high.

And while many democracies – particularly those in Europe – have over the last eighteen months taken stronger positions on China, citing human rights abuses and Beijing's bellicosity abroad, democracies everywhere are not immune from the pressures of aligning with or at least not aggravating China. This is particularly true in developing democracies, whose leaders are under huge pressure to demonstrate tangible advances, particularly in terms of infrastructure, or face ousting. I've seen just how much Malaysia, for instance, needs roads – and how China comes to the table with more money and a willingness to build things faster than anyone else.

This is the case in the Philippines as well, where former president Rodrigo Duterte – and to a lesser extent, current president Ferdinand Marcos Jr – cosied up to China in exchange for investment and other support, despite anti-Chinese sentiment among the public, as well as in Chile, whose new president Gabriel Boric has slammed the United States for missing opportunities in Latin America and extolled China for providing investment without imposing supposedly onerous conditions.[8] It is the case as well in democracies as diverse as Indonesia and South Africa – countries that, like the Philippines and

Chile, if forced to choose between the West (and its partners) and Beijing would likely lean towards the latter.

Even Israel, a country *birthed* in the wake of a genocide, has developed close enough ties with China – despite Beijing's behaviour in Xinjiang – to alarm the United States, Jerusalem's long-time leading supporter.

China is Israel's third-largest trading partner; a Chinese state-owned company has upgraded and will operate the Haifa port, Israel's busiest, until at least 2040.[9] It should alarm democracies everywhere that Israel allowed that port project to continue even after American officials told their Israeli counterparts that 'the United States could not be friends with a country for whom China was building ports'.[10]

Israel was willing to call Washington's bluff, and unwilling to cut its profitable ties with China.

It helps, too, that Beijing – citing its historic foreign policy doctrine of non-interference – offers more complete *carte blanche* for its partners' violation of human rights norms. More than a few Israeli colleagues have told me as much: that while China pays lip service to the Palestinian cause, Chinese criticism is far more measured than what comes out of some segments of the American left and a broader swath of the European body politic. Beijing offers Jerusalem money and friendship without the judgement, which is why in 2017 in Beijing Prime Minister Benjamin Netanyahu went as far as to call the China–Israel relationship 'a marriage made in heaven'.[11]

This is also why Jerusalem, despite its own deep memory of genocide, in 2021 refused to sign on to a French-led UN statement condemning Chinese actions in Xinjiang. One Israeli official said that Jerusalem declined because it has 'other interests that it has to balance' in its relationship with Beijing.[12] Then-foreign minister and future prime minister Yair Lapid was even more blunt, speaking perhaps not only on his country's behalf, but on behalf of fence-sitting nations everywhere – the ones that do not know who will own the future, and are hedging their bets between China and the West.

'China's importance to the Israeli economy is very significant, and we need to find a way to talk about this issue in a way that does not harm Israel's interests,' Lapid said.[13]

* * *

The challenge democracies face today is clear enough. A set of autocracies, China the most powerful among them, is seeking to popularise undemocratic governance the world over. These autocracies want to refashion the existing international order to make it more friendly to their own goals, and thus less friendly to democracies' aims and values. They believe they can bring about such a world because democracies, particularly in the West, are declining – because our politics prevent adequate investments and reforms, resulting in under-performance that brings into power self-defeating leaders like Trump and decisions like Brexit.

An autocratic order might permit some form of free-ish trade. Of course, it is free trade – ironically facilitated by the same order China seeks to now refashion with itself at the centre – that made China rich. But China's vision for free trade is hardly 'free'. Such trade will be highly politicised, with countries like China cutting off partners for purely political reasons.

The result will be stifled economic growth, diminished standards (particularly on human rights issues), and, broadly speaking, a world in which democracies struggle to advance their priorities and values, both at home and abroad. It will be a world in which China and its partners control the flow of key innovations and other goods – one in which no democracy can afford to restrict the import of goods made with forced labour, as the United States has already done with Chinese products from Xinjiang.

Simply put, a world ruled by China will be one in which countries everywhere have little choice but to bend to Beijing's whim or face the economic consequences. It will be a world in which countries must pay fealty to Beijing to both maintain access to key goods like rare earths and export goods to China's massive market, a world in which economic success hinges on countries' willingness to appease China and its partners.

China's decisions in recent years to restrict trade – with South Korea because Seoul deployed the American Terminal High Altitude Area Defense (THAAD) system on its own territory; with Lithuania because Vilnius sought closer ties with Taiwan; and with Australia because Canberra simply called for an investigation into COVID-19's origins – offer a glimpse into what this world would look like.[14] And it's not pretty.

Australia weathered the economic storm well by finding alternative markets for its exports. But not all countries will have such success.[15]

Even South Korea has struggled.

Former president Moon Jae-in normalised trade with Beijing in 2017 by nominally agreeing to a policy known as the 'Three Nos', which pledge that South Korea will (1) not add any new batteries to the THAAD system, (2) not participate in a US missile defence network and (3) not join a military alliance with the United States and Japan. Yet the current South Korean president, Yoon Suk-yeol, came into power promising both a stronger line on China and to deploy another THAAD battery – positions that were evidently popular among the South Korean body politic.

China in August 2022 then demanded that Yoon abide by that policy; Beijing even mispresented a meeting with the two countries' foreign ministers to imply that the South Korean officials had promised to restrict THAAD operations, which they had not. The Yoon administration claimed that the policy 'is neither a promise nor an agreement', but South Korea must ensure at least functional ties with China, which remains Seoul's top trading partner and vital to the South Korean economy.[16]

China, then, could break critical supply chains in Asia and beyond simply because of Beijing's politics. Experience suggests that Xi will not hesitate to do so at some point. That should instil worry – and make clear – what an autocracy-friendly world ruled by China will look like.

This future has not yet been written. China, Russia and their partners do not yet rule the world. The dominant global economic system continues to be the one Washington established. China still relies on that system, and on Western technology, even if Beijing is rapidly trying to make itself less reliant on the world abroad – and thus more able to cut off those that ruffle its feathers.

More power may still reside in Washington than in Beijing, but there is no guarantee that this will be true tomorrow. The world is not static; power ebbs and flows; some great powers decline, becoming relatively normal countries like the United Kingdom. Others, like the Soviet Union, simply collapse.

Democracies should find no comfort in this history. Nothing about it suggests that we'll emerge victorious in our battle for the future. Rather, if the past is a prologue – as it tends to be – democracies have every reason to worry, and to finally get our act together.

We may not yet be in an explicitly armed conflict with autocracy, although the Ukraine crisis has pushed us in that direction, but we are in a world of antagonists who see this competition as zero-sum.

China, Russia and several autocracies believe that their victory must come at our expense. So, while some top policymakers in those countries and their partners may favour coexistence for now, they still aim to defeat us in the long-term, preferably without having to pick up arms. It's all the better for China if Beijing can simply beat us by improving its governance and expanding Chinese international influence while we remain complacent and then decay.

Ultimately, if democracies are to retain their way of life – and if we are to improve the lives of others abroad – we will need to defeat the dictators both at home and abroad. To do so, we must beat autocracies at their own game: not by becoming more authoritarian, but by improving our own governance. We must deliver on the promise that our governance system offers to the people.

China and others may promise economic stability, but we simply offer and can deliver more – more freedom, equality and opportunities to pursue happiness.

For our efforts to be successful, people in democracies and abroad need to know that democracy works. They need to believe in the system, because if democratic citizens revolt against their own system, then elites can hardly hope to promote our values anywhere else. And I firmly believe that for democracies to work, we will need to take the steps outlined in this book.

We must make our systems more meritocratic by investing in early education, paying successful civil servants more competitive wages and containing political patronage.

We will have to become more accountable by prosecuting the powerful (when they clearly deserve it), expanding open records laws and increasing the transparency of money in politics.

We must work to re-establish trust in government by making government more transparent, speaking more about what government *is* doing well, better engaging minority groups, partnering with the private sector in select cases and expanding voter access.

We will also have to think more in the long-term – by legally requiring leaders to focus on the future by developing five- or ten-year plans, encouraging them to speak more honestly about the long-term benefits of their plans, and placing more power in the hands of local communities.

We will need to update our social safety nets for the twenty-first century and beyond by making non-regular workers eligible for high-quality healthcare, making these systems more worker-friendly and streamlining the benefit process.

We must boost our human capital capabilities by offering more undergraduate and graduate scholarships for people studying science and technology, funding and prioritising vocational schools, providing constant skills training to all workers (in a simpler manner than today), supporting companies that invest in human capital development and recruiting more foreign talent.

We have no choice but to invest in our infrastructure – not only by improving our decaying roads and bridges, but by laying high-speed internet cables everywhere, modernising online infrastructure and boosting the cyber-security of cyber-modernised projects already on the grid.

Finally, we must look to accept more immigrants – high-skilled and otherwise – from around the world by reforming our immigration systems, and then priming these migrants for success by training them to solve labour shortages. To make this possible, politicians will need to speak clearly and courageously about the economic benefits of this migration: that immigrants will not take your job but will do the jobs you won't; they will also add to national GDP and tax revenue. Some of them will produce the innovations that change the world, like Google. And of course, their willingness to sacrifice everything to get to us – to get to the democratic world – serves as yet another reminder and powerful demonstration of democracy's superiority.

These steps will make democracies more functional; they will improve democratic citizens' support not only for their governments and countries, but for democracy generally – because when democracy is at its transparent, adaptive and future-focused best, nothing can beat it. And when democracy is at its best at home, it will have a much better shot at winning abroad, both today and tomorrow. And if democracies win, everyone everywhere has a better chance of winning in the long-term.

* * *

Despite what some in Beijing or Moscow think, this competition is not yet a zero-sum game. Just because we need to get our own houses – and model – in order does not mean that China, the United Arab Emirates or Vietnam will or must become democracies tomorrow. Nor does it mean that we cannot have positive ties with Abu Dhabi and Hanoi.

In fact, we can, and we should.

Democracies need friends beyond their own clique, which remains relatively small in the grand scheme of global geopolitics: we need positive ties with Singapore, the United Arab Emirates and Vietnam, even if their domestic successes challenge our values and ideas about what a polity looks like. Defeating autocracy decidedly does not require abandoning all autocratic partners right now.

Rather, we should use these economically and strategically important relationships to advance our respective national interests and produce domestic success in our democracies, such as by engaging in mutually beneficial trade. That success will allow our leaders to do more to support democracy abroad; domestic democratic success alone will surely boost the civil society leaders and democratic-minded folks in autocracies around the world. If we make it clear that our system works, more people will flock to it – and make democracy work for them in the long-term.

Such success offers hope that life can get better, not only in terms of economic growth, but in terms of freedom. By making clear that democracy works, and that it works better than autocracy does, we will lay the groundwork for a more democratic and more harmonious world. That effort will be far more successful than any efforts to topple an autocrat today and replace him with a democrat tomorrow.

My generation may not reap the benefits. But if we play our cards right, perhaps those who come after us will, from Hanoi to Hackney and beyond.

* * *

Autocracy's Afflictions

Democracies' ills dominate the headlines. The disturbing frequency of mass shootings in America makes global news, in Paris and Perth alike. Britain's Brexit vote and autumn 2022 pound crash were panned just about universally. Reports of South Korean presidential corruption make headlines in the *New York Times* and perhaps even the *Telegraph*. So, too, does Japan's ballooning public debt. Stories of our decline are everywhere.

It's understandable why there is so much malaise about democracy, especially in democracies. The narrative of our decline is inescapable; I understand why people everywhere think that we're simply too far gone and slipping into an era of irrelevance. I understand why former classmates in London, peers in Washington and friends from Phnom Penh to Hanoi no longer see democracies as a model. I understand why they look at Singapore or Shanghai and say they want that, rather than San Francisco or Sydney.

There is more than a little truth in these reports. Democracy is in decline around the world; and we do need to do more to get our own houses in order. That's the whole point of this book.

But it's worth spilling some ink about our competitors, too: about the governance mistakes they are making – mistakes that are weakening their own claims to the future and buying us more time to make our necessary fixes. Because in the end, it is good governance, whether by autocracies or democracies, that will win. And good governance remains more likely in democracies, as the examples of autocratic mistakes make clear.

∗ ∗ ∗

Jack Ma, the boy of Hangzhou, is probably China's best-known entrepreneur. The man built Alibaba, the online Chinese retailer worth some USD 165 billion.

In 2014, Ma, as great innovators do, had an idea. He and his partners at Alibaba launched Ant Group, which is best known for its Alipay digital payments app. By 2018, Alipay boasted more than 700 million active users monthly; it also had massive interests in online investing, insurance and consumer lending, all of which gave it almost USD 635 billion under management.[17]

The Chinese government was not pleased. Beijing was already wary of a potential debt crisis, and believed that virtual assets like those held in Alipay were dangerous and risky. Policymakers were growing concerned about the tech sector, too, seeing it as a rival power.

And so, after Ma lightly criticised the Chinese government, Beijing took action, targeting Ant for regulation.[18] China's state media then diminished Ma and criticised Ant for having promoted too much of a consumer culture.[19] And in November, Beijing abruptly halted Ant's USD 37 billion IPO – which would have been the world's largest – citing concerns about the proliferation of unregulated financial-technology services in China and the growing power of China's tech sector more broadly.[20]

Ma went face to face with Beijing's regulators; he promptly found out who was in charge, and it was not him.

But Beijing was not done.

Months later, in April 2021, China's central bank announced that Ant would be undergoing a major restructuring.[21] Ant promised to cut the 'improper' linkage between Alipay and its credit card and consumer loan services.[22]

The damage was done. Alibaba was out of favour with Beijing, and so its profits continued to plummet.[23] Its stock price has steadily declined ever since.

Throughout all of this, Ma disappeared from the public eye. And while he has since returned, the message – 'don't mess with Beijing' – remains obvious.

Ma might have all the money and foreign friends for which one, Chinese or otherwise, could possibly hope, but the Communist Party remains firmly in charge, its guillotine hanging ever ominously over the private sector's neck, ready to drop on a whim.

In late 2021 and into 2022, Xi brought the guillotine down again and again on the tech sector. His government cracked down even further on tech firms, which he blamed for the 'irrational expansion of capital'.[24] Regulators imposed onerous restrictions on them, quietly forcing people like Ma underground. Prominent entrepreneurs stopped posting on social media and hid their previous comments.[25] They saw the writing on the wall: they kept their heads down and essentially disappeared, not so unlike Sergey Brin's parents did in Soviet Moscow.

This is hardly the picture of a comfortable regime, or of a country ready to take over the world. Xi and those around him are clearly overestimating their own abilities – namely, their ability to maintain a strong economy and advance China's model abroad, all while seeking ever-more control of the country's economy and effectively removing many of its animal spirits.

It was on the Chinese people's entrepreneurship that China became economically successful. Beijing's policies played a major role, but Xi's continued repression, state control and foreign assertiveness will undermine China's potential road to greater success. He will stifle potential innovations and force China's best and brightest abroad. He will not, put simply, be able to keep the Chinese economic miracle going if he acts more and more like a totalitarian, seeking control over not only the state, but society and the private sector, too. It is hardly reflective of positive trends that his government has taken aim at 'sissy', effeminate men, who officials blamed for being unable to secure Xi's promised 'national rejuvenation' of China.[26]

So, for all of China's success – and for all the costs China's people have had to bear to get there – the outlook is not particularly bright. The country's economic woes are worsening, thanks both to Xi's misgovernance and to the demographic problems. His compulsion to accumulate ever more power and crack down on those who seemingly challenge it, even in the private sector, is a clear obstacle to growth.

Signs point towards a gradual ending of China's extended honeymoon period. Such stagnation is not the fault of the Chinese people, but of the country's unelected leaders – and one leader alone, who is focused on one thing above all: his own political survival.

Such a singular focus prevents good governance, because it requires chiefly that you focus on the short-term. Mortgaging your future to provide people with benefits now and secure other goals in the name of your legacy may keep you in power, which is one of the reasons why autocracy fails. The rule of one man – one man obsessed with his own power – will stand in the way of a country's future.

* * *

China is not the only powerful autocracy, nor is it the only one with problems.

Russia has issues too obvious to spend much time on. The country is helmed by an unstable dictator who invaded his neighbour, uniting many of the world's most powerful nations against him and bringing economic disaster to his people. Russia's economy has long punched below its weight and will only get worse thanks to the whole swathe of sanctions imposed upon Moscow. The country is facing a demographic disaster, too. With fewer people to power its economy (and immigrants unwilling to move to Russia, while others flee), the country will almost surely experience economic decline – which will in turn weaken not only Russian President Vladimir Putin's claims to power, but also his system's claims to legitimacy at home and abroad. Russia cannot be a model for anyone, if it ever was, without a functional economy.

Saudi Arabia has a better economy and global image, despite its grisly behaviour both at home and abroad. Still, this country, too, faces the problem of an unpredictable dictator: the young Mohammed bin Salman seems temperamentally unfit for the job of leadership he currently holds. Riyadh can also hardly keep control of Islamist terrorism within its own borders; nor can it prevent the violence in neighbouring Yemen from boiling over into Saudi territory.[27] It also remains hard to believe that Saudi Arabia will retain its global importance as the world shifts away from fossil fuels, the country's only important export, and towards renewable energy. Saudi Arabia very well could be in decline.[28]

Something similar is true of many of the world's more powerful, antagonistic and headline-grabbing autocracies – Hungary, Venezuela, Iran, Turkey and Belarus all face substantial economic, social and in some cases security headwinds. Not one of these countries has a positive economic outlook; not one of them has a system of governance anyone is seriously emulating. Their international partners are ones of convenience, not ones based on positive values or admiration. Critically, many of these countries' own people are increasingly dissatisfied and looking to flee. None of them offers a compelling model to the world.

Singapore is the exception.

It is probably the only example of a truly successful autocracy today. It is a rich country, it is a mostly happy one, its government is clean and capable, its people are appreciative – despite evident limits on their freedom – and are not looking to leave. Life there is pretty good, even without democracy. No wonder leaders in developing countries everywhere point to Lee Kuan Yew as an idol.[29]

But Singapore's success is not one that any authoritarian government could truly emulate. Lee Kuan Yew succeeded precisely because he built an effective system from scratch; on the other hand, Putin, Xi and others are dealing with systems too broken by their own design, and that of their predecessors, to ever look like Singapore. There is no way for these and other autocratic leaders to remove the graft or inefficiency that plagues their systems without bringing the systems down entirely. Pulling all the corrupt elites out of power would result in regime collapse. There is no way for them to become Singapore; they would have to burn down their systems to ever build one that looks like the city-state.

Ironically, it is democracies that can most effectively learn lessons from Singapore, the autocratic exception. It is democracies, with our relatively clean governance, and the ability to actually become cleaner, which can look to Singapore to become more meritocratic and accountable, and establish more trust in government, for starters. Democracies can do what Singapore has done even better, thanks to the inherent strength of liberalism.

Singapore may be an autocratic success story. But it is clearly not an autocratic example – its model is not one that any autocracy today can truly follow. Its successes do not offer Xi, Putin and their partners a meaningful off-ramp from decline.

* * *

Let me put it simply: China, Russia and their partners face a whole host of challenges for which they have limited or in some cases no convincing solutions. This does not, however, change the reality that China and other 'successful' autocracies continue to inspire calls to autocracy across the democratic world; nor does it change the fact that democracies are experiencing governance crises on their own merits. Growing authoritarianism in US statehouses and authoritarian-friendly populism in the French countryside have little to do with Beijing or Moscow, despite their disinformation efforts.

But it is to our advantage that these autocracies – including the most 'successful' ones – will struggle because they are not as vibrant as democracies are.

Still, let me be clear: autocracies' problems are not a reason for democratic complacency. China, Russia and others may not necessarily offer as compelling a model of governance as they once did, but they still have enough money, power and weapons to make our lives difficult and to pose a meaningful challenge, in terms of both security and economics. Assuming another state's or systems' decline as a justification for our own inaction is not a good idea.

And while it may take an autocratic challenge to spur action, we should address the problems we face for the simple reason that this will produce better governance at home, fuelling more productivity, more growth and better democracy – because it is not sustainable for people to trust democracy less than ever before. It is not sustainable to ignore our unfavourable demographics, that our infrastructure is in decline and that our climate is in danger.

We can address these problems. We have better tools and a better system to meet them than autocracies do. China and others are currently searching for solutions, which are proving hard to find, thanks to the limitations of their own systems – their inability to root out graft, spur inbound migration and ultimately implement checks and balances.

Democracies, on the other hand, know many of the solutions to their problems, many of which I have shared in this book. It's just politics that is preventing us from turning them into reality. Autocracies' troubles are existential; ours are political.

* * *

Aspirations and Action

This book is admittedly aspirational.

I would love it if the United States redirected funds from wasteful spending towards connecting every American with high-speed internet, but I understand that our politics are too sclerotic for this to happen anytime soon. I would welcome Japan opening its doors to more immigrants, but I understand that cultural concerns prevent this from happening rapidly, too. I understand that no democratic leader – no matter how wise or well intentioned – is going to read this book, run to their bully pulpit and direct their governments to immediately put these plans into action.

That's not how democracy works. Democracy requires deliberation, which is sometimes slow and painful. But liberal, democratic governance has shown resilience over and over again: an ability to meet the problems in front of us, whether that be a world war, another pandemic or an economic crisis. Again and again, democracies rise to meet the moment; we meet the challenge head-on by using it as a motivating factor – as a reason to get things done.

I hope that the autocracy challenge outlined in this book serves as a similar 'stimulus' today, prompting a bold shift in policy for the better. This is not without precedent. It was the 'stimulus' of the Soviet Union that prompted the United States to invest in the human capital that won the space race and eventually the Cold War. Doing so produced innovations like the internet along the way. Of course, the 9/11 attacks 'stimulated' poor decisions, like the wars in Iraq and Afghanistan. But that dark day also led to the creation of the Department of Homeland Security, which while imperfect has played a vital role in preventing another such foreign-directed attack against the United States and is widely understood to be a successful agency.[30]

More recently and far further afield, it was the 2019 Christchurch terrorist attack – in which a white supremacist attacked two mosques, killing fifty-one and injuring forty – that prompted New Zealand to ban just about all semi-automatic weapons.[31] It was this 'stimulus' that resulted not only in a policy change from Auckland, but in the compliance of the population, which turned in some 50,000 guns during a months-long amnesty and buy-back programme.[32]

Troublingly, as in New Zealand, violence is often the most meaningful stimulus, and often not in a positive direction. When people are scared, they tend to vote and act rashly, backing people and policies that promise security, even if they do so with bad ideas, and fail to deliver. It is worth remembering that George W. Bush did not plunge the United States into wars in Iraq and Afghanistan alone; huge majorities of the American public initially supported both wars.[33] So, too, did most of the British population, and a not-insignificant swathe of their Japanese counterparts (a slight majority, according to some polls conducted after 9/11).[34]

One hopes – I certainly do – that it does not take such violence to wake us up to the challenge, if not the threat, posed by the rise of autocracies. Perhaps it's already happened; perhaps the war in Ukraine will ultimately motivate everyone from Australia to Japan to make the large-scale reforms needed to win the twenty-first century.

But it seems more likely that this war will shift most countries' security and energy approach, and probably not much else.

Very few countries seem to have considered the war as an opportunity to seriously reform themselves beyond security and perhaps energy independence. The war has oddly been considered something of a small crisis – one to be responded to with limited action in specific sectors, rather than seen as a stimulus for wholesale reforms to strengthen our democracies. It's viewed not so much as a war between systems and for values, but as a conflict between two Eastern European nations with historical disagreements about which we'd rather forget.

I understand the relative tepidness of this response. I understand that many leaders consider Russia more of a gas station than a state, as the late US Senator John McCain once noted.[35] Nobody fears that Russia, despite its ability to make war in Ukraine, offers a model for governance like China does. Nobody wants to move from Minneapolis to Moscow, or from Busan to Barnaul. Russia's military is something to be combated, sure, but its system of governance is not one to be feared. Moscow cannot refashion the international order in its image.

That much is all true.

But the war could have been an opportunity for countries to seriously reform themselves beyond security and energy independence. There was an opportunity for us to recognise that this *is* a war between systems – between autocracy and democracy – and it seems to be forecasting a future conflict, violent or otherwise. It is unfortunate, then, that the war has oddly become something of a small crisis, rather than a stimulus for wholesale reforms.

Russia may not offer a model to be challenged, but Putin was able to invade Ukraine so recklessly only because he is an autocrat. He was able to wage violent, brutal war because he had dismantled any semblance of checks and balances around him, replacing them with 'yes men' fearful of telling the truth.

His war is a reminder not of Russia's faults and threat alone, but those of autocracy writ large. Putin may have made a drastic miscalculation, but his war should remind us of just how awful autocracy – backed by a nuclear-armed military – can be, and how much worse it could get if a more competent country (say, China) were to pursue such a war.

Putin's war should have motivated wholesale action, but preconceptions of Russia's faults – coupled with a narrow vision of the conflict – have led to limited movement. It is democracies that will be worse off in the long-term for missing this opportunity to galvanise their people and politicians into action. It is democracies that will suffer, even if Russia does, too.

* * *

More likely to motivate a sea change is the China challenge.

Democracies around the world – from Australia to the United States and beyond – increasingly understand that China's push for global supremacy requires action, certainly more action than Russia's war motivated. They recognise the need to act not only in terms of foreign policy and security – with Australia moving to secure nuclear-powered submarines and the United States strengthening its quasi-alliance known as the 'Quad' with Australia, India and Japan – but at home, too. Challenging China is among democracies' leading reasons for investing in infrastructure and research and development.

To their credit, many democratic leaders increasingly understand that making democracy work at home is vital to fending off autocracies like China and Russia and practically promoting democracy abroad – not to mention selling our system more softly, too. They recognise that we are in a governance war, whether they use that language or not. This war has largely remained non-violent so far, the Russian invasion of Ukraine notwithstanding. But that specific war is as much a conflict between democracy and autocracy as it is over contested views of history.

Even if you don't like the 'governance war' framing, let us agree at least that we are in global governance competition – one between the democratic and authoritarian systems of governance, and which one is better not only for today, but for tomorrow, too.

Whether we like it or not, China, Russia and others see us and our success as a threat to their ambitions. That is the main reason why they interfere in our domestic politics by spreading disinformation to cause chaos. Our downfall is their victory; our success is a threat.

This all means that we will, at some point, be forced to respond. And it is better to do so ahead of schedule rather than behind.

* * *

If one looks at the democratic world, it seems that the reality – that we're falling behind in this governance war – is already beginning to take root. That recognition is already motivating even those most sceptical of government spending and involvement to change their tune somewhat, at least on issues directly related to China.

The Republican US Senator John Cornyn of Texas has, for instance, publicly backed and voted for government investment in semiconductors to make the United States less reliant on China, despite admitting that doing so made him uncomfortable. He's an American conservative; he's a strong proponent of the free market, believing that the state should be involved in the economy as little as possible. Government investment in the private sector is generally way out of his wheelhouse. Yet he understands the China challenge and has changed his approach at least somewhat.

'The government, I think, can play some role, as we are, in the semiconductor space,' he told an event I attended at the DC-based Center for Strategic and International Studies (where I'm a fellow) in early 2022. 'This is a little bit of an adjustment for people like me that are sort of free-market conservatives, but I think [it's] absolutely critical to our economy and our national security.'[36]

He's right. Investment like this *is* critical. It will make the United States work better: it will make us less reliant on troubled supply chains, it will make semiconductor-laden products cheaper and it will, ultimately, make people believe more in America, Americans and our democracy.

Cornyn's relative change of tune helps demonstrate the opportunity we must embrace to motivate change on several other fronts. We need to frame the work ahead as necessary initiatives to counter the rise of autocracies, particularly China. Such framing can bring spending-adverse politicians on board. Cornyn himself indicated as much.

There is 'a role for [the] government to play, but not a dominant role, because the worst thing we can do for innovation in America is [for] everything to be run out of Washington, DC by the US government', he said. 'So, we need to give the private sector the encouragement, the incentives, and stand back if we can.'[37]

All that sounds okay to me: government support for – but not control of – the innovations that will strengthen one's country seems like a pretty good step in the right direction.

* * *

Yet, as Cornyn's scepticism of government action indicates, the China challenge may not be enough to get political rivals everywhere on board with sweeping immigration reform or future-focused infrastructure programmes. It may not be enough to establish functional meritocratic and accountable systems. But it very well may motivate more investment in human capital development; I'd argue that it already has, with US spending on semiconductor production a prime example.

And while I'm not naïve enough to believe the China challenge – and the autocracy challenge writ large – will prompt a wholesale change in our dysfunctional politics, there is, as the writer Matt

Yglesias has noted, the potential in the United States and elsewhere that people 'freak out' about China and finally get 'serious about fixing things'.[38] I wouldn't bet on that, but I wouldn't rule it out either.

It's worth remembering that the United States was so motivated to get its own house in order during the Cold War that it acted – on everything from the space race to racial discrimination at home (an issue that is not solved, obviously) – despite never fighting a direct war with the Soviet Union.[39]

The Cold War is not a good model for today's competition; the American and Chinese economies, and the rest of the world for that matter, are too intertwined to fully bifurcate in the way the capitalism and communist worlds were. Splitting the world between US- and China-led blocs is not an option. Neither is dividing the world between democracy and autocracies. Fighting for democracy at home and selling our model abroad does not mean cutting off or even downgrading ties with non-democratic partners like Singapore and Vietnam.

Yet the Cold War can still serve as something of a model for the West – as an example of how a competitor, or a set of competitors, can motivate us to get our own homes in order. Fixing problems at home to improve our democracy helped us to defeat the dictators then; it is key to defeating them again today.

I'm hopeful that it will not take a war over Taiwan for democracies to see the challenge autocracies like China pose and to act accordingly. I'm hopeful that it will not require more violence for democracies to embark on the necessary path of self-strengthening.

To make sure we avoid violence, we must take the first steps on this path now. Readers must hold their representatives to account on these issues and stop getting side-tracked by more minor concerns. The stakes are too high for our politicians to get bogged down in Twitter spats about their opponents' 'sexual frustrations' or feuding with their local sports teams after that team called for 'common sense' gun reform. Such silly spats are a waste of everyone's time and effort and are indicative of a broader trend in our politics away from seriousness.[40]

This is precisely not what we require in this moment – because, put simply, we will need to go onto a war footing if we are to win this governance war and solve problems like climate change. Complacency will not only be damaging. It will be devastating.

* * *

Until the moment that we 'get serious' arrives, I believe that this book can serve as an aspirational roadmap. I'm optimistic that readers across the political spectrum will see at least some of my policy proposals as positive options, as things that can be done in bits and pieces. Any such step in the right direction – even if it's not as big a step as I might want – would be a positive one. But the more urgent and bigger the action, the better; as this book makes clear, we have no time to waste.

I strongly believe in my solutions. I believe that they would make any democracy better. And I believe that if democracies took these steps in aggregate and as quickly as possible, the world would be in a better place.

This book, however, offers just one roadmap; it is not the only roadmap. I do not have a monopoly on good ideas. I am sure that other thinkers out there have a whole host of suggestions for actions democracies can take, on everything from privacy rights to gender equality, that I have not covered in-depth here. These should be debated and considered in good faith, too. That is, after all, the ideal of democracy: competing views can be aired, and the best ideas will survive the competition stronger, meaning that we'll all be better off in the long-run.

Other roadmaps might look different from mine because there

are multiple paths to the good life. What works for Australia may not work in the United States or South Korea and so on. There is no one-size-fits-all fix to democratic distress. Each country will have to chart its own course.

But I hope that this book has at least given us a place to start. I hope that it will be the call to action for both democratic politicians and their publics everywhere to act – to brace for the reality of our current conflict, whether violent or otherwise, and put that sentiment into practice, beginning at home. I hope that it will push governments, companies and advocates to invest in building up the institutions, people and communities vital to democracy – to invest in *us*, so that we, the people powering the democracies of the world, can believe in liberal democracy enough to lay claim to the future on its behalf.

A failure to do so will invite only more autocratic aggression, with dictators considering us unprepared, weak and ultimately unserious. And it will be democracies everywhere – and most importantly, our people – who will pay the price.

Notes

Introduction

1   The World Bank, Intentional homicides (per 100,000 people) (2020), https://data.worldbank.org/indicator/VC.IHR.PSRC.P5

2   Lauren Said-Moorhouse, 'How London's homicide rate stacks up against major US cities', CNN, 18 June 2019, https://www.cnn.com/2019/06/18/world/london-us-cities-homicide-rates-comparison-intl-gbr/index.html.

3   Michael R. Sisak and Jim Mustian, '"Dark period"; Killings spike in NYC amid pandemic, unrest', Associated Press, 29 December 2020, https://apnews.com/article/new-york-shootings-new-york-city-violence-corona-virus-pandemic-b1c52b8071219052fd713a6b83999698

4   Joel Tan, 'I have worked, played and loved in other countries because I can't at home', *New York Times*, 22 September 2022, https://www.nytimes.com/2022/09/22/opinion/international-world/singapore-gay.html

5   Kishore Mahbubani, 'The secret sauce of Singapore', *Dubai Policy Review* Vol. 1 (2019).

6   Ibid.

7   Adrian Wooldridge, 'Meritocracy, not democracy, is the golden ticket to growth', Bloomberg, 16 May 2021, https://www.bloomberg.com/opinion/articles/2021-05-16/china-knows-that-meritocracy-is-the-key-to-boosting-economic-growth

8   Fareed Zakaria, 'A conversation with Lee Kuan Yew', *Foreign Affairs* Vol. 73, No. 2 (March/April 1994).

9   Sean Coughlan, 'Pisa tests: Singapore top in global education rankings', BBC News, 6 December 2016, https://www.bbc.com/news/education-38212070.

10 Zakaria, 'A Conversation with Lee Kuan Yew'.

11 Louis Kraar, 'Singapore, the country run like a corporation', *Fortune* (July 1974), https://fortune.com/2015/03/23/singapore-leekuanyew-corporation-1974/.

12 Ibid.

13 Seth Mydans and Wayne Arnold, 'Modern Singapore's creator is alert to

perils', *New York Times*, 2 September 2007, https://www.nytimes.com/2007/09/02/world/asia/02singapore.html.

14 Kraar, 'Singapore, the country run like a corporation'.

15 Barbara Crossette, 'The Opulence of Singapore', *New York Times Magazine*, 16 December 1984, https://www.nytimes.com/1984/12/16/magazine/the-opulence-of-singapore.html.

16 Lee Kuan Yew, *One Man's View of the World* (Singapore: Straits Times Press Books, 2013), p. 300.

17 Graham Allison, Robert D. Blackwill, and Ali Wyne, *Lee Kuan Yew: The Grand Master's Insights on China, the United States, and the World* (Cambridge: MIT Press, 2013), p. 27.

18 Jonathan Chait, 'Peter Thiel and the authoritarian-libertarian alliance for Trump', *New York Times Magazine*, 31 October 2016, https://nymag.com/intelligencer/2016/10/peter-thiel-the-authoritarian-libertarian-for-trump.html.

19 Tara John, 'Brexiteer fantasy of Singapore-style economy will be hard to achieve', CNN, 27 January 2019, https://www.cnn.com/2019/01/27/uk/singapore-model-brexit-dyson-gbr-intl/index.html.

20 *Parts Unknown*. Season 10, Episode 1. 'Singapore'. Directed by Erik Osterholm. Aired 30 September 2017 on CNN.

21 'GDP per capita', Worldometer, https://www.worldometers.info/gdp/gdp-per-capita/

22 'Life expectancy', Worldometer, https://www.worldometers.info/demographics/life-expectancy/

23 Ibid.

24 *Global Innovation Index 2021* (Geneva: World Intellectual Property Organization, 2021), https://www.wipo.int/edocs/pubdocs/en/wipo_pub_gii_2021.pdf

25 Christopher Hitchens, 'Still red: the last bastions of communism', *Washington Post*, 25 August 1991, https://www.washingtonpost.com/archive/entertainment/books/1991/08/25/still-red-the-last-bastions-of-communism/fa756b42-74ce-424c-8769-0802eaafc776/

26 Laurie Macfarlane, 'A spectre is haunting the West – the spectre of authoritarian capitalism', OpenDemocracy, 16 April 2022, https://www.opendemocracy.net/en/oureconomy/a-spectre-is-haunting-the-west-the-spectre-of-authoritarian-capitalism/

27 Yascha Mounk and Roberto Stefano Foa, 'The end of the democratic century', *Foreign Affairs* Vol. 97, No. 3 (2018).

28 Peter Hille, 'Democracy in decline worldwide', DW, 23 February 2022, https://www.dw.com/en/democracy-in-decline-worldwide/a-60878855

29   Francis Fukuyama, *Origins of Political Order* (London: Profile Books, 2019), p. 482.

30   Edward McAllister, 'Coups cheered in West Africa as Islamist insurgencies sap faith in democracy', Reuters, 1 February 2022, https://www.reuters.com /world/africa/coups-cheered-west-africa-islamist-insurgencies-sap-faith-democracy-2022-02-01/

31   Mounk and Foa, 'The end of the democratic century'.

32   Stephen Walt, 'Why is the United States so bad at foreign policy?', *Foreign Policy*, 13 January 2020, https://foreignpolicy.com/2020/01/13/trump-iran-china-why-united-states-so-bad-foreign-policy/

33   Shadi Hamid and Damir Marusic, 'Is democracy good?', Wisdom of Crowds, 26 January 2022, https://wisdomofcrowds.live/is-democracy-good/.

34   Fukuyama, *Origins of Political Order*.

35   David Himbara, 'In 1960, China was poorer than most African countries. But here is China bankrolling Africa', Medium, 10 September 2018, https:// medium.com/@david.himbara_27884/in-1960-china-was-poorer-than-most-african-countries-but-here-is-china-bankrolling-africa -b7b0b10f41ba

36   Jim Yong Kim, 'World bank group president Jim Yong Kim's remarks at the opening ceremony of the first China international import expo', World Bank, 5 November 2018, https://www.worldbank.org/en/news/speech/2018 /11/05/world-bank-group-president-jim-yong-kims-remarks-at-the-opening-ceremony-of-the-first-china-international-import-expo

37   'The economy that covid-19 could not stop', *The Economist*, 2 September 2021, https://www.economist.com/finance-and-economics/2021/08/30/the -economy-that-covid-19-could-not-stop

38   Halvor Mehlum, Karl Moene, and Ragnar Torvik, 'Institutions and the resource curse', *The Economic Journal* No. 116 (2006), pp. 1–20.

39   Rami Khouri, 'The incredible development of the gulf states', *Agence Global*, 27 August 2008, https://www.belfercenter.org/publication/incredible-development-gulf-states

40   Mounk and Foa, 'The end of the democratic century'.

41   Toh Ee Ming, 'As COVID-19 rages, more in Singapore go hungry', Al Jazeera, 10 November 2021, https://www.aljazeera.com/news/2021/11/10/as-covid-19-rages-more-in-singapore-go-hungry

42   Sui-Lee Wee, 'They had the vaccines and a plan to reopen. instead they got cold feet', *New York Times*, 8 October 2021, https://www.nytimes.com/2021 /10/08/world/asia/singapore-vaccine-covid.html

43   Manu Bhaskaran, 'Getting Singapore in shape: economic challenges and how to meet them', Lowy Institute, 15 June 2018, https://www.lowyinstitute.

org/publications/getting-singapore-shape-economic-challenges-and-how-meet-them

44 'The great hole of China', *The Economist*, 18 October 2014, https://www.economist.com/leaders/2014/10/18/the-great-hole-of-china

45 Ibid.

46 Thomas Piketty, Li Yang, and Gabriel Zucman, 'Capital accumulation, private property, and rising inequality in China, 1978–2015', *American Economic Review* Vol. 109, No. 7 (July 2019), pp. 2469–96, https://www.aeaweb.org/articles?id=10.1257/aer.20170973

47 'China's next debt bomb is an aging population', Bloomberg, 5 February 2018, https://www.bloomberg.com/news/articles/2018-02-05/china-s-next-debt-bomb-is-an-aging-population?sref=TZEt22gR

48 Charlie Campbell, 'China's aging population is a major threat to future', *TIME*, 7 February 2019, https://time.com/5523805/china-aging-population-working-age/

49 Charles Dunst, 'China's leader makes it all about him, and that's dangerous', *Boston Globe*, 3 September 2020, https://www.bostonglobe.com/2020/09/03/opinion/chinas-leader-makes-it-all-about-him-thats-dangerous/

50 Howard French, *Everything Under the Heavens* (New York: Vintage, 2017), p. 264.

51 Robin Minn Khant (@minn_robert), ' "Happiness isn't born in the cage" today sagaing protest people of sagaing keep making their voices to against the junta. Almost one year of the coup and the resistances never stand down. #WhatsHappeningInMyanmar #2022Jan29Coup', Twitter, 29 January 2022, https://twitter.com/minn_robert/status/1487414508746579970?s=11

52 James Crabtree, 'China's radical new vision of globalization', *Noema*, 10 December 2020, https://www.noemamag.com/chinas-radical-new-vision-of-globalization/

53 Thomas L. Friedman, 'We have never been here before', *New York Times*, 25 February 2022, https://www.nytimes.com/2022/02/25/opinion/putin-russia-ukraine.html

54 Trudy Rubin, 'Worldview: democracy at risk', *Philadelphia Inquirer*, 24 March 2013, https://www.inquirer.com/philly/columnists/trudy_rubin/20130224_Worldview__Democracy_at_risk_-_from_West.html; Joshua Kurlantzick, *Democracy in Retreat: The Revolt of the Middle Class and the Worldwide Decline of Representative Democracy* (New Haven: Yale University Press, 2013).

55 Matthew C. MacWilliams, 'Trump is an authoritarian. so are millions of Americans', *POLITICO Magazine*, 23 September 2020, https://www.politico.com/news/magazine/2020/09/23/trump-america-authoritarianism-420681

56   Sohrab Ahmari, 'Against David French-ism', *First Things*, 29 May 2019, https://www.firstthings.com/web-exclusives/2019/05/against-david-french-ism

57   Caleb Crain, 'The case against democracy', *New Yorker*, 31 October 2018, https://www.newyorker.com/magazine/2016/11/07/the-case-against-democracy

58   Jason Brennan, *Against Democracy* (Princeton: Princeton University Press, 2016).

59   Frédéric Lordon, 'For a Neo-Leninism', Verso Books, 10 September 2021, https://www.versobooks.com/blogs/5152-for-a-neo-leninism

60   Ibid.

61   Damir Marusic, 'The missionary position', Wisdom of Crowds, 17 September 2021, https://wisdomofcrowds.live/the-missionary-position/

62   *The Global Satisfaction with Democracy Report 2020*, Centre for the Future of Democracy, 2020, https://www.cam.ac.uk/system/files/report2020_003.pdf

63   Janan Ganesh, 'Beware the downwardly mobile', *Financial Times*, 11 March 2022, https://www.ft.com/content/544171d4-3deb-4ac7-a427-042a106ee43d

64   Fred Lewsey, 'Global dissatisfaction with democracy at a record high', University of Cambridge, 2020, https://www.cam.ac.uk/stories/dissatis-factiondemocracy

65   'Hungary PM: we lied to win election', *The Guardian*, 18 September 2006, https://www.theguardian.com/world/2006/sep/18/1

66   *Magyar Rádió*, 17 September 2006.

67   'Hungary PM': we lied to win election. *The Guardian*.

68   David Chance, 'Thousands protest against Hungarian PM Gyurcsány', Reuters, 23 October 2007, https://www.reuters.com/article/idUSL23297744

69   'Orbán: socialist-liberal gov't turned against people after 2006 Öszöd Speech', Hungary Today, 17 September 2021, https://hungarytoday.hu/orban-gyurcsany-oszod-speech/

70   Ibid.

71   'Quote for this week', *The Atlantic*, 6 November 2008, https://www.theatlantic.com/daily-dish/archive/2008/11/quote-for-this-week/208951/

72   Hamid and Marusic, 'Is democracy good?'

Chapter 1

1   Meo Hüi Goh, 'Becoming *Wen*: the rhetoric in the "final edits" of Han Emperor Wen and Wei Emperor Wen', *Early Medieval China* Vol. 2013, No. 19 (4 April 2014), pp. 58–79; Tan Koon San, *Dynastic China: An Elementary History* (New York: The Other Press, 2014), p. 77.

2   Homer H. Dubs, 'The victory of Han Confucianism', *Journal of the American Oriental Society* Vol. 58, No. 3 (September 1938), pp. 435–49; Theron Corse, 'Ch'in and Han Dynasty China', 2015, https://faculty.tnstate.edu/tcorse/h1210.htm

3   Bernie Yeung, 'Notes on meritocracy: insights from Tang's civil servant exam and poetry', Harvard University, 1 May 2018, https://hcf.fas.harvard.edu/wp-content/uploads/2018/05/Yeung-Bernie-For-May-2018-b.pdf

4   Ibid.

5   Fukuyama, *Origins of Political Order*, p. 371.

6   Ibid., p. 311.

7   Michael Mandelbaum, 'In defense of meritocracy', *American Purpose*, 25 October 2021, https://www.americanpurpose.com/articles/in-defense-of-meritocracy/

8   David Leonhart, 'The N.F.L.'s race problem', *New York Times*, 3 February 2022, https://www.nytimes.com/2022/02/03/briefing/nfl-head-coach-brian-flores-racism.html

9   Wang Pei, 'Debates on political meritocracy in China: a historical perspective', *Philosophy and Public Law Issues (New Series)*, Vol. 7, No. 1 (2017), pp. 53–71.

10 Adrian Wooldridge, *The Aristocracy of Talent: How Meritocracy Made the Modern World* (New York: Skyhorse, 2021), p. 32

11 Yeung, 'Notes on meritocracy'.

12 Wooldridge, *The Aristocracy of Talent*.

13 'Full text: Theresa May's speech on grammar schools', *New Statesman*, 9 September 2016, https://www.newstatesman.com/politics/the-staggers/2016/09/full-text-theresa-mays-speech-grammar-schools

14 'State of the nation 2018-19: social mobility in Great Britain', Social Mobility Commission, April 2019, https://assets.publishing.service.gov.uk/government/uploads/system/uploads/attachment_data/file/798404/SMC_State_of_the_Nation_Report_2018-19.pdf

15 Stephen Bush, 'Musa Okwonga's One of Them: An elegantly written memoir of his Eton days', *New Statesman*, 14 April 2021, https://www.newstatesman.com/international-politics/2021/04/stephen-bush-Musa-Okwonga-one-of-them

16 Rana Foroohar, 'Why meritocracy isn't working', *Financial Times*, 3 September 2020, https://www.ft.com/content/f881fb55-8f06-4508-a812-815a10505077

17 Ibid.

18 Bush, 'Musa Okwonga's One of Them'.

19 Musa Okwonga, *One of Them* (London: Unbound, 2021), p. 188.

20 'Is meritocracy still working in Asia?', Lee Kuan Yew School of Public Policy, 20 August 2019, https://lkyspp.nus.edu.sg/gia/article/is-meritocracy-still-working-in-asia

21 Ibid.

22 Yoo Jung Kim, 'How South Korean society (unfortunately) inspired squid game', *Psychology Today*, 19 October 2021, https://www.psychologytoday.com/us/blog/apple-day/202110/how-south-korean-society-unfortunately-inspired-squid-game

23 Kyle Cheung, 'The "squid game" English subtitle translation doesn't do justice to the story's societal commentary', Salon, 5 October 2021, https://www.salon.com/2021/10/05/squid-game-english-subtitles-mi-nyeo/

24 Eric Schmitt, 'Colin Powell, who shaped U.S. national security, dies at 84', *New York Times*, 18 October 2021, https://www.nytimes.com/2021/10/18/us/politics/colin-powell-dead.html; Daniel Drezner, 'Colin Powell's and the GOP's foreign policy evolution', *Washington Post*, 18 October 2021, https://www.washingtonpost.com/outlook/2021/10/18/colin-powell-gops-foreign-policy-evolution/

25 Brady Rhoades, 'General Powell: life in leadership', *U.S. Veterans Magazine*, 2021, https://usveteransmagazine.com/2017/02/general-colin-powell-life-in-leadership/

26 *Department of Defense Board on Diversity and Inclusion Report: Recommendations to Improve Racial and Ethnicity Diversity and Inclusion in the U.S. Military*, 2020, p. 11 https://media.defense.gov/2020/Dec/18/2002554852/-1/-1/0/DOD-DIVERSITY-AND-INCLUSION-FINAL-BOARD-REPORT.PDF

27 Ibid., p. 11.

28 Ibid., p. 11.

29 Ibid., pp. 10 and 62.

30 Caroline Bechtel, 'Warriors, scholars, diplomats: the role of military officer in foreign policymaking', *New Perspectives in Foreign Policy* No. 14 (Fall 2017), https://www.csis.org/npfp/warriors-scholars-diplomats-role-military-officers-foreign-policymaking

31 Tim Kane, 'Why our best officers are leaving', *The Atlantic*, January/February 2011, https://www.theatlantic.com/magazine/archive/2011/01/why-our-best-officers-are-leaving/308346/

32 Wooldridge, 'Meritocracy, not democracy, is the golden ticket to growth'.

33 Ibid.

34 Jay Mathews, 'Why not lottery admissions for great high schools? It's not church bingo.', *Washington Post*, 16 January 2022, https://www.washingtonpost.com/education/2022/01/16/selective-high-school-lottery/

35   Richard Cano and Nanette Asimov, 'New data shows shift as Lowell High School: More students given failing grades after admissions change', *San Francisco Chronicle*, 25 May 2022, https://www.sfchronicle.com/sf/article/Lowell-High-admissions-17196603.php

36   Philip Shenon, 'Non-aligned movement decides it is still', *New York Times*, 7 September 1992, https://www.nytimes.com/1992/09/07/world/non-aligned-movement-decides-it-is-still-relevant.html

37   Philip Bowring, 'In his father's shoes: Will Singapore's heir turn the ship of state?', *New York Times*, 10 August 2004, https://www.nytimes.com/2004/08/10/opinion/in-his-fathers-shoes-will-singapores-heir-turn-the-ship-of-state.html

38   Goh Chok Tong, 'My urgent mission', *Petir* No. 11-12 (1992), pp. 10–19; Jon S.T. Quah, 'Why Singapore works: five secrets of Singapore's success', *Public Administration and Policy: An Asia-Pacific Journal* Vol. 21, No. 1 (2018), https://www.emerald.com/insight/content/doi/10.1108/PAP-06-2018-002/full/html

39   Quah, 'Why Singapore works'.

40   Naresh C. Saxena, *Virtuous Cycles: The Singapore Public Service and National Development*, United Nations Development Programme (Singapore: 2011), p. 7.

41   Kenneth Paul Tan, 'How Singapore is fixing its meritocracy', *Washington Post*, 16 April 2016, https://www.washingtonpost.com/news/in-theory/wp/2016/04/16/how-singapore-is-fixing-its-meritocracy/

42   Charmaine Ng, 'Meritocracy is best model for Singapore, but needs to evolve to meet new challenges: Ong Ye Kung', *Straits Times*, 25 October 2018, https://www.straitstimes.com/singapore/ong-ye-kung-meritocracy-is-best-model-for-singapore-but-needs-to-evolve-to-meet-new

43   Tiana Desker, 'Meritocracy: time for an update?', Civil Service College Singapore, 14 February 2016, https://www.csc.gov.sg/articles/meritocracy-time-for-an-update

44   'What other countries can learn from Singapore's schools', *The Economist*, 30 August 2018, https://www.economist.com/leaders/2018/08/30/what-other-countries-can-learn-from-singapores-schools

45   'The Global Social Mobility Report 2020', World Economic Forum, January 2020, https://www3.weforum.org/docs/Global_Social_Mobility_Report.pdf

46   'What other countries can learn from Singapore's schools', *The Economist*.

47   'Prime Minister Goh Chok Tong's national day rally 2000 speech in english: transforming Singapore', Ministry of Information and The Arts, 20 August 2000, https://www.nas.gov.sg/archivesonline/data/pdfdoc/2000082001.htm

48   Ibid.

49 Ibid.

50 Mahbubani, 'The secret sauce of Singapore'.

51 Tan, 'How Singapore is fixing its meritocracy'.

52 Mahbubani, 'The secret sauce of Singapore'.

53 Ibid.

54 Jon S.T. Quah, *Public Administration Singapore-Style* (Bingley: Emerald Group Publishing, 2010), pp. 104–10.

55 Saxena, *Virtuous Cycles*, p. 61.

56 Transparency International, *Corruption Perceptions Index 2021* (Berlin 2021), https://images.transparencycdn.org/images/CPI2021_Report_EN-web.pdf

57 Lee Kuan Yew, *From Third World to First: The Singapore Story: 1965-2000* (New York: Harper, 2000), p. 192.

58 Tan, 'How Singapore is fixing its meritocracy'.

59 Justin Ong, 'Civil servants laud tweaks to currently estimated potential system, hope for more holistic and transparent assessment', *TODAY*, 7 October 2020, https://www.todayonline.com/singapore/civil-servants-laud-tweaks-currently-estimated-potential-system-hope-more-holistic-and

60 Navene Elangovan, 'More mid-career entrants from private sector needed to boost diversity in public service: PM Lee', *TODAY*, 17 January 2020, https://www.todayonline.com/singapore/more-mid-career-entrants-private-sector-needed-boost-diversity-public-service-pm-lee

61 Saxena, *Virtuous Cycles*, p. 58.

62 Daniel Kraay, Arat Kraay, and Massimo Mastruzzi, 'The worldwide governance indicators: methodology and analytical issues', 2010, http://info.worldbank.org/governance/wgi/Home/Reports; Saxena, *Virtuous Cycle*.

63 Sean Sullivan and Michael Scherer, 'A family affair: Children and other relatives of Biden aides get administration jobs', *Washington Post*, 18 June 2021, https://www.washingtonpost.com/politics/biden-aides-relatives-jobs/2021/06/17/ab504a22-cea4-11eb-8cd2-4e95230cfac2_story.html

64 'Parliamentary motion "education for our future" response by Minister for Education, Mr Ong Ye Kung', Singapore Ministry of Education, 11 July 2018, https://www.moe.gov.sg/news/speeches/20180711-parliamentary-motion-education-for-our-future-response-by-minister-for-education-mr-ong-ye-kung

65 Vincent Chin, 'Sustaining Singapore's success: lessons of growth and delivery', Center for Public Impact, 11 June 2015, https://www.centreforpublicimpact.org/insights/sustaining-singapores-success

66 Tan, 'How Singapore is fixing its meritocracy'.

67 Jeevan Vasagar, 'Why Singapore's kids are so good at maths', *Financial Times*, 22 July 2016, https://www.ft.com/content/2e4c61f2-4ec8-11e6-8172 -e39ecd3b86fc

68 Shane Markowitz, 'Must try harder: recovering from educational inequality', *Social Europe*, 19 January 2021, https://socialeurope.eu/must-try-harder-recovering-from-educational-inequality

69 Linda Darling-Hammond, 'Unequal opportunity: race and education', Brookings Institution, 1 March 1998, https://www.brookings.edu/articles/ unequal-opportunity-race-and-education/

70 Alana Semuels, 'Good school, rich school; bad school, poor school', *The Atlantic*, 25 August 2016, https://www.theatlantic.com/business/archive/ 2016/08/property-taxes-and-unequal-schools/497333/

71 P.R. Lockhart, '65 years after Brown v. Board of Education, school segregation is getting worse', *Vox*, 10 May 2019, https://www.vox.com/identities/2019/5/10/18566052/school-segregation-brown-board-education -report

72 Kevin Carey, 'Rich schools, poor schools and a plan', *New York Times*, 9 June 2021, https://www.nytimes.com/2021/06/09/upshot/biden-school-funding. html

73 The Crimson Editorial Board, 'High time to end legacy admissions', *The Harvard Crimson*, 28 October 2021, https://www.thecrimson.com/article/ 2021/10/28/high-time-to-end-legacy-admissions/

74 Ibid.; Alex M. Koller and Eric Yan, 'Survey finds class of 2025 disproportionately wealthy', *The Harvard Crimson*, 7 September 2021, https://www. thecrimson.com/article/2021/9/7/class-of-2025-makeup/

75 Jim Pickard and Sebastian Payne, 'Rishi Sunak prepares to cut thousands of civil service jobs', *Financial Times*, 25 December 2001, https://www.ft.com/ content/e42a89cd-0641-434c-a473-a880db9ddae8

76 Walter Olson, 'Fixing the civil service mess', *City Journal*, Autumn 1997, https://www.city-journal.org/html/fixing-civil-service-mess-11892.html

77 Philip Bump, 'How federal workers become the new welfare queens', *The Atlantic*, 20 March 2013, https://www.theatlantic.com/politics/archive/2013 /03/how-federal-workers-became-new-welfare-queens/317156/

78 Eric Katz, 'Firing line', *Government Executive*, 2020, https://www.govexec. com/feature/firing-line/

79 Una Mullally, 'Una Mullally: It's time to challenge the institutionally stagnant Civil Service', *Irish Times*, 10 January 2022, www.irishtimes. com%2Fopinion%2Funa-mullally-it-s-time-to-challenge-the-institutionally-stagnant-civil-service-1.4772381; Lara Marlowe, 'France faces a reckoning over the travails of its civil service,' 16 October 2019, https://www.

irishtimes.com/news/world/europe/france-faces-a-reckoning-over-the-travails-of-its-civil-service-1.4051792; 'Spain's civil servants draw grumbles, and envy', NPR, 11 December 2012, https://www.npr.org/2012/12/11/166958237/spains-civil-servants-draw-grumbles-and-envy

80 Brie K. Buchanan and Jane Z. Li, 'Nearly Three-quarters of harvard grads pursued for-profit jobs in 2018', *The Harvard Crimson*, 22 October 2018, https://www.thecrimson.com/article/2018/10/22/ocs-senior-survey-2018/;   Ken Gewertz, 'Enter to grow in wisdom', *The Harvard Gazette*, 15 December 2005, https://news.harvard.edu/gazette/story/2005/12/enter-to-grow-in-wisdom/

81 Mahbubani, 'The secret sauce of Singapore'.

82 'Prime Minister Goh Chok Tong's National Day Rally 2000 Speech in English', Ministry of Information and The Arts.

83 'Civil service seen as salvation from the private-sector blues', *Korea JoongAng Daily*, 16 August 2021, https://koreajoongangdaily.joins.com/2021/08/16/business/economy/civil-service-exam-civil-servant-public-official/20210816181100415.html

84 Victoria Kim, 'In a tough market, young South Koreans vie for the security of government jobs', *Los Angeles Times*, 6 February 2019, https://www.latimes.com/world/asia/la-fg-south-korea-jobs-20190206-story.html

85 Pan Suk Kim, 'Performance appraisal and performance-related pay in government: the case of South Korea', *International Journal Civil Service Reform & Practice* No. 4 (December 2014).

86 Ibid.

87 Kate Kelly and David D. Kirkpatrick, 'Kushner's and Mnuchin's quick pivots to business with the Gulf', *New York Times*, 22 May 2022, https://www.nytimes.com/2022/05/22/business/jared-kushner-steven-mnuchin-gulf-investments.html

88 Sullivan and Scherer, 'A family affair'.

89 Saxena, *Virtuous Cycles*.

90 Greg Rosalsky, 'Are there too many political appointees?', NPR, 17 November 2020, https://www.npr.org/sections/money/2020/11/17/935430860/are-there-too-many-political-appointees

Chapter 2

1 Shaffiq Alkhatib, 'Two Japanese men jailed for more than five years for corruption', *The New Paper*, 8 June 2018, https://tnp.straitstimes.com/news/singapore/two-japanese-men-jailed-more-five-years-corruption

2 Selina Lum, 'Court cuts jail term for duo who extracted $2m in bribes, imposes nearly $201,000 fine', *Straits Times*, 2 December 2020, https://

www.straitstimes.com/singapore/courts-crime/court-cuts-jail-term-for-duo-who-extracted-2m-in-bribes-imposes-nearly-201000

3   SGHC 265, 2020, https://www.elitigation.sg/gd/s/2020_SGHC_265

4   Lum, 'Court cuts jail term for duo who extracted $2m in bribes, imposes nearly $201,000 fine'.

5   Elena Chong, 'Ex-CPIB assistant director Edwin Yeo jailed 10 years for criminal breach of trust', *Straits Times*, 20 February 2014, https://www.straitstimes.com/singapore/ex-cpib-assistant-director-edwin-yeo-jailed-10-years-for-criminal-breach-of-trust

6   Lydia Lam, 'AMKTC corruption case: Jail terms increased for former general manager, company director after appeals', Channel News Asia, 16 July 2020, https://www.channelnewsasia.com/singapore/ang-mo-kio-town-council-corruption-case-jail-terms-increased-641881

7   Shibani Mahtani, 'Singapore official charged in rare corruption case', *Wall Street Journal*, 6 June 2012, https://www.wsj.com/articles/SB10001424052702303296604577450152007823124

8   Thong Chee Kun and Josephine Chee, 'Anti-Corruption 2022', Chambers and Partners, 7 December 2021, https://practiceguides.chambers.com/practice-guides/anti-corruption-2022/singapore/trends-and-developments

9   Ibid.

10   David Pollock, 'UAE public privately split on key issues, new poll reveals', Fikra Forum, 17 December 2018, https://www.washingtoninstitute.org/policy-analysis/uae-public-privately-split-key-issues-new-poll-reveals; 'Public Trust in Government: 1958-2022', Pew Research Center, 6 June 2022, https://www.pewresearch.org/politics/2021/05/17/public-trust-in-government-1958-2021/

11   'Public Trust in Government: 1958-2022', Pew Research Center.

12   'Revealed: Trust in politicians at lowest level on record', Institute for Public Policy Research, 12 May 2021, https://www.ippr.org/news-and-media/press-releases/revealed-trust-in-politicians-at-lowest-level-on-record

13   Ibid.

14   Richard Wike, Laura Silver, Shannon Schumacher, and Aidan Connaughton, 'Many in U.S., Western Europe say their political system needs major reform', Pew Research Center, 31 March 2021, https://www.pewresearch.org/global/2021/03/31/many-in-us-western-europe-say-their-political-system-needs-major-reform/

15   'Ex-chief of PetroVietnam sentenced to death for embezzlement', Associated Press, 29 September 2017, https://apnews.com/article/b7f63f3b1cf74b10b038996917dd0aec

16   Vu Trong Khanh, 'Vietnam state oil-firm chief arrested on fraud allegations', *Wall Street Journal*, 22 July 2015, https://www.wsj.com/articles/vietnam-state-oil-firm-chief-arrested-on-fraud-allegations-1437563327?

17   'Ex-chief of PetroVietnam sentenced to death for embezzlement', Associated Press.

18   Ibid.

19   Ibid.

20   Hoang Thuy, 'Punishment of high-ranking officials will deter corruption: Party chief', VNExpress, 30 December 2019, https://e.vnexpress.net/news/news/punishment-of-high-ranking-officials-will-deter-corruption-party-chief-4035086.html

21   'Vietnam fires deputy health minister accused of fake meds scam', Reuters, 9 February 2022, https://www.reuters.com/article/vietnam-security/vietnam-fires-deputy-health-minister-accused-of-fake-meds-scam-idUSL1N2UK16H

22   Transparency International, *Corruption Perceptions Index 2021* (Berlin 2021).

23   Patrick Winn, 'Vietnam is sentencing corrupt bankers to death, by firing squad', The World, 3 April 2014, https://theworld.org/stories/2014-04-03/vietnam-sentencing-corrupt-bankers-death-firing-squad

24   My Pham, 'Vietnam punishes officials over Formosa incident', Reuters, 21 April 2017, https://www.reuters.com/article/us-vietnam-formosa/vietnam-punishes-officials-over-formosa-incident-idUSKBN17N26K

25   Ibid.

26   'Vietnam fires southern city party chief for mismanagement', Associated Press, 10 May 2017, https://apnews.com/article/7545ea9a379e432b9fed98bc53930cac

27   Mai Truong, 'Explaining public trust in Vietnam', *Asia Times*, 7 October 2020, https://asiatimes.com/2020/10/explaining-public-trust-in-vietnam/

28   Nicole Naurath, 'Most Vietnamese confident in their government', Gallup, 24 December 2007, https://news.gallup.com/poll/103453/most-vietnamese-confident-their-government.aspx; Zheng-Xu Wang, 'Institutional Trust in East Asia', Asian Barometer Conference on Democracy and Citizen Politics in East Asia, 17-18 June 2013, http://www.asianbarometer.org/publications/e7d4c03698433c4a579ca0132bd28898.pdf

29   Hoang Thuy, 'Party chief to continue fighting corruption, a "disease" of power', VNExpress, 31 January 2021, https://e.vnexpress.net/news/news/party-chief-to-continue-fighting-corruption-a-disease-of-power-4229764.html

30   Ibid.

31 The World Bank, GDP (current US$) (2020), https://data.worldbank.org/indicator/NY.GDP.MKTP.CD

32 The World Bank, Life expectancy at birth, total (years) (2020), https://data.worldbank.org/indicator/SP.DYN.LE00.IN

33 Raed Atef, 'Current UAE government accountability: a business-like orientation', *Journal of Educational Leadership and Policy*, Vol. 2, No. 2 (2017).

34 '14 government officials arrested for corruption', *Gulf News*, 18 February 2001, https://gulfnews.com/uae/14-government-officials-arrested-for-corruption-1.415529

35 Ibid.

36 'UAE issues decree to increase accountability of ministers, officials', Reuters, 31 August 2021, https://www.reuters.com/world/middle-east/uae-issues-decree-increase-accountability-ministers-officials-2021-08-31/

37 Ibid.

38 Transparency International, *Corruption Perceptions Index* (Berlin 2021).

39 'Treasury sanctions six individuals for raising funds in the United Arab Emirates to support Nigeria's Boko Haram terrorist group', U.S. Department of the Treasury, 25 March 2022, https://home.treasury.gov/news/press-releases/jy0678

40 Maggie Michael and Michael Hudson, 'Pandora Papers reveal Emirati royal families' role in secret money flows', International Consortium of Investigative Journalists, 16 November 2021, https://www.icij.org/investigations/pandora-papers/pandora-papers-reveal-emirati-royal-families-role-in-secret-money-flows/

41 'Five best and worst government centres revealed', Emirates News Agency, 14 September 2019, https://wam.ae/en/details/1395302786516

42 'Government performance', United Arab Emirates Ministry of Cabinet Affairs, 2019, https://www.moca.gov.ae/en/area-of-focus/government-performance

43 Abdulaziz Al-Raisa, Saad Amin, and Saad Tahir, 'Determinants of performance management system in UAE public sector', *International Journal of Trade and Global Markets*, Vol. 3, No. 3 (January 2010), pp. 267–79; Sabnam Shaji Razack and Ambitabh Upadhyay, 'Employee Perception of Performance Management Systems in the UAE: An Analysis', 3 February 2017, https://ssrn.com/abstract=2910808

44 'Five best and worst government centres revealed', Emirates News Agency.

45 Grace Ho, 'Singaporeans have high level of confidence in Government but politically uninterested: IPS study', *Straits Times*, 24 March 2021, https://www.straitstimes.com/singapore/politics/singaporeans-have-high-level-of-confidence-in-government-but-politically

46 Mathew Mathews, Teo Kay Key, Melvin Tay, and Alicia Wang, 'Attitudes

toward institutions, politics, and policies: key findings from the world values survey', Institute of Policy Studies No. 17 (March 2021), p. 26, https://lkyspp.nus.edu.sg/docs/default-source/ips/ips-exchange-series-17.pdf,%2026

47 Ho, 'Singaporeans have high level of confidence in Government but politically uninterested'.

48 Mathews, Key, Tay, and Wang, 'Attitudes toward institutions, politics, and policies', p. 26.

49 Pippa Crerar, 'Exclusive: New Partygate image shows Boris Johnson and open bottle of bubbly at No 10 Xmas quiz', *Daily Mirror*, 9 February 2022, https://www.mirror.co.uk/news/politics/new-partygate-image-shows-boris-26181071

50 'The Guardian view on a Covid Christmas: better safe than sorry', *The Guardian*, 15 December 2020, https://www.theguardian.com/commentisfree/2020/dec/15/the-guardian-view-on-a-covid-christmas-safe-not-sorry?

51 Crerar, 'Exclusive'.

52 Lizzy Buchan, 'Partygate: The Downing Street parties Boris Johnson attended – with 6 probed by police', *Daily Mirror*, 29 March 2022, https://www.mirror.co.uk/news/politics/downing-street-parties-boris-johnson-26118738

53 Rajeev Syal, Matthew Weaver, and Peter Walker, 'Johnson's defence of Cummings sparks anger from allies and opponents alike', *The Guardian*, 24 May 2020, https://www.theguardian.com/politics/2020/may/24/boris-johnson-defence-dominic-cummings-anger-from-allies-and-opponents-alike

54 Adam Tooze, *Crashed: How a Decade Of Financial Crises Changed the World* (New York: Penguin, 2019), p. 544.

55 Taryn Luna and Phil Luna, 'Newsom apologizes for French Laundry dinner, says he will practice what he preaches on COVID-19', *Los Angeles Times*, 16 November 2020, https://www.latimes.com/california/story/2020-11-16/gavin-newsom-apology-french-laundry-dinner-covid-19

56 Ben Terris, 'What is Tommy Tuberville doing here?', *Washington Post*, 19 October 2021, https://www.washingtonpost.com/lifestyle/2021/10/19/tommy-tuberville-senator-coach/

57 'Conflicted Congress: Sen. Tommy Tuberville', *INSIDER*, December 2021, https://www.businessinsider.com/financial-conflicts-congress-members-rated-2021-12?page=sen-tommy-tuberville

58 Ibid.

59 Camila DeChalus, Kimberly Leonard, Warren Rojas, and Madison Hall, 'As the pandemic raged, at least 75 lawmakers bought and sold stock in companies that make COVID-19 vaccines, treatments, and tests', *INSIDER*,

13 December 2021, https://www.businessinsider.com/lawmakers-bought-sold-covid-19-related-stocks-during-pandemic-2021-12

60 'Investigation of Political Activities by Senior Trump Administration Officials During the 2020 Presidential Election', U.S. Office of Special Counsel, 9 November 2021, https://osc.gov/Documents/Hatch%20Act/Reports/Investigation%20of%20Political%20Activities%20by%20Senior%20Trump%20Administration%20Officials%20During%20the%202020%20Presidential%20Election.pdf

61 Bryan Metzger, 'The Federal Election Commission let Trump off the hook for allegedly using $2.8 million in charitable donations to veterans for political purposes', *INSIDER*, 24 February 2022, https://www.businessinsider.com/fec-trump-2016-iowa-veterans-campaign-finance-violations-soft-money-2022-2

62 The World Bank, GDP per capita (current US$) (2020), https://data.worldbank.org/indicator/NY.GDP.PCAP.CD

63 Esteban Ortiz-Ospina and Max Roser, 'Trust', Our World In Data, 2016, https://ourworldindata.org/trust

64 William D. Cohen, 'How Wall Street's bankers stayed out of jail', *The Atlantic*, September 2015; Volker Votsmeier, Elisabeth Atzler, and Christopher Cermak, 'Financial crimes, but no punishment', *Handelsblatt*, 7 October 2015, https://amp2.handelsblatt.com/sal-oppenheim-financial-crimes-but-no-punishment/23504414.html

65 Laura Noonan, Cale Tilford, Richard Milne, Ian Mount, and Peter Wise, 'Who went to jail for their role in the financial crisis?', *Financial Times*, 20 September 2018, https://ig.ft.com/jailed-bankers/; Edward Robinson and Omar Valdimarsson, 'This is where bad bankers go to prison', Bloomberg, 31 March 2016, https://www.bloomberg.com/news/features/2016-03-31/welcome-to-iceland-where-bad-bankers-go-to-prison?sref=TZEt22gR; Sjöfn Vilhelmsdóttir, 'Political Trust in Iceland', University of Ireland, February 2020, https://www.researchgate.net/publication/339509059_Political_Trust_in_Iceland_Determinants_and_trends_1983_to_2018

66 David Jiménez, 'There's a simple reason Spain has been hit hard by coronavirus', *New York Times*, 24 September 2020, https://www.nytimes.com/2020/09/24/opinion/spain-pandemic-second-wave.html

67 'Mortality Analyses', Johns Hopkins University of Medicine: Coronavirus Resource Center, accessed August 2022, https://coronavirus.jhu.edu/data/mortality

68 Jiménez, 'There's a simple reason Spain has been hit hard by coronavirus'.

69 'Eurobarometer: Corruption', European Commission, December 2017, https://europa.eu/eurobarometer/surveys/detail/2176

70 Mara Mordecai, '5 facts about public opinion in Spain as its election nears', Pew Research Center, 4 November 2019, https://www.pewresearch.org/fact-tank/2019/11/04/5-facts-about-public-opinion-in-spain-as-its-election-nears/

71 'The 25 most powerful women in the world, 2014', *Forbes*, 28 May 2014, https://www.forbes.com/pictures/lmh45lfdj/geun-hye-park/?sh=60cbf47b69d3; Martin Fackler, 'In a rowdy democracy, a dictator's daughter with an unsoiled aura', *New York Times*, 20 April 2012, https://www.nytimes.com/2012/04/21/world/asia/park-geun-hye-an-unsoiled-leader-in-south-koreas-rowdy-democracy.html?searchResultPosition=66

72 Choe Sang-Hun, 'Claims against South Korean president: extortion, abuse of power and bribery', *New York Times*, 8 December 2016, https://www.nytimes.com/2016/12/08/world/asia/south-korea-park-geun-hye-accusations-impeachment.html

73 Ibid.

74 'Choi-gate: South Korean president's approval rating tanks at 4%', *The Guardian*, 24 November 2016, https://www.theguardian.com/world/2016/nov/25/choi-gate-south-korean-presidents-approval-rating-tanks-at-4

75 Justin McCurry, 'Park Geun-hye: South Korean MPs vote to impeach president', *The Guardian*, 9 December 2016, https://www.theguardian.com/world/2016/dec/09/south-koreas-parliament-votes-to-impeach-president-park-geun-hye; Elise Hu, 'At least 500,000 Seoul protesters demand Korean president resign', NPR, 12 November 2016, https://www.npr.org/sections/thetwo-way/2016/11/12/501818736/at-least-500-000-protest-in-seoul-demanding-korean-presidents-resignation

76 'Park Geun-hye: South Korea's ex-president granted government pardon', BBC News, 24 December 2021, https://www.bbc.com/news/world-asia-59777757

77 Benjamin Haas, 'Former South Korean president jailed for 15 years for corruption', *The Guardian*, 5 October 2018, https://www.theguardian.com/world/2018/oct/05/south-korean-president-jailed-15-years-corruption-lee-myung-bak

78 'South Korea: Roh Tae Woo arrested on corruption charges', Associated Press, 16 November 1995, http://www.aparchive.com/metadata/youtube/611fefa06c50ac029970e1ebe76833e0

79 Patricia Chew, 'Two former S. Korean leaders indicted', CNN, 21 December 1995, http://edition.cnn.com/WORLD/9512/skorea/index.html

80 '2022 Index of Economic Freedom', Heritage Foundation, 2022, https://www.heritage.org/index/ranking

81 Rick Noack, 'Former French president Sarkozy, guilty of illegal campaign

financing, probably will avoid prison', *Washington Post*, 30 September 2021, https://www.washingtonpost.com/world/europe/france-president-sarkozy-convicted-campaign/2021/09/30/b5e8baac-21cc-11ec-a8d9-0827a2a4b915_story.html

82 Adam Taylor, 'Malaysian ex-premier Najib loses appeal, begins 12-year sentence', *Washington Post*, 23 August 2022, https://www.washingtonpost.com/world/2022/08/23/najib-razak-prison-1mdb-appeal-12-years/

83 Free Malaysia Today, 'Corruption is endemic in Malaysia's political system, says Mahathir', Facebook, 8 February 2021, https://m.facebook.com/free-malaysiatoday/videos/845480952678783/?refsrc=deprecated&_rdr; Ipsos Malaysia, 'IPSOS Press Release: What Worries Malaysia?', Ipsos, 19 May 2022, https://www.ipsos.com/sites/default/files/ct/news/documents/2022-05/Ipsos%20Press%20Release%20-%20What%20Worries%20Malaysia%20-%20Thu%2C%2019th%20May%202022%20%28FINAL%29.pdf

84 Jake Lucas, 'How Times reporters use the freedom of information act', *New York Times*, 21 July 2018, https://www.nytimes.com/2018/07/21/insider/information-freedom-reporters-pruitt.html

85 Tom Sasse, 'Government must extend Freedom of Information', Institute for Government, 30 January 2019, https://www.instituteforgovernment.org.uk/blog/government-must-extend-freedom-information-1

86 Tamasin Cave and Andy Rowell, 'The truth about lobbying: 10 ways big business controls government', *The Guardian*, 12 March 2014, https://www.theguardian.com/politics/2014/mar/12/lobbying-10-ways-corprations-influence-government

87 'Influence of big money', Brennan Center for Justice, accessed August 2022, https://www.brennancenter.org/issues/reform-money-politics/influence-big-money

88 Ben Wescott, 'Australia to tackle corrupt lawmakers with new public hearings', Bloomberg, 27 September 2022, https://www.bloomberg.com/news/articles/

89 Frank Anechiarico (ed.), *Legal but Corrupt: A New Perspective on Public Ethics* (Lanham: Lexington Book, 2017).

90 Oguzhan Dincer and Michael Johnston, 'Measuring illegal and legal corruption in American states: some results from the corruption in America survey', Edmond & Lily Safra Center for Ethics, 1 December 2014, https://ethics.harvard.edu/blog/measuring-illegal-and-legal-corruption-american-states-some-results-safra

91 Katya Wachtel, 'Goldman Sachs can't say it didn't get bailed out anymore -- it kept billions from AIG', *INSIDER*, 27 January 2011, http://www.businessinsider.com/goldman-sachs-aig-bailout?IR=T

92 'Germany loses patience with ex-chancellor's Russia lobbying', France24,

13 February 2022, https://www.france24.com/en/live-news/20220213-germany-loses-patience-with-ex-chancellor-s-russia-lobbying

93 Dana Gold, 'Whistleblowers risk everything—lawmakers must protect them', *Government Executive*, 28 October 2021, https://www.govexec.com/oversight/2021/10/whistleblowers-risk-everythinglawmakers-must-protect-them/186441/

94 Transparency International, *Global Corruption Barometer: European Union 2021* (Berlin 2021).

95 Damien Cave, 'Australia may well be the world's most secretive democracy', *New York Times*, 5 June 2019, https://www.nytimes.com/2019/06/05/world/australia/journalist-raids.html

96 Ibid.

97 Damien Cave, 'The secret powers of an Australian Prime Minister, now revealed', *New York Times*, 16 August 2022, https://www.nytimes.com/2022/08/16/world/australia/scott-morrison-minister.html

Chapter 3

1 Anna Jones, 'Coronavirus: How "overreaction" made Vietnam a virus success', BBC News, 15 May 2020, https://www.bbc.com/news/world-asia-52628283

2 Bích Huệ, 'Bộ Y tế chỉ đạo kiểm soát chặt, tránh nguy cơ lây virus qua cửa khẩu', Zing News, 1 April 2020, https://zingnews.vn/bo-y-te-chi-dao-kiem-soat-chat-tranh-nguy-co-lay-virus-qua-cua-khau-post1032354.html

3 John Reed and Pham Hai Cung, 'Vietnam's coronavirus offensive wins praise for low-cost model', *Financial Times*, 23 March 2020, https://www.ft.com/content/0cc3c956-6cb2-11ea-89df-41bea055720b

4 Christine Wilson, ' "There was no confusion" – lessons from Vietnam on COVID-19', British Council, June 2020, https://www.britishcouncil.org/research-policy-insight/insight-articles/lessons-vietnam-covid-19

5 Bre'Anna Grant, 'Vietnam was ranked 2nd for successfully handling the coronavirus pandemic, and its contact tracing was so good it barely had to lock down', *INSIDER*, 20 February 2021, https://www.businessinsider.com/vietnam-coronavirus-measures-among-best-in-world-contact-tracing-masks-2021-2

6 *World Values Survey: Round Seven – Country-Pooled Datafile Version 4.0* (Madrid and Austria: JD Systems Institute and WVSA Secretariat, 2022), doi:10.14281/18241.18

7 Benedict J. Tria Kerkvliet, *Speaking Out in Vietnam: Public Political Criticism in a Communist Party-Ruled Nation* (Ithaca: Cornell University Press, 2019), p. 82.

8   Phạm Quỳnh Phương, 'Covid-19 in Vietnam: social engagement, trust crea-
    tion and political legitimacy', European Commission: Competing Regional
    Integrations in Southeast Asia (December 2020), https://halshs.archives-
    ouvertes.fr/halshs-03151081/document

9   Ibid., p. 3.

10 Ibid., p. 3.

11 Le Vinh Trien and Kris Hartley, 'Vietnam lost public buy-in. its COVID-
    19 struggles followed.', The Diplomat, 1 September 2021, https://thediplo-
    mat.com/2021/09/vietnam-lost-public-buy-in-its-covid-19-struggles-
    followed/

12 Megan Brenan, 'Americans' trust in government remains low', Gallup,
    30 September 2021, https://news.gallup.com/poll/355124/americans-trust-
    government-remains-low.aspx

13 Amy Sippitt, 'Political trust in the UK', Full Fact, June 2019, https://fullfact.
    org/media/uploads/political-trust-in-the-uk.pdf

14 2019 Edelman Trust Barometer: Global Report, Edelman, 2019, p. 42, https:/
    /www.edelman.com/sites/g/files/aatuss191/files/2019-02/2019_Edelman_
    Trust_Barometer_Global_Report.pdf

15 Ibid., p. 42

16 Cary Wu, 'Did the pandemic shake Chinese citizens' trust in their govern-
    ment? We surveyed nearly 20,000 people to find out', Washington Post,
    5 May 2021, https://www.washingtonpost.com/politics/2021/05/05/did-
    pandemic-shake-chinese-citizens-trust-their-government/

17 Edelman Trust Barometer 2021: Global Report, Edelman, 2021, p. 9, https://
    www.edelman.com/sites/g/files/aatuss191/files/2021-01/2021-edelman-
    trust-barometer.pdf; Edelman Trust Barometer 2022: Global Report,
    Edelman, 2022, p. 21, https://www.edelman.com/sites/g/files/aatuss191/
    files/2022-01/2022%20Edelman%20Trust%20Barometer%20FINAL_
    Jan25.pdf

18 Edelman Trust Barometer 2021: Global Report, p. 9; Edelman Trust Barometer
    2022: Global Report, p. 21.

19 Edelman Trust Barometer 2022: Global Report, p. 21.

20 Mark John, 'Autocracies outdo democracies on public trust – survey',
    Reuters, 18 January 2022, https://www.reuters.com/business/autocracies-
    outdo-democracies-public-trust-survey-2022-01-18/

21 Rakhahari Chatterji, 'Trust and democracy', Overseas Research Foundation,
    22 September 2020, https://www.orfonline.org/research/trust-and-democracy/

22 'The American Economy in 1964', U.S. Department of Commerce Office of
    Business Economics, January 1965, https://fraser.stlouisfed.org/files/docs/
    publications/SCB/pages/1965-1969/8106_1965-1969.pdf

23 Ibid.

24 'Public Trust in Government: 1958-2022', Pew Research Center, 6 June 2022, https://www.pewresearch.org/politics/2022/06/06/public-trust-in-government-1958-2022/

25 Jon Talton, ' "It's the economy stupid," and the bad luck of George H.W. Bush', *Seattle Times*, 4 December 2018, https://www.seattletimes.com/business/economy/its-the-economy-stupid-and-the-bad-luck-of-george-h-w-bush/

26 'The Clinton Presidency: historic economic growth', The White House, 2000, https://clintonwhitehouse5.archives.gov/WH/Accomplishments/eightyears-03.html

27 'Public Trust in Government: 1958-2022', Pew Research Center.

28 'Trust in government', Organisation for Economic Co-operation and Development, accessed August 2022, https://data.oecd.org/gga/trust-in-government.htm; The World Bank, GDP per capita (current LCU) – Japan (2020), https://data.worldbank.org/indicator/NY.GDP.PCAP.CN?locations=JP

29 The World Bank, GDP per capita (constant LCU) – Czech Republic (2020), https://data.worldbank.org/indicator/NY.GDP.PCAP.KN?end=2020&locations=CZ; 'Trust in government', Organisation for Economic Co-operation and Development.

30 The World Bank, GDP per capita (constant LCU) – China (2020), https://data.worldbank.org/indicator/NY.GDP.PCAP.KN?end=2020&locations=CN

31 *Edelman Trust Barometer 2021: Global Report*, p. 21.

32 'Trust in government', Organisation for Economic Co-operation and Development.

33 Pippa Norris, 'Trust in government redux: the role of information environments and cognitive skills', Harvard Kennedy School Faculty Research Working Paper Series No. RWP22-001 (January 2022), https://www.hks.harvard.edu/publications/trust-government-redux-role-information-environments-and-cognitive-skills; Bo Rothstein, 'Social capital, economic growth and quality of government: The causal mechanism.' *New Political Economy* Vol. 8, No. 1 (2008), pp. 49–71; Bo Rothstein and Dieter Stolle, 'The state and social capital: An institutional theory of generalized trust', *Comparative Politics* Vol. 33, No. 4 (2008), pp. 401–19; Bo Rothstein and Eric Uslaner, 'All for one: Equality, corruption, and social trust.' *World Politics* Vol. 58, No. 1 (2005), pp. 41–72; Bo Rothstein, *The Quality of Government: Corruption, Social Trust and Inequality in International Perspective* (Chicago: The University of Chicago Press, 2011).

34   Jacqui Thornton, 'Covid-19: Trust in government and other people linked with lower infection rate and higher vaccination uptake', *BMJ* No. 376 (2022), https://www.bmj.com/content/376/bmj.o292

35   Max Stier and Tom Freedman, 'Why democracy's in such trouble: a crisis in public trust of government', *POLITICO Magazine*, 1 March 2022, https://www.politico.com/news/magazine/2022/03/01/democracy-public-crisis-trust-government-faith-00012565

36   OECD, *Government at a Glance 2013* (Paris 2013), p. 23; Anna Tibaijuka, 'Address by Mrs. Anna Tibaijuka Under-Secretary-General of the United Nations and Executive Director of UN-HABITAT On the occasion of World Habitat Day', UN-Habitat, 1 October 2007, https://mirror.unhabitat.org/down-loads/docs/5287_98323_EDwhdSpeechhaguerr07[1].pdf; 'Annual Report: 2009', City of Pittsburgh, Pennsylvania Department of Public Safety, https://apps.pittsburghpa.gov/redtail/images/2511_2009_Annual_Report.pdf

37   *Government at a Glance 2013*, p. 20.

38   Marc J. Hetherington, *Why Trust Matters: Declining Political Trust and the Demise of American Liberalism* (Princeton: Princeton University Press, 2006).

39   Ibid.

40   Kenneth P. Vogel, Jim Rutenberg, and Lisa Lerer, 'The quiet hand of conservative groups in the anti-lockdown protests', *New York Times*, 21 April 2020, https://www.nytimes.com/2020/04/21/us/politics/coronavirus-protests-trump.html

41   David Crow and Patti Waldmeir, 'US anti-lockdown protests: "If you are paranoid about getting sick, just don't go out"', *Financial Times*, 22 April 2020, https://www.ft.com/content/15ca3a5f-bc5c-44a3-99a8-c446f6f6881c

42   Associated Press, 'Idaho residents protest stay-at-home order', YouTube, 17 April 2020, https://youtu.be/2CfxNRV3GHQ?t=15

43   Mike Wilkinson, 'Are your neighbors getting vaccinated? Michigan map shows rates by census tracts', Bridge Michigan, 16 June 2021, https://www.bridgemi.com/michigan-health-watch/are-your-neighbors-vaccinated-michigan-map-shows-rates-census-tracts

44   Nicquel Terry Ellis and Deirdre McPhilipps, 'White people are getting vaccinated at higher rates than Black and Latino Americans', CNN, 26 January 2021, https://www.cnn.com/2021/01/26/us/vaccination-dispari-ties-rollout/index.html

45   Joseph Goldstein and Matthew Sedacca, 'Why only 28 percent of young black new yorkers are vaccinated', *New York Times*, 12 August 2021, https://www.nytimes.com/2021/08/12/nyregion/covid-vaccine-black-young-new-yorkers.html

46 Ibid.

47 Ibid.

48 'Global attitudes towards a COVID-19 vaccine', Imperial College London, May 2021, https://www.imperial.ac.uk/media/imperial-college/institute-of -global-health-innovation/GlobalVaccineInsights_ICL-YouGov-Covid-19- Behaviour-Tracker_20210520_v2.pdf

49 Hyonhee Shin, '"Parasite" reflects deepening social divide in South Korea', Reuters, 10 February 2020, https://www.reuters.com/article/us-awards- oscars-southkorea-inequality/parasite-reflects-deepening-social-divide-in- south-korea-idUSKBN20414L; Hyun Kyung Park, Jie Hye Ham, Deok Hyun Jang, Jin Yong Lee, and Won Mo Jang, 'Political ideologies, government trust, and COVID-19 vaccine hesitancy in South Korea: a cross-sectional survey', *International Journal of Environmental Research and Public Health* Vol. 18, No. 20 (2021).

50 Shuhei Nomura, Akifumi Eguchi, Daisuke Yoneoka, Takayuki Kawashima, and Yuta Tanoue, 'Reasons for being unsure or unwilling regarding inten- tion to take COVID-19 vaccine among Japanese people: A large cross- sectional national survey', *The Lancet Regional Health – Western Pacific* No. 14 (2021), https://www.thelancet.com/pdfs/journals/lanwpc/PIIS2666- 6065(21)00132-2.pdf

51 Makiko Eda, 'Japan must restore trust in the future among the young – here's how', *Japan Times*, 18 January 2022, https://www.japantimes.co.jp/ opinion/2022/01/18/commentary/world-commentary/japans-younger- generation/

52 Keith E. Smith and Adam Mayer, 'A social trap for the climate? Collective action, trust and climate change risk perception in 35 countries', *Global Environmental Change* Vol. 49 (March 2018), pp. 140–53; Joakim Kulin, 'Who do you trust? How trust in partial and impartial government institutions influences climate policy attitudes', *Climate Policy*, Vol. 21, No. 1 (2021), pp. 33–46.

53 Elaine Kamarck, 'The challenging politics of climate change', Brookings Institution, 23 September 2019, https://www.brookings.edu/research/the- challenging-politics-of-climate-change/

54 Nathan Cooper and Amy White, 'IPCC report: urgent climate action needed to halve emissions by 2030', World Economic Forum, 6 April 2022, https:// www.weforum.org/agenda/2022/04/ipcc-report-mitigation-climate-change/

55 'Trust in government', Organisation for Economic Co-operation and Development.

56 Lee Rainie, Scott Keeter, and Andrew Perrin, 'Trust and distrust in America', Pew Research Center, 22 July 2019, https://www.pewresearch.org/poli- tics/2019/07/22/trust-and-distrust-in-america/

57 Joanna Thornborough, 'Trust in local government is still high, and poli-cymakers should take advantage of it', London School of Economics, 19 April 2021, https://blogs.lse.ac.uk/covid19/2021/04/19/trust-in-local-government-is-still-high-and-policymakers-should-take-advantage-of-it/

58 'Edelman trust barometer 2020, spring update: trust and the Covid-19 pandemic', Edelman, 2020, https://www.edelman.com/sites/g/files/aatuss191/files/2020-05/2020%20Edelman%20Trust%20Barometer%20Spring%20Update.pdf

59 Bruce Stokes and Kat Devlin, 'Despite rising economic confidence, Japanese see best days behind them and say children face a bleak future', Pew Research Center, 12 November 2018, https://www.pewresearch.org/global/2018/11/12/views-of-japanese-democracy/

60 Richard Wike, Laura Silver, Shannon Schumacher, and Aidan Connaughton, 'Many in U.S., Western Europe say their political system needs major reform', Pew Research Center, 31 March 2021, https://www.pewresearch.org/global/2021/03/31/many-in-us-western-europe-say-their-political-system-needs-major-reform/

61 Simon Bazelon and Matthew Yglesias, 'The rise and importance of the Secret Congress', Slow Boring, 21 June 2021, https://www.slowboring.com/p/the-rise-and-importance-of-secret

62 Jacob Bogage (@jacobbogage), 'BREAKING: The House passes a major financial overhaul of the USPS, relieving it of $57 billion in liabilities, plus another $50 billion cost savings over the next decade.', Twitter, 8 February 2022, https://twitter.com/jacobbogage/status/1491175544456503298; Helena Bottemiller Evich and Tatyana Monnay, 'In rare bipartisan move, Senate approves bill to help farmers profit on climate action', POLITICO, 4 June 2021, https://www.politico.com/news/2021/06/24/senate-farmers-carbon-agriculture-496029

63 Shim Kyu-Seok, '20th National Assembly dubbed least productive in history', Korea JoongAng Daily, 20 May 2020, https://koreajoongangdaily.joins.com/2020/05/20/politics/National-Assembly-20th-%EA%B5%AD%ED%9A%8C/20200520183200191.html; '2020-21 Korea-U.S. policy dialogue: political polarization', KDI School of Public Policy and Management, 2020, p. 15. https://www.kdevelopedia.org/asset/99202202040168676/1643956900209.pdf

64 Dimiter Toshkov, 'Enhancing access to EU law: Why bother?', European Central Bank Eurosystem Legal Conference 2020, February 2021, pp. 50–54, https://www.ecb.europa.eu/pub/pdf/other/ecb.escblegalconferenceproceedings2020~4c11842967.en.pdf

65 Christian Adam, Steffen Hurka, Christoph Knill, and Yves Steinbebach, 'On democratic intelligence and failure: The vice and virtue of incrementalism under political fragmentation and policy accumulation', *Governance*, Vol. 35, No. 2 (2021), pp. 435–43.

66 'Public Trust in Government: 1958-2022', Pew Research Center, 6 June 2022.

67 *Edelman Trust Barometer 2021: Global Report.*

68 Ibid.

69 Nikita Lalwani, 'When Americans get good government service, they mistakenly give the credit to the private sector', *Washington Post*, 29 August 2019, https://www.washingtonpost.com/politics/2019/08/29/when-americans-get-good-government-service-they-mistakenly-give-credit-private-sector/

70 Elyse Matlin, 'What successful public-private partnerships Do', *Harvard Business Review*, 8 January 2019, https://hbr.org/2019/01/what-successful-public-private-partnerships-do

71 Ibid.

72 Wilfried Wunderlich and Oliver Mayer, 'PPP in Japan's railway system – a success story', *Internationales Verkehrswesen* Vol. 69, Special Edition No. 1 (2017), pp. 21–25; Maria Schulders, 'The potential of German administrative models for the resolution of public-private partnership barriers in Poland', *Studia i Materiały* Vol. 1/2020, No. 32 (2020), pp. 70–80.

73 Arthur Herman, 'Why operation warp speed worked', *Wall Street Journal*, 2 February 2021.

74 Riley Griffin and Drew Armstrong, 'Pfizer vaccine's funding came from Berlin, not Washington', Bloomberg, 9 November 2020, https://www.bloomberg.com/news/articles/2020-11-09/pfizer-vaccine-s-funding-came-from-berlin-not-washington

75 'Bringing transparency to the UK government – why we've launched "open access"', Transparency International UK, 26 November 2018, https://www.transparency.org.uk/bringing-transparency-uk-government-why-we-ve-launched-open-access

76 Andrew Porter, 'David Cameron warns lobbying is next political scandal', *The Telegraph*, 8 February 2010, https://www.telegraph.co.uk/news/election-2010/7189466/David-Cameron-warns-lobbying-is-next-political-scandal.html

77 Ro Khanna, 'Improving government efficiency, transparency, and responsiveness', Ro for Congress, https://www.rokhanna.com/issues/improving-government-efficiency-transparency-and-responsiveness

78 Nancy Soderberg, 'Transforming the security classification system: report to the President from the public interest declassification board', 27 November

2012, https://www.archives.gov/files/declassification/pidb/recommenda-tions/transforming-classification.pdf

79 Senator Ron Wyden and Senator Jerry Moran, 'Time to fix a broken declas-sification system', *Just Security*, 8 September 2020, https://www.justsecurity.org/72326/time-to-fix-a-broken-declassification-system/; Rebecca Beitsch, 'Top Biden official says information classification system undermines national security, public trust', *The Hill*, 27 January 2022, https://thehill.com/policy/national-security/591731-top-biden-official-says-information-clas-sification-system-undermines

80 Robert Panizza, 'Transparency, integrity and accountability in the EU insti-tutions', Briefing to the European Parliament Committee on Petitions, March 2019, p. 1-2 and 6, https://www.europarl.europa.eu/RegData/etudes/BRIE/2019/608873/IPOL_BRI(2019)608873_EN.pdf

81 Nikolaj Nielsen, 'EU Commission promises only minor update on transpar-ency', *EUObserver*, 16 November 2021, https://euobserver.com/democracy/153515

82 Markus Becker, 'The European Commission deletes mass amounts of emails and doesn't archive chats', *DER SPIEGEL*, 11 December 2021, https://www.spiegel.de/international/europe/a-new-controversy-erupts-around-ursula-von-der-leyen-s-text-messages-a-6510951f-e8dc-4468-a0af-2ecd60e77ed9; Nikolaj Nielsen, 'Transparency fight hones in on releasing EU text messages', *EUObserver*, 6 November 2020, https://euobserver.com/institutional/149965

83 Dan Ennis, 'WhatsApp scandal's specter rises again', *Banking Dive*, 1 March 2022, https://www.bankingdive.com/news/whatsapp-citi-goldman-sachs-hsbc-deutsche-bank-jpmorgan-chase-sec-cftc/619609/

84 Nina Katzemich on behalf of the ALTER-EU steering committee, 'Please take action on revised EU Transparency Register', ALTER-EU, 2 February 2022, https://transparency.eu/wp-content/uploads/2022/02/letter_jourova_TR.pdf

85 Nielsen, 'EU Commission promises only minor update on transparency'.

86 Xiaochen Su, 'Lack of transparency complicates Japan's handling of COVID -19', *The Diplomat*, 6 February 2021, https://thediplomat.com/2021/02/lack-of-transparency-complicates-japans-handling-of-covid-19/

87 Adriana García García, 'Transparency in Mexico: An overview of access to information regulations and their effectiveness at the federal and state level', Wilson Center, December 2016, https://www.wilsoncenter.org/publication/transparency-mexico-overview-access-to-information-regulations-and-their-effectiveness

88 'Trust in government by race and ethnicity', Pew Research Center, 10 April

2019, https://www.pewresearch.org/politics/chart/trust-in-government-by-race-and-ethnicity/

89 'Public Trust in Government: 1958-2022', Pew Research Center.

90 Nambi Ndugga, Latoya Hill, Samantha Artiga, and Sweta Halder, 'Latest data on COVID-19 vaccinations by race/ethnicity', Kasier Family Foundation, 14 July 2022, https://www.kff.org/coronavirus-covid-19/issue-brief/latest-data-on-covid-19-vaccinations-by-race-ethnicity/

91 Sophie Trawalter, 'Black Americans are systematically under-treated for pain. why?', University of Virginia Frank Batten School of Leadership and Public Policy, 30 June 2020, https://batten.virginia.edu/about/news/black-americans-are-systematically-under-treated-pain-why

92 Martha Hostetter and Sarah Klein, 'Understanding and ameliorating medical mistrust among Black Americans', The Commonwealth Fund, 14 January 2021, https://www.commonwealthfund.org/publications/newsletter-article/2021/jan/medical-mistrust-among-black-americans

93 Jeffrey M. Jones, 'In U.S., Black confidence in police recovers from 2020 low', Gallup, 14 July 2021, https://news.gallup.com/poll/352304/black-confidence-police-recovers-2020-low.aspx

94 Ibid.

95 Eglė Vaidelytė, Eglė Butkevičienė, Vaidas Morkevičius, and Michiel S. de Vries, 'Familiarity and trust: explaining trust in government through ethno-racial differences', *Viešoji Politika ir Administravimas*, Vol. 20, No. 3 (2021), pp. 397–410.

96 Ibid.

97 Robert Booth, 'BAME Britons less likely to trust Covid health officials – survey', *The Guardian*, 27 August 2020, https://www.theguardian.com/world/2020/aug/27/bame-britons-less-likely-trust-covid-health-officials-survey

98 'Annual poll: Public's faith in institutions, satisfaction in state of country dire', *Times of Israel*, 6 January 2022, https://www.timesofisrael.com/annual-poll-publics-faith-in-institutions-satisfaction-in-state-of-country-dire/

99 Vaidelytė, Butkevičienė, Morkevičius, and S. de Vries, 'Familiarity and Trust'.

100 Mujtaba Ali Isani, 'The effects of discrimination on European Muslim trust in governmental institutions', *POMEPS Studies 32: The Politics of Islam in Europe and North America*, December 2018, https://pomeps.org/the-effects-of-discrimination-on-european-muslim-trust-in-governmental-institutions

101 Josh Smith, 'S. Korea's lack of anti-discrimination laws takes toll on LGBT youth, activists say', Reuters, 13 September 2021, https://www.reuters.com/world/asia-pacific/skoreas-lack-anti-discrimination-laws-takes-toll-lgbt-youth-activists-say-2021-09-14/

102 Jason Strother, 'South Korea's coronavirus contact tracing puts LGBTQ community under surveillance, critics say', The World, 22 May 2020, https://theworld.org/stories/2020-05-22/south-korea-s-coronavirus-contact-tracing-puts-lgbtq-community-under-surveillance

103 Marty Johnson, 'Mistrust of government is significant roadblock to Black American vaccination efforts', The Hill, 23 December 2020, https://thehill.com/policy/healthcare/530947-mistrust-of-government-is-significant-roadblock-to-black-american

104 Ibid.

105 Brandon Tensley, 'America's long history of Black voter suppression', CNN, May 2021, https://www.cnn.com/interactive/2021/05/politics/black-voting-rights-suppression-timeline/

106 'Voting laws roundup: December 2021', Brennan Center for Justice, 21 December 2021, https://www.brennancenter.org/our-work/research-reports/voting-laws-roundup-december-2021

107 Reema Khrais, Hayley Hersman, and Beth Pearlman, 'How Black Americans have been blocked from voting throughout U.S. history', Marketplace, 21 September 2020, https://www.marketplace.org/2020/09/21/how-black-americans-have-been-blocked-from-voting-throughout-u-s-history/

108 Federico Fubini, 'Voter suppression comes to Europe', Project Syndicate, 9 January 2020, https://www.project-syndicate.org/commentary/voter-suppression-in-europe-by-federico-fubini-2020-01; Lili Bayer, 'Viktor Orbán courts voters beyond "fortress Hungary"', POLITICO Europe, 22 August 2017, https://www.politico.eu/article/viktor-orban-courts-voters-in-transylvania-romania-hungarian-election-2018/

109 Bayer, 'Viktor Orbán courts voters beyond "fortress Hungary"'.

110 Lili Rutai, 'A tale of two diasporas: the battle for Hungarian voters abroad', RadioFreeEurope/RadioLiberty, 21 February 2022, https://www.rferl.org/a/hungary-election-diaspora-orban-marki-zay/31712662.html

111 Ibid.

112 Fubini, 'Voter suppression comes to Europe'.

113 Andrew Garber, 'Debunking False Claims About the John Lewis Voting Rights Act', Brennan Center for Justice, 13 January 2022, https://www.brennancenter.org/our-work/research-reports/debunking-false-claims-about-john-lewis-voting-rights-act

114 Nicholas Reimann, 'John Lewis Voting Rights Act fails to pass senate', Forbes, 3 November 2021, https://www.forbes.com/sites/nicholasreimann/2021/11/03/john-lewis-voting-rights-act-fails-to-pass-senate/?sh=6fd72544b3d2

115 Lili Bayer, 'How Orbán broke the EU — and got away with it', *POLITICO Europe*, 24 September 2020, https://www.politico.eu/article/how-viktor-orban-broke-the-eu-and-got-away-with-it-hungary-rule-of-law/

Chapter 4

1 George Dugan, 'Rockefeller eulogizes Gustave Levy Of wall street as "fabulous friend"', *New York Times*, 8 November 1976, https://www.nytimes.com/1976/11/08/archives/rockefeller-eulogizes-gustave-levy-of-wall-street-as-fabulous.html

2 'The New York stock market crash of 1929 preludes the great depression', Goldman Sachs, 2019, https://www.goldmansachs.com/our-firm/history/moments/1929-financial-crash.html

3 William D. Cohen, *Money and Power: How Goldman Sachs Came to Rule the World* (New York: Anchor Books, 2012), pp. 48 and 56.

4 'Average weekly earnings of all employees, total private', U.S. Bureau of Labor Statistics (Federal Reserve Bank of St. Louis), 5 August 2022, https://fred.stlouisfed.org/series/CES0500000011

5 'Goldman Sachs sets block trading record with alcan aluminum trade', Goldman Sachs, 2019, https://www.goldmansachs.com/our-firm/history/moments/1967-alcan-block-trade.html

6 Cohen, *Money and Power*, p. 146.

7 Liz Hoffman, Corrie Driebusch, and Tom McGinty, 'Big stock sales are supposed to be secret. the numbers indicate they aren't', *Wall Street Journal*, 30 March 2022, https://www.wsj.com/articles/big-stock-sales-are-supposed-to-be-secret-the-numbers-indicate-they-arent-11648647914

8 Cohen, *Money and Power*, p. 146.

9 Charles D. Ellis, *The Partnership: The Making of Goldman Sachs* (New York: Penguin), p. 79.

10 Cohen, *Money and Power*, p. 146.

11 Ibid.

12 Ezra Klein, 'At Goldman, short-term greed vs. long-term greed', *Washington Post*, 15 March 2012, https://www.washingtonpost.com/blogs/ezra-klein/post/at-goldman-short-term-greed-vs-long-term-greed/2011/08/25/gIQAxFhhES_blog.html

13 Ibid.

14 Ibid.

15 William Galston, 'Against short-termism', *Democracy Journal* No. 38 (Fall 2015), https://democracyjournal.org/magazine/38/against-short-termism/

16 Jeff Grimshaw, Tanya Mann, Lynne Viscio, and Jennifer Landris, 'Why it

pays to be long-term greedy', *Chief Executive*, 29 July 2019, https://chiefexecutive.net/ceos-pay-long-term-greedy/

17   Roger Fingas, 'Apple has long-term plan, is working on products "way out in the 2020s"', Apple Insider, 21 February 2018, https://appleinsider.com/articles/18/02/21/apple-has-long-term-plan-is-working-on-products-way-out-in-the-2020s

18   Dominic Barton, James Manyika, and Sarah Keohane Williamson, 'Finally, evidence that managing for the long term pays off', *Harvard Business Review*, 9 February 2017, https://hbr.org/2017/02/finally-proof-that-managing-for-the-long-term-pays-off

19   Ann Lee, *What the US Can Learn from China* (Oakland: Berrett-Koehler Publishers, 2012), p. 96.

20   Jane Kinninmont, 'Vision 2030 and Saudi Arabia's social contract', Chatham House, 20 July 2017, https://www.chathamhouse.org/2017/07/vision-2030-and-saudi-arabias-social-contract

21   'What is China's five-year plan?', *The Economist*, 4 March 2021, https://www.economist.com/the-economist-explains/2021/03/04/what-is-chinas-five-year-plan

22   Ibid.

23   Lee, *What the US Can Learn from China*, p. 98.

24   'What is China's five-year plan?', *The Economist*.

25   Ben Murphy (ed.), 'Outline of the People's Republic of China 14th five-year plan for national economic and social development and Long-Range Objectives for 2035', Center for Security and Emerging Technology, 12 May 2021, p. 86, https://cset.georgetown.edu/wp-content/uploads/t0284_14th_Five_Year_Plan_EN.pdf

26   'What is China's five-year plan?', *The Economist*.

27   Keith Bradsher, Chris Buckley, and Vivian Wang, 'A confident China promises robust growth and a hard line on Hong Kong', *New York Times*, 4 March 2021, https://www.nytimes.com/2021/03/04/world/asia/china-economy.html

28   Yuen Yuen Ang, 'Chinese leaders boast about China's rising power. The real story is different', *Washington Post*, 13 April 2021, https://www.washingtonpost.com/politics/2021/04/13/chinese-leaders-boast-about-chinas-rising-power-real-story-is-different/; Thomas L. Friedman, 'China doesn't respect us anymore — for good reason', *New York Times*, 23 March 2021, https://www.nytimes.com/2021/03/23/opinion/china-america.html

29   Murphy (ed.), 'Outline of the People's Republic of China 14th five-year plan'.

30   Benjamin Cooper, 'China's 14th Five-Year Plan (2021-2025) Report', Hill + Knowlton Strategies, 1 April 2021, https://www.hkstrategies.com/en/chinas-14th-five-year-plan-2021-2025-report/

31   Vlad Savov, Debby Wu, and Yuan Gao, 'Biden needs more than $52 billion to counter China in chips', Bloomberg, 9 June 2021, https://www.bloomberg.com/news/articles/2021-06-09/biden-will-need-more-than-52-billion-to-counter-china-in-chips?sref=TZEt22gR

32   Editorial Board, 'The MBS paradox is on full display', *Washington Post*, 27 April 2020, https://www.washingtonpost.com/opinions/global-opinions/the-mbs-paradox-is-on-full-display/2020/04/27/5c3bd8a8-88a4-11ea-ac8a-fe9b8088e101_story.html

33   Samia Nakhoul, William Maclean, and Marwa Rashad, 'Saudi prince unveils sweeping plans to end "addiction" to oil', Reuters, 25 April 2016, https://www.reuters.com/article/us-saudi-economy/saudi-prince-unveils-sweeping-plans-to-end-addiction-to-oil-idUSKCN0XM1CD

34   Marwa Rashad, 'Saudis await prince's vision of future with hope and concern', Reuters, 24 April 2016, https://www.reuters.com/article/us-saudi-plan-idUKKCN0XL0B2

35   Nakhoul, Maclean, and Rashad, 'Saudi prince unveils sweeping plans to end "addiction" to oil'.

36   Rashad, 'Saudis await prince's vision of future with hope and concern'.

37   Nakhoul, Maclean, and Rashad, 'Saudi prince unveils sweeping plans to end "addiction" to oil'.

38   Graeme Wood, 'Absolute Power', *The Atlantic*, April 2022.

39   Ibid.

40   Ibid.

41   Ibid.

42   Stephen Grand and Katherine Wolff, 'Assessing Saudi Vision 2030: A 2020 review', Atlantic Council, 17 June 2020, https://www.atlanticcouncil.org/in-depth-research-reports/report/assessing-saudi-vision-2030-a-2020-review/

43   Ibid.

44   Shadi Hamid, 'What Russia's invasion of Ukraine means for democracy promotion in the Middle East', 23 March 2022, https://www.brookings.edu/blog/order-from-chaos/2022/03/23/what-russias-invasion-of-ukraine-means-for-democracy-promotion-in-the-middle-east/

45   Leo Hickman, 'James Lovelock: Humans are too stupid to prevent climate change', *The Guardian*, 29 March 2010, https://www.theguardian.com/science/2010/mar/29/james-lovelock-climate-change

46   'Are dictatorships better than democracies at fighting climate change?', *The Economist*, 21 September 2019, https://www.economist.com/asia/2019/09/21/are-dictatorships-better-than-democracies-at-fighting-climate-change

47   Ibid.

48   Dambisa Moyo, 'Why democracy doesn't deliver', *Foreign Policy*, 26 April

2018, https://foreignpolicy.com/2018/04/26/why-democracy-doesnt-deliver/; Richard Wike and Janell Fetterolf, 'Global public opinion in an era of democratic anxiety', Pew Research Center, 7 December 2021, https://www.pewresearch.org/global/2021/12/07/global-public-opinion-in-an-era-of-democratic-anxiety/

49 Harry S. Truman, 'Recommendation for assistance to Greece and Turkey', 12 March 1947, https://www.archives.gov/milestone-documents/truman-doctrine

50 Robert Wilde, 'The creation of Britain's welfare state', ThoughtCo., 11 September 2019, https://www.thoughtco.com/creation-of-britains-welfare-state-1221967

51 Ron Fournier and National Journal, 'Eric cantor and the curse of "short-termism" in politics and business', *The Atlantic*, 15 June 2015, https://www.theatlantic.com/politics/archive/2015/06/eric-cantor-and-the-curse-of-short-termism-in-politics-and-business/460512/

52 Therese Raphael | Bloomberg, 'Boris Johnson rearranges his cabinet. It could use a redesign', *Washington Post*, 17 September 2021, https://www.washingtonpost.com/business/boris-johnson-rearranges-his-cabinet-it-could-use-a-redesign/2021/09/16/a19a9b76-16b7-11ec-a019-cb-193b28aa73_story.html

53 Ibid. Peter Landers, 'Japan's love of debt offers a view of U.S. future', *Wall Street Journal*, 22 August 2021, https://www.wsj.com/articles/japans-love-of-debt-offers-a-view-of-u-s-future-11629640800; Lenora Chu, 'Japan's conundrum: It needs foreign workers. It doesn't want immigrants.', *Christian Science Monitor*, 10 July 2019, https://www.csmonitor.com/World/Asia-Pacific/2019/0710/Japan-s-conundrum-It-needs-foreign-workers.-It-doesn-t-want-immigrants

54 Carlo Bastasin, 'Even after Mattarella's reelection, Italy's political system remains unstable', Brookings Institution, 14 February 2022, https://www.brookings.edu/blog/order-from-chaos/2022/02/14/even-after-mattarellas-reelection-italys-political-system-remains-unstable/

55 Isabel Kershner, 'Israel passes first budget in more than 3 years in lifeline for government', *New York Times*, 4 November 2021, https://www.nytimes.com/2021/11/04/world/middleeast/israel-budget.html

56 'Merkel rejects calls for new stimulus package before G20 meeting', DW, 13 March 2009, https://www.dw.com/en/merkel-rejects-calls-for-new-stimulus-package-before-g20-meeting/a-4095549

57 Nicholas Kulish, 'Germany looks to its own costly reunification in resisting stimulus for Greece', *New York Times*, 25 May 2012, https://www.nytimes.com/2012/05/26/world/europe/german-reunification-pains-inform-stance-on-greece.html

58 Marcus Walker and Matthew Karnitschnig, 'Merkel rejects Obama's call to spend', *Wall Street Journal*, 23 June 2010, https://www.wsj.com/articles/SB10 001424052748703900004575324941614808602

59 Jon Cohen, 'White House releases $65 billion pandemic prepardeness proposal', *Science*, 3 September 2021, https://www.science.org/content/article/white-house-releases-65-billion-pandemic-preparedness-proposal

60 Maggie Fox, 'The world is unprepared for the next pandemic, study find', CNN, 9 December 2021, https://www.cnn.com/2021/12/08/health/world-unprepared-pandemic-report/index.html

61 Ezra Klein, '7 reasons America will fail on climate change', *Vox*, 5 June 2014, https://www.vox.com/2014/6/5/5779040/7-reasons-America-fail-global-warming

62 Michael Kimmelman, 'What does it mean to save a neighborhood?', *New York Times*, 2 December 2021, https://www.nytimes.com/2021/12/02/us/hurricane-sandy-lower-manhattan-nyc.html

63 Donna Lu, 'Satellite data shows entire Conger ice shelf has collapsed in Antarctica', *The Guardian*, 24 March 2022, https://www.theguardian.com/world/2022/mar/25/satellite-data-shows-entire-conger-ice-shelf-has-collapsed-in-antarctica

64 John Geddes, 'For Gerald Butts, climate change isn't like other policy', *Maclean's*, 19 February 2019, https://www.macleans.ca/politics/ottawa/for-gerald-butts-climate-change-isnt-like-other-policy/

65 'Romania fears that whatever happens in Ukraine, it will end up more vulnerable', *The Economist*, 22 March 2022, https://www.economist.com/europe/2022/03/22/romania-fears-that-whatever-happens-in-ukraine-it-will-end-up-more-vulnerable

66 Hilary Matfess, 'The progressive case for free trade', *Vox*, 1 August 2019, https://www.vox.com/policy-and-politics/2019/8/1/20750506/elizabeth-warren-trade-policy-bernie-sanders-tpp-2020-democrats-progressives

67 Andy Barr, 'Tea partiers told to "drop by" Perriello's home', *POLITICO*, 22 March 2010, https://www.politico.com/story/2010/03/tea-partiers-told-to-drop-by-perriellos-home-034843

68 Michael Cooper, 'Accusations fly between parties over threats and vandalism', *New York Times*, 25 March 2010, https://www.nytimes.com/2010/03/26/us/politics/26threat.html

69 'Former Dem. Rep.: Losing seat is "much less important" than giving Americans health care coverage', MSNBC, 22 March 2021, https://www.msnbc.com/the-last-word/watch/former-dem-rep-losing-seat-is-much-less-important-than-giving-americans-health-care-coverage

-108950597513; Tom Perriello, 'I lost my election after voting for Obamacare. Democrats need to back Biden's agenda', *Washington Post*, 29 September 2021, https://www.washingtonpost.com/opinions/2021/09/29/tom-perriello-biden-agenda-democrats-aca-vote/

70 Margot Sanger-Katz, 'Missing from Biden's budget: his signature policy agenda', *New York Times*, 28 March 2022, https://www.nytimes.com/2022/03/28/upshot/budget-biden-policy-agenda.html

71 Peter Scoblic, 'We can't prevent tomorrow's catastrophes unless we imagine them today', *Washington Post*, 18 March 2021.

72 Janna Anderson and Lee Rainie, 'Many tech experts say digital disruption will hurt democracy', Pew Research Center, 21 February 2020, https://www.pewresearch.org/internet/2020/02/21/many-tech-experts-say-digital-disruption-will-hurt-democracy/

73 President Biden (@POTUS), 'My Build Back Better Agenda costs zero dollars. Instead of wasting money on tax breaks, loopholes, and tax evasion for big corporations and the wealthy, we can make a once-in-a-generation investment in working America. And it adds zero dollars to the national debt', Twitter, 25 September 2021, https://twitter.com/potus/status/1441924106765602819; Glenn Kessler, 'Biden's claim that his spending plan "costs zero dollars"', *Washington Post*, 28 September 2021, https://www.washingtonpost.com/politics/2021/09/28/bidens-claim-that-his-spending-plan-costs-zero-dollars/

74 L. Yoon, 'Voter turnout in presidential elections in South Korea from 1987 to 2022', Statista, March 2022, https://www.statista.com/statistics/704937/south-korea-presidential-election-turnout/; D. Clark, 'Voter turnout in general elections and in the Brexit referendum in the United Kingdom from 1918 to 2019', Statista, December 2019, https://www.statista.com/statistics/1050929/voter-turnout-in-the-uk/

75 'Politicians should take citizens' assemblies seriously', *The Economist*, 17 September 2020, https://www.economist.com/leaders/2020/09/17/politicians-should-take-citizens-assemblies-seriously

76 Katariina Kulha, Mikko Leino, Maija Setälä, Maija Jäske, and Staffan Himmelroos, 'For the sake of the future: can democratic deliberation help thinking and caring about future generations?', *Sustainability*, Vol. 13, No. 5487 (2021).

77 Ibid.

Chapter 5

1 Ingrid Henriksen, 'An Economic History of Denmark', EH.Net, 6 October 2006, https://eh.net/encyclopedia/an-economic-history-of-denmark/

2   Byron Rom-Jensen, 'Saving the American Farmer: The Impact of Danish Agricultural Practices on American Policy Direction', *The Bridge* Vol. 39, No. 2 (2006), Article 9.

3   D.R. Bergsmark, 'Agriculture in Denmark: A land of specialized farming and cooperation', *Journal of Geography* Vol. 37, No. 129 (1938), p. 141.

4   Niels-Henrik Topp, 'Unemployment in Denmark in the 1930s', *Scandinavian Economic History Review* Vol. 45, No. 2 (1997), pp. 131–41.

5   'The Recession of 2007–2009', U.S. Bureau of Labor Statistics, February 2012, https://www.bls.gov/spotlight/2012/recession/pdf/recession_bls_spotlight.pdf

6   Michael I.A. Linton and Christian Nokkentved, 'The 20th century: Parliamentary democracy and war, c. 1900–45', Britannica, accessed August 2022, https://www.britannica.com/place/Denmark/The-20th-century

7   Ibid.

8   Klaus Petersen, 'The social welfare state', Danish Agency for Culture and The Heritage Agency of Denmark, accessed August 2022, http://www.kulturarv.dk/1001fortaellinger/en_GB/theme/the-social-welfare-state/article

9   Kazimierz Musial, 'On some aspects of the Danish welfare state from 1960s to 1990s', *Polia Scandinavica* Vol. 3 (1996), p. 47; Claus Friisberg, *Den nordiske velfærdsstat: velfærdsdebat og politik efter 1945* (Copenhagen: Gyldendal, 1977).

10 Ibid.

11 The World Bank, GDP growth (annual %) – Denmark (2020), https://data.worldbank.org/indicator/NY.GDP.MKTP.KD.ZG?locations=DK

12 Petersen, 'The Social Welfare State'.

13 Ibid.

14 Ibid.

15 'Poverty rate in the United States from 1990 to 2020', Statista, 27 July 2022, https://www.statista.com/statistics/200463/us-poverty-rate-since-1990/; The World Bank, Poverty headcount ratio at $5.50 a day (2011 PPP) (% of population) – Denmark (2020), https://data.worldbank.org/indicator/SI.POV.UMIC?locations=DK

16 Neil Irwin, 'A big safety net and strong job market can coexist. Just ask Scandinavia', *New York Times*, 17 December 2014, https://www.nytimes.com/2014/12/18/upshot/nordic-nations-show-that-big-safety-net-can-allow-for-leap-in-employment-rate-.html

17 OECD, 'General government spending', 2022, accessed August 2022, https://data.oecd.org/gga/general-government-spending.htm; OECD, 'Employment rate: aged 15-64: all persons for Denmark', retrieved from Federal Reserve Bank of St. Louis, accessed August 2022, https://fred.

stlouisfed.org/graph/?g=kTfL; Liz Alderman and Steven Greenhouse, 'Living wages, rarity for U.S. fast-food workers, served up in Denmark', *New York Times*, 27 October 2014, https://www.nytimes.com/2014/10/28/business/international/living-wages-served-in-denmark-fast-food-restaurants.html; OECD, 'Life expectancy at birth', 2022, accessed August 2022, https://data.oecd.org/healthstat/life-expectancy-at-birth.htm

18   Francis Fukuyama, ' "Getting to Denmark": how societies build capable, democratic and law-bound states', Center for Development and Enterprise, 1 August 2019, https://www.africaportal.org/publications/getting-denmark-how-societies-build-capable-democratic-and-law-bound-states/; Martin Selseo Sorensen, 'Fox business took a shot at Denmark. Denmark fired back', *New York Times*, 15 August 2018, https://www.nytimes.com/2018/08/15/world/europe/trish-regan-fox-denmark-venezuela.html

19   Chris Moody, 'Bernie Sanders' American Dream is in Denmark', CNN, 17 February 2016, https://www.cnn.com/2016/02/17/politics/bernie-sanders-2016-denmark-democratic-socialism/index.html

20   Kevin Roberts, 'Two Views: The American Dream is alive and well in Texas', *Austin American-Statesman*, 2 March 2020, https://www.statesman.com/story/opinion/editorials/2020/03/02/two-views-american-dream-is-alive-and-well-in-texas/1604411007/

21   'The Danes are feeling bleak', *The Economist*, 5 March 1998, https://www.economist.com/europe/1998/03/05/the-danes-are-feeling-bleak

22   Rasmus Landersø and James J. Heckman, 'The Scandinavian Fantasy: The sources of intergenerational mobility in Denmark and the U.S.', National Bureau of Economic Research Working Paper 22465 (July 2016), https://www.nber.org/papers/w22465

23   Ibid., p. 55.

24   Ida Auken, 'We Danes aren't living the "American Dream." And we still aren't socialist', *Washington Post*, 22 February 2020, https://www.washingtonpost.com/outlook/2020/02/22/we-danes-arent-living-american-dream-we-still-arent-socialist/

25   The World Bank, Poverty headcount ratio at $5.50 a day (2011 PPP) (% of population) – Denmark.

26   'The welfare state needs updating', *The Economist*, 12 July 2018, https://www.economist.com/international/2018/07/12/the-welfare-state-needs-updating

27   Areeba Haider, Rose Khattar, Nicole Rapfogel, Jocelyn Frye, Juli Adhikari, and Emily Gee, 'Census data show historic investments in social safety net alleviated poverty in 2020', Center for American Progress, 14 September

2021, https://www.americanprogress.org/article/census-data-show-historic
-investments-social-safety-net-alleviated-poverty-2020/

28 Ibid.

29 Henry J. Aaron, 'The social safety net: The gaps that COVID-19 spotlights',
Brookings Institution, 23 June 2020, https://www.brookings.edu/blog/up-
front/2020/06/23/the-social-safety-net-the-gaps-that-covid-19-spotlights/

30 Mattathias Schwartz, 'A shadow medical safety net, stretched to the limit',
New York Times Magazine, 6 May 2020, https://www.nytimes.com/2020/05/
06/magazine/community-health-centers-covid.html

31 Haider, Khattar, Rapfogel, Frye, Adhikari, and Gee, 'Census data show
historic investments in social safety net alleviated poverty in 2020'.

32 Aaron, 'The social safety net'.

33 Haider, Khattar, Rapfogel, Frye, Adhikari, and Gee, 'Census data show
historic investments in social safety net alleviated poverty in 2020'; CBPP
Staff, 'Robust COVID relief achieved historic gains against poverty and
hardship, bolstered economy', Center for Budget and Policy Priorities,
24 February 2022, https://www.cbpp.org/research/poverty-and-inequality/
robust-covid-relief-achieved-historic-gains-against-poverty-and

34 Ashraf Kalil and Lisa Mascaro, 'Two anchors of COVID safety net ending,
affecting millions', Associated Press, 5 September 2021, https://www.usnews.
com/news/business/articles/2021-09-05/two-anchors-of-covid-safety-net-
ending-affecting-millions

35 Cory Turner, 'The expanded child tax credit briefly slashed child poverty.
Here's what else it did', NPR, 27 January 2022, https://www.npr.org/2022/01
/27/1075299510/the-expanded-child-tax-credit-briefly-slashed-child-
poverty-heres-what-else-it-d

36 Kelsey Ramirez, 'Expanded Child Tax Credit expiration results in nearly
4 million children falling into poverty: report', Fox Business, 21 March 2022,
https://www.foxbusiness.com/personal-finance/child-tax-credit-expired
-poverty

37 Margherita Stancati and Paul Hannon, 'As U.S. throws workers a lifeline,
Europe's safety net leaves many behind', *Wall Street Journal*, 8 March 2021,
https://www.wsj.com/articles/as-u-s-throws-workers-a-lifeline-europes-
safety-net-leaves-many-behind-11615202977

38 Ibid.; Emma Reynolds, 'Europe's social safety net is often considered the
gold standard. Coronavirus has exposed its holes', CNN, 6 December 2020,
https://www.cnn.com/2020/12/06/business/europe-covid-inequality-bene-
fits-intl/index.html

39 Stancati and Hannon, 'As U.S. throws workers a lifeline'.

40 Ibid.

41 Ibid.

42 Onisi Yuka, 'Safety net fails as pandemic puts thousands out of work', NHK WORLD-JAPAN, 23 November 2020, https://www3.nhk.or.jp/nhkworld/en/news/backstories/1387/; 'Japan: 40 percent of workers in irregular employment, with low pay and little stability', Business & Human Rights Resource Centre, 4 January 2016, https://www.business-humanrights.org/en/latest-news/japan-40-percent-of-workers-in-irregular-employment-with-low-pay-and-little-stability/

43 Yuka, 'Safety net fails', NHK WORLD-JAPAN.

44 Harumi Kimoto and Satoshi Fukutomi, 'Non-regular worker's sudden plunge into poverty exposes Japan's toxic labor environment', *The Mainichi Shimbun*, 28 January 2021, https://mainichi.jp/english/articles/20210128/p2a/00m/0na/043000c

45 Ibid.

46 Harumi Ozawa, 'Pandemic reveals hidden poverty in wealthy Japan', *Barron's*, 19 January 2021, https://www.barrons.com/news/pandemic-reveals-hidden-poverty-in-wealthy-japan-01611035439

47 Ibid.

48 Ibid.

49 Jae-jin Yang, 'South Korea's social safety net wasn't prepared for coronavirus', *The National Interest*, 4 October 2020, https://nationalinterest.org/blog/korea-watch/south-koreas-social-safety-net-wasnt-prepared-coronavirus-169993

50 '2021년8월경제활동인구조사 비임금근로및비경제활동인구 부가조사결과', 통계청이작성한, 4 November 2021, http://kostat.go.kr/assist/synap/preview/skin/miri.html?fn=c4727172593386804090841&rs=/assist/synap/preview

51 Lee, 'South Korea's self-employment crisis', *The Diplomat*, 12 March 2022, https://thediplomat.com/2022/03/south-koreas-self-employment-crisis/

52 Yang, 'South Korea's social safety net wasn't prepared for coronavirus'.

53 Yonhap, 'S. Korea to further expand scope of beneficiaries of employment insurance system', *The Korea Herald*, 24 September 2021, http://www.korea-herald.com/view.php?ud=20210924000231

54 Lee, 'South Korea's self-employment crisis'.

55 Ibid.; Presidential Commission on Policy Planning, March 2020, http://pcpp.go.kr/images/webzine/202003/s61.html

56 Ibid.

57 Yonhap, '40% of self-employed consider biz closure amid pandemic: survey', *The Korea Herald*, 16 January 2022, http://www.koreaherald.com/view.php?ud=20220116000073

58 이종현 기자, '서울 자영업자 94% "코로나로 타격"…매출 42% 줄었다', ChosunBiz, 5 January 2022, https://biz.chosun.com/topics/topics_social/2022/01/05/K4GMOXN44ZBKLDMU6ZQ42ICIAY/

59 노경민 기자, '"수백명 극단 선택…살려 주세요" 자영업자들, -8도 한파에도 '생존집회', *NewDaily*, 11 January 2022, https://www.newdaily.co.kr/site/data/html/2022/01/11/2022011100110.html

60 Ibid.

61 The World Bank, Life expectancy at birth, total (years) (2020), https://data.worldbank.org/indicator/SP.DYN.LE00.IN?most_recent_value_desc=true&year_high_desc=true; The World Bank, Mortality rate, infant (per 1,000 live births) – Singapore, United States, Germany, Netherlands, Japan, France, Australia, Korea Rep. (2020), https://data.worldbank.org/indicator/SP.DYN.IMRT.IN?locations=SG-US-DE-NL-JP-FR-AU-KR&most_recent_value_desc=true&year_high_desc=true

62 The World Bank, Mortality rate, infant (per 1,000 live births) – Singapore, United States, Germany, Netherlands, Japan, France, Australia, Korea Rep. (2020).

63 Donovan Choy, 'What America could learn from Singapore's social welfare system', Foundation for Economic Education, 5 January 2019, https://fee.org/articles/what-america-could-learn-from-singapores-social-welfare-system/

64 Ron Haskins, 'Social policy in Singapore: A crucible of individual responsibility', Brookings Institution, 1 June 2011, https://www.brookings.edu/articles/social-policy-in-singapore-a-crucible-of-individual-responsibility/

65 Ezra Klein, 'Is Singapore's "miracle" health care system the answer for America?', *Vox*, 25 April 2017, https://www.vox.com/policy-and-politics/2017/4/25/15356118/singapore-health-care-system-explained

66 'Households', Department of Statistics Singapore, 15 February 2022, https://www.singstat.gov.sg/find-data/search-by-theme/households/households/latest-data%20gives%20it%20at%2088.9%

67 'Homeownership rate in the U.S. 1990-2021', Statista, 17 February 2022, https://www.statista.com/statistics/184902/homeownership-rate-in-the-us-since-2003/#:~:text=The%20homeownership%20rate%20in%20the,and%20decimated%20the%20housing%20market; Ministry of Housing, Communities and Local Government, 'Home ownership', Gov.UK, 15 September 2020, https://www.ethnicity-facts-figures.service.gov.uk/housing/owning-and-renting/home-ownership/latest; 'Japan home ownership rate', Trading Economics, accessed August 2022, https://tradingeconomics.com/japan/home-ownership-rate; 'Canada home ownership rate', Trading Economics, accessed August 2022, https://tradingeconomics.com/canada/home-ownership-rate.

68 Adam Majendie, 'Why Singapore has one of the highest home ownership rates', Bloomberg, 14 July 2020, https://www.bloomberg.com/news/articles/2020-07-08/behind-the-design-of-singapore-s-low-cost-housing?sref=TZEt22gR

69 Haskins, 'Social policy in Singapore'.

70 Aya Batrawy, 'Half the Saudi population receiving welfare in new system', Seattle Times, 21 December 2017, https://www.seattletimes.com/business/half-the-saudi-population-receiving-welfare-in-new-system/

71 The World Bank, Life expectancy at birth, total (years) (2020), https://data.worldbank.org/indicator/SP.DYN.LE00.IN?most_recent_value_desc=true

72 Elizabeth Arias, Betzaida Tejada-Vera, Kenneth D. Kochanek, and Farida B. Ahmad, 'Provisional life expectancy estimates for 2021', Vital Statistics Rapid Release No. 23 (Hyattsville: National Center for Health Statistics, August 2022), https://www.cdc.gov/nchs/data/vsrr/vsrr023.pdf

73 Claus Frelle-Petersen, Andreas Hein, and Mathias Christiansen, 'The Nordic social welfare model', Deloitte Insights, January 2020, https://www2.deloitte.com/content/dam/insights/us/articles/43149-the-nordic-social-welfare-model/DI_The-Nordic-social-welfare-model.pdf

74 Ibid.; Hon Andrew Little, Hon Peeni Henare, and Hon Dr Ayesha Verrall, 'Major reforms will make healthcare accessible for all NZers', Beehive.govt.nz, 21 April 2021, https://www.beehive.govt.nz/release/major-reforms-will-make-healthcare-accessible-all-nzers

75 The World Bank, Life expectancy at birth, total (years) (2020).

76 Sanghoon Park, 'Why do authoritarian regimes provide welfare?', The Annual Meeting of Midwest Political Science Association (February 2020), https://www.researchgate.net/publication/339513278_Why_Do_Authoritarian_Regimes_Provide_Welfare; Xian Huang, Social Protection under Authoritarianism: Health Politics and Policy in China (Oxford: Oxford University Press, 2020).

77 Adam D.K., 'How COVID-19 has exposed holes in our social-safety net', TVO Today, 15 April 2020, https://www.tvo.org/article/how-covid-19-has-exposed-holes-in-our-social-safety-net; Louise Humpage, 'If New Zealand can radically reform its health system, why not do the same for welfare?', The Conversation, 4 May 2021, https://theconversation.com/if-new-zealand-can-radically-reform-its-health-system-why-not-do-the-same-for-welfare-160247

78 Matthew Stanley, '"We are not Denmark": Hillary Clinton and Liberal American exceptionalism', Common Dreams, 26 February 2016, https://www.commondreams.org/views/2016/02/26/we-are-not-denmark-hillary-clinton-and-liberal-american-exceptionalism

79 'Denmark: Individual – Taxes on personal income', PWC, 21 February 2022, https://taxsummaries.pwc.com/denmark/individual/taxes-on-personal-income

80 'Covid-19 has transformed the welfare state. Which changes will endure?', *The Economist*, 6 March 2021, https://www.economist.com/briefing/2021/03/06/covid-19-has-transformed-the-welfare-state-which-changes-will-endure

81 André Dua, Kweilin Ellingrud, Michael Lazar, Ryan Luby, Matthew Petric, Alex Ulyett, and Tucker Van Aken, 'Unequal America: Ten insights on the state of economic opportunity', McKinsey & Company, 26 May 2021, https://www.mckinsey.com/featured-insights/sustainable-inclusive-growth/unequal-america-ten-insights-on-the-state-of-economic-opportunity; Alex Rosenblat, 'Gig workers are here to stay. it's time to give them benefits', *Harvard Business Review*, 3 July 2020, https://hbr.org/2020/07/gig-workers-are-here-to-stay-its-time-to-give-them-benefits

82 Ally Schweitzer, 'What gig workers need to know about collecting unemployment', NPR, 13 April 2020, https://www.npr.org/local/305/2020/04/13/833332449/what-gig-workers-need-to-know-about-collecting-unemployment

83 Emma Charlton, 'What is the gig economy and what's the deal for gig workers?', World Economic Forum, 26 May 2021, https://www.weforum.org/agenda/2021/05/what-gig-economy-workers

84 Steven Hill, 'Opinion: How California can create a safety net for gig workers', *The Mercury News*, 9 December 2020, https://www.mercurynews.com/2020/12/09/opinion-how-california-can-create-a-safety-net-for-gig-workers/

85 Anne Underwood, 'Health care abroad: Taiwan', *New York Times*, 3 November 2009, https://prescriptions.blogs.nytimes.com/2009/11/03/health-care-abroad-taiwan/

86 'Health insurance', Taiwan Gold Card Community, accessed August 2022, https://taiwangoldcard.com/goldcard-holders-faq/health-insurance/

87 'Residence permit for a freelance employment – Issuance', Berlin.de, accessed August 2022, https://service.berlin.de/dienstleistung/328332/en/

88 David Owen, 'A freelancer's forty-three years in the American health-care system', *New Yorker*, 26 March 2022, https://www.newyorker.com/culture/personal-history/a-freelancers-forty-three-years-in-the-american-health-care-system

89 Maria Castellucci, 'Lack of insurance is tied to higher death rates, new study shows', *Modern Healthcare*, 26 June 2017, https://www.modernhealthcare.com/article/20170626/NEWS/170629912/lack-of-insurance-is-tied-to-higher-death-rates-new-study-shows

90 Fred Kramer, 'The cost of not having a safety net is higher', *Washington Post*, 3 May 2021, https://www.washingtonpost.com/opinions/letters-to-the-editor/the-cost-of-not-having-a-safety-net-is-higher/2021/05/03/7a0f5a82-a9cb-11eb-a8a7-5f45ddcdf364_story.html

91 Glen Whitman and Raymond Raad, 'Bending the productivity curve: why America leads the world in medical innovation', CATO Institute Policy Analysis No. 654, 18 November 2009, https://www.cato.org/policy-analysis/bending-productivity-curve-why-america-leads-world-medical-innovation; 'U.S. healthcare system ranks sixth worldwide – innovative but fiscally unsustainable', Peter G. Peterson Foundation, 3 February 2022, https://www.pgpf.org/blog/2022/01/us-healthcare-system-ranks-sixth-worldwide-innovative-but-fiscally-unsustainable

92 Akshat Rathi, 'The British seem less likely to get cancer than Americans but are also less likely to survive. Why?', *Quartz*, 20 July 2022, https://qz.com/397419/the-british-seem-less-likely-to-get-cancer-than-americans-yet-less-likely-to-survive-why/

93 Anita Andreano, Michael D. Peake, Samuel M. Janes, Maria Grazia Valsecchi, Kathy Pritchard-Jones, Jessica R. Hoag, and Cary P. Gross, 'The care and outcomes of older persons with lung cancer in England and the United States, 2008–2012', *Journal of Thoracic Oncology* Vol. 13, No. 7 (July 2018), pp. 904–14.

94 Ed Dolan, 'Universal catastrophic coverage: principles for Bipartisan health care reform', *Medium*, 25 June 2019, https://medium.com/swlh/universal-catastrophic-coverage-principles-for-bipartisan-health-care-reform-d33f0e1176e

95 Leah Shepherd, 'EU proposes new protections for gig workers', Society for Human Resource Management, 2 February 2022, https://www.shrm.org/resourcesandtools/hr-topics/global-hr/pages/eu-proposed-protections-gig-workers.aspx

96 David Rolf, Dara Khosrowshahi, and Nick Hanauer, 'An open letter to leaders in business, labor and government', SEIU 775 and Uber, 23 January 2018, https://ubernewsroomapi.10upcdn.com/wp-content/uploads/2018/01/Portable-Benefits-Principles-FINAL2.pdf

97 Joel Berg, 'Classism and the politics of SNAP', *Democracy Journal*, 14 July 2016, https://democracyjournal.org/arguments/classism-and-the-politics-of-snap/

98 Jonnelle Marte and Andy Sullivan, 'Millions filed for U.S. unemployment – many are still waiting for the cash', Reuters, 10 April 2020, https://www.reuters.com/article/us-health-coronavirus-usa-unemployment/millions-filed-for-u-s-unemployment-many-are-still-waiting-for-the-cash-idUSKCN21S1YD

99 David H. Slater and Sara Ikebe, 'Social distancing from the problem of Japanese homelessness under Covid-19', *The Asia Pacific Journal* Vol. 18, Issue 18, No. 4 (2020).

100 Ibid.

101 Ibid.

102 'Leave no family behind: strengthening local welfare assistance during Covid-19', The Children's Society, October 2020, https://www.childrenssociety.org.uk/sites/default/files/2020-10/leave-no-family-behind.pdf

103 Gareth Duffield, 'Ensure local welfare assistance is the lifeline it needs to be, during this crisis and in the future', Greater Manchester Poverty Action, 12 August 2020, https://www.gmpovertyaction.org/local-welfare-assistance/

104 'Policy implementation analysis on disability grant of Thailand', Faculty of Social Administration and Thammasat University United Nations Children's Fund, 2019, https://www.unicef.org/thailand/media/5511/file/Policy%20Implementation%20Analysis%20on%20Disability%20Grant%20of%20Thailand%20EN.pdf; Reinhard Busse and Miriam Blümel, 'Germany: health system review', *Health Systems in Transition* Vol. 16, No. 2 (2014), pp. 1–296.

105 Ryan Cooper, 'The right kind of welfare reform', *The Week*, 17 March 2021, https://theweek.com/articles/972318/right-kind-welfare-reform

106 David Ribar, 'How to improve participation in social assistance programs', *IZA World of Labor: 2014*, No. 104 (2014), https://wol.iza.org/uploads/articles/104/pdfs/how-to-improve-participation-in-social-assistance-programs.pdf

107 Chad Smith and Sara Soka, 'Technology, data, and design-enabled approaches for a more responsive, effective social safety net', Beeck Center for Social Impact and Innovation, October 2020, https://beeckcenter.georgetown.edu/wp-content/uploads/2020/10/SSNB_October_v3.pdf

108 Ibid.

109 Ibid.

110 Lauren Harrison, 'A blueprint for human-centered change', *Government Technology*, June 2018, https://www.govtech.com/civic/a-blueprint-for-human-centered-change.html

111 'The welfare state needs updating', *The Economist*, 12 July 2018, https://www.economist.com/international/2018/07/12/the-welfare-state-needs-updating

112 Ibid.

113 Ibid.

114 Ibid.

115 Jeremy Davison and Ito Peng, 'Views on immigration in Japan: identities,

interests, and pragmatic divergence', *Journal of Ethnic and Migration Studies*, Vol. 47, No. 11 (2021), pp. 2578–95.

116 Agnes Constante, 'Largest U.S. refugee group struggling with poverty 45 years after resettlement', NBC News, 4 March 2020, https://www.nbcnews. com/news/asian-america/largest-u-s-refugee-group-struggling-poverty-45 -years-after-n1150031

117 'The welfare state needs updating', *The Economist*; Annie Lowrey, 'Are immigrants a drain on government resources?', *The Atlantic*, 29 September 2018, https://www.theatlantic.com/ideas/archive/2018/09/are-immigrants-drain-government-resources/571582/; Gretchen Frazee, '4 myths about how immigrants affect the U.S. economy', PBS, 2 November 2018, https://www.pbs.org/newshour/economy/making-sense/4-myths-about-how-immigrants-affect-the-u-s-economy; Ana Damas de Matos, 'The fiscal impact of immigration in OECD countries since the mid-2000s' in *International Migrant Outlook 2021* (Paris: OECD Publishing, 2021), pp. 111–62.

118 'UNI Global Union: "Qatar must protect the income of low-wage migrants during pandemic"', UNI Global Union, 13 May 2020, https://uniglobalunion.org/news/uni-global-union-qatar-must-protect-the-income-of-low-wage-migrants-during-pandemic/; Pete Pattisson, Niamh McIntyre, Imran Mukhtar, Nikhil Eapen, Imran Mukhtar, Md Owasim Uddin Bhuyan, Udwab Bhattarai, and Aanya Piyari in Colombo, 'Revealed: 6500 migrant workers have died in Qatar since World Cup Awarded', *The Guardian*, 23 February 2021, https://www.theguardian.com/global-development/2021/feb/23/revealed-migrant-worker-deaths-qatar-fifa-world-cup-2022

119 'The welfare state needs updating', *The Economist*.

120 'Capitalism needs a welfare state to survive', *The Economist*, 12 July 2018, https://www.economist.com/leaders/2018/07/12/capitalism-needs-a-welfare-state-to-survive

121 'In their own words: behind Americans' views of "socialism" and "capitalism"', Pew Research Center, 7 October 2019, https://www.pewresearch.org/politics/2019/10/07/in-their-own-words-behind-americans-views-of-socialism-and-capitalism/; Julia Manchester, 'Majority of young adults in US hold negative view of capitalism: poll', *The Hill*, 28 June 2021, https://thehill.com/homenews/campaign/560493-majority-of-young-adults-in-us-hold-negative-view-of-capitalism-poll/; 'The welfare state needs updating', *The Economist*.

122 Minouche Shafik, *What We Owe Each Other: A New Social Contract for a Better Society* (Princeton: Princeton University Press, 2021), p. 26.

Chapter 6

1   The World Bank, GDP per capita (current US$) – China, Cambodia (2020), https://data.worldbank.org/indicator/NY.GDP.PCAP. CD?end=1964&locations=CN-KH&most_recent_value_ desc=false&start=1961; Aaron Hseuh, 'Jiangnan journey', *The World of Chinese*, 22 February 2020, https://www.theworldofchinese.com/post/deli- cate-jiangnan/

2   'Memorabilia from China's Cultural Revolution', BBC News, 16 May 2016, https://www.bbc.com/news/in-pictures-36274660

3   Xiaogang Wu and Zhuoni Zhang, 'Changes in educational inequality in China, 1990-2005: evidence from the population census data', *Research in the Sociology of Education* Vol. 17 (2010), p. 139.

4   Keith Bradsher, 'Next Made-in-China boom: college graduates', *New York Times*, 16 January 2013, https://www.nytimes.com/2013/01/17/business/ chinas-ambitious-goal-for-boom-in-college-graduates.html

5   Ibid.

6   Ibid.

7   Ibid.

8   Ibid.

9   Ibid.

10 Abby Jackson, 'Here's the one big problem with China's supposedly amazing schools', *INSIDER*, 9 May 2015, https://www.businessinsider.com/china-has -a-major-issue-with-its-educational-system-2015-5; Brian Wu, ' "Invisible China": The hidden human capital crisis that threatens common prosperity', *SupChina*, 17 December 2021, https://supchina.com/2021/12/17/invisible- china-the-hidden-human-capital-crisis-that-threatens-common-prosper- ity/; Jay Mathews, 'Big hole in popular view that China beats U.S. in educa- tion', *Washington Post*, 13 June 2021, https://www.washingtonpost.com/ local/education/chinese-students-math-ability/2021/06/11/6fb1d94c-c92a- 11eb-81b1-34796c7393af_story.html

11 David Smith, 'What is the Chinese government doing to improve educa- tion?', *Times of Higher Education*, 4 May 2018, https://www.timeshigheredu- cation.com/blog/what-chinese-government-doing-improve-education

12 Hongbin Li, Prashant Loyalka, Scott Rozelle, and Binzhen Wu, 'Human capital and China's future growth', *The Journal of Economic Perspectives* Vol. 31, No. 1 (Winter 2017), p. 25–47.

13 Ibid., p. 27.

14 Ibid., p. 27.

15 Ibid., p. 27; Hongbin Li, Yueyuan Ma, Lingsheng Meng, Xue Qiao and

Xinzheng Shi, 'Skill complementarities and returns to higher education: Evidence from the college enrollment expansion in China', *China Economic Review* Vol. 26 (2017), pp. 10–26; Hongbin Li, Lei Li, Binzhen Wu, and Yanvan Xiong, 'The end of cheap Chinese labor', *Journal of Economic Perspectives*, Vol. 26, No. 4 (2012), p. 5.

16   Liqing Tao, Margaret Berci, and Wayne He, 'Education as a social ladder', *New York Times*, 2006, https://archive.nytimes.com/www.nytimes.com/ref/college/coll-china-education-004.html

17   The Editorial Board, 'Industrial policy, same old politics', *Wall Street Journal*, 25 May 2021, https://www.wsj.com/articles/industrial-policy-same-old-politics-11621981515

18   'Executives', TSMC, accessed August 2022, https://www.tsmc.com/english/aboutTSMC/executives

19   Elsa B. Kania, ' "AI weapons" in China's military innovation', Brookings Institution, April 2020, https://www.brookings.edu/wp-content/uploads/2020/04/FP_20200427_ai_weapons_kania_v2.pdf

20   Zichen Wang, 'Xi Jinping's speech on science & tech on May 28, 2021', *Pekingnology*, 8 June 2021, https://www.pekingnology.com/p/xi-jinpings-speech-on-science-and

21   新华社, '习近平出席中央人才工作会议并发表重要讲话', 28 September 2021, http://www.gov.cn/xinwen/2021-09/28/content_5639868.htm

22   President Joe Biden, 'Remarks by President Biden at the office of the director of national intelligence', The White House, 27 July 2021, https://www.whitehouse.gov/briefing-room/speeches-remarks/2021/07/27/remarks-by-president-biden-at-the-office-of-the-director-of-national-intelligence/

23   'Federal R&D as a percent of GDP', American Association for the Advancement of Science, 2020, https://www.aaas.org/sites/default/files/2020-10/RDGDP.png?adobe_mc=MCMID%3D53335390786803844983358839118233552568%7CMCORGID%3D242B6472541199F70A4C98A6%2540AdobeOrg%7CTS%3D1649799381

24   Erin Duffin, 'Federal funds for education and research 1970-2020', Statista, 7 January 2022, https://www.statista.com/statistics/184069/federal-funds-for-education-and-research/

25   Erin Duffin, 'U.S. education – total expenditure per pupil in public schools 1990-2019', Statista, 21 February 2022, https://www.statista.com/statistics/203118/expenditures-per-pupil-in-public-schools-in-the-us-since-1990/

26   Paul Bolton, 'Education spending in the UK', UK Parliament: House of Commons Library, 15 November 2021, https://commonslibrary.parliament.uk/research-briefings/sn01078/#:~:text=When%20expressed%20as%20a%20proportion,the%20first%20since%202010%2D11; Ikuku Tsuboya-

Newell, 'Education: Best investment for our future', *Japan Times*, 26 November 2017, https://www.japantimes.co.jp/opinion/2017/11/26/ commentary/japan-commentary/education-best-investment-future/; OECD, 'Education at a Glance 2012: OECD Indictators', Country Note, 11 September 2012, https://www.oecd.org/france/EAG2012%20- %20Country%20note%20-%20France%20(EN).pdf

27 Ryan Haas and Jude Blanchette, 'The U.S. is still beating China in human capital—for now', *Foreign Policy*, 4 November 2021, https://foreignpolicy. com/2021/11/04/china-human-capital-stem-graduates-competition/

28 Thomas J. Duesterberg, 'Economic cracks in the Great Wall of China: Is China's current economic model sustainable?', Hudson Institute, December 2021, https://www.hudson.org/research/17443-economic-cracks-in-the- great-wall-of-china-is-china-s-current-economic-model-sustainable

29 Stein Emil Vollset, Emily Goren, Chun-Wei Yuan, Jackie Cao, Amanda E. Smith, Thomas Hsiao, et al., 'Fertility, mortality, migration, and population scenarios for 195 countries and territories from 2017 to 2100: a forecasting analysis for the Global Burden of Disease Study', *The Lancet* Vol. 398, No. 10258 (2020), p. 1285.

30 Eamonn Fingleton, 'America the innovative?', *New York Times*, 30 March 2013, https://www.nytimes.com/2013/03/31/sunday-review/america-the- innovative.html

31 Joshua J. Mark, 'Mesopotamian inventions', *World History*, 20 October 2021, https://www.worldhistory.org/article/1859/mesopotamian-inventions/

32 Joshua J. Mark, 'Ancient Egyptian government', *World History*, 13 October 2016, https://www.worldhistory.org/Egyptian_Government/

33 Robert Greene and Paul Triolo, 'Will China control the global internet via its Digital Silk Road?', *SupChina*, 8 May 2020, https://carnegieendowment. org/2020/05/08/will-china-control-global-internet-via-its-digital-silk-road -pub-81857

34 Graham Allison and Eric Schmidt, 'China's 5G soars over America's', *Wall Street Journal*, 16 February 2022, https://www.wsj.com/articles/chinas-5g- america-streaming-speed-midband-investment-innovation-competition- act-semiconductor-biotech-ai-11645046867

35 Ibid.

36 Congressional Research Service, 'National security implications of fifth generation (5g) mobile technologies', In Focus, 5 April 2022, https://sgp.fas. org/crs/natsec/IF11251.pdf

37 Goldman Sachs, '5G's future in China', *BRIEFINGS*, 1 July 2019, https:// www.goldmansachs.com/insights/pages/from_briefings_01-july-2019.html

38 Alex Rossino, 'Department of Defense 5G Investment in Fiscal 2022',

GovWin, 8 December 2021, https://iq.govwin.com/neo/marketAnalysis/view/Department-of-Defense-5G-Investment-in-Fiscal-2022/6297?researchTypeId=1&researchMarket=

39 Allison and Schmidt, 'China's 5G soars over America's'.

40 Bharat Sharma, '5G in 2021: more countries adopted 5g, but global speeds took a hit', *India Times*, 29 December 2021, https://www.indiatimes.com/technology/news/5g-connectivity-trends-557413.html; Ian Fogg, 'Benchmarking the global 5G experience', Open Signal, 3 February 2021, https://www.opensignal.com/2021/02/03/benchmarking-the-global-5g-experience

41 Linda Hardesty, '5G download speeds in U.S. at meager 47-58 Mbps range, per Opensignal', Fierce Wireless, 25 January 2021, https://www.fiercewireless.com/5g/5g-download-speeds-u-s-at-meager-47-58-mbps-range-per-opensignal; Allison and Schmidt, 'China's 5G Soars over America's'.

42 Statista Research Department, 'Countries with the highest number of cities in which 5G is available 2022', Statista, 11 August 2022, https://www.statista.com/statistics/1215456/5g-cities-by-country/

43 Allison and Schmidt, 'China's 5G soars over America's'

44 Klint Finley, 'Does it matter if China beats the US to build a 5G network?', *WIRED*, 6 June 20218, https://www.wired.com/story/does-it-matter-if-china-beats-the-us-to-build-a-5g-network/

45 Kaleigh Rogers, 'Everything you need to know about a nationalized 5G wireless network', *VICE*, 29 January 2018, https://www.vice.com/en/article/yw5yv7/everything-you-need-to-know-about-a-nationalized-5g-wireless-network

46 Amanda Lee, 'China gains ground on US in hi-tech "tug of war", as Beijing spends billions on national champions', *South China Morning Post*, 8 June 2022, https://www.scmp.com/economy/china-economy/article/3180753/china-gains-ground-us-hi-tech-tug-war-beijing-spends-billions

47 Allison and Schmidt, 'China's 5G soars over America's'

48 G.S. White, *Memoir of Samuel Slater* (Philadelphia, 1836), p. 74, https://books.google.com/books?id=K79AAAAAcAAJ&source=gbs_navlinks_s

49 Emily Mahoney, *The Industrial Revolution: The Birth of Modern America* (New York: Greenhaven Publishing, 2017).

50 Ryōji Itō, 'Education as a basic factor in Japan's economic growth', *The Developing Economies* Vol. 1, No. 1 (1963), p. 51.

51 Lee Jong-Wha, 'Lessons of East Asia's human-capital development', *Project Syndicate*, 29 January 2019, https://www.project-syndicate.org/commentary/human-capital-east-asia-development-strategy-education-by-lee-jong-wha-2019-01

52 'The Human Capital Index 2020 Update: human capital in the time of COVID-19', The World Bank, accessed August 2022.

53　Jandhyala B. G. Tilak, 'Building human capital in East Asia: what others can learn', International Bank for Reconstruction and Development/The World Bank, 2002, p. 2, https://citeseerx.ist.psu.edu/viewdoc/download?doi=10.1.1.195.2238&rep=rep1&type=pdf

54　The Human Capital Index 2020 update; Cheng Ting-Fang and Lauly Li, 'Vietnam to make Apple Watch and MacBook for first time ever', *Nikkei Asia*, 17 August 2022, https://asia.nikkei.com/Business/Technology/Vietnam-to-make-Apple-Watch-and-MacBook-for-first-time-ever

55　Jong-Wha Lee, Santosh Mehrotra, Ruth Francisco, and Dainn Wie, 'Human capital development in South Asia', Asian Development Bank, December 2017, https://www.adb.org/publications/human-capital-development-achievements-prospects-policy-challenges

56　Elena Pelinescu, 'The impact of human capital on economic growth', *Procedia Economics and Finance* Vol. 22 (2015), pp. 184–90.

57　Andrea Bassanini and Stefano Scarpetta, 'Does human capital matter for growth in OECD countries? evidence from pooled mean-group estimates', OECD Economics Department Working Papers No. 282 (2001), p. 19; Ibid.

58　Ibid., p. 189.

59　'How much does your country invest in R&D?', UNESCO Institute for Statistics, accessed August 2022, http://uis.unesco.org/apps/visualisations/research-and-development-spending/

60　Ibid.

61　The World Bank, Research and development expenditure (% of GDP) – United States, United Kingdom, China, United Arab Emirates, Singapore, France, Canada, Australia, New Zealand, India, Japan Korea, Rep., Israel (2020), https://data.worldbank.org/indicator/GB.XPD.RSDV.GD.ZS?end=2018&locations=US-GB-CN-AE-SG-FR-CA-AU-NZ-IN-JP-KR-IL&most_recent_value_desc=true&start=1996; 'How Much Does Your Country Invest in R&D?'

62　The World Bank, Research and development expenditure (% of GDP) – Australia, New Zealand, United Kingdom (2020), https://data.worldbank.org/indicator/GB.XPD.RSDV.GD.ZS?end=2018&locations=US-GB-CN-AE-SG-FR-CA-AU-NZ&start=1996; 'How Much Does Your Country Invest in R&D'.

63　The World Bank, Research and development expenditure (% of GDP) – United States, United Kingdom, China, United Arab Emirates, Singapore, France, Canada, Australia, New Zealand, India, Japan Korea, Rep., Israel (2020).

64　'Research And Development Expenditure (% Of GDP) By Country', Trading Economics, accessed August 2022, https://tradingeconomics.com/country-list/research-and-development-expenditure-percent-of-gdp-wb-data.html

65   Ibid.
66   'United Arab Emirates', UNESCO Institute for Statistics, accessed August 2022, http://uis.unesco.org/en/country/ae?theme=science-technology-and -innovation
67   Briana Boland, Kevin Dong, Jude Blanchette, and Ryan Hass, 'How China's human capital impacts its national competitiveness', Center for Strategic and International Studies, 16 May 2022, https://www.csis.org/analysis/how -chinas-human-capital-impacts-its-national-competitiveness
68   Ibid.
69   *Global Innovation Index 2021*, p. 20.
70   Luke Dascoli, 'Fact of the week: China sourced the most stem articles in 2020, but the United States had the highest share in the top 1 percent that were most cited,' Information Technology and Innovation Foundation, 15 November 2021, https://itif.org/publications/2021/11/15/fact-week- china-sourced-most-stem-articles-2020-united-states-had-highest/; Karen White, 'Publications Output: U.S. trends and international comparisons', National Science Board, October 2021, https://ncses.nsf.gov/pubs/nsb20214 /executive-summary; and Caroline S. Wagner, Lin Zhang, and Loet Leydesdorff, 'A discussion of measuring the top-1% most-highly cited publications: Quality and impact of Chinese papers', *Scientometrics*, Vol. 127 (2022), pp. 1825–39.
71   Wagner, Zhang, and Leydesdorff, 'A discussion of measuring the top-1% most-highly cited publications'; Jeff Grabmeier, 'Analysis suggests China has passed U.S. on one research measure', Ohio State University, 8 March 2022, https://news.osu.edu/analysis-suggests-china-has-passed-us-on-one- research-measure/
72   Boland, Dong, Blanchette, and Hass, 'How China's human capital impacts its national competitiveness'.
73   The World Bank, Government expenditure on education, total (% of GDP) – China (2020), https://data.worldbank.org/indicator/SE.XPD.TOTL.GD.Z S?end=2018&locations=CN&start=1994&view=chart
74   OECD, 'Education spending at a glance: Education finance indicators', accessed August 2022, https://data.oecd.org/eduresource/education-spend- ing.htm
75   Ibid.
76   Remco Zwetsloot, Jack Corrigan, Emily S. Weinstein, Dahlia Peterson, Diana Gehlhaus, and Ryan Fedasiuk, 'China is Fast Outpacing U.S. STEM PhD Growth', Center for Security and Emerging Technology, August 2021, p. 2, https://cset.georgetown.edu/publication/china-is-fast-outpacing-u-s- stem-phd-growth/

77 Andreas Schleicher, *PISA 2018* (Paris: OECD, 2018), pp. 6–9, https://www. oecd.org/pisa/PISA%202018%20Insights%20and%20Interpretations%20 FINAL%20PDF.pdf

78 *PISA 2018*, pp. 6–9; 'PISA 2018 Worldwide Ranking – average score of mathematics, science and reading'.

79 Duong Tam, 'Vietnam students impress with math-science Olympiad medal haul', *VNExpress*, 25 January 2021, https://e.vnexpress.net/news/news/viet-nam-students-impress-with-math-science-olympiad-medal-haul-4226351. html; Lee Crawfurd, Susannah Hares, Alexis Le Nestour, and Ana Luiza Minardi, 'PISA 2018: A few reactions to the new global education rankings', Center for Global Development, 3 December 2019, https://www.cgdev.org/ blog/pisa-2018-few-reactions-new-global-education-rankings

80 James Pethokoukis, 'The keys to American ingenuity: a short-read Q&A with Author Kevin Baker', American Enterprise Institute, 13 March 2018, https://www.aei.org/economics/the-keys-to-american-ingenuity-a-short-read-qa-with-author-kevin-baker/

81 Ibid.

82 Zócalo Public Square, 'Why does America prize creativity and invention?', *Smithsonian Magazine*, 12 November 2015, https://www.smithsonianmag. com/innovation/why-does-america-prize-creativity-and-invention-180957256/

83 *Global Innovation Index 2021* (Geneva: World Intellectual Property Organization, 2021).

84 Ufuk Akcigit, John Gribsby, and Tom Nicholas, 'When America was most innovative, and why', *Harvard Business Review*, 6 March 2017, https://hbr. org/2017/03/when-america-was-most-innovative-and-why

85 Mark J. Perry, 'U.S. culture rewards innovation and risk-taking', American Enterprise Institute, 7 February 2007, https://www.aei.org/carpe-diem/u-s-culture-rewards-innovation-and-risk-taking/; 'All prizes in economic sciences', The Nobel Prize, accessed August 2022, https://www.nobelprize. org/prizes/lists/all-prizes-in-economic-sciences/

86 Fingleton, 'America the Innovative?'

87 Suzanne Mettler, 'How the G.I. bill built the middle class and enhanced democracy', Scholar Strategy Network, 2005, https://scholars.org/sites/ scholars/files/ssn_key_findings_mettler_on_gi_bill.pdf; Suzanne Mettler, *Soldiers to Citizens: The G.I. Bill and the Making of the Greatest Generation* (Oxford: Oxford University Press, 2005).

88 Mettler, 'How the G.I. bill built the middle class and enhanced democracy'; Julia Wells, 'Jerome Kohlberg Jr., businessman who challenged Wall Street, owner of Gazette, dies', *Vineyard Gazette*, 1 August 2015, https://

vineyardgazette.com/news/2015/08/01/jerome-kohlberg-jr-businessman-who-challenged-wall-street-owner-gazette-dies

89   Thalia Assuras, 'How the GI bill changed America', CBS News, 22 June 2008, https://www.cbsnews.com/news/how-the-gi-bill-changed-america/

90   Arthur Krock, 'In the nation', *New York Times*, 10 October 1957, https://timesmachine.nytimes.com/timesmachine/1957/10/10/84771136.html?pageNumber=32

91   Brandon Kirk Williams, 'America's past offers the model for topping China in science and technology', *Washington Post*, 14 April 2022, https://www.washingtonpost.com/outlook/2022/04/14/americas-past-offers-model-topping-china-science-technology/

92   Ibid.

93   Ibid.

94   John F. Sargent Jr., 'U.S. research and development funding and performance: fact sheet', Congressional Research Service, 4 October 2021, https://sgp.fas.org/crs/misc/R44307.pdf

95   Ibid.

96   Ibid.

97   James Pethokoukis, 'US federal research spending is at a 60-year low. should we be concerned?', American Enterprise Institute, 11 May 2020, https://www.aei.org/economics/us-federal-research-spending-is-at-a-60-year-low-should-we-be-concerned/

98   Williams, 'America's past offers the model for topping China'.

99   The World Bank, *2020 Human Capital Index*.

100   Fingleton, 'America the Innovative?'

101   Ibid.

102   The World Bank, 'The World Bank In Singapore', 9 April 2019, https://www.worldbank.org/en/country/singapore/overview#1; The World Bank, *2020 Human Capital Index*.

103   https://www.oecd-ilibrary.org/sites/9789264281394-6-en/index.html?itemId=/content/component/9789264281394-6-en

104   The World Bank, 'The World Bank In Singapore'.

105   WAM, 'UAE strives towards future, relying on human capital – our true wealth, says Sheikh Mohamed bin Zayed', *Khaleej Times*, 1 December 2021, https://www.khaleejtimes.com/year-of-the-50th/uae-strives-towards-future-relying-on-human-capital-our-true-wealth-says-sheikh-mohamed-bin-zaye; Ambassador Abdullah bin Rashid Al Khalifa, 'Bahrain makes a big leap toward fintech and human capital', RealClearMarkets, 18 March 2022, https://www.realclearmarkets.com/articles/2022/03/18/bahrain_makes_a_big_leap_toward_fintech_and_human_capital_822323.html

106   Eric C. C. Chang and Wen-Chin Wu, 'Autocracy and human capital', *World Development* Vol. 157 (September 2022).

107   Haas and Blanchette, 'The U.S. is still beating China'.

108   Zwetsloot, Corrigan, Weinstein, Peterson, Gehlhaus, and Fedasiuk, 'China is fast outpacing U.S. STEM PhD Growth'.

109   Wu, ' "Invisible China" '.

110   Rebecca Fannin, *Tech Titans of China: How China's Tech Sector is Challenging the World by Innovating Faster, Working Harder & Going Global* (Boston: Nicholas Brealey, 2019).

111   '15 Years of The Most Innovative Companies', Boston Consulting Group, 2021, accessed August 2022, https://www.bcg.com/publications/most-innovative-companies-historical-rankings; '16 years of the most innovative companies', Boston Consulting Group, accessed October 2022, https://www.bcg.com/publications/most-innovative-companies-historical-rankings

112   *Global Innovation Index 2021*; 'Exploring the Interactive Database of the GII 2021 Indicators', Portulans Institute, accessed August 2022, https://www.globalinnovationindex.org/analysis-indicator; 'Analysis', Global Innovation Index, 2022, https://www.globalinnovationindex.org/analysis-indicator

113   'GDP per Capita by Country 2022', World Population Review, accessed August 2022, https://worldpopulationreview.com/country-rankings/gdp-per-capita-by-country; The World Bank, GDP per capita (current US$) – 2020, https://data.worldbank.org/indicator/ny.gdp.pcap.cd?most_recent_value_desc=true

114   'GDP per Capita by Country 2022', World Population Review; The World Bank, GDP per capita (current US$) – 2020.

115   Jim Yong Kim, 'The human capital gap', *Foreign Affairs* Vol. 97, No. 4 (July/August 2018).

116   Andy Robinson, 'What's the point of saving for retirement in your 20s?', *Harvard Business Review*, 15 September 2020, https://hbr.org/2020/09/whats-the-point-of-saving-for-retirement-in-your-20s

117   Tim Whitney (@TimWhitney), 'Another week, another PhD student has come to my office in tears as they can't afford to live in London on £18k. And this is before the price cap increase. @UKRI_News this time – can I ask what you are doing to support the next-generation so there is a next-generation?! Pls RT', Twitter, 22 August 2022, https://twitter.com/timwitney/status/1561678397612457985?s=11&t=RPlfmDXGdFQVJS2e_yowAA

118   Adam Taylor, 'Long closed to most immigration, Japan looks to open up amid labor shortage', *Washington Post*, 18 November 2021, https://www.washingtonpost.com/world/2021/11/18/japan-labor-shortage-immigration/; Luke Sophinos, 'To close the skills gap, we all need to empower vocational

educators', *Forbes*, 2 March 2022, https://www.forbes.com/sites/forbestech-council/2022/03/02/to-close-the-skills-gap-we-all-need-to-empower-voca-tional-educators/?sh=57e0d5657d99; Heekyong Yang and Cynthia Kim, 'South Korea's latest big export: Jobless college graduates', Reuters, 12 May 2019, https://www.reuters.com/article/us-southkorea-jobs-kmove-insight/south-koreas-latest-big-export-jobless-college-graduates-idUSKCN-1SI0QE; Mitsuru Obe, 'Japan turns to tech to help foreign blue-collar work-ers', *Nikkei Asia*, 10 September 2021, https://asia.nikkei.com/Spotlight/Japan-immigration/Japan-turns-to-tech-to-help-foreign-blue-collar-worker; 'As in the US, labor shortages are rising in most of Europe', The Conference Board, 30 September 2021, https://www.conference-board.org/topics/labor-markets-charts/europe-labor-shortages

119   Yang and Kim, 'South Korea's latest big export'; Taylor, 'Long closed to most immigration.

120   Sophinos, 'To close the skills gap'.

121   Marius R. Busemeyer, Julian L. Garritzmann, Erik Neimanns, and Roula Nezi, 'Investing in education in Europe: Evidence from a new survey of public opinion', *Journal of European Social Policy* Vol. 28, No. 1 (2018), pp. 34–54.

122   'Poll: Americans are more open to vocational school', *Richmond Times-Dispatch*, 3 February 2020, https://richmond.com/news/video_c4e634c7-1fa0-5b74-a119-fd8d968ad3d0.html; Dr. Nivea Torres, Jay Ramsey, and David Ferreira, 'The increasing demand for career and technical education', New England Association of Schools and Colleges, June 2016, https://www.neasc.org/about/member-stories/demand-for-cte

123   Stephen Steigleder and Louis Soares, 'Let's get serious about our nation's human capital', Center for American Progress, 19 June 2012, https://www.americanprogress.org/article/lets-get-serious-about-our-nations-human-capital/

124   AAhad M. Osman-Gani, 'Human capital development in Singapore: an analysis of national policy perspectives', *Advances in Developing Human Resources* Vol. 6, No. 3 (2004), p. 278.

125   Singapore Government, 'Skills Development Levy Act', Singapore Statutes Online, 31 May 2012, https://sso.agc.gov.sg/Act-Rev/SDLA1979/Published/20120531?DocDate=20120531&WholeDoc=1; Singapore Government, 'Skills development fund is established', HistorySG, 2013, https://eresources.nlb.gov.sg/history/events/98e1b55f-093d-4d44-b219-d51f6a38c313

126   Richard Johanson, 'A review of national training funds', SP Discussion Paper No. 0922, Social Protection Unit (Washington, DC: World Bank, 2009).

127   Sarosh Kuruvilla and Rodney Chua, 'How do nations increase workforce

skills? factors influencing the success of the Singapore skills development system', *Global Business Review* Vol. 1, No. 1 (2000), pp. 11–47; Johanson, 'Review of national training funds'.

128 'Ontario providing additional investment into skills development fund', Ontario, 28 September 2021, https://news.ontario.ca/en/release/1000887/ontario-providing-additional-investment-into-skills-development-fund; 'Skills Development Fund', Texas Workforce Commission, accessed August 2022, https://www.twc.texas.gov/partners/skills-development-fund

129 Alastair Fitzpayne and Ethan Pollack, 'Worker training tax credit: promoting employer investments in the workforce', Aspen Institute, 16 August 2018, pp. 1–2, https://www.aspeninstitute.org/publications/worker-training-tax-credit-update-august-2018/

130 Ibid.

131 'Equipping people to stay ahead of technological change', *The Economist*, 14 January 2017, https://www.economist.com/leaders/2017/01/14/equipping-people-to-stay-ahead-of-technological-change

132 Ibid.

133 Ian Bremmer, 'The Technopolar Moment', *Foreign Affairs* Vo. 100, No. 6 (November/December 2021).

134 Ibid.

135 'CHIPS for America & FABS Act', Semiconductor Industry Association, accessed August 2022, https://www.semiconductors.org/chips/; 'FACT SHEET: Biden-Harris administration bringing semiconductor manufacturing Back to America', The White House, 21 January 2022, https://www.whitehouse.gov/briefing-room/statements-releases/2022/01/21/fact-sheet-biden-harris-administration-bringing-semiconductor-manufacturing-back-to-america-2/

136 Remco Zwetsloot, 'Winning the tech talent competition', Center for Strategic and International Studies, 28 October 2021, https://www.csis.org/analysis/winning-tech-talent-competition

137 Itō Kenji, 'Making Japan a top destination for international students', Nippon.com, 27 February 2019, https://www.nippon.com/en/in-depth/d00465/making-japan-a-top-destination-for-international-students.html; John Amari for The ACCJ Journal, 'Dream big: Japanese students seek new paths to overseas study', *Japan Today*, 9 December 2019, https://japantoday.com/category/features/lifestyle/dream-big-japanese-students-seek-new-paths-to-overseas-study

138 'New American Fortune 500 in 2019: Top American companies and their immigrant roots', New American Economy, 22 July 2019, https://data.newamericaneconomy.org/en/fortune500-2019/

139   David Gelles, 'The Husband-and-Wife team behind the leading vaccine to solve Covid-19', *New York Times*, 10 November 2020, https://www.nytimes.com/2020/11/10/business/biontech-covid-vaccine.html

140   Federico Caviggioli, Paul Jensen, and Giuseppe Scellato, 'Highly skilled migrants and technological diversification in the US and Europe', *Technology Forecasting and Social Change* Vol. 154 (2020), p. 14.

141   Marion Walsmann, 'Europe's IPR rules need to be strengthened to ensure they meet current and future challenges, explains Marion Walsmann', *The Parliament*, 13 October 2021, https://www.theparliamentmagazine.eu/news/article/the-key-to-innovation

Chapter 7

1   Cheng Yunjie, 'China's economic zones evolve to spearhead future reforms', Consulate-General of the People's Republic of China in Cape Town, accessed August 2022, http://capetown.china-consulate.gov.cn/eng/zt/201009/t20100925_7014482.htm

2   'Top 1979 movies at the domestic box office', The Numbers, accessed August 2022, https://www.the-numbers.com/box-office-records/domestic/all-movies/cumulative/released-in-1979

3   Christopher S. Wren, 'China unleashes a capitalist tool', *New York Times*, 25 April 1982, https://www.nytimes.com/1982/04/25/business/china-unleases-a-capitalist-tool.html?searchResultPosition=3

4   Ibid.

5   Ilaria Maria Sala, 'Story of cities #39: Shenzhen – from rural village to the world's largest megalopolis', *The Guardian*, 10 May 2016, https://www.theguardian.com/cities/2016/may/10/story-of-cities-39-shenzhen-from-rural-village-to-the-worlds-largest-megalopolis

6   Christopher S. Wren, 'Hong Kong spurs China's first superhighway', 16 May 1982, https://www.nytimes.com/1982/05/16/world/hong-kong-spurs-china-s-first-superhighway.html?searchResultPosition=4

7   Ibid.

8   *The Story of Shenzhen* (Nairobi: UN-Habitat, 2019), p. 2.

9   Wren, 'Hong Kong spurs China's first superhighway'.

10   Ibid.

11   Willa Wu, 'Infrastructure paves the way to glory', *China Daily*, 6 November 2020, https://global.chinadaily.com.cn/a/202011/06/WS5fa50a64a31024ad0ba8397d_1.html

12   *The Story of Shenzhen*, p. 7.

13   Ibid., p. 7.

14 Keith Bradsher, 'The attraction that Is Southern China', *New York Times*, 5 November 2003, https://www.nytimes.com/2003/11/05/business/the-attraction-that-is-southern-china.html?searchResultPosition=14

15 Ibid.

16 *The Story of Shenzhen*, p. 9.

17 Ibid., p. 9.

18 Ibid., p. 16.

19 Ibid., p. 16.

20 Wu, 'Infrastructure paves the way to glory'.

21 Mike Wardle and Michael Mainelli, 'The Global Financial Centres Index 29', Long Finance and Financial Centre Futures, March 2021, p. 4, https://papers.ssrn.com/sol3/papers.cfm?abstract_id=3869776

22 'The Top 50 Container Ports', World Shipping Council, accessed August 2022, https://www.worldshipping.org/top-50-ports

23 Juan Du, 'The Shenzhen Effect', *Weapons of Reason*, 24 November 2015, https://medium.com/the-megacities-issue/the-shenzhen-effect-e0db4a71c0ad

24 Evenlyn Cheng, 'China's fastest growing city wants to be the next Silicon Valley — local systems may get in the way', CNBC, 1 April 2021, https://www.cnbc.com/2021/04/02/chinas-fastest-growing-city-wants-to-be-the-next-silicon-valley.html; Rick Gladstone, 'Shenzhen: the city where China's transformation began', *New York Times*, 21 December 2015, https://www.nytimes.com/2015/12/22/world/asia/shenzhen-site-of-landslide-embodies-chinas-rapid-growth.html

25 'GDP Cartogram', Visual Capitalism, April 2021, https://www.visualcapitalist.com/wp-content/uploads/2021/08/Global-Wealth-Distribution.html; C. Textor, 'GDP value of Shenzhen city, China 2011-2021', Statista, 11 May 2021, https://www.statista.com/statistics/1025207/china-gdp-of-shenzhen/

26 'GDP Cartogram', Visual Capitalism.

27 Ibid.

28 Du, 'The Shenzhen Effect'.

29 'How modern is the infrastructure of China?', Quora, accessed August 2022, https://www.quora.com/How-modern-is-the-infrastructure-of-China

30 Shira Ovide, 'America's internet has China envy', *New York Times*, 16 November 2020, https://www.nytimes.com/2020/11/16/technology/internet-china.html

31 '2021 report card for America's infrastructure', American Society of Civil Engineers and American Society of Civil Engineers Foundation, 2022, https://infrastructurereportcard.org/

32 James T. Areddy, 'What the U.S. can learn from China's infatuation with

infrastructure', *Wall Street Journal*, 3 April 2021, https://www.wsj.com/articles/what-the-u-s-can-learn-from-chinas-infatuation-with-infrastructure-11617442201

33   Amir Vera, Jason Hanna, and Nouran Salahieh, 'The water crisis in Jackson, Mississippi, has gotten so bad, the city temporarily ran out of bottled water to give to residents', CNN, 31 August 2022, https://www.cnn.com/2022/08/30/us/jackson-water-system-failing-tuesday/index.html

34   'Infrastructure and the economy', Congressional Research Service, 29 November 2021, p. 9, https://sgp.fas.org/crs/misc/R46826.pdf; *Failure to Act: Economic Impacts of Status Quo Investment Across Infrastructure System*; Ron Temple and Apratim Gautam, 'What America can learn from China about infrastructure investment', *Barron's*, 15 March 2021, https://www.barrons.com/articles/what-america-can-learn-from-china-about-infrastructure-investment-51615822894

35   *Failure to Act: Economic Impacts of Status Quo Investment Across Infrastructure System.*

36   Temple and Gautam, 'What America can learn from China'.

37   'Give people more control over their energy bills', Confederation of British Industry, 7 June 2022, https://www.cbi.org.uk/media-centre/articles/give-people-more-control-over-their-energy-bills/; 'SME guide to energy efficiency', UK Department of Energy and Climate Change, 2020, p.4, https://assets.publishing.service.gov.uk/government/uploads/system/uploads/attachment_data/file/417410/DECC_advice_guide.pdf; Fiona Harvey, 'Fuel-poor homes face taking £250 energy hit due to poor insulation', *The Guardian*, 30 June 2022, https://www.theguardian.com/environment/2022/jul/01/fuel-poor-homes-face-taking-250-energy-hit-due-to-poor-insulation; Colm Britchfield and Pedro Guertler, 'Responding to the UK gas crisis', E3G, October 2021, https://9tj4025ol53byww26jdkao0x-wpengine.netdna-ssl.com/wp-content/uploads/Responding-to-the-UK-gas-crisis-E3G-Briefing.pdf

38   'Germany's low investment rate leaves its infrastructure creaking', *The Economist*, 17 June 2017, https://www.economist.com/europe/2017/06/17/germanys-low-investment-rate-leaves-its-infrastructure-creaking

39   Sarah Martin, '$600bn of spending needed over next 15 years, Infrastructure Australia says', *The Guardian*, 12 August 2019, https://www.theguardian.com/australia-news/2019/aug/13/600bn-of-spending-needed-over-next-15-years-infrastructure-australia-says

40   Ibid.

41   Martin Kornejew, Jun Retnschler, and Stéphane Hallegatte, 'Well spent: how governance determines the effectiveness of infrastructure investments', The World Bank (Policy Research Working Paper No. 8894, 2019).

42   Samuel Sherraden and Shayne Henry, 'Costs of the infrastructure deficit', New America, 2 March 2011, https://www.newamerica.org/economic-growth/policy-papers/costs-of-the-infrastructure-deficit/

43   Areddy, 'What the U.S. can learn from China's infatuation with infrastructure'.

44   Howard W. French, 'What the U.S. can learn from China's economy recovery', *World Politics Review*, 17 March 2021, https://www.worldpoliticsreview.com/articles/29498/what-the-u-s-can-learn-from-chinese-stimulus

45   Ed Pilkington, 'Pittsburgh bridge collapses hours before Biden's infrastructure speech in city', *The Guardian*, 28 January 2022, https://www.theguardian.com/us-news/2022/jan/28/pittsburgh-bridge-collapse-biden-infrastructure-speech

46   Ibid.

47   Ibid.

48   Josh Boak and Colleen Long, 'Biden signs $1T infrastructure deal with bipartisan crowd', Associated Press, 15 November 2021, https://apnews.com/article/joe-biden-congress-infrastructure-bill-signing-b5b8cca-843133de060778f049861b144; Andrew Gawthorpe, 'Biden scored a major victory on infrastructure. But is it enough?', *The Guardian*, 7 November 2021, https://www.theguardian.com/commentisfree/2021/nov/07/biden-scored-a-major-victory-on-infrastructure-but-is-it-enough; Madeleine Ngo, 'Skilled Workers Are Scarce, Posing a Challenge for Biden's Infrastructure Plan', *New York Times*, 9 September 2021, https://www.nytimes.com/2021/09/09/us/politics/biden-infrastructure-plan.html; Li Zhou, 'The bipartisan infrastructure law is both historic and not nearly enough', *Vox*, 15 November 2021, https://www.vox.com/22770447/infrastructure-bill-democrats-biden-water-broadband-roads-buses

49   Mark Beech, 'COVID-19 pushes up internet use 70% and streaming more than 12%, first figures reveal', *Forbes*, 25 March 2020, https://www.forbes.com/sites/markbeech/2020/03/25/covid-19-pushes-up-internet-use-70-streaming-more-than-12-first-figures-reveal/?sh=5ec707723104; Colleean McClain, Emily A. Vogels, Andrew Perrin, Stella Sechopoulos, and Lee Raine, 'The internet and the pandemic', Pew Research Center, 1 September 2021, https://www.pewresearch.org/internet/2021/09/01/the-internet-and-the-pandemic/#:~:text=The%20vast%20majority%20of%20adults,from%2053%25%20in%20April%202020

50   Abidemi Adisa, Bhaskar Chakravorti, Ravi Shankar Chaturvedi, and Christina Filipovic, 'The impact of internet access on covid-19 mortality in the United States', Digital Planet (The Fletcher School at Tufts University),

22 June 2022, https://sites.tufts.edu/digitalplanet/the-impact-of-internet-access-on-covid-19-deaths-in-the-us/

51   Ibid.

52   Sebastian Ibold, 'BRI Projects', Belt and Road Initiative, accessed August 2022, https://www.beltroad-initiative.com/projects/; Andrew Chatzsky and James McBride, 'China's massive belt and road initiative', Council on Foreign Relations, 28 January 2020, https://www.cfr.org/backgrounder/chinas-massive-belt-and-road-initiative

53   Charles Dunst, 'Where China isn't sending its best and brightest', *Washington Monthly*, 25 November 2019, https://washingtonmonthly.com/2019/11/25/where-china-isnt-sending-its-best-and-brightest/

54   Ibid.

55   Ryan Manuel, 'Twists in the belt and road', *China Leadership Monitor*, 1 September 2019, https://www.prcleader.org/_files/ugd/10535f_60ed8e44eba14dffb628131596fdd408.pdf

56   Lily Kuo, 'A Chinese-built bridge collapsed in Kenya two weeks after it was inspected by the president', *Quartz Africa*, 28 June 2017, https://qz.com/africa/1015554/a-chinese-built-bridge-collapsed-in-kenya-two-weeks-after-it-was-inspected-by-the-president/

57   'Rains damage Lusaka-Chirundu road', *Lusaka Times*, 20 March 2009, https://www.lusakatimes.com/2009/03/20/rains-damage-lusaka-chirundu-road/; Rafael Marques de Morais, 'Growing wealth, shrinking democracy', *New York Times*, August 29, 2012, https://www.nytimes.com/2012/08/30/opinion/in-angola-growing-wealth-but-shrinking-democracy.html

58   Martin Farrer and agencies, 'Five Chinese charged as toll in Cambodia building collapse rises to 28', *The Guardian*, 25 June 2019, https://www.theguardian.com/world/2019/jun/24/chinese-builders-arrested-as-toll-in-cambodia-building-collapse-rises-to-24; Bradley Murg, 'Sihanoukville tragedy and China: Time for a serious discussion', *Phnom Penh Post*, 27 June 2019, https://www.phnompenhpost.com/opinion/sihanoukville-tragedy-and-china-time-serious-discussion

59   'Coronavirus: Ten dead in China quarantine hotel collapse', BBC News, 8 March 2020, https://www.bbc.com/news/world-asia-china-51787936

60   The Associated Press, 'The death toll from a building collapse in China soars past 50', NPR, 6 May 2022, https://www.npr.org/2022/05/05/1096810346/survivor-found-almost-6-days-after-china-building-collapse; 'Four people killed in expressway bridge collapse in China's Hubei province', Reuters, 19 December 2019, https://www.reuters.com/world/china/four-people-killed-expressway-bridge-collapse-chinas-hubei-province-2021-12-19/

61   Gavin Gibbon, 'Two killed and 13 injured after university building collapse

in Riyadh', *Arabian Business*, 18 December 2019, https://www.arabianbusiness.com/industries/industries-culture-society/435621-two-killed-13-injured-after-university-building-collapses-in-riyadh; omarsc, 'Reports: Building collapses in Musheireb this morning', *Doha News*, 24 October 2021, https://dohanews.tumblr.com/post/11862277819/reports-building-collapses-in-musheireb-this

62 Owen Hatherley, ' "A lethal failure of oversight, like at Grenfell Tower, was going to happen sooner or later"', *dezeen*, 16 June 2017, https://www.dezeen.com/2017/06/16/grenfell-tower-fire-lethal-failure-oversight-opinion-column-owen-hatherley/; Mike Baker, Anjali Singhvi, and Patricia Mazzei, 'Engineer warned of "major structural damage" at Florida Condo Complex', *New York Times*, 26 June 2021, https://www.nytimes.com/2021/06/26/us/miami-building-collapse-investigation.html

63 Huong Le Thu and Malcolm Cook, 'Abe leaves top job with Japan a leading light in the Indo-Pacific', *The Strategist*, 9 September 2020, https://www.aspistrategist.org.au/abe-leaves-top-job-with-japan-a-leading-light-in-the-indo-pacific/

64 'Gross Domestic Product, 1st Quarter 2020 (Third Estimate); Corporate Profits, 1st Quarter 2020 (Revised Estimate)', Bureau of Economic Analysis (U.S. Department of Commerce), 25 June 2020, https://www.bea.gov/news/2020/gross-domestic-product-1st-quarter-2020-third-estimate-corporate-profits-1st-quarter-2020#:~:text=Current%E2%80%91dollar%20GDP%20decreased%203.4,(tables%201%20and%203)

65 'G20 GDP Growth – First quarter of 2020, OECD', OECD, 11 June 2020, https://www.oecd.org/economy/g20-gdp-growth-first-quarter-2020-oecd.htm

66 Éanna Kelly, 'Germany unveils €50B stimulus for 'future-focused' technologies', *Science|Business*, 4 June 2020, https://sciencebusiness.net/covid-19/news/germany-unveils-eu50b-stimulus-future-focused-technologies

67 Edward White and Song Jung-a, 'South Korea boosts coronavirus crisis stimulus package to $200bn', *Financial Times*, 22 April 2020, https://www.ft.com/content/54f5513e-c2fc-4062-acae-538f986a5f65

68 Laure He, 'China unveils $500 billion stimulus for the economy as it scraps growth target due to the pandemic', CNN Business, 22 May 2020, https://www.cnn.com/2020/05/21/economy/china-economy-growth-target-intl-hnk/index.html

69 Kevin Yao, 'Exclusive: China to ramp up spending to revive economy, could cut growth target – sources', Reuters, 19 March 2020, https://www.reuters.com/article/us-china-economy-stimulus-exclusive/exclusive-china-to-ramp-up-spending-to-revive-economy-could-cut-growth-target-sources-idUSKBN2161NW

70 Temple and Gautam, 'What America can learn from China'.

71 Linda Qui, 'Fact Check: Just how big is the infrastructure package?', *New York Times*, 11 August 2021, https://www.nytimes.com/2021/08/11/us/politics/infrastructure-fact-check.html

72 Adie Tomer, Joseph W. Kane, and Robert Puentes, 'How historic would a $1 trillion infrastructure program be?', Brookings Institution, 27 May 2017, https://www.brookings.edu/blog/the-avenue/2017/05/12/how-historic-would-a-1-trillion-infrastructure-program-be/

73 " 'What a waste": Video of 15 skyscrapers being simultaneously demolished in China stuns all online', *Indian Express*, 17 September 2021, https://indian-express.com/article/trending/trending-globally/video-of-15-skyscrapers-being-simultaneously-demolished-in-china-viral-7513147/

74 Tom Hancock, 'China's $2.3 trillion infrastructure plan puts America's to shame', Bloomberg, 6 April 2022, https://www.bloomberg.com/news/articles/2022-04-06/china-infrastructure-push-dwarfs-u-s-spending?sref=TZEt22gR

75 Ibid.

76 Ibid.

77 Ibid.

78 'Singapore funds new infrastructure', International Trade Ministration, 26 February 2021, https://www.trade.gov/market-intelligence/singapore-funds-new-infrastructure

79 Ibid.

80 Masood Afridi and Adite Aloke, 'The energy regulation and markets review: United Arab Emirates', *The Energy Regulation and Markets Review* No. 11 (2022), https://thelawreviews.co.uk/title/the-energy-regulation-and-markets-review/united-arab-emirates; Ahmad Ali Azari, 'How did the UAE manage its renewable energy investments during COVID?', Boston University Institute for Global Sustainability', 24 September 2020, https://energycentral.com/c/ec/how-did-uae-manage-its-renewable-energy-investments-during-covid; 'United Arab Emirates', KPMG, 18 November 2020, https://home.kpmg/xx/en/home/insights/2020/04/united-arab-emirates-government-and-institution-measures-in-response-to-covid.html; Colin Foreman, 'UAE moves to accelerate major infrastructure schemes', *MEED*, 23 March 2020, https://www.meed.com/uae-moves-to-accelerate-major-infrastructure-schemes; David Sit, 'Interview with H.E. Ms Mariam Alshamsi, Acting Consul General of the United Arab Emirates in Hong Kong', HKTDC Research, 23 September 2021, https://research.hktdc.com/en/article/ODU4MjA1Nzg3

81 Dana Khraiche, 'UAE approves four-year federal budget focused on social spending', Bloomberg, 12 October 2021, https://www.bloomberg.com/news

/articles/2021-10-12/uae-approves-four-year-federal-budget-focused-on-social-spending?sref=TZEt22gR; 'Federal Budget 2021', United Arab Emirates Ministry of Finance, accessed August 2022, https://www.mof.gov.ae/en/resourcesAndBudget/fedralBudget/Pages/budget2021.aspx

82 Statista Research Department, 'Top 100: Ranking of countries according to their quality of infrastructure in 2019', Statista, 5 August 2022, https://www.statista.com/statistics/264753/ranking-of-countries-according-to-the-general-quality-of-infrastructure/

83 'These countries have the most well-developed digital infrastructure', *U.S. News*, accessed August 2022, https://www.usnews.com/news/best-countries/rankings/well-developed-digital-infrastructure

84 Ibid.

85 Harold C. Schonberg, 'Japan journal', *New York Times*, 21 March 1982.

86 Nick Serafino, Curt Tarnoff, and Dick K. Nanto, 'U.S. occupation assistance: Iraq, Germany and Japan compared', Congressional Research Service, 23 March 2006, p. CRS-5, https://sgp.fas.org/crs/natsec/RL33331.pdf

87 Robert C. Orr (ed.), *Winning the Peace: An American Strategy for Post-conflict Reconstruction* (Washington, DC: The CSIS Press, 2004), p. 183.

88 Hiroko Tabuchi, 'In Japan, a growth strategy with echoes of the past', *New York Times*, 12 June 2013, https://www.nytimes.com/2013/06/13/business/global/in-japan-a-growth-strategy-with-echoes-of-the-past.html

89 Ibid.

90 'New highway in Japan aids economic growth', *New York Times*, 18 April 1965, https://timesmachine.nytimes.com/timesmachine/1965/04/18/101538944.html?pageNumber=8

91 'Tokaido Shinkansen', japan-guide.com, 2018, https://www.japan-guide.com/e/e2018_tokaido.html

92 Eisuke Sakakibara, *Beyond Capitalism: The Japanese Model of Market Economics* (New York: University Press of America, 1993), p. 29 and 31.

93 Martin Fackler, 'Japan's big-works stimulus is lesson', *New York Times*, 5 February 2009, https://www.nytimes.com/2009/02/06/world/asia/06japan.html

94 Ibid.

95 Kana Inagaki, 'Japan to unleash $350bn stimulus as west unwinds state spending', *Financial Times*, 17 November 2021, https://www.ft.com/content/52216cb9-0505-4fde-824a-58c7778d07e1; Leika Kihara and Tetsushi Kajimoto, 'Japan unveils $708 billion in fresh stimulus with eye on post-COVID growth', Reuters, 7 December 2020, https://www.reuters.com/article/us-japan-economy-stimulus/japan-unveils-708-billion-in-fresh-stimulus-with-eye-on-post-covid-growth-idUSKBN28I02Y; 'Japan stimulus

package', International Energy Agency, 11 February 2022, https://www.iea.org/policies/14466-japanese-stimulus-package

96 Kihara and Kajimoto, 'Japan unveils $708 billion in fresh stimulus with eye on post-COVID growth'.

97 *The Global Competitiveness Report 2019* (Geneva: World Economic Forum, 2019),p.17,https://www3.weforum.org/docs/WEF_TheGlobalCompetitiveness Report2019.pdf.

98 Carl-Johan Dalgaard, Nicolai Kaarsen, Ola Olsson, and Pablo Selaya, 'Roman roads to prosperity: Persistence and non-persistence of public infrastructure', *Journal of Comparative Economics*, 14 June 2022, https://www.sciencedirect.com/science/article/pii/S0147596722000269

99 Devrim Demirel, Jeffrey Kling, and Chad Shirle, 'Effects of physical infrastructure spending on the economy and the budget under two illustrative scenarios', Congressional Budget Office, August 2021, https://www.cbo.gov/publication/57407

100 Ibid.

101 *Legacies, Clouds, Uncertainties* (Washington: International Monetary Fund, October 2014), pp. 87–88.

102 Chief Economist Directorate, 'Infrastructure investment: evidence summary', Scottish Government, 13 December 2018, https://www.gov.scot/publications/exploring-economic-rationale-infrastructure-investment/

103 Jean-Marc Fournier, 'The positive effect of public investment on potential growth', The World Bank Economics Department Working Papers No. 1347 (22 November 2016), p. 15, https://www.oecd.org/economy/public-finance/The-positive-effect-of-public-investment-on-potential-growth.pdf

104 Christophe Hurlin, 'Network effects of the productivity of infrastructure in developing countries', World Bank Policy Research Working Paper No. 3808 (2006), https://openknowledge.worldbank.org/handle/10986/8836?show=full

105 BER staff, 'Analysis of Taiwanese economic history and policies', *Berkeley Economic Review*, 17 February 2020, https://econreview.berkeley.edu/analysis-of-taiwanese-economic-history-and-policies/; Jennie Hay Woo, 'Education and economic growth in Taiwan: A case of successful planning', *World Development* Vol. 19, No. 8 (August 1991), pp. 1029–44; Michael J. Seth, 'An unpromising recovery: South Korea's Post-Korean war economic development: 1953-1961', *Education About Asia* Vol. 18, No. 3 (Winter 2013), pp.42–45,https://www.asianstudies.org/publications/eaa/archives/an-unpromising-recovery-south-koreas-post-korea; Andrea Matles Savada and William Shaw (ed.), *South Korea: A Country Study* (Collingdale: DIANE Publishing, p. 141).

106 'Infrastructure in Indonesia', PWC, accessed August 2022, https://www.pwc.com/id/en/industry-sectors/cpi/infrastructure-in-indonesia.html

107 Rajat Agarwal, Antonious Santoso, Khoon Tee Tan, and Phillia Wibowo, 'Ten ideas to unlock Indonesia's growth after COVID-19', McKinsey, accessed August 2022, https://www.mckinsey.com/featured-insights/asia-pacific/ten-ideas-to-unlock-indonesias-growth-after-covid-19

108 Abhishek Dangra, 'The missing piece in India's economic growth story: robust infrastructure', S&P Global, 2 August 2016, https://www.spglobal.com/en/research-insights/articles/the-missing-piece-in-indias-economic-growth-story-robust-infrastructure; 'Why Mexico's economy underperforms', The Economist, 19 March 2022, https://www.economist.com/the-americas/2022/03/19/why-mexicos-economy-underperforms; Oxford Analytica, 'Poor infrastructure will weigh on South African Growth', Expert Briefings, 23 March 2020, https://doi.org/10.1108/OXAN-DB251336

109 Lester Gunnion, 'Infrastructure investment: An economist's view from the ground up', Deloitte, July 2021, https://www2.deloitte.com/us/en/insights/economy/spotlight/impact-of-us-infrastructure-investment.html

110 Jim Glassman, 'How a big infrastructure investment could pay off', J.P. Morgan | Chase, 8 September 2021, https://www.jpmorgan.com/commercial-banking/insights/the-economic-case-for-infrastructure-spending

111 Miriam Jordan and Robert Gebeloff, 'Amid slowdown, immigration is driving U.S. population growth', New York Times, 5 February 2022, https://www.nytimes.com/2022/02/05/us/immigration-census-population.html

112 James McBride and Anshu Siripurapu, 'The state of U.S. infrastructure', Council on Foreing Relations, 8 November 2021, https://www.cfr.org/backgrounder/state-us-infrastructure

113 Gabby Birenbaum, 'The bipartisan infrastructure bill provides historic funding for transit. It's not enough', Vox, 23 August 2021, https://www.vox.com/22621793/public-transit-funding-bipartisan-infrastructure-bill

114 Jacob Funk Kirkegaard, 'Europe is falling behind on infrastructure spending', Peterson Institute for International Economics, 22 May 2019, https://www.piie.com/research/piie-charts/europe-falling-behind-infrastructure-spending; The Associated Press, 'In global 5G race, European Union is told to step up pace', ABC News, 24 January 2022, https://abcnews.go.com/International/wireStory/global-5g-race-european-union-told-step-pace-82440872; Philiip-Bastian Brutscher and Andreas Kappeler, 'Addressing Europe's infrastructure gaps: Fiscal constraints and planning capacity matter', VoxEU at the Centre for Economic Policy Research, 18 April 2018, https://voxeu.org/article/addressing-europe-s-infrastructure-gaps; Takanori Okabe, 'Aging infrastructure a major roadblock to Japan's future',

Nikkei Asia, 10 February 2022, https://asia.nikkei.com/Spotlight/Datawatch /Aging-infrastructure-a-major-roadblock-to-Japan-s-future

115 Thomas L. Friedman, 'Post-pandemic, here's how America rises again', *New York Times*, 14 April 2020, https://www.nytimes.com/2020/04/14/opinion/ stimulus-infrastructure-covid.html

116 Viiveck Verma, 'Transcending the urban: incubating rural innovation', *BW Businessworld*, 27 May 2021, https://www.businessworld.in/article/ Transcending-The-Urban-Incubating-Rural-Innovation/27-05-2021- 391116/; Ibid.

117 Friedman, 'Post-Pandemic'.

118 Raul Katz, *Impact of Broadband on the Economy* (Geneva: International Telecommunication Union, April 2012).

119 'Connectivity: key to revitalising rural areas', European Commission, 30 June 2021, https://digital-strategy.ec.europa.eu/en/news/connectivity- key-revitalising-rural-areas

120 Monica Anderson, 'About a quarter of rural Americans say access to high- speed internet is a major problem', Pew Research Center, 10 September 2018, https://www.pewresearch.org/fact-tank/2018/09/10/about-a-quarter-of- rural-americans-say-access-to-high-speed-internet-is-a-major-problem/

121 'The global cost of connectivity', Compare The Market Limited, accessed August 2022, https://www.comparethemarket.com/broadband/content/ global-broadband-index/

122 Tom Wheeler, '5 steps to get the internet to all Americans', Brookings Institution, 27 May 2020, https://www.brookings.edu/research/5-steps-to- get-the-internet-to-all-americans/

123 Ibid.

124 Nina Jobst, 'Internet usage in South Korea - statistics & facts', Statista, 29 April 2022, https://www.statista.com/topics/2230/internet-usage-in-south- korea/#dossierKeyfigures

125 Robert D. Atkinson, ' "Building back better" requires building in digital', Information Technology & Innovation Foundation, 10 May 2021, https:// itif.org/publications/2021/05/10/building-back-better-requires-building -digital

126 Ibid.

127 Jed Pressgrove, 'How should governments plan for the latest network tech?', *Government Technology*, 5 February 2021, https://www.govtech.com/ network/how-should-governments-plan-for-the-latest-network-tech.html

128 Frank Nagle, 'Digital infrastructure is more than just broadband: What the US can learn from Europe's open source technology policy study', Brookings Institution, 9 November 2021, https://www.brookings.edu/research/digital

-infrastructure-is-more-than-just-broadband-what-the-u-s-can-learn-from-europes-open-source-technology-policy-study/

129 Jed Pressgrove, 'Cybersecurity: the latest challenge for local water utilities', *Government Technology*, 30 March 2021, https://www.govtech.com/security/cybersecurity-the-latest-challenge-for-local-water-utilities.html

130 Joseph Berger, 'A dam, small and unsung, is caught up in an Iranian hacking case', *New York Times*, 25 March 2016, https://www.nytimes.com/2016/03/26/nyregion/rye-brook-dam-caught-in-computer-hacking-case.html

131 Ibid.

132 Matt Burgess, 'A hacking spree against Iran spills out into the physical world', *WIRED*, 29 November 2021, https://www.wired.com/story/hacking-iran-critical-infrastructure-israel/

133 AP and TOI Staff, "'Cyber winter is coming", warns Israel cyber chief after attack on water systems', *Times of Israel*, 28 May 2020, https://www.timesofisrael.com/israeli-cyber-chief-attack-on-water-systems-a-changing-point-in-cyber-warfare/

134 Ibid.

135 Mark Montgomery, 'Congress invests in national cyber resilience but misses important opportunities in the consolidated appropriations act', *Lawfare*, 1 April 2022, https://www.lawfareblog.com/congress-invests-national-cyber-resilience-misses-important-opportunities-consolidated

136 Jessica Davis, 'Healthcare cybersecurity investment critical to national security, says CISA official', SC Media, 10 March 2022, https://www.scmagazine.com/analysis/ransomware/healthcare-cybersecurity-investment-critical-to-national-security-says-cisa-official

137 William Ralston, 'The untold story of a cyberattack, a hospital and a dying woman', *WIRED*, 11 November 2020, https://www.wired.co.uk/article/ransomware-hospital-death-germany; Debora Irene Christine, 'Improving cybersecurity means understanding how cyberattacks affect both governments and civilians', *The Conversation*, 19 July 2021, https://theconversation.com/improving-cybersecurity-means-understanding-how-cyberattacks-affect-both-governments-and-civilians-163261

138 Michael Chertoff and Jeremy Grant, '8 ways governments can improve their cybersecurity', *Harvard Business Review*, 25 April 2017, https://hbr.org/2017/04/8-ways-governments-can-improve-their-cybersecurity

139 Ryan Harkins and Erin English, 'Guarding the public sector: seven ways state governments can boost their cybersecurity', MarshMcLennan, October 2018, https://www.marshmclennan.com/insights/publications/2018/oct/guarding-the-public-sector--seven-ways-state-governments-can-boo.html

140 Ralston, 'The untold story of a cyberattack, a hospital and a dying woman'.

Chapter 8

1   Olga Carlisle, 'Literary life in Moscow', *New York Times*, 14 March 1965, https://www.nytimes.com/1965/03/14/archives/literary-life-in-moscow-moscow-moscow.html?searchResultPosition=3

2   Mark Malseed, 'The story of Sergey Brin', *Moment*, February-March 2007, https://momentmag.com/the-story-of-sergey-brin/

3   Ibid.

4   Ibid.

5   Ibid.

6   Ibid.

7   Ibid.

8   Ibid.

9   Verge Staff, 'Google turns 20: how an internet search engine reshaped the world', *The Verge*, 27 September 2018, https://www.theverge.com/2018/9/5/17823490/google-20th-birthday-anniversary-history-milestones

10 Scott Austin, 'About Eric Schmidt's "adult supervision" comment', *Wall Street Journal*, 20 January 2011, https://blogs.wsj.com/venturecapital/2011/01/20/about-eric-schmidts-adult-supervision-comment/

11 Fred Vogelstein, 'How Yahoo blew it', *Wired*, 1 February 2007, https://www.wired.com/2007/02/yahoo-3/

12 Staff, 'Google turns 20'.

13 'Google goes public', *New York Times*, 20 August 2004, https://www.nytimes.com/2004/08/20/opinion/google-goes-public.html

14 Andrew Ross Sorkin and Jeremy W. Peters, 'Google to acquire YouTube for $1.65 billion', *New York Times*, 9 October 2006, https://www.nytimes.com/2006/10/09/business/09cnd-deal.html

15 'Fortune 500', *Fortune*, accessed August 2022, https://fortune.com/fortune500/

16 Sundair Pichai, 'Our plans to invest $9.5 billion in the U.S. in 2022', Google, 13 April 2022, https://blog.google/inside-google/company-announcements/investing-america-2022/

17 Joan Levinstein, 'Dr. David Ho: 1996', *TIME*, 2019, http://content.time.com/time/specials/packages/article/0,28804,2019712_2019703_2019666,00.html

18 'First- and second-generation share of the population, 1900-2017', Pew Research Center, 3 June 2019, https://www.pewresearch.org/hispanic/chart/first-and-second-generation-share-of-the-population/

19 Pierre Azoulay, Benjamin Jones, J. Daniel Kim, and Javier Miranda, 'Immigration and entrepreneurship in the United States', National Bureau of Economic Research Working Paper No. 27778, p. 13, https://www.nber.org/papers/w27778

20 Ibid.

21 *The Economic and Fiscal Consequences of Immigration* (Washington: National Academies of Sciences, Engineering, and Medicine, 2017), https:// doi.org/10.17226/23550; 'Immigrants and the economy in: United States of America', New American Economy, accessed August 2022, https://www. newamericaneconomy.org/locations/national/

22 Willian N. Evans and Daniel Fitzgerald, 'The economic and social outcomes of refugees in the United States: Evidence from the ACS', National Bureau of Economic Research Working Paper No. 23498, June 2017, p. 6, https://www. nber.org/papers/w23498

23 'Immigrants and the economy in: United States of America'.

24 'How are immigration and GDP growth connected?', fwd.us, 29 June 2021, https://www.fwd.us/news/immigration-and-gdp-growth/; 'Increasing future immigration grows the U.S.' Competitive Advantage', fwd.us, 7 April 2021, https://www.fwd.us/news/future-immigration/

25 Ibid. (Raw dollar amount comes from multiplying fwd.us's per capita GDP additions by population numbers, as of 2022.)

26 Sean O'Grady, 'Ten things that immigration has done for Britain', *Independent*, 4 November 2014, https://www.independent.co.uk/voices/comment/ten-things-that-immigration-has-done-for-britain-9839549.html

27 Ibid.

28 Jonathan Liew, 'The England squad is built on immigration – yet our xenophobic government dares to cheer it on', *New Statesman*, 7 July 2021, https://www.newstatesman.com/politics/2021/07/england-squad-built-immigration-yet-our-xenophobic-government-dares-cheer-it

29 Philip Salter, 'Half Of UK's fastest growing businesses have a foreign-born founder', *Forbes*, 11 July 2019, https://www.forbes.com/sites/philipsalter/2019/07/11/half-of-uks-fastest-growing-businesses-have-a-foreign-born-founder/?sh=496ccb74d3ae

30 Rupert Neate, 'About a quarter of the UK's top earners are migrants, data shows', *The Guardian*, 20 September 2020, https://www.theguardian.com/money/2020/sep/20/about-a-quarter-of-the-uks-top-earners-are-migrants-data-shows

31 'Migrants contribute more to Britain than they take, and will carry on doing so', *The Economist*, 26 September 2018, https://www.economist.com/graphic-detail/2018/09/26/migrants-contribute-more-to-britain-than-they-take-and-will-carry-on-doing-so; 'EAA migration in the UK: Final report', Migration Advisory Commission, September 2018, https://assets.publishing.service.gov.uk/government/uploads/system/uploads/attachment_data/file/741926/Final_EEA_report.PDF

32 Ibid.

33 Christian Dustmann and Tommaso Frattini, 'The fiscal effects of immigration to the UK', *The Economic Journal* Vol. 124, No. 580 (2014), pp. F593 -F643.

34 Siobhan Dowling, 'Germany welcomed refugees. Now it's reaping the economic benefits', Al Jazeera, 20 June 2019, https://www.aljazeera.com/ economy/2019/6/20/germany-welcomed-refugees-now-its-reaping-the-economic-benefits

35 Marc Desormeaux, 'Why Canada is prioritizing immigration during the pandemic', CIC News, 30 June 2021, https://www.cicnews.com/2021/06/why -canada-is-prioritizing-immigration-during-the-pandemic-0618502.html

36 'The economic impact of migration', Migration Council Australia, April 2021, p. 2, https://migrationcouncil.org.au/wp-content/uploads/2021/04/ The-Economic-Impact-of-Migration.pdf

37 Jonathan Coleman, 'Immigration New Zealand's contribution to growing the economy', Beehive.govt.nz, 7 May 2011, https://www.beehive.govt.nz/ speech/immigration-new-zealands-contribution-growing-economy; ANZ Research, "NZ Insight: How does immigration affect the New Zealand economy?', ANZ, 29 June 2021, https://www.anz.co.nz/content/dam/ anzconz/documents/economics-and-market-research/2021/ANZ-Immigration-Insight-20210629.pdf

38 Kazumasa Oguru and Manabu Shimasawa, 'The impact of immigration on the Japanese economy: A multi-country simulation model', The Research Institute of Economy, Trade and Industry Discussion Paper Series 09-E-2020, 13 April 2009, https://www.rieti.go.jp/jp/publications/ dp/09e020.pdf

39 Ivan Krastev, 'Eastern Europe's illiberal revolution', *Foreign Affairs*, Vol. 97, No. 3 (May/June 2018).

40 Ibid.

41 Kyodo, 'Elderly citizens accounted for record 28.4% of Japan's population in 2018, data show', *Japan Times*, 15 September 2019, https://www.japantimes. co.jp/news/2019/09/15/national/elderly-citizens-accounted-record-28-4-japans-population-2018-data-show/

42 'Asia's advanced economies now have lower birth rates than Japan', *The Economist*, 19 May 2022 https://www.economist.com/asia/2022/05/19/asias -advanced-economies-now-have-lower-birth-rates-than-japan

43 Sashan Ingber, 'Japan's population is in rapid decline', NPR, 21 December 2018, https://www.npr.org/2018/12/21/679103541/japans-population-is-in -rapid-decline#:~:text=About%20127%20million%20people%20 live,aging%20out%20of%20the%20workforce

44 'Demographic change in Japan', World Demographic and Ageing Forum, May 2012, https://demographic-challenge.com/demographic-change-in-japan.html

45 Ingber, 'Japan's population is in rapid decline'.

46 San Kim, 'Korea shatters its own record for world's lowest fertility rate', Bloomberg, 23 August 2022, https://www.bloomberg.com/news/articles/2022-08-24/fastest-aging-wealthy-economy-breaks-own-fertility-record-again?sref=TZEt22gR

47 Richard Harding, 'Japanese employers struggle to fill jobs', *Financial Times*, 13 May 2019, https://www.ft.com/content/3412cc78-72f8-11e9-bf5c-6eeb837566c5

48 'Health at a Glance 2021: OECD Indicators', OECD, 2021, https://www.oecd.org/japan/health-at-a-glance-japan-EN.pdf

49 Ibid., p. 2; Enrico D'Ambrogio, 'Japan's ageing society', European Parliamentary Research Service, December 2020, https://www.europarl.europa.eu/RegData/etudes/BRIE/2020/659419/EPRS_BRI(2020)659419_EN.pdf

50 Mariana Colacelli and Emilio Fernández Corugedo, 'Macroeconomic effects of Japan's demographics: can structural reforms reverse them?', International Monetary Fund Working Paper No. 248, 28 November 2018, p. 5, https://www.imf.org/en/Publications/WP/Issues/2018/11/28/Macroeconomic-Effects-of-Japans-Demographics-Can-Structural-Reforms-Reverse-Them-46356

51 Sungjin Cho and Jan R. Kim, 'Population aging in Korea: implications for fiscal sustainability', *Seoul Journal of Economics* Vol. 34, No. 2 (2021), p. 253.

52 The World Bank, GDP growth (annual %) – Korea, Rep. (2020), https://data.worldbank.org/indicator/NY.GDP.MKTP.KD.ZG?end=2009&locations=KR&start=2000; Markit, 'South Korean economy boosted by exports', Seeking Alpha, 21 February 2022, https://seekingalpha.com/article/4488815-south-korean-economy-boosted-by-strong-exports; Kyooho Kwon, 'Korea's demographic transition and long-term growth projection based on an overlapping generations model', *KDI Journal of Economic Policy* Vol. 39, No. 2 (2017), pp. 27 and 41.

53 Kwon, 'Korea's Demographic Transition', p. 27 and 41.

54 'Korea', *International Migration Outlook 2020* (Paris: OECD 2020), https://www.oecd-ilibrary.org/sites/22b3b254-en/index.html?itemId=/content/component/22b3b254-en#

55 'Japan', *International Migration Outlook 2020* (Paris: OECD 2020), https://www.oecd-ilibrary.org/sites/b140958b-en/index.html?itemId=/content/component/b140958b-en#

56   'United States', *International Migration Outlook 2020* (Paris: OECD 2020), https://www.oecd-ilibrary.org/social-issues-migration-health/international-migration-outlook-2020_927d2d27-en

57   'Austria', *International Migration Outlook 2020* (Paris: OECD 2020), https://www.oecd-ilibrary.org/social-issues-migration-health/international-migration-outlook-2020_55e6b202-en

58   'Hungary', *International Migration Outlook 2020* (Paris: OECD 2020), https://www.oecd-ilibrary.org/social-issues-migration-health/international-migration-outlook-2020_2c9eaf3f-en

59   Markus Bell, 'Japan's self-destructive immigration policy', *The Diplomat*, 4 January 2022, https://thediplomat.com/2022/01/japans-self-destructive-immigration-policy/; Darcie Draudt, 'Korea's immigration policy backlash', Council on Foreign Relations, 15 April 2015, https://www.cfr.org/blog/koreas-immigration-policy-backlash; Choe Sang-Hun, 'How "multiculturalism" became a bad word in South Korea', *New York Times*, 1 March 2022, https://www.nytimes.com/2022/03/01/world/asia/south-korea-diversity-muslims.html

60   Matt Katz, 'What happens when Japan stops looking "Japanese"?', *The Atlantic*, 23 December 2019, https://www.theatlantic.com/international/archive/2019/12/immigration-japan-national-identity/603568/

61   Rick Gladstone, 'As birthrate falls, South Korea's population declines, posing threat to economy', *New York Times*, 4 January 2021, https://www.nytimes.com/2021/01/04/world/asia/south-korea-population.html

62   Ibid.

63   Casey Baseel, 'Tokyo's latest plan to boost birth rate: Pay people 100,000 yen per baby they give birth to', *Japan Today*, 21 January 2021, https://japantoday.com/category/features/lifestyle/Tokyo%E2%80%99s-latest-plan-to-boost-birth-rate-Pay-people-100-000-yen-per-baby-they-give-birth-to

64   Alex Williams, 'To breed or not to breed?', *New York Times*, 20 November 2021, https://www.nytimes.com/2021/11/20/style/breed-children-climate-change.html

65   Cindy Sui, 'Taiwanese birth rate plummets despite measures', BBC News, 15 August 2011, https://www.bbc.com/news/world-asia-pacific-14525525

66   Cybil Chou, 'Taiwan's falling birthrate "threatens its economic security"', *Nikkei Asia*, 18 July 2021, https://asia.nikkei.com/Life-Arts/Life/Taiwan-s-falling-birthrate-threatens-its-economic-security2

67   Gladstone, 'As birthrate falls'.

68   Justin McCurry and Nemo Kim, '"Luxuries I can't afford": why fewer women in South Korea are having children', *The Guardian*, 15 January 2021, https://www.theguardian.com/world/2021/jan/15/luxuries-i-cant-afford-why-fewer-women-in-south-korea-are-having-children

69   The World Bank, Fertility rate, total (births per woman) (2020), https://data.worldbank.org/indicator/SP.DYN.TFRT.IN

70   Ibid.

71   Ibid.

72   Claire Cain Miller, 'Americans are having fewer babies. They told us why', *New York Times*, 5 July 2018, https://www.nytimes.com/2018/07/05/upshot/americans-are-having-fewer-babies-they-told-us-why.html

73   Gretchen Livingston, 'Birth rates lag in Europe and the U.S., but the desire for kids does not', Pew Research Center, 11 April 2014, https://www.pewresearch.org/fact-tank/2014/04/11/birth-rates-lag-in-europe-and-the-u-s-but-the-desire-for-kids-does-not/

74   Ibid.

75   Ibid.

76   Cain Miller, 'Americans are having fewer babies'.

77   Ibid.

78   Corinne Purtill and Dan Kopf, 'The reason the richest women in the US are the ones having the most kids', *Quartz*, 11 November 2017, https://qz.com/1125805/the-reason-the-richest-women-in-the-us-are-the-ones-having-the-most-kids/; Dan A. Black, Natalia Kolesnikova, Seth G. Sanders, and Lowell J. Taylor, 'Are children "normal"?', *The Review of Economics and Statistics* Vol. 95, No. 1 (2013), pp. 21–33; Joseph Price, 'How income affects fertility', Institute for Family Studies, 8 October 2013, https://ifstudies.org/blog/how-income-affects-fertility

79   'World population by region', Our World in Data, 2019, https://ourworldindata.org/grapher/historical-and-projected-population-by-region

80   José Graziano Da Silva, 'Feeding the world sustainably', United Nations, June 2012, https://www.un.org/en/chronicle/article/feeding-world-sustainably#; Robinson Meyer, 'There's no scenario in which 2050 is "normal"', *The Atlantic*, 27 April 2022, https://www.theatlantic.com/science/archive/2022/04/ipcc-report-climate-change-2050/629691/

81   Laura Spinney, 'Why declining birth rates are good news for life on Earth', *The Guardian*, 8 July 2021, https://www.theguardian.com/commentisfree/2021/jul/08/why-declining-birth-rates-are-good-news-for-life-on-earth

82   'China's young elite are considering moving abroad', *The Economist*, 5 May 2022, https://www.economist.com/china/2022/05/05/chinas-young-elite-are-considering-moving-abroad

83   Ibid.

84   Vivian Wang and Alexandra Stevenson, 'As China doubles down on lockdowns, some Chinese seek an exit', *New York Times*, 20 May 2022, https://

www.nytimes.com/2022/05/20/world/asia/china-lockdown-migration.
html

85 Ibid.

86 'China's young elite are considering moving abroad'.

87 'China Immigration Statistics 1960-2022', Macrotrends, accessed August 2022, https://www.macrotrends.net/countries/CHN/china/immigration -statistics

88 Ibid.

89 Rachel Wang, 'Why China's rich want to leave', *The Atlantic*, 11 April 2017, https://www.theatlantic.com/china/archive/2013/04/why-chinas-rich-want -to-leave/274920/

90 Ibid.

91 'China Immigration Statistics 1960-2022'.

92 Robert Frank, 'More than a third of Chinese millionaires want to leave China, here's where they want to go', CNBC, 5 July 2018, https://www.cnbc. com/2018/07/05/more-than-a-third-of-chinese-millionaires-want-to-leave -china.html

93 'China Net Migration Rate 1950-2022', Macrotrends, accessed August 2022, https://www.macrotrends.net/countries/CHN/china/net-migration

94 'U.S. Net Migration Rate 1950-2022', Macrotrends, accessed August 2022, https://www.macrotrends.net/countries/USA/united-states/net-migra-tion#; 'Germany Net Migration Rate 1950-2022', Macrotrends, accessed August 2022, https://www.macrotrends.net/countries/DEU/germany/net-migration#; 'U.K. Net Migration Rate 1950-2022', Macrotrends, accessed August 2022, https://www.macrotrends.net/countries/GBR/united-king-dom/net-migration

95 国家移民管理局,'国家移民管理局：对非必要、非紧急出境事由暂不签发普通护照等出入境证件', WeChat, 4 August 2021, https://mp.weixin. qq.com/s/iU2rSXnnC1Yad7bRtI4Kig

96 李京泽, '国家移民管理局：上半年全国普通护照签发量为2019年同期的 2%', 中国新闻网, 30 July 2021, https://www.chinanews.com.cn/gn/2021 /07-30/9532310.shtml

97 国家移民管理局微信公号, '国家移民管理局：从严限制中国公民非必要出境活动', 澎湃新闻, 12 May 2022, https://m.thepaper.cn/ newsDetail_forward_18053022

98 Wang and Stevenson, 'As China doubles down on lockdown'.

99 Julie Ray and Neli Esipova, 'Record numbers of Americans want to leave the U.S.', Gallup, 4 January 2019, https://news.gallup.com/poll/245789/record-numbers-americans-leave.aspx

100 William Yang, 'How has the one-child policy affected China?', DW, 19 July

2018, https://www.dw.com/en/how-has-the-one-child-policy-affected-china/a-44749604

101   Ibid.

102   Steve LeVine, 'Demographics may decide the U.S.-China rivalry', Axios 3 July 2019, https://www.axios.com/demographics-decide-us-china-rivalry-64ef68fb-b34e-4216-870b-0a6cf0d8b946.ht

103   Campbell, 'China's aging population is a major threat to future'.

104   'Asia's advanced economies now have lower birth rates than Japan'.

105   Ibid.

106   Ibid.

107   Ibid.

108   Mike Ives, 'China wants to attract more foreigners (of a certain kind)', New York Times, 23 February 2017, https://www.nytimes.com/2017/02/23/world/asia/china-green-card-stephon-marbury.html; 'Special report: over 3,000 Cambodian students graduate and study in China (Video inside)', Fresh News, 15 July 2020, http://m.en.freshnewsasia.com/index.php/en/localnews/18807-2020-07-15-08-11-24.html; 'China emerging as a major destination for African students', ICEF Monitor, 21 April 2021, https://monitor.icef.com/2021/04/china-emerging-as-a-major-destination-for-african-students/

109   'Russia Net Migration Rate 1950-2022', Macrotrends, accessed August 2022, https://www.macrotrends.net/countries/RUS/russia/net-migration#

110   'Thailand Net Migration Rate 1950-2022', Macrotrends, accessed August 2022, https://www.macrotrends.net/countries/THA/thailand/net-migration

111   'Kazakhstan Net Migration Rate 1950-2022', Macrotrends, accessed August 2022, https://www.macrotrends.net/countries/KAZ/kazakhstan/net-migration#

112   'Qatar Net Migration Rate 1950-2022', Macrotrends, accessed August 2022, https://www.macrotrends.net/countries/QAT/qatar/net-migration#

113   'Hong Kong net migration rate 1950-2022', Macrotrends, accessed August 2022, https://www.macrotrends.net/countries/HKG/hong-kong/net-migration#

114   Kari Soo Lindberg, 'Hong Kong population drops by record as people flee covid curbs', Bloomberg, 11 August 2022, https://www.bloomberg.com/news/articles/2022-08-11/hong-kong-population-drops-by-record-as-people-flee-covid-curbs?srnd=asia-politics

115   The World Bank, GDP per capita (current US$) – 2020, https://data.worldbank.org/indicator/NY.GDP.PCAP.CD?most_recent_value_desc=true

116   Anna Platonova and Giuliana Urso, 'Asian immigration to the European Union, United States and Canada: an initial comparison', Journal of Global Policy and Governance Vol. 1 (2013), pp. 143–56; 'At least a million Sub-Saharan Africans moved to Europe since 2010', Pew Research Center,

22 March 2018, https://www.pewresearch.org/global/2018/03/22/at-least-a
-million-sub-saharan-africans-moved-to-europe-since-2010/

117   Neli Esipova, Anita Pugliese, and Julie Ray, 'More than 750 million worldwide would migrate if they could', Gallup, 10 December 2018, https://news.
gallup.com/poll/245255/750-million-worldwide-migrate.aspx

118   Ibid.

119   Warsan Shire, 'Home' in *Teaching My Mother How to Give Birth* (London:
Flipped eye, 2011).

120   Dylan Matthews, 'The case for open borders', *Vox*, 15 December 2014, https:
//www.vox.com/2014/9/13/6135905/open-borders-bryan-caplan-interview
-gdp-double

121   Jens Manuel Krogstad, Mark Hugo Lopez, and Jeffrey S. Passel, 'A majority
of Americans say immigrants mostly fill jobs U.S. citizens do not want', Pew
Research Center, 10 June 2020, https://www.pewresearch.org/fact-tank/
2020/06/10/a-majority-of-americans-say-immigrants-mostly-fill-jobs-u-s-
citizens-do-not-want/

122   Zefitret Abera Molla, 'Ending the title 42 expulsion policy is the right thing
to do', Center for American Progress, 6 April 2022, https://www.american-
progress.org/article/ending-the-title-42-expulsion-policy-is-the-right-
thing-to-do/

123   Re-elect Rashida, 'Racial and immigration justice', accessed August
2022, https://rashidaforcongress.com/issues/racial-and-immigration-
justice/; 'Immigration reform', The Office of Hillary Rodham Clinton,
accessed August 2022, https://www.hillaryclinton.com/issues/immigra-
tion-reform/

124   Ana Gonzalez-Barrera and Phillip Connor, 'Around the world, more says
immigrants are a strength than a burden', Pew Research Center, 14 March
2019, https://www.pewresearch.org/global/2019/03/14/around-the-world-
more-say-immigrants-are-a-strength-than-a-burden/

125   'Why have Danes turned against immigration?', *The Economist*,
18 December 2021, https://www.economist.com/europe/2021/12/18/why
-have-danes-turned-against-immigration

126   David J. Bier, 'Why the legal immigration system is broken: a short list of
problems', CATO Institute, 10 July 2018, https://www.cato.org/blog/why-
legal-immigration-system-broken-short-list-problems

127   Andrew Small, 'Japan's failing immigration system', *Northeastern University
Political Review*, 31 March 2022, https://www.nupoliticalreview.com/2022/
03/31/japans-failing-immigration-system/

128   Virginie Guiraudon, 'Immigration policy in France', Brookings Institution,
1 July 2018, https://www.brookings.edu/articles/immigration-policy-in

-france/; Norimitsu Onishi, 'France announces tough new measures on immigration', *New York Times*, 6 November 2019, https://www.nytimes.com/2019/11/06/world/europe/france-macron-immigration.html; Adam Nossiter, 'Macron aims to keep migrants, and far right, at bay in France', *New York Times*, 22 February 2018, https://www.nytimes.com/2018/02/22/world/europe/france-immigration-law.html

129   Eleanor Davey, 'The humanitarian disgrace of Australia's immigration regime', *Boston Review*, 18 January 2022, https://bostonreview.net/articles/the-humanitarian-disgrace-of-australias-immigration-regime/

130   Michelle Jamrisko, 'Singapore unveils long-term work visas to end talent crunch', Bloomberg, 29 August 2022, https://www.bloomberg.com/news/articles/2022-08-29/singapore-unveils-long-term-work-visas-to-end-talent-crunch?sref=TZEt22gR

131   Charles Dunst, 'Cambodian deportees return to a "home" they've never known', *The Atlantic*, 16 January 2019, https://www.theatlantic.com/international/archive/2019/01/america-deports-cambodian-refugees/580393/

132   Sonja Haug, Edda Currle, Susanne Lochner, Dominik Huber, and Amelie Altenbuchner, 'Asylsuchende in Bayern', Hanns Seidel Stiftung and Ostbayerische Technische Hochschule Regensburg, 3 April 2017, p. 68, https://www.hss.de/download/publications/Asylsuchende_in_Bayern.pdf; Günther Jikeli, 'Attitudes of Syrian and Iraqi refugees in Germany toward Jews' in *Confronting Antisemitism in Modern Media, the Legal and Political Worlds* (Berlin: De Gruyter, 2021), p. 243.

133   Antje Röder, 'Immigrants' attitudes toward homosexuality: socialization religion, and acculturation in European host societies', *International Migration Review* Vol. 49, No. 4 (2015), p. 22, https://d-nb.info/1200547411/34

134   Ibid., p. 23.

135   Ibid., p. 23.

136   Nino Simic, Kristin Marklund, Ann Jönsson, Helena Lagercrantz, Caroline Lagercrantz, David Erichsen, Joan Rask, Jeanette Björkqvist, Bjørn Kvaal, and Annska Ólafsdóttir, *New in the Nordic Countries* (Copenhagen: Nordic Council of Ministers, 2018), pp. 10–11 and 21–22.

137   Mette Foged, Janis Kreuder & Giovanni Peri, 'Integrating refugees by addressing labor shortages? A policy evaluation', National Bureau of Economic Research Working Paper No. 29781 (February 2022), p. 3.

138   Silvia M. Radulescu, 'Embracing refugees: a revival solution for shrinking American Cities', *Georgetown Immigration Law General* Vol. 36, No. 2 (2022), pp. 783 and 793.

139   U.S. Bureau of Economic Analysis, 'Total real gross domestic product for

Utica-Rome, NY (MSA)', Federal Reserve Bank of St. Louis, accessed August 2022, https://fred.stlouisfed.org/series/RGMP46540

140 Yusaku Yoshikawa, 'Combatting Japan's agricultural worker shortage', *East Asia Forum*, 3 March 2022, https://www.eastasiaforum.org/2022/03/03/combatting-japans-agricultural-worker-shortage/; Claire Marshall, 'Farming labour shortage could mean price rises, MPs warn', BBC, 6 April 2022, https://www.bbc.com/news/science-environment-60999236

141 Stephanie Ferguson, 'Understanding America's labor shortage: the most impacted industries', U.S. Chamber of Commerce, 19 August 2022, https://www.uschamber.com/workforce/understanding-americas-labor-shortage-the-most-impacted-industries

142 'Estonia: adequate labour supply in the manufacturing industry for economic growth', European Centre for the Development of Vocational Training, 26 November 2021, https://www.cedefop.europa.eu/en/news/estonia-adequate-labour-supply-manufacturing-industry-economic-growth

143 Hannah Miao, 'Facing shortage of high-skilled workers, employers are seeking more immigrant talent, study finds,' CNBC, 10 June 2021, https://www.cnbc.com/2021/06/10/study-employers-seek-immigrants-amid-shortage-of-high-skilled-workers.html

144 Robert Plummer, 'Where are Britain's missing million workers?', BBC News, 28 January 2022, https://www.bbc.com/news/business-60039923

145 Anne Proch, 'UK to run out of highly skilled workers by 2030', Statista, 24 February 2022, https://www.statista.com/press/p/labour_shortage20200224/

146 Sally Herships, 'Japan tackles skilled labor shortage with free education', Marketplace, 15 March 2017, https://www.marketplace.org/2017/03/15/japan-tackles-skilled-labor-shortage-free-education/

147 Mathias Czaika and Christopher Parsons, 'The gravity of high-skilled migration policies', VoxEU at the Centre for Economic Policy Research, 7 June 2015, https://voxeu.org/article/attracting-high-skilled-migrants

148 'H-1B Specialty Occupations, DOD cooperative research and development project workers, and fashion models', U.S. Citizenship and Immigration Services', accessed August 2022, https://www.uscis.gov/working-in-the-united-states/h-1b-specialty-occupations

149 'H-1B Visa', Harvard International Office, accessed August 2022, http://www.hio.harvard.edu/h-1b-visa

150 'Skilled Worker Visa', Gov.UK, accessed August 2022, https://www.gov.uk/skilled-worker-visa

151 Kyodo, 'Chinese man gets Japan's first skilled worker visa with no time limit', *Japan Times*, 14 April 2022, https://www.japantimes.co.jp/news/2022/04/14/national/chinese-japan-first-skilled-worker-visa-no-time-limit/

152   Noah Smith, 'Japan wants immigrants. The feeling isn't mutual', Bloomberg, 29 November 2017, https://www.bloomberg.com/opinion/articles/2017-11 -30/japan-wants-immigrants-the-feeling-isn-t-mutual

153   Phillip Connor and Neil G. Ruiz, 'Majority of U.S. public supports high-skilled immigration', Pew Research Center, 22 January 2019, https://www.pewresearch.org/global/2019/01/22/majority-of-u-s-public-supports-high-skilled-immigration/; Ashley Cowburn, 'Half of British public support more immigration of highly skilled workers, poll suggests', Independent, 18 April 2017, https://www.independent.co.uk/news/uk/politics/half-of-british-public-support-more-immigration-of-highly-skilled-workers-poll-suggests-a7687086.html; Claire Slattery and Emma Brancatisano, 'Majority of Australians support path to permanent residency for migrants, new survey shows', SBS News, 2 February 2022, https://www.sbs.com.au/news/article/majority-of-australians-support-path-to-permanent-residency-for-migrants -new-survey-shows/boegy11vl

154   Michael A. Clemens, 'Economics and emigration: trillion-dollar bills on the sidewalk?', Journal of Economic Perspectives Vol. 25, No. 3 (Summer 2011), pp. 84 and 87.

Conclusion

1   Ye Nee Lee, '2 charts show how much the world depends on Taiwan for semiconductors', CNBC, 15 March 2021, https://www.cnbc.com/2021/03/16/2-charts-show-how-much-the-world-depends-on-taiwan-for-semiconductors.html; Yimou Lee, Norihoko Shirouzi, and David Lague, 'T-DAY: the battle for Taiwan', Reuters, 27 December 2021, https://www.reuters.com/investigates/special-report/taiwan-china-chips/; June Teufel Dreyer, 'China's monopoly on rare earth elements–and why we should care', Foreign Policy Research Institute, 7 October 2020, https://www.fpri.org/article/2020/10/chinas-monopoly-on-rare-earth-elements-and-why-we-should-care/

2   Dreyer, 'China's monopoly on rare earth elements'.

3   James Fernyhough, 'Pentagon bankrolls rare earths plant as US plays catch -up to China', Financial Times, 14 June 2022, https://www.ft.com/content/5a974ea5-c863-406f-bab1-3cc6fe8d6ad2

4   'China's share of global chip sales now surpasses Taiwan's, closing in on Europe's and Japan's', Semiconductor Industry Association, 10 January 2022, https://www.semiconductors.org/chinas-share-of-global-chip-sales-now-surpasses-taiwan-closing-in-on-europe-and-japan/

5   Phred Dvorak and Matthew Dalton, 'Solar-energy supply chain depends on region where China is accused of genocide', Wall Street Journal,

11 April 2021, https://www.wsj.com/articles/solar-energy-supply-chain
-depends-on-region-where-china-is-accused-of-genocide-11618147228

6   'Pakistan's Khan backs China on Uighurs, praises one-party system',
    Al Jazeera, 2 July 2021, https://www.aljazeera.com/news/2021/7/2/paki-
    stan-imran-khan-china-uighurs; 'Pakistan aiding Chinese repression of
    Uyghurs in Xinjiang: Report', *Times of India*, 22 January 2022, https://
    timesofindia.indiatimes.com/world/pakistan/pakistan-aiding-chinese-
    repression-of-uyghurs-in-xinjiang-report/articleshow/89054392.cms

7   HRH Bergen, 'Cambodia deported twenty Uyghurs back to China', Human
    Rights House, 4 January 10, https://humanrightshouse.org/articles/cambo-
    dia-deported-twenty-uyghurs-back-to-china/; 'April 13, 2022 Saudi Arabia:
    Uyghur child among four "booked for deportation" to China tonight',
    Amnesty International, 13 April 2022, https://www.amnesty.org/en/latest/
    news/2022/04/saudi-arabia-uyghur-child-among-four-booked-for-depor-
    tation-to-china-tonight/

8   Missy Ryan, 'U.S. missing opportunities with Latin America, Chile's leader
    says', *Washington Post*, 9 June 2022, https://www.washingtonpost.com/
    national-security/2022/06/09/united-states-chile-president-boric/

9   Ricky Ben-David, 'Israel inaugurates Chinese-run Haifa port terminal, in
    likely boost for economy', *Times of Israel*, 2 September 2021, https://www.
    timesofisrael.com/israel-inaugurates-new-haifa-port-terminal-in-expected
    -boost-for-economy/

10 Amir Tibon and Amos Harel, 'U.S. Senate warns Israel over deepening ties
    with China, citing "serious security concerns"', *Haaretz*, 14 June 2019, https:
    //www.haaretz.com/us-news/2019-06-14/ty-article/.premium/u-s-senate-
    condemns-deepening-israel-china-ties-cites-serious-security-concerns/
    0000017f-e6ce-da9b-a1ff-eeefc3550000

11 Shannon Tiezzi, 'Israel and China a "marriage made in heaven," says
    Netanyahu', *The Diplomat*, 22 March 2017, https://thediplomat.com/2017/
    03/israel-and-china-a-marriage-made-in-heaven-says-netanyahu/

12 Jacob Magid, 'In effort to placate China, Israel refrains from signing UN
    statement on Uighurs', *Times of Israel*, 26 October 2021, https://www.
    timesofisrael.com/in-effort-to-placate-china-israel-refrains-from-signing-
    un-statement-on-uighurs/

13 Ibid.

14 Weizhen Tan, 'Australia's growth may "never return" to its pre-virus path
    after trade trouble with China, says economist', CNBC, 29 December 2020,
    https://www.cnbc.com/2020/12/29/trade-war-with-china-australias-econ-
    omy-after-covid-19-pandemic.html

15 Chris Buckley and Damien Cave, 'Australia took on China. Did it get it

right?', *New York Times*, 27 September 2021, https://www.nytimes.com/2021/09/27/world/australia/australia-china-relations.html

16 Christian Davies and Kang Buseong, 'South Korea disputes China's account of foreign minister talks', *Financial Times*, 12 August 2022, https://www.ft.com/content/a42ba772-32fc-477f-957d-01ad763d8f08

17 Zeyi Yang, 'Ant Group gets rectified', *Protocol*, 12 April 2021, https://www.protocol.com/bulletins/ant-financial

18 Lingling Wei and Jing Yang, 'Ant Founder Jack Ma faces backlash from regulators', *Wall Street Journal*, 3 November 2020, https://www.wsj.com/articles/ant-founder-jack-ma-faces-backlash-from-regulators-11604442018

19 Ibid.

20 Christopher Zara, 'Ant Group's record-breaking IPO has been suspended', *Fast Company*, 3 November 2020, https://www.fastcompany.com/90571537/ant-groups-record-breaking-ipo-has-been-suspended

21 Christopher Zara, 'Jack Ma's Ant Group was ordered to restructure by Chinese regulators: Here's how things will change', *Fast Company*, 4 December 2021, https://www.fastcompany.com/90624273/jack-mas-ant-group-ordered-to-restructure-by-chinese-regulators-heres-how-things-will-change

22 'China forces Jack Ma's Ant Group to restructure', BBC News, 13 April 2021, https://www.bbc.com/news/business-56728038

23 Jack Denton, 'Alibaba's quarterly profit is set to plummet 60%. here's why', *Barron's*, 23 February 2022, https://www.barrons.com/articles/alibaba-stock-price-earnings-report-preview-51645621558?tesla=y#; Tracy Qu, 'Alibaba net income plummets 87 per cent, with first adjusted profit decline in more than five years', *South China Morning Post*, 18 November 2021, https://www.scmp.com/tech/big-tech/article/3156560/alibaba-net-income-plummets-87-cent-resulting-first-adjusted-profit

24 Jun Mai, '"Irrational expansion of capital" behind China's fan culture and tech monopolies, says Beijing expert', *South China Morning Post*, 31 August 2021, https://www.scmp.com/news/china/politics/article/3147059/irrational-expansion-capital-behind-chinas-fan-culture-and-tech

25 Eva Dou and Pei Lin Wu, 'Once China's darling, tech industry is burdened by covid and crackdowns', *Washington Post*, 16 May 2022, https://www.washingtonpost.com/world/2022/05/16/china-tech-challenges-covid-crackdown/

26 Associated Press, 'China bans effeminate men from TV', NPR, 2 September 2021, https://www.npr.org/2021/09/02/1033687586/china-ban-effeminate-men-tv-official-morality

27 Yoel Guzansky, 'Challenges confronting Saudi Arabia' in *Strategic Survey for*

Israel 2016-17 (Tel Aviv: Institute for National Security Studies, 2016), p. 137; 'Houthis launch multiple strikes on Saudi sites', Al Jazeera, 20 March 2022, https://www.aljazeera.com/news/2022/3/20/houthis-launch-attacks-on-saudi-energy-desalination-facilities

28 Marwan Bishara, 'The end of the Saudi era', Al Jazeera, 22 September 2020,https://www.aljazeera.com/opinions/2020/9/22/the-end-of-the-saudi-era

29 Richard Javad Heydarian, 'What is behind the resurgence of the Marcos dynasty?', Al Jazeera, 14 December 2021, https://www.aljazeera.com/opinions/2021/12/14/what-is-behind-the-resurgence-of-the-marcos-dynasty

30 Peter Bergen, David Sterman, and Melissa Salyk-Virk, 'Terrorism in America 18 Years after 9/11', New America, 18 September 2019, https://www.newamerica.org/international-security/reports/terrorism-america-18-years-after-911/; Katie Gibson, '15 years after 9/11, how has national security changed?', Harvard Kennedy School, 2016, https://www.hks.harvard.edu/faculty-research/policy-topics/international-relations-security/15-years-after-911-how-has-national

31 Karen Zraick, 'New Zealand ban on most semiautomatic weapons takes effect', *New York Times*, 20 December 2019, https://www.nytimes.com/2019/12/20/world/australia/new-zealand-gun-ban.html

32 Kat Lonsdorf, 'New Zealanders hand In more than 50,000 weapons as the country's buyback program ends', NPR, 21 December 2019, https://www.npr.org/2019/12/21/790466492/new-zealanders-hand-in-more-than-50-000-weapons-as-the-countrys-buyback-program-

33 Frank Newport, 'Public opinion of the war in Afghanistan', Gallup, 31 October 2001, https://news.gallup.com/poll/9994/public-opinion-war-afghanistan.aspx; Robert Kagan, 'It wasn't hubris that drove America into Afghanistan. It was fear', *Washington Post*, 26 August 2021.

34 William Dahlgreen, 'Memories of Iraq: did we ever support the war?', YouGov, 3 June 2015, https://yougov.co.uk/topics/politics/articles-reports/2015/06/03/remembering-iraq; https://www.ipsos.com/en-uk/war-afghanistan-poll-1; 'War in Afghanistan Poll', Ipsos, 4 November 2001, https://www.ipsos.com/en-uk/war-afghanistan-poll-1; *Asahi Shimbun*, 4 October 2001 (morning edition), p. 4; *Asahi Shimbun*, 27 November 2001 (morning edition), p. 4; 'Asia Public Opinion Still Divided on War in Iraq', VOA, 25 March 2003, https://www.voanews.com/a/a-13-a-2003-03-25-48-asia/393189.html; Paul Midford, 'Japanese Public Opinion and the War on Terrorism: Implications for Japan's Security Strategy', Policy Studies No. 27 (Washington: East-West Center in Washington, 2006), p. 28.

35   John McCain (@SenJohnMcCain), 'I say again: #Russia is a gas station masquerading as a country. Must-read @WSJ : "Putin's Potemkin Economy"', Twitter, 24 March 2014, https://twitter.com/senjohnmccain/status/448126001865052160?lang=en

36   'Fireside chat with Senator John Cornyn', Center for Strategic and International Studies, 6 April 2022, p. 10, https://csis-website-prod.s3.amazonaws.com/s3fs-public/event/220406_Indo_John_Cornyn.pdf?Se3BjW49z3dnJ3seamItVHq71833BOMF

37   Ibid.

38   Matthew Yglesias, 'Mancur Olson', *Slow Boring*, 7 April 2022, https://www.slowboring.com/p/mancur-olson-end-of-history?

39   Meredith L. Roman, *Opposing Jim Crow: African Americans and the Soviet Indictment of U.S. Racism, 1928-1937* (Lincoln: University of Nebraska Press, 2012).

40   Gary Fineout, 'Rubio's feud with his hometown NBA team', *POLITICO*, 27 May 2022, https://www.politico.com/newsletters/florida-playbook/2022/05/27/rubios-feud-with-his-hometown-nba-team-00035642; Houston Keene, 'AOC claims Republicans motivated by "sexual frustrations" in Twitter rant amid Florida trip controversy', Fox News, 31 December 2022, https://www.foxnews.com/politics/aoc-republicans-motivated-sexual-frustration-florida-trip

Acknowledgements

On March 5, 2020, I grabbed coffee with a literary agent – Jack Ramm – at the Delaunay Counter in London, steps from the Thames. Jack and I did not know each other; we had been introduced by a colleague of mine, Stephen Paduano, with whom I worked at LSE IDEAS, the London School of Economics' foreign policy think tank. Jack and I hit it off. I remember leaving my coffee with Jack, calling my parents and telling them how excited I was to have found an agent and that a book would be coming – *eventually*.

Less than a month later, COVID-19 had shut down London and I had returned to New York. Everything, the nascent idea of a book included, came to a halt.

Yet Jack and I persisted. More aptly, Jack stuck with me as I put together a proposal for a Southeast Asia-focused book that never materialised. But Jack believed in me. So, when Hodder & Stoughton approached him about a book on autocracy, he reached out and asked simply: 'Would you be interested?' And more importantly, 'Could you do it?' I was, and promised I could. And we did, managing to produce a polished draft within a year.

It is Jack's belief – coupled with his brilliant edits and those of his colleague, Sofia Smith-Laing – that made this book possible. Without Jack (and without Stephen), there is no *Defeating the Dictators*. The same is true both of my editors Izzy Everington and Rupert Lancaster, who oversaw and championed the project at Hodder & Stoughton, and Harriet Poland, who commissioned it. Nick Fawcett's edits were similarly vital, as was the work of Purvi Gadia, my fact-checker Laura Mauro, and several other folks on the Hodder team. For their support and work on this project, I will forever be grateful.

There are several other people to whom I owe a debt and without whom this book would not be possible.

There is nobody I owe more than my parents, Lisbeth Diringer and Lee Dunst – my first and forever champions, a front on which they are challenged only by my grandparents, Diane and Laurence Dunst (Nana and Papa), and my late grandparents, Lila and Owen 'Buddy' Diringer (Grandma and Grandpa). My brother, Josh Dunst, graciously read every chapter I put in front of him and told me, bluntly, when I had erred. I am grateful, too, for the several other family members who helped with this project, including Isabel 'Liz' Dunst, Melissa Dunst Lipman, Elliot Diringer and Edmund and Nancy Dunst.

Several friends of mine played a key role in this book, if only by listening to me prattle on about ways to defeat the dictators, including Shahn Louis, Jack Zivitofsky, Tyler Khilnani, Jacob Judah, Samantha Benevelli, Ryan DelGaudio, Conor O'Shea, Eleni Neyland, Michael DeFeo, Aaron McIntyre, Steven Barker, Osman Awad, James Bryan, Sara Abbassi, Yasmeen Serhan, David Gevarter, Jake Wasserstein, and Coby Goldberg. Congressman Jim Cooper – who has been truly gracious with his time in supporting me and this book – and his interns were kind enough to read the whole thing, line by line, and offer smart edits. Congressman Don Beyer did much the same, reading the book in its entirety and taking the time to discuss it with me over breakfast in Arlington. Writing this book was possible because of the support I received from each and every one of you.

And, of course, thank you to my partner, Matthew Minor, for supporting me every step of the way, including much of 2022 – when I was writing this book on the weekends and evenings while working a full-time job (and maintaining a think-tank fellowship). None of this was easy, but your daily support played a truly crucial role in making *Defeating the Dictators* a reality. Thank you for loving me, each and every day.

I am grateful, too, to my colleagues at The Asia Group. They are the best in the business and have helped shape my thinking not only on Asia but on the world. I owe a particular gratitude to Ambassador Kurt Tong, Nirav Patel, Jim Loi, Rexon Ryu, Jonah Lefkoe, Rachel Lambert, and Rhea Menon. I am grateful as well to my colleagues past and present at the Center for Strategic and International Studies, including Greg Poling, Simon Tran Hudes, Andreyka Natalegawa, Karen Lee, and Danielle Fallin, from whom I learn more about Southeast Asia every day.

I also owe thanks to several other mentors and friends: Jeff Gedmin, David Wippman, Sharon Rivera, Nicholas Rostow, Ambassador Ted Osius, Chris Alden, James Walters, Ambassador Scot Marciel, Cory Cowles, Ambassador David Saperstein, Ryan Heath, Brian Harding, Francisco Bencosme, Satu Limaye, Josh Kurlantzick, Ali Wyne and Prashant Rao.

Sincere thanks are due also to everyone not yet mentioned who graciously read and offered advanced praise for *Defeating the Dictators*. Your support means more than you could possibly imagine.

This book was a labour of love. Its message is one in which I believe strongly and which I know to be incredibly important, particularly at our perilous moment. I can only hope that *Defeating the Dictators* leaves a mark and plays a small role in ensuring democracy's victory, both today and tomorrow.

Index